What Current Research Says
to the Middle Level Practitioner

National Middle School Association is dedicated to improving the educational experiences of young adolescents by providing vision, knowledge, and resources to all who serve them in order to develop healthy, productive, and ethical citizens.

What Current Research Says
to the Middle Level Practitioner

Judith L. Irvin, Editor

National Middle School Association
Columbus, OH

National Middle School Association
2600 Corporate Exchange Drive, Suite 370
Columbus, Ohio 43231
Telephone (800) 528-NMSA

Printed in the United States of America

Sue Swaim, Executive Director
Jeff Ward, Director of Business Services
John Lounsbury, Editor
Mary Mitchell, Copy Editor/Designer
Marcia Meade, Publications Sales

ISBN: 1-56090-120-9   NMSA Stock Number: 1244

Library of Congress Cataloging-in-Publication Data
What current research says to the middle level practitioner/Judith
    L. Irvin, editor
        p.   cm.
    Includes bibliographical references.
    ISBN 1-56090-120-9 (pbk.)
    1. Middle schools--United States. 2. Middle school teaching--
United States. 3. Middle school students--United States.
4. Middle schools--United States--Curricula.   I. Irvin, Judith L.,
date.   II. National Middle School Association.
LB1623.W43   1997   97-26451
373.236--dc21   CIP

Table of Contents

III
CURRICULUM

IV
TEACHER EDUCATION

V
SOCIAL CONTEXT

Sue Swaim

Foreword

E ducation is at an important crossroad; and middle level education in particular is receiving new scrutiny. *What Current Research Says to the Middle Level Practitioner*, therefore, is a most timely publication. National Middle School Association is proud to be able to facilitate the preparation and publishing of this important volume. It is another demonstration of the association's commitment to the importance of middle level research and its impact on the implementation of high performance, developmentally responsive middle level schools. NMSA's other research initiatives and resources include:

- the ongoing work of NMSA's Research Committee,
- the expansion and publication of *Research in Middle Level Education Quarterly*, a journal dedicated to sharing quality research concerning young adolescents and their schooling,
- the publication and distribution, via the internet and fax-on-demand, of *Research Summaries* that synthesize research and answer questions most frequently raised about middle level schools,
- the publication and dissemination of the *Middle Level Research Agenda* that was developed by a blue ribbon task force of researchers and middle level practitioners to help encourage and facilitate the continued focus on quality middle level research.

Collectively, these initiatives are building a body of knowledge which is easily accessible to middle level practitioners. It is important that we combine what we are learning through relevant research with the cumulative experiences of thousands of middle level educators so that the critical work of reforming and improving middle level education will continue to move forward.

I encourage you to read this publication very carefully and share it with others, including board members and citizens generally. It touches on a wide variety of important middle level topics and is written in a clear voice directed to middle level practitioners. Now is the time to rise to the challenge of implementing middle level schools that expect high academic achievement from all students through the implementation of developmentally responsive practices. The young adolescents with whom we work and live on a daily basis deserve our best efforts if each is to have the chance to become all he or she can and should be.

> *The importance of achieving developmentally responsive middle level schools cannot be overemphasized. The nature of the educational programs young adolescents experience during this formative period of life will, in large measure, determine the future for all of us.*
> — ***This We Believe,*** 1995.

John H. Lounsbury

Foreword

The middle school movement is an educational success story unparalleled in our history. In little over three decades the face of American education has been remade; the intermediate level of education has been given a long overdue identity and has, in fact, been recognized as the level leading in instituting significant educational reform.

To maintain the momentum, however, the clear light of solid research is needed. As a presumably new idea, the middle school has faced hard questions, ones neither the elementary school nor the high school has had to answer. Because the middle school advocacy included practices and programs that were not a part of established school practices, parents and board members have been skeptical and wanted evidence. Citizens demanded research data to justify implementation of middle school practices, although no research studies could be cited to justify maintaining the status quo. Now, however, there are data to give credibility to advocated middle level practices.

For many years, there was little relevant research available, and the studies that existed were scattered. Middle school advocates were certain about the validity of their educational philosophy and sufficiently committed to implement their beliefs on faith. The positive responses of students gave them further assurance, but subjective judgments about "doing the right thing for kids" failed to satisfy critics and skeptics. Fortunately, research studies that focus on young adolescents and middle school practices have begun to accumulate, with prospects for more in the immediate future. While the definitive, no qualification results that some would like are not available, a body of solid research data to undergird middle school practices is now present. In education it is never possible to control sufficiently all the variables as can be done in a scientific laboratory. However, about the weight of evidence supporting middle school practices there can be little doubt.

This volume is a testament to that fact, and its publication is a matter of real importance to the still-expanding middle school movement. Never before has there been assembled and presented in clear, understandable terms so much research data on so many facets of middle level education. In the 31 chapters, topics ranging from young adolescent development, to teaming, to inclusion, to grouping, to urban schools, to organizational issues are examined.

What Current Research Says to the Middle Level Practitioner is a carefully crafted melding of research findings and understandable prose. Judith Irvin and the forty competent authors/researchers are to be commended for providing this much-needed volume. Filling admirably the gap that has existed in middle level professional literature, this resource deserves to be studied, quoted, referred to, and otherwise put to use in the continuing campaign to improve the educational experience of young adolescents.

Judith L. Irvin

Preface

What *Research Says to the Middle Level Practitioner,* released by NMSA in 1986, filled a critical need. Since that time, considerable activity in the field of middle level research has occurred. *Research in Middle Level Education Quarterly* was established, and quality research concerning young adolescents and their schooling can be found in a variety of other journals both inside and outside of education. Although *RMLEQ* makes a deliberate effort to report implications of research to the field of practice, the reality is that teachers, administrators, school district personnel, school board members, and other practitioners have neither the time nor the inclination to locate and pour through research articles on topics of interest in middle level education. NMSA attempts to fill the gap between research and practice by producing a series of *Research Summaries* that synthesize research and answer questions most frequently raised by middle level practitioners.

This all new volume, *What Current Research Says to the Middle Level Practitioner,* is a result of discussions between the Research Committee and the Publications Committee of NMSA, both of which recognized the need to provide a ready source of the most recent research findings, in a readable fashion, on important topics. The table of contents was shaped by the Research Committee and members of the American Educational Research Association's (AERA) Special Interest Group in Middle Level Education; then, highly knowledgeable researchers in the field were asked to submit chapters. This volume represents the collaborative efforts of 40 separate authors with guidance from NMSA's Research Committee members Joanne Arhar, Ronald Klemp, Laurie Hart, Rebecca Mills, David Hough, Nancy Mizelle, and Jill Van Ness. It was, indeed, a pleasure for me to work with this entire group of dedicated scholars.

Introduction

Irvin | *Judith L. Irvin*
Florida State University
Tallahassee, Florida

Hough | *David Hough*
Southwest Missouri
State University
Springfield, Missouri

Judith L. Irvin and David Hough

Research in Middle Level Education

The success of middle level education over the past two decades is more the result of courageous efforts by adventuresome educators than reliance on a research base supporting such signature practices as interdisciplinary team organization, small group guidance, or an exploratory curriculum. In fact, some middle level practitioners have shunned research as being impractical, difficult to understand, and somewhat intimidating. The 1990s, however, have brought new sophistication to middle level education among school board members and site-based decision makers. These policy makers in the educational process now demand to consider research findings that may make an impact on decisions made in individual schools or districts. Research in middle level education seems to be coming of age.

Much of the educational restructuring rhetoric seems to be focused, in general, on practices such as team organization, interdisciplinary instruction, and an advisory role for teachers – practices first designed for and practiced in middle level schools. In the next decade, it is already clear that educators are sure to witness in elementary and high schools the implementation of practices that have been traditionally identified as middle school practices. More than ever, then, research supporting or raising questions about the effectiveness of these practices is imperative.

❏ Research Methodologies ❏

Reluctant research consumers cite their lack of statistical sophistication as a reason not to use the results of systematic study in their daily decision making. Generally, they associate numbers, formulas, and convoluted sets of findings with articles that rarely discuss the implications of such findings. Until recently, reluctant consumers of research may have been justified in their hesitancy.

New research methodologies have liberated educators from these intimidations. We will briefly describe five methodologies most commonly used to study education that are extremely useful to middle level practitioners: surveys, shadow studies, quantitative, qualitative, and action research. Each methodology differs in its observational and analytical techniques, the role of the researcher, and the emphasis on the context of the phenomenon studied. We conclude this chapter by discussing the identity of middle level education research and efforts to disseminate research to the field of practice.

❏ Survey research

The most useful aspect of survey research is the ability to gain insights and information from people covering vast distances in a reasonable amount of time. Samples are generally large, yet information about context is limited. Survey research is particularly useful to track trends, practices, and issues over time and across numerous sites.

At least four large survey efforts have provided useful descriptive data addressing the degree to which middle school programs and practices are implemented across the country. *Schools in the Middle: Status and Progress* (Alexander & McEwin, 1989) compares and contrasts the results between a 1968 and 1988 survey of trends in grade configuration, enrollment numbers, reasons for establishing a middle school, subject offerings, evaluations, and attitudes towards middle schools. In *Education in the Middle Grades: National Practices and Trends,* Epstein & Mac Iver (1990) surveyed 2400 middle level schools with a response rate of 73%. This study addressed the practices surveyed in the Alexander and McEwin survey and asked respondents to project possible future practices.

The most recent survey and the most comprehensive provided status data derived from a 1993 random sample of 1,798 middle level schools together with comparisons from the 1968 and 1988 surveys cited above. *America's Middle Schools: Practices and Progress—A 25 Year Perspective* (McEwin, Dickinson, & Jenkins, 1996) supplies detailed information on nearly every aspect of middle level schooling. One hundred and twelve tables and figures supplement the narrative. Especially valuable is the ability to see the shifts that have occurred since the initial Alexander survey of 1968 and the subsequent 1988 study.

Another important large scale survey effort was conducted by the National Association of Secondary School Principals (NASSP) through their publication of three studies: *The Junior High Principalship* (Rock & Hemphill, 1966), *The Middle Level Principalship: A Survey of Middle Level Principals and Programs* (Valentine, Clark, Nickerson, & Keefe, 1981), and *Leadership in Middle Level Education: A National Survey of Middle Level Leaders and Schools* (Valentine, Clark, Irvin, Melton, & Keefe, 1993). These large-scale surveys obtained information about practices of principals and assistant principals and the degree of implementation of middle school programs and practices. The latest two studies included a second volume which consisted of a multiple cross-site analysis of certain programs and practices. Teams of researchers actually visited selected sites to verify and extend information learned through the survey (Keefe, Clark, Nickerson, & Valentine, 1983; Keefe, Valentine, Clark, & Irvin, 1994). Taken together, these surveys (spanning 27 years from 1966 to 1993) have been useful in tracking middle level education to understand better the level of implementation of signature practices.

❏ Shadow studies

Five shadow studies of middle level grades have been conducted on a national level. They have provided a realistic look at what students experience in school: *The Junior High School We Saw: One Day in the Eighth Grade* (Lounsbury & Marani, 1964); *The Middle School in Profile: A Day in the Seventh Grade* (Lounsbury, Marani, & Compton, 1980); *How Fares the Ninth Grade?* (Lounsbury & Johnston, 1985); *Life in the Three Sixth Grades* (Lounsbury & Johnston, 1988); and *Inside Grade Eight: From Apathy to Excitement* (Lounsbury & Clark, 1990). By following or "shadowing" students throughout a particular school day, researchers have helped practitioners understand the unique experiences of young adolescents at each middle level grade and from the standpoint of the consumer. Shadow studies provide a revealing picture of life in the schools and classrooms that serve young adolescent students.

❏ Quantitative research

Numbers and formulas are trademarks of quantitative research methodologies. Comparison between treatment and control groups and significance of results are important elements. One of the difficulties with quantitative research is that to understand the conclusions drawn, one must understand each of the variables and how it was measured as well as the statistical procedures used to analyze the data in this deductive approach.

❏ Qualitative research

Interviews, observations, and document analysis are the major forms of data collection in this research methodology. Samples are generally small, but context becomes extremely important. Volumes of data are collected, analyzed, and synthesized because qualitative researchers usually spend long periods of time "in the field." Themes often emerge inductively and are often used to draw conclusions. Just as quantitative research has checks for validity and rigor, qualitative methodology establishes validity and rigor through such techniques as member checks (returning to the source of information for accuracy) and triangulation (validating information from more than one source). Despite the difficulty of drawing generalizations from qualitative research, this methodology is popular and has facilitated the study of many of the phenomena in middle level schools that are difficult to quantify.

❏ Action research

Collaboration among university, school faculty, and students make this type of research meaningful, context driven, and of specific use to local sites. Qualitative, quantitative, or a combination of the two methodologies can be used in action research which is most often used to study such issues as curricular innovations, instructional strategies, or student attitudes peculiar to one situation in time. Results are not necessarily intended to be generalized to other settings.

All of these research techniques have validity and rigor built into their methodologies. All have been used (and sometimes misused) by researchers and practitioners, and all have their place in adding pieces to the middle level education puzzle. Occasionally, we are asked the question "which study proves what we do in middle school is right for young adolescents?" No one study and no one methodology answers that complex question. Building a research agenda is the first step toward asking the "right questions" so that bona fide answers might be found.

❏ Identity of Middle Level Research ❏

In a comprehensive review of the research literature, Hough (1989, 1991) found pre-1980 middle level education research "weak in design and methodologically flawed. During the 1980s, however, [he found] a growing level of sophistication in the design and conduct of many studies [which] produced a higher quality of research" (p. 8). Middle level research of the

1990s is of higher quality than in the 1970s or 1980s, and there is considerably more of it.

Identity may be a key factor in improving both the quality and the amount of research pertinent to middle level education. A Delphi Study conducted by the National Middle School Association (Jenkins & Jenkins, 1991) revealed that achieving legitimacy for the middle school was the leading issue among its members. Educators voiced an imperative for middle level education to be recognized as a distinctly separate entity, not an addition to either elementary or high school education.

While middle level education has a long legacy, its forming identity, especially to those "outside" the movement, is fairly new. Middle school identity can be understood best, perhaps, through a series of publications beginning with Donald Eichhorn's *The Middle School* (1966), after which a flurry of middle school activity ensued. *This We Believe* (1982), the first official position statement of the National Middle School Association, and *This We Believe: Developmentally Responsive Middle Level Schools* (1995), the newer NMSA position paper, both have had wide distribution and influence. *Turning Points: Preparing American Youth for the 21st Century* (Carnegie Council on Adolescent Development, 1989) brought national attention to the middle level of education and endorsed the premises of earlier efforts and publications. These publications and, of course, the writing and implementing of three decades of middle level educators, and the efforts of the National Middle School Association have provided a model, an identity, that makes this level of education distinct from all others.

The time has finally come for researchers to examine closely the key middle school issues. It took three decades for these issues to emerge and be clearly defined, regardless of methodology.

Johnston (1984) emphasized the importance of "looking outside middle school research per se to identify information that is useful in making professional decisions that enhance the educational program for young adolescents" (p. 135). Research in middle level education has become a sub-specialty field in the broader context of educational research. In a chapter on middle level research, Strahan (1992) stated: "if we think of education as a field of study, we can begin to think of the various formal disciplines and other areas of inquiry as strands that pass through the field. We can begin to think of the middle level as a major 'zone' of the field that encompasses these areas of inquiry" (p. 382).

Two kinds of questions beg to be answered: (1) What significance do broad areas such as grouping practices, integrated curriculum, and literacy learning have for middle level education? (2) What is the evidence supporting the identifying practices found to be unique in the middle level school such as interdisciplinary team organization, small group guidance, and an emphasis on exploratory experiences? A research agenda includes lines of inquiry with collections of studies that point to a common solution or need for change. For example, hundreds of studies pointing to the perils of ability grouping (see e.g., Oakes, 1985) have prompted school personnel to begin to change these practices in the last five years. Hundreds of studies on cooperative learning have given confidence to many educators that this instructional strategy is supported by a substantial research base.

❏ Efforts to Disseminate Research Findings ❏

In his chapter in *Perspectives: Middle School Education 1964-1984*, Johnston (1984) presented a synopsis of research in middle level education in nine clusters of studies. The "What Research Says to the Middle Level Practitioner" department in *Middle School Journal* has been helpful in keeping practitioners attentive to new research developments. *What Research Says to the Middle Level Practitioner* (Johnston & Markle, 1986) was essentially a collection of these articles. The all-new chapters for this volume were solicited from the most knowledgeable researchers in the field around topics of importance to middle level practitioners.

The Research Committee of the National Middle School Association has diligently disseminated research findings to its membership through the publication of 43 issues of *Research in Middle Level Education Quarterly* (first called *The Research Annual* and then *Research in Middle Level Education*) and through sponsored Research Symposia at each NMSA annual conference. *Research in Middle Level Education Quarterly* is currently recognized by the Special Interest Group in Middle Level Education of the American Educational Research Association (AERA) as its preferred outlet for publication of middle level education research.

The National Middle School Association has engaged in other efforts to disseminate research findings to practitioners including a growing number of sessions at conferences earmarked as research-based strands and the wide distribution of "Research Summaries" addressing the most frequently asked questions by practitioners. (These summaries are available by calling 1-800-528-NMSA). In addition, a Research Agenda Task Force has met and collaborated with AERA to articulate a Research Agenda for middle level education that can guide development and funding efforts through in the next decade.

Setting a research agenda for middle level education is not a simple task. Schooling in general is complex, and middle level education research has traditionally had to create its own identity. In the now limited waking hours before the new century arrives, we have the opportunity to create environments that respond to the needs of young adolescents and engage them actively in learning. We have the option of grouping students in ways that are fair to all. We have the understanding needed to develop a curriculum that is fully integrated and relevant to students. We have adequate reasons for seeking legitimacy for education's middle level so that the proper education and certification of teachers for young adolescent students is ensured. We have the skills needed to establish a solid research base for this distinct level of education. In a review of middle level research, Van Zandt and Totten (1995) stated that "the pursuit of middle level reforms that enhance students' educational experiences and opportunities is well underway. While research prior to 1990 focused on *how* to meet student needs, the current decade is witnessing a shift toward the importance of documenting the *effectiveness* of these programs" (p. 20). Setting and implementing a research agenda for middle level education is imperative, and from all appearances it is an idea whose time has come. ℝ

References

Alexander, W., & McEwin, K. (1989). *Schools in the middle: Status and progress*. Columbus, OH: National Middle School Association.

Carnegie Council on Adolescent Development. (1989). *Turning points: Preparing American youth for the 21st century.* New York: Carnegie Corporation.

Eichhorn, D. H. (1966). *The middle school.* New York: Center for Applied Research.

Epstein, J. L., & Mac Iver, D. J. (1990). *Education in the middle grades: National practices and trends.* Columbus, OH: National Middle School Association.

Hough, D. L. (1989). *Middle level education in California: A survey of programs and organization.* Riverside, CA: University of California, Educational Research Cooperative.

Hough, D. L. (1991). Setting a research agenda for middle level education. *Crossroads: The California Journal of Middle Grades Research, 1* (1), 4-11.

Jenkins, D., & Jenkins, K. (1991). The NMSA Delphi report. *Middle School Journal, 22* (4), 23-36.

Johnston, J. H. (1984). A synthesis of research findings on middle level education. In J. Lounsbury (Ed.), *Perspectives: Middle school education 1964-1984* (pp. 135-156). Columbus, OH: National Middle School Association.

Johnston, J. H., & Markle, G. C. (1986). *What research says to the middle level practitioner.* Columbus, OH: National Middle School Association.

Keefe, J. W., Clark, D. C., Nickerson, N. C., & Valentine, J. (1983). *The effective middle level principal.* Reston, VA: National Association of Secondary School Principals.

Keefe, J. W., Valentine, J., Clark, D. C., & Irvin, J. L. (1994). *Leadership in middle level education: Volume II: Leadership in successfully restructuring middle level schools.* Reston, VA: National Association of Secondary School Principals.

Lounsbury, J. H., & Clark, D. C. (1990). *Inside grade eight: From apathy to excitement.* Reston, VA: National Association of Secondary School Principals.

Lounsbury, J. H., & Johnston, J. H. (1985). *How fares the ninth grade?* Reston, VA: National Association of Secondary School Principals.

Lounsbury, J. H., & Johnston, J. H. (1988). *Life in the three sixth grades.* Reston, VA: National Association of Secondary School Principals.

Lounsbury, J. H., & Marani, J. (1964). *The junior high school we saw: One day in the eighth grade.* Alexandria, VA: Association for Supervision and Curriculum Development.

Lounsbury, J. H., Marani, J., & Compton, M. (1980). *The middle school in profile: A day in the seventh grade.* Columbus, OH: National Middle School Association.

McEwin, C. K., Dickinson, T. S., & Jenkins, D. M. (1996). *America's middle Schools: Practices and progress—A 25 year perspective.* Columbus, OH: National Middle School Association.

National Middle School Association. (1982). *This we believe.* Columbus, OH: Author.

National Middle School Association. (1995). *This we believe: Developmentally responsive middle level schools.* Columbus, OH: Author.

Oakes, J. (1985). *Keeping track: How schools structure inequality.* New Haven, CT: Yale University Press.

Rock, D.A., & Hemphill, J.K. (1966). *The junior high-school principalship.* Reston, VA: National Association of Secondary School Principals.

Strahan, D. B. (1992). Turning points and beyond: Coming of age in middle level research. In J. L. Irvin (Ed.), *Transforming middle level education: Perspectives and possibilities* (pp. 381-399). Boston: Allyn and Bacon.

Valentine, J. W. , Clark, D. C., Nickerson, N. C., & Keefe, J. W. (1981). *The middle level principalship: A survey of middle level principals and programs (Vol. I).* Reston, VA: National Association of Secondary School Principals.

Valentine, J. W., Clark, D. C., Irvin, J. L., Keefe, J. W., & Melton, G. (1993). *Leadership in middle level education: Volume I: A national survey of middle level leaders and schools*. Reston, VA: National Association of Secondary School Principals.

Van Zandt, L. M., & Totten, S. (1995). The current status of middle level education research: A critical review. *Research in Middle Level Education, 18* (3), 1-26.

II

Teaching and Learning

Eccles	*Jacquelynne S. Eccles* *University of Michigan,* *Ann Arbor, Michigan*
Wigfield	*Allan F. Wigfield* *University of Maryland,* *Baltimore, Maryland*
Lipka	*Richard P. Lipka* *Pittsburg State University* *Pittsburg, Kansas*
Anderman	*Lynley Hicks Anderman* *Univeristy of Missouri* *Kansas City, Missouri*
Midgley	*Carol Midgley* *University of Michigan* *Ann Arbor, Michigan*
Arhar	*Joanne M. Arhar* *Kent State University* *Kent, Ohio*
McLaughlin	*H. James McLaughlin* *University of Georgia* *Athens, Georgia*
Doda	*Nancy Doda* *National-Louis University* *Washington, D.C.*
Bennett	*Betty J. Bennett* *Florida State University* *Tallahassee, Florida*
Mills	*Rebecca Mills* *University of Nevada* *Las Vegas, Nevada*

Rosselli | Hilda C. Rosselli
University of South Florida
Tampa, Florida

Hines | Rebecca A. Hines
Southeast Missouri
State University
Cape Girardeau, Missouri

Johnston | J. Howard Johnston
University of South Florida
Tampa, Florida

VanNess | Jill VanNess
Florida State University
Tallahassee, Florida

Platt | Elizabeth Platt
Florida State University
Tallahassee, Florida

McDaniel | Janet E. McDaniel
California State University
San Marcos, California

Stowell | Laura P. Stowell
California State University
San Marcos, California

Swaim | John H. Swaim
Otterbein College
Westerfield, Ohio

McEwin | C. Kenneth McEwin
Appalachian State University
Boone, North Carolina

Jacquelynne S. Eccles and Allan Wigfield

Young Adolescent Development

Early adolescence is a time of great change, the biological changes associated with puberty, the social/educational changes associated with the transitions from elementary to secondary school, the social and psychological changes associated with the emergence of sexuality to name a few. In fact, very few developmental periods are characterized by as many changes in as many areas. With rapid change comes a heightened potential for both positive and negative outcomes. Although most individuals pass through this developmental period without excessively high levels of "storm and stress," a substantial number of individuals experience difficulty. For example, between 15 and 30 percent (depending on ethnic group) drop out of school before completing high school; further, adolescents as a group have the highest arrest rate of any age group; and increasing numbers of adolescents consume alcohol and other drugs on regular basis (Office of Educational Research and Improvement, 1988). Many of these problems begin during the young adolescent years (Carnegie Council on Adolescent Development, 1989). In addition, because individuals make many choices and engage in a variety of behaviors during this period that can influence the rest of their lives, it is critical that educators understand what factors influence whether young people stay on a healthy, productive pathway or move onto a problematic, and potentially destructive pathway as they pass through this important developmental period. In this chapter, we summarize the major changes and, given that most of our own theoretical and empirical work has focused on young adolescents' achievement motivation and school performance (e.g., Eccles, Midgley, Buchanan, Wigfield, Reuman & Mac Iver, 1993; Wigfield & Eccles, 1992; Wigfield, Eccles,

Mac Iver, Reuman, & Midgley, 1991), we emphasize this aspect of development and its relation to changes in school experiences. We begin with a consideration of the biological changes that occur during early adolescence.

❏ Biological changes associated with puberty

A complete review of the biological changes associated with puberty is beyond the scope of this chapter (see Adams, Montemayor, & Gullotta, 1989; Brooks-Gunn & Reiter, 1990; Buchanan, Eccles, & Becker, 1992). Briefly, as a result of the activation of the hormones controlling these physical developments, most children undergo a growth spurt, develop primary and secondary sex characteristics, become fertile, and experience increased sexual libido during early adolescence. Because girls begin to experience these pubertal changes approximately 18 months younger than boys, girls and boys of the same chronological age are likely to be at quite different points in physical and social development during early adolescence, a fact that both complicates social interactions in middle grades classrooms and creates different psychological dilemmas for early maturing girls versus boys. While early maturation tends to be advantageous for boys, particularly with respect to their participation in sports activities and social standing in school, early maturation can be problematic for girls because they are the first individuals in their cohort to begin changing and because the kinds of physical changes girls experience (such as getting fatter) are not highly valued among many white American groups who value the slim, androgynous female body characteristic of white fashion models (see Petersen, 1998; Simmons & Blyth, 1987). In fact, early maturing white females have the lowest self-esteem and the most difficulty adjusting to school transitions, particularly the transition from elementary to junior high school (e.g., Eccles, Lord, Roeser, Barber, Jozefowicz, 1996; Simmons & Blyth, 1979). African American females do not evidence this same pattern perhaps because the African American culture places higher value on the secondary sex characteristics associated with female maturation.

Magnusson and Stattin traced the long-term consequences of early maturation in females (Magnusson, 1988; Stattin & Magnusson, 1990). The early maturing girls in these studies obtained less education and married earlier than their later maturing peers despite the lack of any differences in achievement levels prior to the onset of puberty. These researchers attributed this difference to the fact that the early maturing females were more likely to join older peer groups and to begin dating older males; in turn, the early maturing girls in these peer groups were more likely to drop out of school and get married, perhaps because school achievement was not valued by their peer social network while early entry into the job market and early marriage were valued.

Recently, researchers have studied exactly how the hormonal changes occurring during early adolescence (ages 9-13) relate to changes in children's behavior (e.g., see Buchanan et al., 1992; Petersen & Taylor, 1980). Some evidence exists for direct effects of hormones on behaviors such as aggression, sexuality and mood swings (e.g., Buchanan et al., 1992; Olweus, Mattssoon, Schalling, & Low, 1988; Susman, Inoff-Germain, Nottelmann, Loriaux, Cutler, & Chrousos, 1987). Hormones can also affect behavior indirectly through their impact on the emergence of secondary sex characteristics, which, in turn, can influence social experiences and psychological well-being. For example, when breast development is associated with increases in girls' body image, it is also related to better psychological adjustment, more positive peer relations, and better school achievement (Brooks-Gunn & Warren, 1988).

In addition to physical changes, young adolescents experience major school transitions and important social changes as well. Several researchers (e.g., Simmons & Blyth, 1987) have argued that it is the combination of so many changes occurring simultaneously during early adolescence that is problematic for so many young adolescents. Individuals who must cope with several stressful changes (such as those associated with pubertal change, school transitions, and the social-role changes associated with dating) at the same time are at risk for developmental problems such as lowered self-esteem and early sexual activity. Again, because girls enter puberty earlier than boys, they are more likely than boys to be coping with pubertal changes at the same time they make the middle grades school transition and thus are more likely to face multiple transitions simultaneously.

This perspective raises the question of when students should make the transition from elementary to secondary school. Given the difficulties of coping with several transitions at once, some researchers have argued that middle grades school should begin earlier, so that all students make the school transition before they enter puberty. Others have argued that a K-8 organizational structure may be most beneficial to young adolescents. The recent movement to make middle grades schools more like elementary schools and less like traditional junior high schools also reflects concern over the variety of changes young adolescents must face.

❏ Changes in cognition

The most important cognitive changes during this period relate to the increasing ability of children to think abstractly, consider the hypothetical as well as the real, engage in more sophisticated and elaborate information processing strategies, consider multiple dimensions of a problem at once, and reflect on oneself and on complicated problems (see Keating, 1990). Indeed, such abstract and hypothetical thinking is the hallmark of Piaget's formal operations stage assumed to begin during early adolescence (e.g., Piaget & Inhelder, 1973). Although there is still considerable debate about when exactly these kinds of cognitive processes emerge and whether their emergence reflects global stage-like changes in cognitive skills as described by Piaget, most theorists do agree that these kinds of thought processes are more characteristic of adolescents' cognition than of younger children's cognition.

Many cognitive theorists have also assessed how more specific information processing skills, cognitive learning strategies, and metacognitive skills change (e.g., Bjorklund, 1989; Siegler, 1986). A steady increase occurs in children's information processing skills and learning strategies, in their knowledge of a variety of different topics and subject areas, their ability to apply their knowledge to new learning situations, and in their awareness of their strengths and weaknesses as learners. Although one would think that these types of cognitive changes ought to allow young adolescents to be more efficient, sophisticated learners, ready to cope with relatively advanced topics in many different subject areas, Keating (1990) argued that these changes do not necessarily make them better thinkers, particularly during the period of early adolescence. They need at lot of experience exercising these skills before they can use the skills efficiently.

Researchers have also suggested that these kinds of cognitive changes could affect how children and young adolescents regulate their behavior in educational settings (e.g., Zimmerman, 1989). For example, as children's cognitive skills increase and they have more experience in educational settings, they should be able to regulate their learning better and so do more complicated and elaborate achievement tasks.

Along with the implications for learning, these kinds of cognitive changes can also affect an individual's self-concept, thoughts about the future, and understanding of others. Theorists from Erikson (1963) to Harter (1990) have suggested that the young adolescent years are a time of change in a young person's self-concept as young people consider what possibilities are available to them and try to come to a deeper understanding of themselves. These sorts of self-reflections require the kinds of higher-order cognitive processes just discussed. During early adolescence and adolescence individuals also become much more interested in understanding others' internal psychological characteristics, and friendships become based

18

more on perceived similarity in these characteristics (see Selman, 1980). Again, these sorts of changes in person perception reflect the broader changes in cognition that occur at this time.

Before leaving this topic, it is important to acknowledge the continuing debate about how much schooling can facilitate these kinds of cognitive changes. In discussing secondary schools' effects on educational attainment, Entwisle (1990) concluded that the effects of school quality on achievement test gains in high school are relatively small. Keating (1990) also discussed how the increase in knowledge and cognitive skills slows during adolescence. However, he also argued that there are a number of factors in the school setting that can influence cognitive development and success in school such as: the amount of meaningful material introduced, how the training of thinking skills is (or isn't) embedded in detailed content knowledge, and the ways in which teachers foster (or don't foster) critical thinking skills. In addition, these changes in cognitive skills and the ability to regulate behavior are often used as a rationale for special middle schools in which students purportedly learn more challenging material.

❏ Friendships and peer groups

Probably the most controversial changes during early adolescence involve the increase in peer focus and involvement in peer-related social, sports, and other extracurricular activities. Many young adolescents attach great importance to these types of activities – substantially more importance than they attach to academic activities (Wigfield et al., 1991). Indeed, often to the chagrin of parents and teachers, activities with peers, peer acceptance, and appearance can take precedence over school activities, particularly during early adolescence. Further, young adolescents' confidence in their physical appearance and social acceptance is often a more important predictor of self-esteem than confidence in their cognitive/academic competence (Harter, 1990).

In part because of the importance of social acceptance during early adolescence, friendship networks during this period often are organized into relatively rigid cliques that differ in social status within the school setting (see Brown, 1990). The existence of these cliques seems to reflect young adolescents' need to establish a sense of identity; belonging to a group is one way to answer the "Who am I?" question.

Also, in part because of the importance of social acceptance, children's conformity to their peers peaks during early adolescence (Brown, 1990). Much has been written about how this peer conformity can create many problems for young adolescents, and about how "good" children often are corrupted by the negative influences of peers, particularly by adolescent gangs – and indeed gangs do pose serious social problems in many cities. However, although pressure from peers to engage in misconduct does increase during early adolescence (see Brown, 1990), most researchers do not accept the simplistic view that peer groups are mostly a bad influence during early adolescence. More often than not young adolescents tend to agree more with their parents' views on "major" issues such as morality, the importance of education, politics, and religion. Peers have more influence on things such as dress and clothing styles, music, and activity choice. In addition, young adolescents usually seek out similar peers; this means that those involved in sports will have other athletes as friends; those serious about school will seek those kinds of friends. Consequently, young adolescents also tend to hang around with peers who hold similar views as their parents on the major issues listed above. Brown (1990) concluded that it is poor parenting that usually leads children to get in with a "bad" peer group, rather than the peer group pulling a "good" child into difficulties. In most cases, the peer group acts more to reinforce existing strengths and weakness than to change young adolescents' characteristics.

Finally, the quality of children's friendships also undergoes some important changes during adolescence (see Berndt & Perry, 1990). As suggested by Sullivan (1953), young adolescents' friendships are more focused on fulfilling intimacy needs than younger children's friendship. This is particularly true for girls.

❏ Changes in family relations

Although the extent of actual disruption in parent-adolescent relations is still being debated, little question exists that parent-child relations change during early adolescence (e.g., Buchanan et al., 1992; Collins, 1990; Petersen, 1988). As young adolescents become physically mature they often seek more independence and autonomy, and may begin to question family rules and roles, leading to conflicts particularly around issues like dress and appearance, chores, and dating (see Collins, 1990). However, despite these conflicts over day to day issues, parents and adolescents agree more than they disagree regarding core values linked to education, politics, and spirituality.

Parents and young adolescents also have fewer interactions and do fewer things together outside the home than they did at an earlier period – as illustrated by the horror many young adolescents express at seeing their parents at places like shopping malls. Steinberg (1990) argued that this "distancing" in the relations between young adolescents and parents is a natural part of pubertal development, citing evidence from nonhuman primates that puberty is the time at which parents and offspring often go their separate ways. Because parents and young adolescents in our culture usually continue to live together for a long time after puberty, distancing rather than complete separation may be the evolutionary vestige in humans. Although he did not take an evolutionary perspective, Collins (1990) also concluded that the distancing in parent-adolescent relations has great functional value for young adolescents, in that it fosters their individuation from their parents, allows them to try more things on their own, and develops their own competencies and efficacy.

❑ School transitions and young adolescent development

For some, early adolescence marks the beginning of a downward spiral leading to academic failure and school dropout. For example, Simmons and Blyth (1987) found a marked decline in some young adolescents' school grades as they moved into junior high school – a decline that was predictive of subsequent school failure and dropout. Similar declines have been documented for such motivational constructs as: interest in school, intrinsic motivation, self-concepts/self-perceptions, and confidence in one's intellectual abilities, especially following failure. Finally, there are also increases during early adolescence in such negative motivational and behavioral characteristics as test anxiety, learned helpless responses to failure, focus on self-evaluation rather than task mastery, and both truancy and school dropout (See Eccles & Midgley, 1989; Wigfield, Eccles & Pintrich, 1996). Although these changes are not extreme for most students, there is sufficient evidence of gradual decline in various indicators of academic motivation, behavior, and self-perception over these years to make one wonder what is happening. Although few researchers have gathered information on ethnic or social class differences in these declines, we know that academic failure and dropping out are especially problematic among some ethnic groups and among youth from low SES communities and families; thus, it is likely that these groups are particularly likely to show these declines in academic motivation and self-perception as they move into, and through, the secondary school years.

A variety of explanations have been offered for these "negative" changes. Some have suggested that declines such as these result from the intraspsychic upheaval assumed to be associated with young adolescent development (e.g. Blos, 1979). Others have suggested that it is the coincidence of the timing of multiple life changes (e.g., Simmons & Blyth, 1987). Still others have suggested that it is the nature of the junior high school

21

environment itself rather than the transition per se that is important. Drawing upon Person-Environment Fit theory, Eccles and Midgley (1989) proposed that the negative motivational and behavioral changes associated with early adolescence could result from traditional junior high schools not providing appropriate educational environments for young adolescents. According to Person-Environment Fit theory, behavior, motivation, and mental health are influenced by the fit between the characteristics individuals bring to their social environments and the characteristics of these social environments. Individuals are not likely to do very well, or be very moti vated if they are in social environments that do not fit their psychological needs. If the social environments in the typical middle grades schools do not fit very well with the psychological needs of young adolescents, then Person-Environment Fit theory predicts a decline in their motivation, interest, performance, and behavior as they move into this environment. Some evidence exists for each of these perspectives. Given our own research we will focus on the evidence for the Person-Environment Fit theory.

❏ The relation of changes in school environments to motivational changes during early adolescence

Researchers have documented the impact of classroom and school environmental characteristics on motivation. For example, the big school/ small schools literature has demonstrated the motivational advantages of small secondary schools especially for marginal students (Barker & Gump, 1964). Similarly, the teacher efficacy literature has documented the positive student motivational consequences of high teacher efficacy (Ashton, 1985; Brookover, Beady, Flood, Schweitzer & Wisenbaker, 1979). Finally, organizational psychology has demonstrated the importance of participatory work structures on worker motivation (Lawler, 1976). The list of such influences could, of course, go on for several pages. The point is that there may be systematic differences between the academic environments in typical elementary schools and those in typical junior high schools and middle schools; if so, these differences could account for some of the motivational changes seen among young adolescents as they make the transition into junior high school or middle school. In other words, the motivational problems seen during early adolescence may be a consequence of the type of change in the school environment rather than characteristics of the developmental period per se.

Eccles and her colleagues (e.g., Eccles et al., 1993) called this phenomenon "Stage-Environment Fit." At the most basic level, this perspective suggests the importance of looking at the fit between the needs of young adolescents and the opportunities afforded them in their middle grades school environment. A poor fit would help explain the declines in motivation associated with the transition to either junior high or middle school. More specifically, these researchers suggested that different types of educational environments may be needed for different age groups to meet the individual's developmental needs and to foster continued developmental growth. Exposure to the developmentally appropriate environment would facilitate both motivation and continued growth; in contrast, exposure to a developmentally inappropriate environment, especially a developmentally regressive environment would create a particularly poor person-environment fit, which, in turn, would lead to declines in motivation as well as in the attachment to the goals of the institution. Imagine two trajectories: one a developmental trajectory of individual growth, the other a trajectory of environmental change across the school years. Positive motivational consequences are predicted when these two trajectories are in synchrony with each other; that is, when the environment is both responsive to the changing needs of the individual and offers the kinds of stimulation that will propel continued positive growth. In other words, transition to a facilitative and developmentally appropriate environment, even at this vulnerable age, should have a positive impact on children's perceptions of themselves and their educational environment. In contrast, negative motivational consequences are predicted when these two trajectories are out of synchrony. If this is true, then a transition into a developmentally inappropriate educational environment should result in the types of motivational declines that have been identified as occurring with the transition into junior high school.

Eccles and Midgley (1989) further argued that many young adolescents experience developmentally inappropriate changes in a cluster of classroom organizational, instructional, and climate variables, including task structure, task complexity, grouping practices, evaluation techniques, motivational strategies, locus of responsibility for learning, and quality of teacher-student and student-student relationships as they move into either middle school or junior high school. They argued, in turn, that these experiences contribute to the negative change in students' motivation and achievement-related beliefs assumed to coincide with the transition into junior high school. Research supports these suggestions. For example, Simmons & Blyth (1987) pointed out that most junior high schools are substantially larger than elementary schools and instruction is also more likely to be organized and taught departmentally. As a result of both of these differences, junior high school teachers typically teach several different groups of students each day and are unlikely to teach any particular students for more than one year. In addition, students typically have several teachers each day with little opportunity to interact with any one teacher on any dimension except the academic content of what is being taught and disciplinary issues. Thus, the opportunity for forming close relationships between students and teachers is effectively eliminated at precisely the point in the students' development when they have a great need for guidance and support from non-familial adults (see Carnegie Council on Adolescent Development, 1989). Such changes in student-teacher relationships, in turn, are likely to undermine the sense of community and trust between students and teachers – leading to a lowered sense of efficacy among the teachers, an increased reliance on authoritarian control practices by the teachers, and an increased sense of alienation among the students. Such changes are also likely to decrease the probability that any particular student's difficulties will be noticed early enough to get the student necessary help - thus increasing the likelihood that students on the edge will be allowed to slip onto negative trajectories leading to increased school failure and dropout.

Consistent evidence also exists of the kinds of changes at the classroom level that would undermine young adolescents' school motivation. Further, evidence is beginning to emerge documenting the negative impact of these changes in school experience on motivation (see Eccles & Midgley, 1989 and Eccles et al., 1993, for details of particular studies). First, despite the increasing maturity of students, junior high school classrooms, compared to elementary school classrooms, are characterized by a greater emphasis on teacher control and discipline, and fewer opportunities for student decision making, choice, and self-management. Such a mismatch between young adolescents' desires for autonomy and control and their perception of the opportunities in their environments should result in a decline in the adolescents' intrinsic motivation and interest in school; and this is exactly what happens (see Mac Iver & Reuman, 1988).

Second, junior high school classrooms are characterized by a less personal and positive teacher/student relationship than elementary school classrooms. The implications of this decline were discussed earlier.

Third, junior high schools are more likely to use whole class task organization and between classroom ability grouping than elementary schools. Differences such as these are likely to lead to increases in social comparison, in concerns about evaluation, and in competitiveness (e.g., see Rosenholtz & Simpson, 1984). They may also increase the likelihood that teachers will use normative grading criteria and more public forms of evaluation, both of which are likely to impact negatively on many young adolescents' self-perceptions and motivation. These differences may also make

24

aptitude differences more salient to junior high school teachers and students, leading to increased teacher expectancy effects and decreased feelings of efficacy among teachers (see Eccles & Wigfield, 1989).

Fourth, junior high school teachers feel less effective as teachers, especially for low-ability students. Several studies have documented the impact of teacher efficacy on student beliefs, attitudes, motivation, and achievement (e.g., Ashton, 1985; Brookover et al., 1979). Given these associations, it is not surprising that differences in teachers' sense of efficacy before and after the transition to junior high school contribute to the decline in young adolescents' beliefs about their academic competency and potential (see Midgley, Feldlaufer, & Eccles, 1989).

Finally, junior high school teachers appear to use a higher standard in judging students' competence and in grading their performance than do elementary school teachers. There is no stronger predictor of students' self-confidence and efficacy than the grades they receive. If grades change, then we would expect to see a concomitant shift in the students' self-perceptions and academic motivation. Junior high school teachers use stricter and more social comparison-based standards than elementary school teachers to assess student competency and to evaluate student performance, leading to a drop in grades for many young adolescents as they make the junior high school transition (e.g., Simmons & Blyth, 1987).

❏ Summary

Changes such as those reviewed above are likely to have a negative effect on many children's motivational orientation toward school at any grade level. But Eccles and Midgley (1989) have argued that these types of school environmental changes are particularly harmful during early adolescence given what is known about psychological development during this stage of life. Young adolescent development is characterized by increases in desire for autonomy, peer orientation, self-focus and self-consciousness, salience of identity issues, concern over heterosexual relationships, and capacity for abstract cognitive activity (see Brown, 1990; Eccles & Midgley, 1989; Keating, 1990; Simmons & Blyth, 1987). Simmons and Blyth (1987) argued that young adolescents need a reasonably safe, as well as an intellectually challenging environment to adapt to these shifts – an environment that provides a "zone of comfort" as well as challenging new opportunities for growth. In light of these needs, the environmental changes often associated with transition to middle grade schools are likely to be particularly harmful in that they emphasize competition, social comparison, and ability self-assessment at a time of heightened self-focus; they decrease decision making and choice at a time when the desire for control is growing; they emphasize lower level cognitive strategies at a time when the ability to use higher level strategies is increasing; and they disrupt social networks at a time when adolescents are especially concerned with peer relationships and may be in special need of close adult relationships outside of the home. The nature of these environmental changes, coupled with the normal course of individual development, is likely to result in a developmental mismatch so that the "fit" between the young adolescent and the classroom environment is particularly poor, increasing the risk of negative motivational outcomes, especially for those students who are having difficulty succeeding in school academically. Ⓡ

References

Adams, G. R., Montemayor, R., & Gullotta, T. P. (Eds.). (1989). *Biology of adolescent behavior and development.* Newbury Park, CA: Sage.

Ashton, P. (1985). Motivation and the teacher's sense of efficacy. In C. Ames & R. Ames (Eds.), *Research on motivation in education* (Vol. 2, pp. 141-171). Orlando: Academic Press.

Barker, R., & Gump, P. (1964). *Big school, small school: High school size and student behavior.* Stanford, CA: Stanford University Press.

Berndt, T. J., & Perry, T. B. (1990). Distinctive features of early adolescent friendships. In R Montemayor, G. R. Adams, & T. P. Gullotta (Eds.), *From childhood to adolescence: A transitional period?* (pp. 269-287). Newbury Park, CA: Sage.

Bjorklund, D. (1989). *Children's thinking: Developmental function and individual differences.* Pacific Grove CA: Brooks-Cole.

Blos, P. (1979). *The adolescent passage.* New York: International Universities Press.

Brookover, W., Beady, C., Flood, P., Schweitzer, J., & Wisenbaker, J. (1979). *School social systems and student achievement: Schools can make a difference.* New York: Praeger.

Brooks-Gunn, J., & Reiter, E. O. (1990). The role of pubertal processes. In S. S. Feldman & G. R. Elliott (Eds.), *At the threshold: The developing adolescent* (pp. 16-53). Cambridge, MA: Harvard University Press.

Brooks-Gunn, J., & Warren, M. P. (1988). The psychological significance of secondary sexual characteristics in 9- to 11-year old girls. *Child Development, 59* (4), 161-169.

Brown, B. B. (1990). Peer groups and peer cultures. In S. S. Feldman & G. R. Elliott (Eds.), *At the threshold: The developing adolescent* (pp. 171-196). Cambridge, MA: Harvard University Press.

Buchanan, C. M., Eccles, J. S., & Becker, J. B. (1992). Are adolescents the victims of raging hormones? Evidence for activational effects of hormones on moods and behaviors at adolescence. *Psychological Bulletin, 111* (1), 62-107.

Carnegie Council on Adolescent Development (1989). *Turning points: Preparing American youth for the 21st century*. New York: Carnegie Corporation.

Collins, W. A. (1990). Parent-child relationships in the transition to adolescence: Continuity and change in interaction, affect, and cognition. In R. Montemayor, G. R. Adams, & T. P. Gullotta (Eds.), *From childhood to adolescence: A transitional period?* (pp. 85-106). Beverly Hills, CA: Sage.

Eccles, J. S., Lord, S. E., Roeser, R. W., Barber, B. L., & Jozefowicz, D. M. H. (1996). The association of school transitions in early adolescence with developmental trajectories through high school. In J. Schulenberg, J. Maggs, & K. Hurrelmann, (Eds.), *Health risks and developmental transitions during adolescence.* (pp. 283-320). New York: Cambridge University Press.

Eccles, J. S., & Midgley, C. (1989). Stage - environment fit: Developmentally appropriate classrooms for young adolescents. In C. Ames & R. Ames (Eds.), *Research on motivation in education* (Vol. 3, pp. 139-186). San Diego, CA: Academic Press.

Eccles, J. S., Midgley, C., Buchanan, C. M., Wigfield, A., Reuman, D., & Mac Iver, D. (1993). Development during adolescence: The impact of stage/environment fit. *American Psychologist, 48* (2), 90-101.

Entwisle, D. R. (1990). Schooling and the adolescent. In S. S. Feldman & G. R. Elliott (Eds.), *At the threshold: The developing adolescent* (pp. 197-224). Cambridge, MA: Harvard University Press.

Erikson, E. H. (1963). *Childhood and society*. New York: Norton.

Harter, S. (1990). Causes, correlates and the functional role of self-worth: A life-span perspective. In R. J. Sternberg & J. Kolligian (Eds.), *Competence considered* (pp. 67-97). New Haven, CT: Yale University Press.

Keating, D. P. (1990). Adolescent thinking. In S. S. Feldman & G. R. Elliott (Eds.), *At the threshold: The developing adolescent* (pp. 54-89). Cambridge, MA: Harvard University Press.

Lawler, E. E. (1976). Control systems in organizations. In M. D. Dunnette (Ed.), *Handbook of industrial and organizational psychology* (pp. 1247-1293). Chicago: Rand McNally.

Mac Iver, D., & Reuman, D. A. (1988, April). *Decision making in the classroom and early adolescents' valuing of mathematics.* Paper presented at the annual meeting of the American Educational Research Association, New Orleans.

Magnusson, D. (1988). *Individual development from an interactional perspective.* Hillsdale, NJ: Lawrence Erlbaum Associates.

Midgley, C. M., Feldlaufer, H., & Eccles, J. S. (1989). Changes in teacher efficacy and student self- and task-related beliefs during the transition to junior high school. *Journal of Educational Psychology, 81* (2), 247-258.

Office of Educational Research and Improvement (1988). *Youth indicators 1988.* Washington, DC: U.S. Government Printing Office.

Olweus, D., Mattssoon, A., Schalling, D., & Low, H. (1988). Circulating testosterone levels and aggression in adolescent males: A causal analysis. *Psychosomatic Medicine, 50* (3), 261-272.

Petersen, A. (1988). Adolescent development. *Annual Review of Psychology, 39,* 583-607.

Petersen, A., & Taylor, B. (1980). The biological approach to adolescence: Biological change and psychosocial adaptation. In Adelson, J. (Ed.), *Handbook of the psychology of adolescence* (pp. 117-155). New York: Wiley.

Piaget, J., & Inhelder, B. (1973). *Memory and intelligence.* London: Routledge and Kegan Paul.

Rosenholtz, S. J., & Simpson, C. (1984). The formation of ability conceptions: Developmental trend or social construction? *Review of Educational Research, 54* (1), 301-325.

Selman, R. L. (1980). *The growth of interpersonal understanding.* New York: Academic Press.

Siegler, R. S. (1986). *Children's thinking.* Englewood Cliffs, NJ: Prentice Hall.

Simmons, R. G., & Blyth, D. A. (1987). *Moving into adolescence: The impact of pubertal change and school context.* Hawthorn, NY: Aldine de Gruyler.

Stattin, H., & Magnusson, D. (1990). *Pubertal maturation in female development.* Hillsdale, NJ: Lawrence Erlbaum Associates.

Steinberg, L. (1990). Autonomy, conflict, and harmony in the family relationship. In S. S. Feldman & G. R. Elliott (Eds.), *At the threshold: The developing adolescent* (pp. 255-276). Cambridge, MA: Harvard University Press.

Sullivan, H. S. (1953). *The interpersonal theory of psychiatry.* New York: Norton.

Susman, E. J., Inoff-Germain, G., Nottelmann, E. D., Loriaux, D. L., Cutler, C. B., & Chrousos, G. P. (1987). Hormones, emotional dispositions, and aggressive attributes in young adolescents. *Child Development, 58* (4), 1114-1134.

Wigfield, A., & Eccles, J. S. (1992). The development of achievement task values: A theoretical analysis. *Developmental Review, 12* (2), 265-310.

Wigfield, A., Eccles, J., Mac Iver, D., Reuman, D., & Midgley, C. (1991). Transitions at early adolescence: Changes in children's domain-specific self-perceptions and general self-esteem across the transition to junior high school. *Developmental Psychology, 27* (4), 552-565.

Wigfield, A., Eccles, J. S., & Pintrich, P. R. (1996). Development between the ages of eleven and twenty-five. In D. C. Berliner and R. C. Calfee (Eds.), *The handbook of educational psychology* (pp. 148-155). New York: Macmillan Publishing.

Zimmerman, B. J. (1989). A social cognitive view of self-regulated learning. *Journal of Educational Psychology, 81* (3), 329-339.

Richard Lipka

Enhancing Self-Concept/Self-Esteem in Young Adolescents

ognitive learning is hard-won by someone whose life is in affective disarray! At the very heart of those affective concerns is the development of clear self-concept and positive self-esteem. These dimensions of self represent the central feature of the human personality which in the case of young adolescents unifies the physical, social, and cognitive characteristics into a sense of identity, adequacy, and affirmation. From an understanding of self springs a host of other variables such as behavior, motivation, and the perception of others. Understanding the self brings us closer to understanding the young adolescent. Attending to the self in school brings us closer to developing the kind of middle school young adolescents need and deserve.

I will attempt four purposes within this very short chapter: (1) clarification of the terms self-concept and self-esteem, which are often erroneously used interchangeably, (2) discussion of recent developments in our knowledge base concerning self-concept, self-esteem, and the young adolescent, (3) identification of where the middle school should fit in promoting clear self-concept and positive self-esteem, and (4) recognition of challenges that exist for practitioners and researchers.

❏ Self-concept and self-esteem defined

The ability to interpret, generalize, and apply the findings of self-perception research can be directly attributed to the lack of clear definitions for the constructs of self-concept and self-esteem. Self-concept is defined as the perception(s) one has of oneself in terms of personal attributes and the various roles which are played or fulfilled by the indi-

31

vidual. Thus, a young adolescent might perceive self as a son or daughter, fat or thin, as a "successful" student or a poor basketball player. Self-concept then is a descriptive perception of self in terms of one's various roles and attributes. Self-esteem, on the other hand, is the valuative assessment one makes regarding personal satisfaction with roles, attributes, and/or the quality of one's performances. These decisions are made on the basis of personal values, although given the cognitive development of young adolescents, these decisions will, to a large degree, be considered environmentally induced. A young adolescent might view him/herself as lacking oral language skills and describe self as a poor English student. Depending upon personal values, however, he/she may desire to change this situation, keep it the same, or may simply not care enough to change. As noted, this valuing process is most likely a function of the environmental context within which the role is played. Many of these contexts are defined in terms of "significant others" whom the individual recognizes as influential. While in the early years parents are the "most" significant others, during early adolescence peers and teachers emerge as significant in a host of specific situations.

The process of self-perceiving is best described as an interaction between self-concept and self-esteem as various roles are played or fulfilled in situations through which feedback and influence are received. In this way, the young adolescent may develop or refine self-concept descriptions and/or make valuation decisions with regard to self-esteem. Actual self-esteem can only be ascertained by eliciting the value or relative priority which the individual attaches to the attribute.

❑ Self in early adolescence

Shirk and Renouf's (1992) contribution has been to place the development of self in early adolescence into a context of pivotal socio-emotional developmental tasks. Using the guiding framework of Erikson (1963), Shirk and Renouf identified two tasks that are the purview of early adolescence. These tasks are the conservation of self and maintenance of positive self-esteem. Conservation of self is the ability to promote continuity by linking change to existing self structures. It appears that early adolescence is the period when issues of continuity in the self-concept are most salient to the individual. This is due in large part to a movement from self-understanding based on behaviors, physical attributes, and physical competencies to self understanding based upon psychological traits and more abstract skills such as communication and social skills. While the maintenance of positive self-esteem is important throughout one's life, developmental transitions make early adolescence an especially critical period. These transitions include biological, social, and cognitive challenges. Biologically, the transition to puberty in relationship to one's cohort is most profound. That is, to be "off-time" either early or late in relation to one's peers has the potential to erode positive self-esteem.

In the social arena, young adolescents acquire three additional domains important to self-esteem. The three additional domains are job competence, romantic appeal, and close friendships – domains that suggest the need for the acquisition and coordination of new skills. Acquiring new skills not only provides a venue for new successes but also new failures, and as such represent new challenges for young adolescent self-esteem.

The emergence of increased cognitive abilities also provides a challenge to young adolescent self-esteem. The young person literally begins to develop an awareness of his or her own self-awareness. As the individual begins to view self in terms of abstractions or psychological traits, new demands are made upon his or her self-esteem.

During a recent effort to disentangle the effects of chronological age from school experience on self-esteem, Lipka, Hurford, and Litten (1992) analyzed data that suggested middle school students were indeed aware that society is age-graded and has a set of expectations regarding age and appropriate behavior. To perceive oneself as "on-time" with regard to one's life span makes for a sense of predictable life cycle and positive self-esteem. To perceive oneself as "off-time" and having fallen short of the goals or the expectations held by significant others in their lives may lead to a resultant decay in self-esteem. Individuals in this latter case may misperceive, distort, or avoid any new situations or experiences that accentuate the perception that they hold of being off-time. This may be a key ingredient in understanding at-risk or potential dropouts in middle school environments.

One of the most exciting areas of research is that which is calling into question the "storm and stress" characterization of young adolescent and adolescent development. Evidence is amassing (see Demo & Savin-Williams, 1992; Shirk & Renouf, 1992) that Rosenberg's (1985) distinction between the barometric self-concept and the baseline self-concept is critical in understanding early adolescence. The barometric self refers to moment to moment fluctuations, and clearly early adolescence has the widest array of peaks and valleys of any age period. Baseline self, on the other hand, refers to a underlying self-concept that changes slowly, over an extended period of time, and is focused upon striving towards healthy self-development. To continue to focus solely upon the barometric self (e.g.

"hormones with feet") at the expense of the baseline self is both wrong-headed and wrong hearted! Our challenge, then, as middle level educators is to acknowledge barometric self yet expend our efforts and resources to facilitate the striving towards healthy self-development represented by the baseline self.

❏ The middle school we need

At present, the treatment of self-concept and self-esteem in middle schools can be viewed as on a continuum with four points from least effective to most effective practices. At the lowest level we see the utilization of techniques that promote self-revelation and affirmation as evidenced by group "raps" and classroom posters and prizes that encourage a "feel good about yourself" orientation. The value in such approaches is that young people may view themselves as being surrounded by "nice" rather than "mean" people. However, the day to day realities of competition, grading, sorting, and labeling quickly have young people viewing these group activities and posters as short side trips in the journey through school. The second level involves the treatment of affective education as a program or unit – two weeks on self-esteem followed by a two-week unit on farm products of Kansas. To make a real difference the self-direction, personal decision- making, goal-setting objectives of such units would need to extend throughout the school, school day, and school year. The relative ineffectiveness of these first two levels in the continuum have made middle level educators easy targets for critics (e.g. Krauthammer, 1990) and have increased resistance to examining the human condition in our middle schools.

The third approach on the continuum is one known as the ecological approach (see Beane & Lipka, 1986, 1987). This approach begins with the question of whether the school as a whole is a self-enhancing environment and then proceeds to examine every facet of the school in light of that question. To date, this questioning process has led to the advocacy, empirically based, of a number of practices in the school setting. Such practices include cooperative learning, an approach that encourages young adolescents to learn how to work well with others. As noted earlier in the chapter, young adolescents have a powerful drive to form relationships with peers, to find a place in the group, and to earn some degree of status. To be "one with others" is so powerful that young men and women will risk conflict with adults and give up some aspects (e.g. clothing, language) of their individuality for it.

The emergence of the needs of job competence, self-worth, and altruism are ably addressed by placing young people in projects that involve service to others. Under the auspices of the school, service learning projects take young adolescents out of the school into the community where they may assist preschoolers, help the elderly, help with environmental problems, work to improve community recreation opportunities, and so on. In addition to all the positive aspects of self-esteem associated with "earning one's way," service learning projects have the real potential to enlighten citizens about the competence of young adolescents and their capability to care for and about others. Teacher-student planning means working in a partnership to articulate a problem/concern, develop objectives, locate resources, and evaluate progress in fulfilling objectives. While the foci of such efforts may be many and varied, the value of the method is that it helps young adolescents gradually exercise more control over their lives in school. Exercising more control over one's life reduces feelings of powerlessness and enhances self-esteem. Advisor-advisee programs with an emphasis upon personal, social growth, and the attempts to work closely with parents of the age group, are additional elements of a self-enhancing school.

The final stop on this continuum is the one that addresses the shortcoming of the ecological position which is not addressing conditions outside the school that enter into the ongoing formation and alteration of self-perceptions. Jim Beane titled this the integrated approach (see Beane, 1991, 1992, 1993, 1994) where the curriculum is centered on helping young adolescents search for self and social meaning in their lives.

Planning of the curriculum begins with young people identifying questions and concerns they have about themselves and the larger world in which they (and we) live. Common questions and concerns are shared in small groups, and an attempt is made to connect questions about self with related questions about the world; for example, issues about personal health are connected to concerns about environmental problems. Clusters of questions are organized by themes, and the whole group then decides upon activities they will do to address the themes and answer the questions. Themes that have emerged from such planning have included "living in the future," "jobs, careers, and money," "sex, health, genetics," "conflict, gangs, and violence," "cultures," and many more.

It does not take much imagination to see how self-perceptions are at the very center of such a curriculum. More than that, this kind of curriculum brings questions of the self into connection with the larger world, thus integrating self and social interests. And giving young people a powerful voice in planning the curriculum is a direct attempt to develop authentic efficacy: what young people have to say counts for something. Furthermore, young people will be in a continuing process of constructing personal and social meanings rather than having themselves and their world defined exclusively for them by adults (Beane, 1994). As middle level educators, we must examine where we are on the continuum and gather the resources necessary to move to the most effective practices.

❏ The teachers we need

What type of teachers will be required to move middle schools to the third and fourth positions on the continuum? Historically, part of the answer can be found in the writings of Jersild (1952, 1955) and Combs (1962). Borich (in press) explored the dimensions of teacher self-concept and self-esteem that have the potential to expand current conceptions of effective teaching. As in the past, Borich demonstrated that teachers with clear self-concept and positive self-esteem function within the teaching role as significant others for young adolescents and create a classroom environment that fosters clear self-concept and positive self-esteem in their pupils. The power in his present work is the determination of the absolute necessity for teachers to have work environments and significant others (e.g. administrators, teacher educators, colleagues) in their lives providing the facilitating conditions necessary for the promotion of a healthy, functional view of "self as teacher."

Hamachek (in press) made a strong case for teachers developing their "emotional intelligence" which is comprised of the five components of self-awareness, mood management, self-motivation, empathic skills, and relationship skills. Teachers who focus upon their emotional intelligence and have a clear and coherent picture of themselves as persons/professionals are most likely to have their professional lives characterized by the following behavioral descriptions:

1. They are inclined to combine a warm and friendly attitude with firm, but reasonable, expectations.
2. They project an enthusiasm for their work that lends excitement to their teaching.
3. They are by no means perfect, in the sense of doing and saying just the right thing at all times. (This has less to do with something that teachers consciously do, and more to do, perhaps, with the wide latitude of teacher imperfections that students can live with as long as the core person is basically fair and decent.)
4. Intellectually, they are thoroughly grounded in their subject area, which, by virtue of a broad base of interests, they are able to connect to related areas of knowledge.

5. They are ready to assume responsibility for student outcomes, which they reflect in their efforts to make sure that all students have a chance to learn.

6. They make a point to know their students as individuals and to respond to them as individuals; they go beyond simply seeing them as "students."

7. They provide definite study guidelines; they are as interested in getting their students prepared to know as they are in evaluating what they know.

8. They are able to challenge without being offensive and to encourage without being condescending; more importantly, they challenge when that is appropriate and they encourage when that is needed. Neither behavior is indiscriminately practiced.

9. They give feedback that is personalized, an effect that makes the feedback more believable and powerful.

10. They take time to reflect about their work, their students, and themselves as teachers; they are, in a word, thoughtful.

11. They work on developing a positive rapport that serves as the interpersonal medium within which high, but reasonable expectations and constructive, critical feedback can be transmitted.

12. They are able to be flexibly adaptive in terms of using direct or indirect methods of teaching to meet various students' abilities and needs. — pp. 21-22

For a very compatible set of behavioral descriptions of "the effective middle school teacher" see *Middle Level Teachers: Protraits of Excellence* (Arth, Lounsbury, McEwin, & Swaim, 1995). In addition to identifying sixteen characteristics, this book provides the firsthand views of 48 teachers about how these characteristics are manifested in their teaching and their reflections on the special nature of middle level teaching.

❏ The challenges

As with any complex educational issue the challenges are many. For practitioners, I urge more public declarations of the fact that cognitive learning is hard-won by someone whose life is in affective disarray. I urge more utilization of our growing knowledge base about self-concept and self-esteem. I urge more ownership of this knowledge base by participating in the selection of research questions of interest and value to our day to day lives in school. For researchers, I urge a better understanding of the philosophy and features of the middle school. I urge a clear focus upon "self" as primary variables of interest and not as secondary concerns in research with other agendas. And, finally I urge constructive dialogues between practitioners and researchers about the assets and liabilities inherit in the "practice of research" versus the "research of practice." ℝ

References

Arth, A., Lounsbury, J., McEwin, K., & Swaim, J. (1995). *Middle level teachers: Portraits of excellence.* Columbus, OH: National Middle School Association/ National Association of Secondary School Principals.

Beane, J. A. (1991). The middle school: The natural home of integrated curriculum. *Educational Leadership, 49* (2), 943.

Beane, J. A. (1992). Turning the floor over: Reflections on a middle school curriculum. *Middle School Journal, 23* (3), 34-40.

Beane, J. A. (1993). *A middle school curriculum: From rhetoric to reality.* Columbus, OH: National Middle School Association

Beane, J. A. (1994). Cluttered terrain: The school's interest in the self. In T. M. Brinthaupt & R. P. Lipka (Eds.), *Changing the self: Philosophies, techniques, and experiences.* (pp. 69-87). Albany, NY: State University of New York Press.

Beane, J. A., & Lipka, R. P. (1986). *Self-concept and self-esteem and the curriculum.* New York: Teachers College Press.

Beane, J. A., & Lipka R. P. (1987). *When the kids come first: Enhancing self-esteem.* Columbus, OH: National Middle School Association.

Borich, G. D. (in press). Dimensions of self that influence effective teaching. In R. P. Lipka & T. M. Brinthaupt (Eds.), *The role of self in teacher development.* Albany, NY: State University of New York Press.

Combs, A. W. (Ed.). (1962). *Perceiving, behaving, becoming.* Washington, DC: Association for Supervision and Curriculum Development.

Demo, D. H., & Savin-Williams, R. C. (1992). Self-concept, stability and change during adolescence. In R. P. Lipka & T. M. Brinthaupt (Eds.), *Self-perspectives across the life span* (pp.116-148). Albany, NY: State University of New York Press.

Erikson, E. (1963). *Childhood and society.* (2nd ed.) New York: Norton.

Hamachek, D. (in press). Effective teachers: What they do, how they do it, and the importance of self knowledge. In R. P. Lipka & T. M. Brinthaupt (Eds.), *The role of self in teacher development.* Albany, NY: State University at New York Press.

Jersild, A. T. (1952). *In search of self.* New York: Teachers College Press.

Jersild, A. T. (1955). *When teachers face themselves.* New York: Teachers College Press.

Krauthammer, C. (1990, February 5). Education: Doing bad and feeling good. *Time,* 78.

Lipka, R. P., Hurford, D. P., & Litten, M. J. (1992). Self in school: Age and school experience effects. In R. P. Lipka and T. M. Brinthaupt (Eds.), *Self- perspective across the life-span* (pp.93-115). Albany, NY: State University of New York Press.

Rosenberg, M. (1985). Self-concept and psychological well-being in adolescence. In R. Leahy (Ed.), *The development of self* (pp. 205-242). New York: Academic Press.

Shirk, S. R., & Renouf, A. G. (1992). The tasks of self-development in middle childhood and early adolescence. In R. P. Lipka & T. M. Brinthaupt (Eds.), *Self-perspective across the life span* (pp.53-90). Albany, NY: State University of New York Press.

Lynley Hicks Anderman and Carol Midgley

Motivation and Middle School Students

F ew educators would argue with the premise that student motivation is an important influence on learning. Whether students select advanced courses of study or drop out of school; whether they work intensively and persist in the face of difficulty or procrastinate and work halfheartedly; whether they set realistic goals for themselves and then set about achieving them in an efficient manner or flounder through their days with little sense of direction; these behaviors reflect important aspects of student motivation. Student motivation is of particular importance for those who work with young adolescents.

Considerable research has shown a decline in motivation and performance for many children as they move from elementary school into middle school (see Eccles & Midgley, 1989, for a review). Often it has been assumed that this decline is largely due to physiological and psychological changes associated with puberty and, therefore, is somewhat inevitable. This assumption has been challenged, however, by research that demonstrates that the nature of motivational change on entry to middle school depends on characteristics of the learning environment in which students find themselves (see Midgley, 1993). That is, when students make a transition into a facilitative school environment, motivation and performance can be maintained or even improved. These findings represent an important aspect of current thinking in motivational theory. That is, any given student's quality of motivation reflects an interaction of characteristics of the individual and of the environment surrounding her or him. Differences in students' academic histories, their values and interests, and especially their beliefs about the purpose of school and the reasons for their own achievement are crucial to consider. Thus, it is difficult to prescribe a "one size fits all" approach to motivating students. Nevertheless, based on many research studies, some general patterns do appear to hold true for a wide range of students. Schools and teachers are not completely responsible for their students' motivation but neither are they powerless to influence it. The aim of this chapter, therefore, is to outline some suggestions for enhancing student motivation, supported by research findings, that are particularly relevant for middle school teachers and administrators. Currently, a number of different approaches to the study of motivation exist, including expectancy-value, self-efficacy, self-worth, and intrinsic motivation theories. It is not our purpose here to review all of these; they are described in detail elsewhere (see Pintrich & Schunk, 1996; Stipek, 1988, for reviews). Here we discuss three theories that are currently prominent and that have particular relevance for young adolescent students and their teachers.

❏ Attribution theory

The first point to be emphasized is that students' *perceptions* of their educational experiences are generally more influential for their motivation than the actual, objective reality of those experiences. For example, a history of success in a given subject area is generally assumed to lead one to continue persisting in that area. Weiner (1985, 1986), however, pointed out that students' beliefs about the reasons for their success (i.e., their attributions for success) will determine whether this is true. Imagine a 7th grade girl who has always done well in math but who, seemingly inexplicably, lacks the confidence to elect a challenging math class. Pointing out this student's previous achievements in math may have little effect if she believes that her prior success was mainly due to luck or to the relatively easy work in her earlier classes. In contrast, if the same student believes that her past success resulted from a combination of good work habits and consistent effort, she is more likely to take up the challenge of an advanced class. Students' attributions for failure are also important influences on motivation. When students have a history of failure in school, it is particularly difficult for them to sustain the motivation to keep trying. Students who believe that their poor performance is due to factors out of their control (e.g., their own lack of ability or the perceived animosity of teachers) are unlikely to see any reason to hope for an improvement. In contrast, if students attribute their poor performance to a lack of important skills or to poor study habits (i.e., to something they can control), they are more likely to persist in the future. The implications of attribution theory for teachers revolve around the importance of understanding what students believe about the reasons for their academic performance. It is clearly important for classroom teachers to listen to students' explanations for past successes and failures and to be prepared to challenge, if necessary, maladaptive patterns of beliefs. In addition, research has demonstrated (e.g., Graham & Barker, 1990) that students make decisions about the ability and effort of one another from surprisingly scant evidence in classroom settings. Teachers can unknowingly communicate a range of attitudes about whether ability is fixed or modifiable and their expectations for individual students through their instructional practices (see Graham, 1990). We need to ask ourselves what assumptions our behavior is reinforcing: Do we communicate to our students that everyone has the ability to succeed, that effort and appropriate strategies are necessary components of improvement, that errors are an essential part of progress and something to be learned from? This emphasis on the "messages" that students perceive about the meaning of academic tasks also constitutes an important theme in the next theory to be discussed, known as goal theory.

❏ Goal theory

While attribution theory focuses on the reasons students perceive for their successes and failures in school, goal theory focuses on the reasons or purposes students perceive for achieving (e.g., Ames, 1992; Dweck & Leggett, 1988; Maehr & Midgley, 1991; Midgley, 1993; Nicholls, 1989). While different researchers define the constructs slightly differently, two main goal orientations are generally discussed. These are: 1. Task goals (also referred to as mastery goals, or learning goals). A task goal orientation represents the belief that the purpose of achieving is personal improvement and understanding. Students with a task goal orientation focus on their own progress in mastering skills and knowledge, and define success in those terms. 2. Ability goals (also referred to as performance goals or ego goals). An ability goal orientation represents the belief that the purpose of achieving is the demonstration of ability (or, alternatively, the concealment of a lack of ability). Students with an ability goal orientation focus on appearing competent, often in comparison to others, and define success accordingly. Studies of students' goal orientations generally find that the adoption of task goals is associated with more adaptive patterns of learning than is the adoption of ability goals, including the use of more effective cognitive strategies, a willingness to seek help when it is needed, a greater tendency to engage in challenging tasks, and more positive feelings about school and oneself as a learner (See Anderman & Maehr, 1994, for a review. See also Ryan, Hicks, & Midgley, 1997). If adopting a task goal orientation is related to positive educational outcomes for students, the question then arises as to how such an orientation can be fostered. Recent studies suggest that the policies and practices in classrooms and schools influence students' goal orientations (e.g., Ames & Archer, 1988; Maehr & Midgley, 1991). Table 1 includes specific suggestions for moving away from an ability-focus and toward a task-focus in middle schools. As described by Ames (1992), a task or ability focus is conveyed through a constellation of policies and practices. That is, students' motivation is not only influenced by, for example, the ways in which rewards are allocated. Rather, teachers communicate messages to their students about the meaning of achievement and effort through the full range of instructional decisions they make on a daily basis.

❑ Self-determination theory

A third motivational theory of particular importance for middle school educators is self-determination theory (Deci & Ryan, 1985). This theory describes students as having three categories of needs: needing a sense of competence, of relatedness to others, and of autonomy (or self-determination). Competence involves understanding how to, and believing that one can achieve various outcomes. Relatedness involves developing satisfactory connections to others in one's social group. Autonomy involves initiating and regulating one's own actions. Most of the research in self-determination theory focuses on the latter of these three needs. Within the classroom, autonomy needs could be addressed through allowing some student choice and input on classroom decision making. For young adolescent students, with their increased cognitive abilities and developing sense of identity, a sense of autonomy may be particularly important. Furthermore, students at this stage say that they want to be included in decision making and to have some sense of control over their activities. Unfortunately, research suggests that students in middle schools actually experience fewer opportunities for self-determination than they did in elementary school (e.g., Midgley & Feldlaufer, 1987). When students' developmental needs are not well met in their classrooms, their interest in and valuing of academic work can suffer. How, then, might classrooms support student autonomy, in adaptive ways? Deci, Vallerand, Pelletier, & Ryan (1991) summarized contextual factors that support student autonomy. Features such as the provision of choice over what types of tasks to engage in and how much time to allot to each, are associated with students' feelings of self-determination. In contrast, the use of extrinsic rewards, the imposition of deadlines, and an emphasis on evaluations detract from a feeling of self-determination and lead

TABLE 1
Strategies to Move Toward a Task-Focused Middle School Environment

	Move away from	Move toward
Grouping	Grouping by ability Over-use of standardized tests	Grouping by topic, interest, student choice Frequent reformation of groups
Competition/Cooperation	Competition between students Contests with limited winners	Cooperative Learning
Assessment	Using test data as a basis for comparison	Using test data for diagnosis Alternatives to tests such as portfolios
Grading	Normative grading Public display of grades	Grading for progress, improvement Involving students in determining their grades
Recognition/Rewards/Incentives	Recognition for relative performance Honor rolls for high grades Over-use of praise, especially for the completion of short, easy tasks	Recognition of progress improvement An emphasis on learning for its own sake
Student Input	Decisions made exclusively by administrators and teachers	Opportunities for choice, electives Student decision making, self-scheduling, self-regulation
Approaches to the Curriculum	Departmentalized approach to curriculum	Thematic approaches/interdisciplinary focus Viewing mistakes as a part of learning Allowing students to redo work Encouraging students to take academic risks
Academic Tasks	Rote learning and memorization Over-use of work sheets and textbooks Decontextualized facts	Providing challenging, complex work to students Giving homework that is enriching, challenging Encouraging problem solving, comprehension
Remediation	Pull out programs Retention	Cross-age tutoring, peer tutoring Enrichment

Reprinted from *Middle School Journal*, Nov, 1992

to a decrease in intrinsic motivation. These findings have been well known for some time and many educators are aware of such recommendations. In practice, however, providing for students' autonomy in the classroom is not easy. We recognize that the constraints of grading policies, curricula demands, and scheduling make it very difficult for many teachers to build flexibility into their programs. Furthermore, classroom management concerns often increase when students first attempt to regulate their own learning. It is important to recognize, however, that supporting student autonomy does not require major upheaval in the classroom or that teachers relinquish the management of students' behavior. Even small opportunities for choice, such as whether to work with a partner or independently, or whether to present a book review as a paper, poster, or class presentation, can increase students' sense of self-determination. Students can also be included in classroom decision making around issues such as seating arrangements, displays of work, and class rules. Finally, it is important to recognize that students' early attempts at regulating their own work may not always be successful. Good decision making and time management require practice. Teachers can help their students develop their self-regulation by providing limited choices between acceptable options, by assisting with breaking large tasks into manageable pieces, and by providing guidelines for students to use in monitoring their own progress. Thus, the teacher's role is less one of controlling students' learning and more one of supporting their efforts toward self-determination.

❏ Conclusion

Middle school teachers often teach many students over the course of a school day, and for a relatively short period of time. Given such brief contact with so many, it is easy to underestimate the influence that one's teaching practices can have on any one individual. We hope current moves to implement the middle school philosophy (e.g., Carnegie Council on Adolescent Development, 1989) will provide a more facilitative schedule for both teachers and students. But even in a highly structured and departmentalized middle school, teachers can take specific steps to provide a learning environment that will promote the motivation of all students. ℝ

References

Ames, C. (1992). Classrooms: Goals, structures, and student motivation. *Journal of Educational Psychology, 84* (3), 261-271.

Ames, C., & Archer, J. (1988). Achievement goals in the classroom: Students' learning strategies and motivation processes. *Journal of Educational Psychology, 80* (3), 260-267.

Anderman, E. M., & Maehr, M. L. (1994). Motivation and schooling in the middle grades. *Review of Educational Research, 64* (2), 287-309.

Carnegie Council on Adolescent Development. (1989). *Turning points: Preparing American youth for the 21st century.* New York: Carnegie Corporation.

Deci, E. L., & Ryan, R. M. (1985). *Intrinsic motivation and self-determination in human behavior.* New York: Plenum.

Deci, E. L., Vallerand, R. J., Pelletier, L. G., & Ryan, R. M. (1991). Motivation and education: The self-determination perspective. *Educational Psychologist, 26* (3 & 4), 325-346.

Dweck, C. S., & Leggett, E. L. (1988). A social-cognitive approach to motivation and personality. *Psychological Review, 95* (2), 256-273.

Eccles, J. S., & Midgley, C. (1989). Stage/environment fit: Developmentally appropriate classrooms for early adolescents. In R. E. Ames & C. Ames (Eds.), *Research on motivation in education* (Vol. 3, pp. 139-186). New York: Academic.

Graham, S. (1990). Communicating low ability in the classroom: Bad things good teachers sometimes do. In S. Graham and V. Folkes (Eds.), *Attribution theory: Applications to achievement, mental health, and interpersonal conflict* (pp. 17 - 36). Hillsdale, NJ: Erlbaum.

Graham, S., & Barker, G. (1990). The downside of help: An attributional-developmental analysis of helping behavior as a low ability cue. *Journal of Educational Psychology, 82* (1), 7-14.

Maehr, M. L., & Midgley, C. (1991). Enhancing student motivation: A schoolwide approach. *Educational Psychologist, 26* (3 & 4), 399-427.

Midgley, C. (1993). Motivation and middle level schools. In P. R. Pintrich & M. L. Maehr (Eds.), *Advances in motivation and achievement, Vol. 8: Motivation in the adolescent years* (pp. 219- 276). Greenwich, CT: JAI Press.

Midgley, C., & Feldlaufer, H. (1987). Students' and teachers' decision-making fit before and after the transition to junior high school. *Journal of Early Adolescence, 7* (2), 225-241.

Midgley, C., & Urdan, T. C. (1992). The transition to middle level schools: Making it a good experience for all students. *Middle School Journal, 24* (2) 5-14.

Nicholls, J. G. (1989). *The competitive ethos and democratic education.* Cambridge, MA: Harvard University Press.

Pintrich, P. R., & Schunk, D. H. (1996). *Motivation in education: Theory, research, and applications.* Englewood Cliffs, NJ: Prentice Hall.

Ryan, A. M., Hicks, L., & Midgley, C. (1997). Social goals, academic goals, and avoiding seeking help in the classroom. *Journal of Early Adolescence, 17* (2), 152-171.

Stipek, D. J. (1988). *Motivation to learn: From theory to practice.* 2nd ed. Needham Heights, MA: Allyn & Bacon.

Weiner, B. (1985). An attributional theory of achievement motivation and emotion. *Psychological Review, 92* (4) 548-573.

Weiner, B. (1986). *An attributional theory of motivation and emotion.* New York: Springer-Verlag.

Joanne M. Arhar

The Effects of Interdisciplinary Teaming on Teachers and Students

Reflecting the admonitions of John Dewey that "The school must itself be a community life" (Dewey, 1966, p. 358), middle school reformers advocate interdisciplinary teaming to create a "small community of learning" (Carnegie Council on Adolescent Development, 1989). Most middle level educators consider interdisciplinary team organization, in which teachers share students, space and schedule, an essential component in meeting the needs of young adolescents. According to a 1993 survey, 85% of the schools that have implemented the major components of the middle school believe teaming has contributed to the long-term effectiveness of their program (George & Shewey, 1994, p. 80).

In this review of literature, I will briefly examine the history, design, and incidence of interdisciplinary teams. I will then examine the effects of interdisciplinary teaming on teacher and student outcomes. Interdisciplinary teaming, as an organizational feature of middle schools, involves areas such as how authority is organized, how the work of teachers and students is organized, and how the social relations are structured. These relationships have an effect on teacher and student outcomes. Two strands of research – on teacher professionalism and student learning – help define the outcomes of this review.

❏ History of interdisciplinary teaming

Interdisciplinary teaming is not a recent innovation. Its historical roots lie, in part, in the Pontoon Transitional Design of the early 1960s that involved teacher autonomy in the decision-making process, flexible scheduling using large blocks of time, correlated subject matter, common planning time, and teacher collaboration (Clark & Clark, 1992). Early research on this comprehensive model of teaming showed students scoring higher on such achievement measures as math, reading, and social studies tests. Unfortunately, most systematic research on teaming was sporadic during the next two decades, and the topic did not reappear until the first reviews of teaming as a structural arrangement were published in *Middle School Journal* (Arhar, Johnston & Markle, 1988; Arhar, Johnston & Markle, 1989).

❏ Design and incidence of interdisciplinary teaming

Interdisciplinary team organization is "a way of organizing the faculty so that a group of teachers share: (1) the same group of students; (2) the responsibility for planning, teaching, and evaluating curriculum and instruction in more than one academic area; (3) the same schedule; and (4) the same area of the building" (George & Alexander, 1993, p. 249). Four large scale surveys have examined the incidence of teaming in middle-level schools (Alexander & McEwin, 1989; Epstein & Mac Iver, 1990; McEwin, Dickinson, & Jenkins,1996; Valentine, Clark, Irvin, Keefe & Melton, 1993). Teaming has increased from 33% (1989) to 42% (1990) to 57% (1992). The greatest percentage of teams are found in schools with a 6-7-8 grade configuration (66%), while the smallest percentage of teams are found in the 7-8-9 grade configuration (40%). Sixth grade has the greatest percentage of teams (55%), whereas the ninth grade has the fewest teams (9%).

Results of the 1992 study and the other national surveys indicate that the use of common planning time and individual planning time has also increased in the past years indicating an increased commitment to teaming. In addition it was found that most students in teamed schools were grouped heterogeneously indicating a commitment to equity and opportunity for all students. The subjects most commonly taught within teams are math, science, social studies language arts, and reading. These surveys have added a great deal to our awareness of the commitment schools are making to this "signature" middle school practice.

❏ Outcomes for teachers

Several recent studies add empirical support for the benefits of collaborative work for teacher professionalism, particularly in terms of satisfaction, efficacy, and commitment. McLaughlin's study of eight high schools (1993) portrayed professional communities of teachers as cohesive, collegial environments in which "teachers report a high level of innovativeness, high levels of energy and enthusiasm ...support for personal growth and learning...[and a] high level of commitment to teaching and to all of the students with whom they work" (p. 94). This portrait is similar to reports by Lee, Dedrick, and Smith (1991) and Raudenbush, Rowan, and Cheong (1992) who found that collaboration among high school teachers was positively related to teachers' feelings of efficacy and satisfaction.

Several studies conducted in middle schools add support to the belief that interdisciplinary teaming has the potential to enhance teacher professionalism. Mills, Powell, and Pollack (1992) investigated three teams in a junior high school. In their qualitative investigation, they describe how the personal isolation so characteristic of teachers' school lives is diminished within months after teams are formed. Gatewood, Cline, Green, and Harris (1992) found that teaming enhanced teachers' personal sense of professionalism. Husband and Short (1994) found that interdisciplinary team members felt significantly more empowered in all six factors under investigation (decision making, professional growth, status, self-efficacy, autonomy, and impact) than departmentally organized teachers. These studies in middle level schools indicate the importance of this organizational arrangement for enhancing the appeal of teaching as a profession.

In another study of restructuring in four middle schools, teachers reported that teaming undermined faculty ability to deal with issues related to the whole school. The dilemmas that interfered include: time conflicts between team or whole-school issues; increased involvement with their group of students; limited time for peer observation; competition between teams; and the tendency within teams to compromise rather than risk serious disagreement – leading important issues to be diluted. These dilemmas detracted from the development of a school-wide professional community (Kruse & Louis, 1995).

The positive outcomes of teaming will not occur by simply placing teachers together on teams. These outcomes are the result of preparing and supporting teachers through this process of change. Team processes are the subject of another review in this volume.

❏ Outcomes for students

The positive outcomes of collaboration for students include increased engagement in academic and school-related work, achievement, student attendance and behavior, and student belonging. While there are difficulties associated with team work, the increased feelings of efficacy and professional satisfaction that accompany well-structured collaboration has payoff for students. Ashton & Webb (1986) and Rosenholtz (1989) found that efficacy and satisfaction for teachers is associated with increased student achievement. Using a subsample of the NELS:88 data, Lee and Smith (1993) found that students in restructured middle level schools (less departmentalization, more heterogeneous grouping, more team teaching, and a composite index of other restructuring factors) scored significantly higher on achievement and engagement than students in non-restructured schools. Restructuring also equalized achievement and engagement among students of differing social backgrounds. These positive results were small, but statistically significant. Although this study does not isolate the impact of interdisciplinary teaming on student achievement and engagement, it portrays teaming as part of a larger and more complex realm of restructuring, a realm that is difficult to separate out into components parts. As reported in a review of literature on the effects of teaming on students (Arhar, Johnston, & Markle, 1989), teachers' collaboration is also associated in more direct ways with reduced disciplinary problems, increased student engagement in academic tasks, and clarification of learning goals. These outcomes are important in themselves, but they also act as mediating variables interacting with students in ways to enhance their academic learning.

The role of teaming in reducing student alienation is the subject of a series of studies. In a study of fourteen alternative high schools for students who were not succeeding in regular schools, Wehlage, Rutter, Smith, Lesko, and Fernandez (1989) found that the school-within-a school was an innovation that allowed teachers the flexibility, autonomy, and control that they needed to succeed with these students. They found that this structural arrangement enabled the kinds of relationships between teachers and students that encouraged both school membership and academic engagement for students as well as a supportive and collegial culture for teachers.

In Arhar's (1992, 1994) study of the relationship between student belonging and interdisciplinary teaming, 5000 students in teamed and non-teamed schools were compared on belonging to peers, teachers, and school. Students in teamed schools scored higher on belonging to teachers and to school than their non-teamed counterparts. There was no significant difference in scores of teamed and non-teamed students on bonding to peers.

In a follow-up study, Arhar and Kromrey (1995) divided the schools from the 1992 study into high-income pairs (teamed and non-teamed schools matched on a variety of variables) and low-income pairs (teamed and non-teamed). There was no significant difference between the belonging scores of students in teamed and non-teamed high-income schools. However, there was a significant difference between belonging to teacher scores in teamed and non-teamed schools that were categorized as low income schools. There was also a significant difference between belonging to peer scores in teamed and non-teamed low-income schools. These findings suggest that interdisciplinary teaming has the potential to create a sense of belonging for students who come from communities that do not provide the kind of social and economic support found in more affluent areas.

McPartland (1987) found that increased departmentalization has a negative effect on teacher-student relations, particularly for low-income students. He suggested that interdisciplinary teaming may partially ameliorate the negative effects of departmentalization on student-teacher relations while preserving the academic benefits of working with teachers who have specialized content expertise.

Bradock and McPartland's (1993) review of the literature on schooling and early adolescence offer an explanation for the importance of a caring climate and supportive school structures for disadvantaged youth. Disadvantaged youth are often found in lower tracks and in larger departmentalized schools in which teachers have daily contact with large numbers of students. In such schools, students have a difficult time finding the kind of environment that they need in order to be successful in their academic work. Teaming, with its possibility for flexibility (multi-age, time, space, etc.), autonomy, and personal advising, has the potential to decrease the feelings of alienation experienced by so many students.

Increased achievement, engagement, and belonging and decreased incidence of behavioral problems do not always occur when teaming is implemented. Wehlage, Smith, and Lipman (1992) reported that restructuring interventions that included teaming in urban middle schools were "supplemental" at best, leaving basic curricular and instructional practices, as well as relationships with students unchanged. Conditions which foster positive outcomes for students are the subject of a review on team processes.

❑ Summary and conclusion

Although current studies do not report a relationship between teaming and student dropout rates, a recent study of middle school dropouts (Rumberger, 1995) reports that high absenteeism, misbehavior, and poor academic performance are predictive of middle school students dropping out of school. Teaming, with its potential to minimize student social behavior problems and increase achievement though positive relationships and teacher professionalism, may have an indirect effect on the number of students who drop out.

The search for a positive relationship between interdisciplinary teaming and student achievement continues. The longitudinal study of levels of implementation of reform elements conducted by Felner, Jackson, Kasak, Mulhall, Brand, and Flowers (1997) suggests that higher levels of implementation are associated with increased achievement, fewer behavior problems, and student adjustment to school, particularly for "at-risk" students. While these outcomes are important, social elements of team communities such as the ability to care for one another, depend on one another, and share responsibility for problem solving and learning are also important ends in themselves. These social elements are much more than mechanisms to be manipulated for accomplishing academic aims – they are the valued *ends* of a middle school education. ⓡ

References

Alexander, W. M., & McEwin, C. K. (1989). *Schools in the middle: Status and progress.* Columbus, OH: National Middle School Association.

Arhar, J. M. (1992). Interdisciplinary teaming and the social bonding of middle level students. In J. Irvin (Ed.), *Transforming middle level education: Perspectives and possibilities* (pp. 139-161). Boston: Allyn and Bacon.

Arhar, J. M. (1994). Personalizing the social organization of middle-level schools: Does interdisciplinary teaming make a difference? In K. M. Borman and N. P. Greenman (Eds.), *Changing America education: Recapturing the past or inventing the future?* (pp. 325-350) Albany NY: SUNY.

Arhar, J. M., & Kromrey, J. (1995). Interdisciplinary teaming and the demographics of membership: A comparison of student belonging in high SES and low SES middle-level schools. *Research in Middle Level Education, 18* (2), 71-88.

Arhar, J. M., Johnston, J. H., & Markle, G. C. (1988). The effects of teaming and other collaborative arrangements. *Middle School Journal, 19* (4), 22-25.

Arhar, J. M., Johnston, J. H., & Markle, G. C. (1989). The effects of teaming on students. *Middle School Journal, 20* (3), 21-27.

Ashton P. T., & Webb, R.B. (1986). *Making a difference: Teachers' sense of efficacy and student achievement.* New York: Longman.

Bradock J. H., & McPartland, J. M. (1993). Education of early adolescents. In L. Darling-Hammond (Ed.), *Review of Research in Education, 19,* (pp.135-170). Washington, DC: American Educational Research Association.

Carnegie Council on Adolescent Development. (1989). *Turning points: Preparing American youth for the 21st century.* New York: Carnegie Corporation.

Clark, S. N., & Clark, D. C. (1992). The pontoon transitional design: A missing link in research on interdisciplinary teaming. *Research in Middle Level Education, 15* (2), 57-81.

Dewey, J. (1966). *Democracy and education.* New York: Macmillan.

Epstein, J. L., & Mac Iver, D. J. (1990). *Education in the middle grades: National practices and trends.* Columbus, OH: National Middle School Association.

Felner, R.D., Jackson, A.W., Kasak, D., Mulhall, P., Brand, S., & Flowers, N. (1997). The impact of school reform for the middle years. *Phi Delta Kappan, 78* (7) 528-549.

Gatewood, T.E., Cline, G., Green, G., & Harris, S.E. (1992). The middle school interdisciplinary team organization and its relationship to teacher stress. *Research in Middle Level Education, 15* (2), (27-40)

George P. S., & Alexander, W. M. (1993). *The exemplary middle school* (2nd Edition). New York: Holt, Reinhart and Winston, Inc.

George, P. S., & Shewey, K. (1994). *New evidence for the middle school.* Columbus, OH: National Middle School Association.

Husband, R. E., & Short, P. M. (1994). Interdisciplinary teams lead to greater teacher empowerment. *Middle School Journal, 26* (2), 58-60.

Johnston, J. H., Markle, G. C., & Arhar, J. M. (1988). Cooperation, collaboration, and the professional development of teachers. *Middle School Journal, 19* (3), 28-32.

Kruse, S., & Louis, K. S. (1995). Teacher teaming—opportunities and dilemmas. *Brief to principals.* (Brief No.11). Madison, WI: Center on Organization and Restructuring of Schools.

Lee, V. E., Dedrick, R. F., & Smith, J. B. (1991). The effects of the social organization of schools on teachers' efficacy and satisfaction. *Sociology of Education, 64* (3), 190-208.

Lee V., & Smith, J. (1993). Effects of school restructuring on the achievement and engagement of middle-grades students. *Sociology of Education, 66,* (3)164-187.

McLaughlin, M. W. (1993). What matters most in teachers' workplace context? In J. W. Little & M. W. McLaughlin (Eds.), *Teachers' work* (pp. 79-103). New York: Teachers College Press.

McPartland, J. M. (1987). *Balancing high quality subject matter instruction with positive teacher-student relations in the middle grades.* Baltimore, MD: Johns Hopkins University Center of Research on Elementary and Middle Schools.

Mills, R.A., Powell, R.R., & Pollack, J.P. (1992). The influence of interdisciplinary teaming on teacher isolation: A case study. *Research in Middle Level Education, 15* (2), 9-26.

Raudenbush, S. W., Rowan, B., & Cheon, Y. F. (1992). Contextual effects of the self-perceived efficacy of high school teachers. *Sociology of Education, 65,* (2), 150-167.

Rosenholtz, S. (1989). *Teacher's workplace: The social organization of schools.* New York: Longman.

Rumberger, R. W. (1995). Dropping out of middle school: A multilevel analysis of students and schools. *American Educational Research Journal, 32* (3), 583-625.

Valentine, J. W., Clark, D. C., Irvin, J. L., Keefe, J. W., & Melton, G. (1993). *Leadership in middle level education Volume 1: A national survey of middle level leaders and schools*. Reston, VA: National Association of Secondary School Principals.

Wehlage, G. G., Rutter, R. A., Smith, G. A., Lesko, N., & Fernandez, R. R. (1989). *Reducing the risk: Schools as communities of support*. New York: Falmer.

Wehlage, G. G., Smith, G. A., & Lipman, P. (1992). Restructuring urban schools: The New Futures experience. *American Educational Research Journal, 29* (1), 51-93.

H. James McLaughlin and Nancy M. Doda

Teaching with Time on Your Side: Developing Long-Term Relationships in Schools

*Alas, I have finally arrived at a place of comfort
with my students and now I must bid them farewell.*

This middle school teacher's comment reflects the sentiments of many who recognize that by the close of a school year strong classroom relationships and in many cases productive work patterns have evolved. Few would deny that time can offer amazing dividends in a teaching-learning context.

In spite of the fact that nearly all teachers readily acknowledge the hard-won gifts of a year's time with young adolescents, most middle schools march on in the tradition of grouping children by grade or age and moving them on with each passing year to start the process all over again. In exchange for the novelty each new school year brings, teachers and children must wipe the slate clean and begin anew with the challenge of cultivating the best context for learning – often the one they left behind.

The multiyear classroom has a long and illustrious history in American education. As late as 1918, there were close to 200,000 one-room schools in the United States, which accounted for 71% of all public schools (Miller, 1990). It can be gathered from stories told and research conducted that these schools, in which children of different ages learned together for many years, were small, familiar, communal settings. Students were known exceedingly well, and continuous and individual progress was more readily managed. Families were directly involved in children's schooling. Teachers could not easily give up on even the most challenging child, knowing that with each passing day there were years to follow. Whatever the school's shortcomings, there was a sense of community that can only be developed through continuous years of living out days together (Fogarty, 1993). These attributes constitute some of the same reasons stated by proponents of modern versions of multiyear teaching.

There is no question, however, that the appeal of the one-room school remains fantasy, given the financial and human limitations of having one teacher under one roof with multiaged learners. Currently, fewer than 1,000 one-room schools remain in the United States. The promise of multiyear arrangements, however, is not fantasy at all. Many elementary schools today use multiage and multiyear classroom formats. Rural communities and villages depend on such groupings to manage small school populations. Likewise, increasing numbers of elementary and middle level schools have embraced the alternatives to traditional grouping by single ages and single years, and it is encouraging to note that the support for such a change is found in a rich history of practice and research.

❏ Why We Need Long-Term Relationships ❏ in Middle Schools

More than curiosity or nostalgia brings middle school practitioners into conversations about multiyear grouping. One original rationale emerged when Eichhorn (1966) documented the absence of any correlation between grade level and student development during early adolescence. That variability remains, and it is compounded by the staggering diversity of the children we serve now. Such diversity has led some to reexamine the assumptions from which we group and teach children. What purposes do grade levels serve? Is the single year the optimal amount of time for the teaching-learning process? What grouping best serves the needs of our children preparing for today's society?

While Eichhorn's rationale piqued some interest, today's middle school educators are intrigued for additional reasons. One of the numerous changes in family life is that young adolescents spend less time outside of school with adults, and their social environment is often unstable (Scales, 1991). Scales asserted that the number one concern for educators in the 1990s is: "How can we ensure that young adolescents establish reliable and caring attachments, particularly with adults?" (p. 42) Scales goes on to say that to establish stronger attachments, schools for young adolescents must be places in which there is "informality, flexibility, and intimacy" (pp. 8-9).

Citizens and educators alike express a growing concern for the preservation of democracy and an accompanying demand for improved cooperative citizenship. Some see multiyear grouping as a way to create school settings in which children are encouraged by adults to participate in community life and to develop cooperative social skills and attitudes. Young adolescents need to experience community, and they need to participate in mentoring and cross-age relationships (Scales, 1991).

Educators are also concerned that it is increasingly difficult to reach disaffected students in the confines of a single year's time, and they are eager to examine ways to salvage time in the teaching-learning equation. Teachers worry that today's young adolescents are increasingly vulnerable to declining self-esteem. Students' motivation, their self-concept related to their abilities, and their attitudes toward school decrease as they move from 6th to 8th grades (see Anderman & Maehr, 1995, and the work of Eccles, Wigfield, Midgley, Reuman, Mac Iver, & Feldlaufer, 1993 for the negative effects of traditional middle level schools.) According to Beane and Lipka (1986), the cultivation of a humanistic (relationship-centered) rather than a custodial (control-centered) climate is critical to the self-esteem of young adolescents. When teachers and students spend repeated years together, it is reasonable to believe that a humanistic climate can be achieved and that positive relationships would reduce the need for control-centered teaching.

In light of diminished adult support and an accompanying decline in students' positive attitudes toward school, it is no surprise that problems associated with retention and dropping out have come to the forefront. Recently, Roderick (1994) reviewed the research on retention of students and related it to dropout rates. She called for "promotion with remediation" (p. 749) and offered alternatives to retaining students in the elementary and middle grades. One alternative that Roderick did not consider is multiyear grouping, because long-term relationships are essential if we are to engage struggling students who are otherwise passed along with little accountability or retained with little hope of gaining ground.

Finally, as practices like interdisciplinary teaming, curriculum integration, heterogeneous grouping, special education inclusion, cooperative learning, and alternative assessment have found their way into the middle school, practitioners have been more prone to explore experimental grouping arrangements that resist separating, labeling, and sorting children by predefined descriptors. All of these and other issues have coaxed many middle school educators into examining alternatives to single-grade and single-year grouping.

❏ Four Ways to Develop Long-Term Relationships ❏

Educators have tried to strengthen the long-term bonds between families and schools in four ways. Perhaps the most well known is that of the mixed-age classroom, a modern day analog of the traditional one-room school. Before continuing, a clarification of terminology may be helpful. Veenman (1995) used the word *multigraded* to mean a grouping of multiple age students that is created out of convenience or necessity (such as combining 6 third-graders with 15 fourth-graders to stay within mandated class sizes). The strategy of combining students from several grade levels has often been used in small villages, rural communities, or developing nations to manage small numbers of students or shifting school enrollments (Veenman, 1995). In the U. S., this arrangement is most common in elementary schools that have self-contained classes; middle grades students are rarely combined in this manner.

Multiage is a term commonly used today to connote mixed-age groups. In most cases where this term is applied to the grouping pattern, it is driven by pedagogical rather than economic reasons. During the 1960s and 1970s in the United Kingdom, during the heyday of the British infant schools, mixed-age grouping was known as "vertical" or "family" grouping. Multiage differs slightly from ungraded or nongraded grouping (primarily an elementary school idea) which does not differentiate between different grade levels and allows for students' continuous progress through the curriculum. Unlike the historic one-room schools, multiage classrooms rarely include students from more than three grades. In this chapter we address the value of intentional multiage and multiyear grouping, and we prefer Miller's (1996) simple definition of the term: "I use multiage to mean two or more grade levels that have been intentionally blended together to improve learning" (p. 12).

Whether it is instituted for administrative or pedagogical reasons, multigrade and multiage grouping enable interaction across age groups and may involve a long-term relationship among students and teachers. In a multiyear program of this sort, children in different grade levels learn side-by-side and the oldest children move on at the close of their stay, to be replaced by a new group of younger students each year. For example, in a sixth, seventh, and eighth grade multiage team, as eighth graders complete their three-year residency, new incoming sixth graders take their place. Some programs have arranged for a multiage class in only one subject. In this plan, students are grouped and regrouped in specific subjects by needs rather than grade, thus providing enormous flexibility for grouping and regrouping that would otherwise not be available.

Though not dramatically different from multiage grouping, developmental age grouping is another arrangement of several grade level groups that are combined according to developmental growth indicators. Based on the work of Eichhorn (1966), this plan works to create communities in a middle school that share common developmental needs and concerns in a mixed age setting. Spring Hill Middle School, in Spring Hill, Florida was originally designed for developmental age grouping. The plan organized students into three learning units or communities. Unit I housed the fifth graders and the developmentally younger sixth graders. Unit II housed the older sixth graders and younger seventh graders. Finally, Unit III housed the older seventh graders and eighth graders. This plan functioned so that each child spent a period of two years with the same group of teachers and with one-half of the same student group.

In more recent years, schools have experimented with a concept in which students from a single grade-level group stay intact and remain with their class or team of teachers for several consecutive years. In this arrangement, students do not experience instruction in mixed-age groups. Rather, the focus is on the long-term relationships facilitated by a continuous, year-to-year instructional plan. This arrangement has a long history. It was described as "teacher rotation" in a Department of Interior random memo from 1913. In the 1970s, Paul George and educators at Lincoln Middle School in Gainesville, Florida, wrote a monograph published by National Middle School Association (1987) describing this approach as "student-teacher progression." More recently, writers have referred to this organizational plan as "looping," a term that probably originated in the United Kingdom or Canada. The idea is international in scope. Koln-Holweide Comprehensive School is the most famous of several schools in Germany that have used looping for the last 20 years (Ratzki, 1988). While there is very little research on looping, practitioners claim it reduces wasted time at the start of each year, increases stability and routine, facilitates the membership of reticent students, and enhances classroom cooperation.

A fourth approach entails grouping teams of students together for several years to create a "school-within-a-school." This approach has also been referred to as the "house plan" or the "community" system. The students are not necessarily in multiage groups and they may not stay with exactly the same cohort for years. This structure has often been used in large high schools, though it is also seen in middle schools. For example, within a school comprised of 2,000 students, grades 6-8, there might be six "communities" located in different areas of the school facility. Each community could incorporate one 6th, one 7th, and one 8th grade team with an entire community population of over 300 students. In some schools, students would then stay within that community from 6th to 8th grades, though their teachers might change from year to year (see Oxley, 1989).

❏ What We Know From Research ❏

While the the pedagogy and practices are intriguing, how worthy are they? Many possible benefits of establishing long-term relationships exist in school communities, but the research on different approaches is spotty. We know of no full-scale reviews on looping, developmental age grouping, or schools-within-a-school. The majority of the research on multiage/multigrade classrooms has been at the elementary level, but many of the studies to date have included grades which serve young adolescents, and the research is varied and illuminating. To simplify, we have synthesized findings by large issues of concern, drawing mainly from four comprehensive reviews of research conducted by Miller (1990; 1991), Pavan (1992), Gutiérrez and Slavin (1992), and Veenman (1995). When examined collectively, these reviews provide a rich picture of what is known about multigrade, multiage, and multiyear grouping.

Miller (1990, 1991) summarized the findings of quantitative and qualitative research studies on multiage grouping. Miller's reviews featured data from rural schools, and he contributed to our understanding by trying to examine qualitative data, something that few reviewers have attempted. Gutiérrez and Slavin (1992) helped us to differentiate among "Joplin-like" grouping, in which students are grouped across ages only for reading; "comprehensive" grouping that mixes the ages for most or all classes, but uses whole-class and small-group instruction; and "individualized" grouping in which students primarily work alone. Pavan (1992) asserted the importance of considering "nongradedness" or "multiage" not merely as a structure, but as a set of instructional practices such as cooperative learning and peer tutoring. Veenman (1995) distinguished between "multigrade" and "multiage" groups, as noted earlier, and incorporated international studies in his review.

❏ Achievement

In all four reviews, the majority of studies point to the largely neutral and occasionally positive effects of multiage and multigraded grouping on achievement. Children in nongraded classrooms fare as well or better than children in single-graded classrooms on standardized measures of achievement (Gutiérrez & Slavin, 1992; Miller, 1990; Pavan, 1992). According to Pavan's review (1992), 91% of the 57 reviewed U. S. and Canadian studies revealed that students in nongraded settings did as well as or outperformed students in graded classes. Since many have challenged the viability of mixed-age teaching in terms of curriculum mastery, Pavan's observation that students in nongraded programs performed as well as or better on standardized achievement tests is noteworthy. In Miller's review (1990), students in multiaged settings outperformed their graded counterparts on reading, but did not do as well as graded students on mathematics.

Since a grouping arrangement alone may not be sufficient to make an impact on achievement, what Gutiérrez and Slavin (1992) found in their "best evidence synthesis" of research makes sense. They reported that " the effects of nongraded programs depend on the types of programs being implemented" (p. 366). Only two types of nongraded programs seemed to show significant achievement gains when compared with graded programs:

1. "Joplin-like programs, in which students are grouped across age lines in just one subject, usually reading;
2. Programs that utilize cross-age grouping in many subjects but do not rely on individualized instruction at the expense of more comprehensive approaches to instruction, including cooperative and teacher-led methods" (p. 368).

When teachers employed comprehensive instructional methods, no study supported the single graded group (p. 352). Moreover, once again, language and reading showed the most positive gains, with mixed results in mathematics. This success in the language areas is not surprising, since language acquisition is enhanced by a rich and diverse context of exposure. Conducting the most comprehensively international review to date, Veenman (1995) reviewed 56 studies, 37 of them U. S. or Canadian and the remainder from various international sites. Veenman's review examined the cognitive and noncognitive effects of multigrade and multiage classrooms. Veenman concluded that the effects on achievement were neutral.

In nearly all cases where single-grade students outperformed mixed-grade students, the achievement gains appeared related to factors other than the grouping. Although differences between two schools were not considered when comparing achievement results in two U. S. middle schools, Marsh (1980) found her single-grade students did better on measures of achievement. In a study of multigraded versus graded schools in West Germany, Fippinger (1967) found that students in single-grade classes outperformed their multigrade counterparts. The difference appeared to be related to the fact that students in the graded schools were from markedly higher socioeconomic levels than students in the nongraded schools. In numerous other U.S. cases, the superiority of graded students' achievement was connected with parents' self-selection or location (suburban vs. rural) and the consequent social class and ability issues that such differences can create (Miller, 1990; Veenman, 1995). Moreover, several of these studies were conducted in situations that deliberately placed highly successful students in the single-graded contexts.

In reviewing these findings, it is important to recall that none of the studies actually controlled for teaching practice, so it is difficult to know to what extent differences in instruction played a role. As one researcher speculated, where single grade classes outperformed mixed-grade classes, there were enormous differences in teacher preparation, with far more extensive training provided for the teachers who were to teach grade level classes (Rowley, 1992).

❏ Affective and social outcomes

While the jury is out with regard to the relationship between multiage and multigrade grouping and achievement, the picture is clearer for affective outcomes. As Miller (1989) asserted at the close of his review:

"These studies indicate that being a student in a multigraded classroom does not negatively affect academic performance nor student social relationships and attitudes. . . When it comes to student affect, the case for multigrade organizations appears much stronger, with multigrade students outperforming single-grade students in over 75 percent of the measures used" (p. 13).

Although it is not one of the primary reviews included here, one of the more provocative reviews was written by Pratt (1986). From his review of experimental studies, Pratt could make no conclusions about achievement. He did claim, however, that students' self-concepts were strengthened by multiage arrangements. After analyzing pertinent anthropological studies, he also concluded that multiage classrooms are "socially and psychologically healthy places" because they promote "children's friendships" and provide extended contact with adults and peers of varying ages" (p. 114). He further stated that one vital aspect of multiage grouping's effects was the availability of cross-age tutoring, which may be correlated with higher academic achievement and enhanced self-esteem for both the tutor and the tutee.

Pavan (1992) reached similar conclusions regarding student affect. She noted that students in multigraded schools scored higher than graded school students on the Coopersmith Self-Esteem Inventory and Piers-Harris Children's Self-Concept Scale. In addition to improved self-esteem, students in nongraded schools had superior attitudes towards self and school. One would expect this increase in attitude would translate into improved discipline and in one study it did. Students in that study spent five years in a nongraded junior high/middle school setting and significantly fewer students were referred for discipline procedures. Moreover, in that study underachievers from nongraded schools had better self-concepts, attitudes towards school, and academic achievement than underachievers in graded schools (Pavan, 1992).

With young adolescents, issues of peer relationships could have an impact on the outcomes of any initiative. In a study of the effect of grade-level status on student perceptions about their interactions in cross-age pairs in a combined third and fifth grade classroom, Young and Boyle (1994) uncovered what they called the "Lady Bountiful Syndrome." Based on an analysis of interviews, results showed that fifth graders perceived the third graders as incapable and did things for the third graders rather than helping them learn to work independently. In cross-age situations where such status/ knowledge perceptions are at work, Young and Boyle concluded that peer interactions could interfere with the learning process. Also addressing peer interactions, a case study of cross-race friendships in two racially diverse graded and multigraded schools showed encouraging results favoring the multigraded school (D'Amico & Bell-Nathaniel, 1981).

Another intriguing study (Smith, 1993) focused on student attitudes towards multiage classrooms based on gender and grade level in two multiage classrooms (grades 3-4 and 5-6). Results showed no significant difference based on gender, but students in the two upper grades had more negative attitudes towards multiage grouping than did the younger students in each class. It is not clear from the study whether this practice was recently instituted and thus would have been new to the fourth and sixth grade youngsters. If that were the case, the negative attitudes seem understandable. Where grade level carries status, older students new to multiage grouping might feel demoted. On the other hand, French, Waas, Stright, and Baker (1986) noted that in a multiyear structure, more students had the opportunity to be leaders including older students who otherwise might not have assumed leadership positions.

While there are very few studies of looping, the results of those few that have been concluded are quite positive. George (1987) indicated that teachers and students saw many benefits in staying together. Mizelle (1993) described the Delta Project, an interdisciplinary team of four teachers who followed a group of students for three consecutive years. During the two years when the study was conducted, students' self-esteem and attitudes towards school improved. Mizelle described how looping offered students: (1) opportunities for working in groups that accept diversity; (2) opportunities for personally significant learning experiences; (3) opportunities for self-evaluation; and (4) opportunities to view mistakes as a normal part of the learning process. In addition, Pate, Mizelle, Hart, Jordan, Matthews, Matthews, Scott, and Brantley (1993) asserted that looping enhanced student collaboration, enabled long-term curricular projects to flourish, and "created a positive working and learning environment for both teachers and students" (p. 27).

❏ Limitations of the research

We have already made the point obliquely, but will state it more clearly: there is a startling lack of research evidence mustered on behalf of multiage grouping, looping, and schools-within-a-school in American middle schools. Quite a bit of research exists on multiage grouping in elementary schools and some research on schools-within-a-school in high schools. We can find almost no substantive research on looping at any grade level, though there are a growing number of descriptions of practice. What is more, even the research that has been conducted often fails to track students and teachers over two or more years; most of the studies are one-year snapshots that fail to capture the complexity of multiyear learning. For all the talk and anecdotal evidence about these grouping ideas, in the coming years we must conduct much more substantive research about the benefits of multiyear teaming and learning. Educational relationships are based in part on the participants' perceptions of students' educational success. If teachers, parents, and students cannot be shown that looping and multiage teaching arrangements yield positive affective and cognitive gains, then multiyear grouping may not last.

❏ What Hinders or Facilitates ❏ Long-Term Educational Relationships?

❏ Instructional issues

While research on specific outcomes is essential to program decision-making, practitioners are often most concerned with the implementation. As one interested teacher put it, "Sounds wonderful, but would it work?" Fortunately, we have many credible reports that describe what hinders and facilitates new grouping arrangements.

Miller's (1991) qualitative review focused on how teachers and administrators view the job of working in multiage situations and how instruction is carried out. Most teachers believed that teaching in a multiage classroom was more difficult than teaching in a graded classroom, and that it required special preparation. In particular, teachers highlighted individualizing instruction, unit planning, classroom organization, and curriculum development as the most challenging tasks that must be performed well in a multiage teaching situation. Anderson and Pavan (1993) and Gutiérrez and Slavin (1994) asserted that students should be engaged in learning from one another, they should be regrouped for instruction within and across age or grade levels, and any cross-age grouping should be flexible. Veenman (1995) believed that frequent assessment of mastery, increased amounts of teaching time for homogeneous instructional groups, and the organization of subject areas by levels (not age groups) are also important features (p. 373). All of these authors offer vital ideas for teachers and administrators to consider.

Different approaches may have different problems of implementation. For some teachers, looping may be less intimidating than multiage teaching. With looping, teachers can maintain a grade-level approach to curriculum as they follow students from year to year. In addition, some parents may be uncomfortable with the notion of eighth graders and sixth graders in one room and many teachers worry that they will be spread too thin with the diverse demands of various age and grade levels. Looping does require that teachers adjust to new curricula for the first cycle of years, but they may do so with fewer struggles in the process.

All innovations in curriculum and instruction require leadership if they are to succeed. Miller (1996) emphasized the "common traits" of leadership in developing greater parent and teacher support for multiage grouping. He proposed a set of key principles that enable multiage grouping to work. We believe his principles apply to any effort to establish long-term relationships in schools.

1. Find research-based information and descriptive stories of practice before beginning planning.
2. No single model of practice will suffice.
3. Change comes top-down and bottom-up, at the same time.
4. Teachers must challenge their preconceived notions of student grouping and the most appropriate instructional strategies.

5. "Strategic, incremental steps" are more important than "large leaps that are not well thought out and articulated" (p. 17).

❏ A matter of continuity

A central feature of any multiyear grouping, whether it is looping or a multiage team that stays together for more than one year, is that teachers develop a curriculum articulated across the years. This feature has great promise because it can provide for what Miller (1994) called "social and academic continuity" (p. 94). This sort of curriculum articulation requires that teachers be provided additional time and resources for planning.

For teachers engaged in looping or multiage, multiyear teaming, the opportunity to know students and their families closely is of paramount importance. Anne Bingham (1993) talked about the power of a "shared history" (p. 77). Parents can come to know teachers better, in terms of their expectations, their teaching styles, and their ways of communicating. Parents also have a chance to participate in long-term projects over a period of years (Alioto, 1994). Varying types of family involvement are possible, and many benefits of a real "family-school-community partnership" exist (National Education Goals Report, 1996). Multiyear arrangements can help such partnerships to flourish, but the school educators have to develop plans that incorporate creative ideas about how to engage parents and families.

❏ Final Reflections ❏

In some respects these are desperate times. Increasing numbers of educators express concern about the ever-emerging population of youngsters who are more difficult to reach and teach. Embarrassing numbers of young adolescents in the United States do not fare well in school. Remedial and punitive measures have failed miserably. Many have a sense that one new innovation after the next has done little to change the foundation and fabric of school relationships upon which all teaching and learning is built. *The National Education Goals Report* (1996) described the progress or lack of progress in key educational areas over the last two years, and then calls for new approaches to long-term assessment, the use of textbooks, the use of themes, and long-term projects. We believe that teachers constructing a multiyear curriculum have a greater chance to develop those approaches because they are able to develop social and academic continuity and to emphasize students' progress over time.

Ways to facilitate stronger relationships in schools are many; we have examined only a few. From our perspective, and in light of the research we've shared, there is great promise in long-term teaching relationships. We must move from a reliance on short-term affection or control to a renewal of long-term respect between young adolescents and adults. With time on our side, using creative grouping alternatives, we open a whole world of possibilities. ⓡ

References

The references are categorized according to whether they are individual research studies about the three approaches, research summaries, descriptions of programs and practices, or miscellaneous books and articles.

Research Studies

Anderman, E. M., & Maehr, M. L. (1995). Motivation and schooling in the middle grades. *Review of Educational Research, 64* (2), 287-309.

D'Amico, S. B., & Bell-Nathaniel, D. (1981, April). *Facilitating interracial contact: Let the structure do it for you.* Paper presented at the annual meeting of the American Educational Research Association, Los Angeles, CA.

Eccles, J. S., Wigfield, A., Midgley, C., Reuman, D., Mac Iver, D., & Feldlaufer, H. (1993). Negative effects of traditional middle schools on students' motivation. *Elementary School Journal, 93* (5), 553-574.

Fippinger, F. (1967). An empirical study of scholastic achievement of pupils in fully and partially grade-differentiated schools. *School and Psychology, 14* (4), 97-104.

French, D. C., Waas, G. A., Stright, A. L., & Baker, J. A. (1986). Leadership asymmetries in mixed-age children's groups. *Child Development, 57* (5), 1277-1283.

George, P. S. (1987). *Long-term teacher-student relationships: A middle school case study.* Columbus, OH: National Middle School Association.

Marsh, M. M. (1980). *Academic achievement and school-wide grouping of students in two middle schools.* Unpublished doctoral dissertation, University of Florida, Gainesville, FL.

Mizelle, N. B. (1993, April). *Classroom structures and student motivation: A study of the Delta Project.* Paper presented at the Annual Meeting of the American Educational Research Association, Atlanta, GA.

Pate, P. E., Mizelle, N. B., Hart, L. E., Jordan, J., Matthews, R., Matthews, S., Scott, V., & Brantley, V. (1993). The Delta Project: A three year longitudinal study of middle school change. *Middle School Journal, 25* (1), 24-27.

Roderick, M. (1994). Grade retention and school dropout: Investigating the association. *American Educational Research Journal, 31* (4), 729-759.

Rowley, S. D. (1992). *Multigrade classrooms in Pakistan: How teacher conditions and practices affect student achievement.* Unpublished doctoral dissertation, Harvard University, Cambridge, MA.

Smith, K. A. (1993). *Attitudes towards multiple aged classrooms of third, fourth, fifth, and sixth grade students.* (ERIC Document Reproduction Service No. ED 361088).

Young, S. J., & Boyle, R. A. (1994, April). *Grade level status effects in multiage groupwork: The Lady Bountiful syndrome.* Paper presented at the Annual Meeting of the American Educational Research Association, New Orleans, LA.

Research Summaries

Gutiérrez , R., & Slavin, R. E. (1992). Achievement effects of nongraded elementary schools: A best evidence synthesis. *Review of Educational Research, 62* (4), 333-376.

Miller, B. A. (1989). *The multigrade classroom: A resource handbook for small rural schools.* Portland, OR: Northwest Regional Educational Lab. (ERIC Document 320-719).

Miller, B. A. (1990). A review of the quantitative research on multigrade instruction. *Journal of Research in Rural Education, 7* (1), 1-8.

Miller, B. A. (1991). A review of the qualitative research on multigrade instruction. *Journal of Research in Rural Education, 7* (2), 3-12.

Pavan, B. N. (1992). The benefits of nongraded schools. *Educational Leadership, 50* (2), 22-25.

Pratt, D. (1986). On the merits of multiage classrooms. *Journal of Research in Rural Education, 3* (3), 111-115.

Veenman, S. (1995). Cognitive and noncognitive effects of multigrade and multiage classes: A best-evidence synthesis. *Review of Educational Research, 65* (4), 319-381.

Descriptions of Practice and Programs

Alioto, K. (1994). Multiage: A parent's view. In P. Chase & J. Doan (Eds.), *Full circle: A new look at multiage education* (pp. 107-114). Portsmouth, NH: Heinemann.

Bingham, A. (1993). Snapshots of a multiage community. In C. Rathbone (Ed.), *Multiage portraits: Teaching and learning in mixed-age classrooms* (pp. 65-84). Peterborough, NH: Crystal Springs Books.

Miller, B. (1994). *Children at the center: Implementing the multiage classroom.* Portland, OR: Northwest Regional Educational Laboratory.

Oxley, D. (1989). Smaller is better. *American Educator, 13* (1), 28-31, 51-52.

Ratzki, A. (1988). The remarkable impact of creating a school community. *American Educator, 12* (1), 10-17, 38-39.

Miscellaneous Resources

Anderson, R. H., & Pavan, B. N. (1993). *Nongradedness: Helping it to happen.* Lancaster, PA: Technomic.

Author. (1996). *The national educational goals report: Building a nation of learners.* Washington, DC: U. S. Government Printing Office.

Beane, J., & Lipka, R. (1986). *Self-concept, self-esteem, and the curriculum.* New York: Teachers College Press.

Eichhorn, D. H. (1966). *The middle school.* New York: Center for Applied Research in Education.

Fogarty, R. (Ed.). (1993). *The multiage classroom: A collection.* Palatine, IL: IRI/Skylight Publishers.

Miller, B. A. (1996). A basic understanding of multiage grouping. *The School Administrator, 53* (1), 12-17.

Scales, P. C. (1991). *A portrait of young adolescents in the 1990s.* Carrboro, NC: Center for Early Adolescence.

Betty J. Bennett

Middle Level Discipline and Young Adolescents: Making the Connection

Concern about classroom management and school discipline is not new. Since the first public opinion Gallup poll involving education in 1969, school discipline has been represented as the number one concern on 14 of 15 occasions. In the twenty-first annual Gallup poll of the public attitude toward public schools, "lack of school discipline" ranked number two, second only to drug problems (Evanac, 1993). Numerous methods and materials have been developed on disciplinary approaches because the problem of discipline in the schools is so immediate. Few proposed discipline methods or models, however, deal specifically with the unique needs of young adolescents even though most teachers who work with middle school age students usually feel that, in reference to classroom discipline, this particular age group is the most difficult group with which to work (Stradley & Aspinall, 1975).

Perhaps this lack of a specific middle school discipline model is partially due to the fact that there is no single model of the All-American Young Adolescent because of the vast physical, social, emotional, and intellectual differences between them. Because of this variability, especially emotional development, attempts have been made to consider these needs and provide a unique program for students of this age group. It is particularly important for middle schools to strive to achieve an effective plan for discipline that not only serves the school environment, but also assists young adolescents in making a successful transition through these trying years.

Through my review of the relevant literature on discipline effectiveness, I have identified eight themes that were most prominent in the literature: (1) development of a school-wide discipline plan; (2) inservice programs; (3) classroom discipline plans; (4) a repertoire of discipline models for teachers; (5) educating students; (6) implementation; (7) leadership; and (8) positive school climate.

❑ Development of a school-wide discipline plan

Discipline, to be effective, must be a school-wide effort (Evanac, 1993). This effort begins with an awareness of all of those involved of the need for school-wide procedures for preventing and/or responding to disruptive student behavior. In fact, it has been estimated that three out of every four schools have some form of printed disciplinary code. The development of a school-wide management program not only raises expectations and increases the visibility of student management issues, but can reduce disruptive behavior and improve student achievement (Jones, 1984).

Much literature exists describing procedures necessary for developing effective discipline plans. The one recommendation that is most frequently mentioned among the plethora of literature on developing discipline plans is that of the plan's development being of a collaborative nature. Burns (1985) stated that "the key to effective discipline" is in collaboration between the teachers and the administration in the development of the school-wide discipline plan (p. 3). A plan single-handedly devised by the administration would likely meet with immediate opposition from those faculty members who might feel that the plan was being imposed upon them (Lane, 1989).

A majority of the literature reviewed indicated a need for involving teachers and administrators, as well as including input from students and parents in developing a school-wide discipline plan (Blendinger, Cornelious, McGrath, & Rose, 1993; Evanac, 1993; Gaustad, 1992; Gilchrist, 1989; Gottfredson, Gottfredson, & Hybl, 1990; Hartzell & Petrie, 1992; Jones, 1984; Lane, 1989; Lasley & Wayson, 1982; MacNaughton & Johns, 1991; Menacker, Hurwitz, & Weldon, 1988; Short, 1988). When parents are more involved in the decision making process at the school, they will be more supportive. Parent interest and concern needs to be revitalized to help modify their youngsters' behavior (Evanac, 1993). Student input is also important. Furtwengler and Konnert (1982) demonstrated a relationship between student involvement in the discipline policy formation and improved student conduct levels. "People want to be involved they want to know what's going on, they want to be associated with excellence, and they will work hard to make it happen – if you let them" (Gilchrist, 1989, p. 143).

❏ Inservice programs

In a survey conducted by Youngblood (1989), principals identified discipline as one of the subjects that they wanted to learn more about. Likewise, 48 percent of the teachers and 52 percent of the administrators identified the principles in classroom management and discipline as their top choice of topics to be covered during certification preparation in a questionnaire conducted by DeMedio and Mazur-Stewart (1990).

"We believe that an effective inservice program should provide for a degree of school-wide uniformity and still allow for sufficient diversity to meet the needs of individual teachers" (MacNaughton & Johns, 1991, p. 52). The three steps recommended are (1) knowledge of the basic principles learned through effective teacher research; (2) a background in the range of management and discipline models available to teachers; and (3) training in the school-wide discipline plan itself. Wolfgang (1995) is also a proponent of teachers being familiar with a variety of management and discipline models from which to draw methods, depending on the teacher's personality, teaching style, and the situation at hand. Many of the teacher training programs dealing with discipline are outdated and ineffective and provide teachers with one-dimensional strategies for solving discipline problems after they occur. It is recommended that inservice training on effective discipline focus on methods that are both preventive and corrective.

Finally, it is important that teachers clearly understand the school-wide discipline plan, itself, as well as its implementation and their roles and responsibilities in this implementation (Gaustad, 1992; Gottfredson, Karweit, & Gottfredson, 1989; Jones, 1984; Short, 1988). Gottfredson, Karweit, & Gottfredson (1989) stated that research on the sources of school disruption clearly indicated that schools in which the teachers say they understand what the school rules are experience less disruption than others.

❏ Classroom discipline plans

School-wide discipline policies should be developed that are also included in the individual classroom governance plans. "In order to achieve a positive school culture, the principal, teachers, and parents must present a united front on discipline matters" (Blendinger et al., 1993). Classroom rules must be consistent and coordinated with the school-wide discipline plan (Blendinger et al., 1993; Gottfredson et al., 1989; Lane, 1989). Lane (1989) suggested that the same set of classroom rules and management procedures be followed in every classroom in the school. Wolfgang (1995) disagreed and insisted that for a teacher to have effective classroom management, the system of discipline must relate to his/her personality, teaching style, and the present classroom situation.

Arhar (1992) suggested that for middle grades students, since the teaming concept is used in many of these, consistent procedures for handling student disruptions and setting of rules be implemented on a team basis. George and Oldaker (1985) reported improvement in school discipline and student personal development as a result of their enrollment in middle schools, a principal component of which was team teaching. In middle schools organized into "gradewide interdisciplinary teams," it is recommended that teachers develop common grade level rules and procedures for dealing with discipline (George & Alexander, 1993).

Classrooms that exhibit effective management are described as being characterized by a sense of purpose, relative quiet, and pleasure in learning. In addition, teacher behaviors are present that produce high levels of student involvement in classroom activities, minimal amounts of student behaviors that interfere with the teacher's or other students' work, and efficient use of instructional time (Emmer & Evertson, 1981). Within these classrooms, the rules and expectations are clearly posted (Blendinger et al., 1993; Lane, 1989). In addition, these rules must be clearly defined and communicated (Blendinger et al., 1993; Gottfredson et al., 1990).

Classroom discipline rules and procedures should be developed with the unique needs of students in mind. This recommendation pertains particularly to young adolescents who are experiencing many physical, cognitive, and psychological changes that may effect their behavior, as well as their attitudes toward themselves (George & Alexander, 1993). The classroom discipline plans must include positive reinforcers that encourage good behavior (Lasley & Wayson, 1982).

Finally, educators should not assume that students come to school with common ideas about proper behavior. In addition to learning the schoolwide and classroom discipline policies, students must also be made aware of what behaviors are appropriate in varying circumstances and environments. Part of middle school educators' responsibilities involve teaching students how to behave (Greenlee & Ogletree, 1993).

❏ A repertoire of discipline models for teachers

Just as individual young adolescents differ immensely from one another, so do the discipline-related incidents in which they become involved. In addition, vast differences exist between individual teachers' philosophies, styles, personal preferences, and personalities. The wide variation among these factors pose difficulties when it comes to trying to incorporate one discipline model throughout the entire school.

A principal may decide on one of the many packaged discipline models available, have a consultant deliver an inservice workshop to the teachers and provide them with reading materials about how to enforce the model, and then to tell the teachers, "Now go back to your classrooms and discipline those kids!" Unfortunately, this "one model approach" leaves the teacher with "a limited range of techniques for dealing with the limitless range of behaviors in children" (Wolfgang, 1995). One approach to discipline will not work with all students or for all teachers. Teachers need a diverse "bag of tricks" which includes knowledge of a variety of discipline models and techniques.

As mentioned earlier, for a discipline plan to be effective, it must be consistent and be a school wide effort. This consistency is possible even while allowing for various situations, teachers' personalities, and the diverse nature of the students. By setting school-wide, or team-wide, rules and procedures, more consistency is assured. Teachers should be allowed a certain degree of latitude in how these rules are enforced and procedures carried out in their individual classrooms. When a teacher has an abundant repertoire of discipline models, he/she can make suitable decisions as to what strategies will be most effective in various situations and develops his or her own style.

An abundance of discipline models exist ranging from those that emphasize verbal communication to models that advocate corporal punishment as a means of disciplining unruly students. Most models have their good and less desirable attributes. Teachers may pick and choose certain elements from models that fit their philosophy of classroom discipline. The key to success is whether or not a particular method facilitates the desired outcome.

In *Solving Discipline Problems: Methods and Models For Today's Teachers* (1995), Wolfgang described eight popular discipline models and included a section describing the strengths and limitations of each. Each of these models is placed on a continuum of teacher behaviors in dealing with discipline incidents that reflects a graduated scale of teacher control. This allows for a comparison of the techniques and strategies involved in each model. In addition, the models are arranged in order from types that encourage the student to do his/her own problem solving to types where the belief is held that students develop only by the conditioning of outside forces (Wolfgang, 1995). In the following paragraphs, these models will be briefly described in order from emphasizing student control to emphasizing teacher control.

In the first model Thomas Gordon's Teacher Effectiveness Training (T.E.T), the role of the teacher is to be a supportive, noncritical facilitator who believes that the student has the ability to identify and solve his or her own unique problems (Gordon, 1974). The second model, Berne (1964) and Harris' (1969) Transactional Analysis, concludes that in all people there exist three states of being; the child, adult, and parent. The teacher's role in this model is to determine which state the child is operating in when he/she is misbehaving and then to choose the correct way to respond based upon the responses recommended in the model (Harris, 1969).

In Raths and Simon's Values Clarification model, teachers attempt to provide students with activities that allow them to investigate their own ways of behaving (Raths, Harmin, & Simon, 1966). In the Social Discipline model of Rudolf Dreikurs (1968), it is believed that students misbehave because of their failure to gain social acceptance. Each student is described to have one of four subconscious goals that motivate his/her misbehavior and subsequent desire for social acceptance. In this model, teachers identify whether the misbehaving student's goal is to get attention, to gain power and control, to get revenge, or to show helplessness or inadequacy. Teachers then respond with techniques described in the model to fit the student's goal.

The Reality Model by William Glasser (1975) requires that the misbehaving student be made aware of and become responsible for the consequences of his or her actions. This approach involves behavior contracts and logical consequences. Next, behavior modification techniques are described which operate under the premise that all children will learn to abide by certain standards if they receive proper reinforcements. Ideally, behaviors that are inappropriate should be ignored and acceptable behavior rewarded. If these means fail, then the teacher resorts to actions such as isolation (Blackham & Silberman, 1975).

The Assertiveness Model of Lee and Marlene Canter (1976) is suggested as a discipline approach to be used only after the students already know the rules. This model focuses on the idea that the teacher has a right to teach and a right to expect the students to behave. The model involves a structured plan involving consequences for misbehaviors, even if they occur more than once. The consequences include withholding privileges, isolation, or a visit to the principal. Positive reinforcers are also used in the form of free time, games, or trips. Finally, the Behaviorism/Punishment Model by Englemann (1969) and Dobson (1970) advocates physical punishment in order for students to learn standards of behavior. Engleman and Dobson believe that the most effective practice a teacher has available to him or her is inflicting physical pain.

A wide variety of models are available to teachers and the models discussed here are a mere sample of those available. The key point here is that the more knowledge that a teacher has of types of discipline approaches, the greater the chance that he/she will have something in his/her repertoire that will most effectively address discipline situations.

❏ Educating students

Discipline problems are not only of concern to teachers, parents, and administrators, they are a major concern to the students as well. Much of the literature on school discipline suggests that students should actually be taught the school-wide as well as the classroom discipline rules and procedures (Blendinger et al., 1993; Burns, 1985; Emmer & Evertson, 1981; Gaustad, 1992; Gottfredson et al., 1989; Lane, 1989; Short, 1988).

In addition to school rules and procedures, students should also be taught how to behave. "Students need to learn to behave in a socially approved manner in order for a healthy learning environment to exist" (Greenlee & Ogletree, 1993, p. 4). Gaustad (1992) referred to this need for students to be taught to behave and urged administrators to regard disciplinary referrals as opportunities to teach students social skills. Much of the literature on school discipline describes schools with effective discipline as being ones in which students learn how to behave (Blendinger et al., 1993: Burns, 1985; Emmer & Evertson, 1981; Hartzell & Petrie, 1992; Jones, 1984). Hartzell and Petrie (1992) suggested that students learn how to behave through modeling by teachers, administrators, and parents. Lane (1989) referred to encouraging the development of responsible students when he stated, "Teaching discipline as a skill has resulted in fewer discipline related school problems" (p. 8).

Other areas that needed to be included in the curriculum aimed at improving school discipline involve teaching students responsibility and values. Burns (1985) suggested that expectations of behavior such as respect for adults, patriotic behavior, or not stealing be taught. Other teaching suggestions include deference, civility, courtesy, and accountability which need to be reinforced both in the home and at school (Hartzell & Petrie, 1992). George and Alexander (1993) suggested that educating students in values can be accomplished through the advisor/advisee program at the middle school level. They state that with the support of parents and community members, teachers can successfully teach school-oriented values. Such values as honesty, cleanliness, punctuality, tolerance, friendliness, endurance, and loyalty are included in effective advisory programs.

Another way in which to educate students in values and moral development is through character education. Character education began at the beginning of this century as a way to teach character. A form of character education widely used at that time was called the Children's Morality Code which stressed the ten laws of right living. These were self control, good health, kindness, sportsmanship, self-reliance, duty, reliability, truth, good workmanship, and teamwork (Hutchins, 1917).

Character education curricula all but disappeared by the 1950s. However, in 1966, Lawrence Kohlberg's application of his work in cognitive-development theory of moral reasoning to moral education in schools brought about the rebirth of character education. Moral reasoning and values clarification dominated the field of character education for the next twenty years (Leming, 1993).

Generally, it is suggested in the research that the teaching of values and moral thinking begin in the early elementary grades. However, the middle school years are not too late. Considering the massive cognitive, social, emotional, intellectual, and physical changes that adolescents face, early adolescence is a crucial time for forming life long self-concepts and positive identities (Davis, 1993). Presently, character education involves a holistic approach where all aspects of school life are involved in the teaching of morals and values. This character education curriculum involves the teacher acting as a caregiver, model, and mentor; creating a moral community; practicing moral discipline; creating a democratic classroom environment; teaching values through the curriculum; using cooperative learning; encouraging moral reflection; teaching conflict resolution; fostering caring beyond the classroom; creating a positive moral culture in the school; and recruiting the parents and community as partners (Lickona, 1991). These areas are age-appropriate for middle level students and could be easily integrated into current advisor/advisee activities. Some suggested strategies for delivering character education include brainstorming activities, exercises where students think of possible consequences of immoral behavior such as "what would happen if...," students imagining themselves in other roles and discussing their feelings, and problem solving in which students clarify and find solutions to affective problems (Davis, 1993).

Historically, public schools have viewed character development as an integral part of the education process. Today, more than ever, there is a need for schools to take a comprehensive approach in order to positively influence the moral development of students (Lickona, 1991). Schools cannot develop discipline plans or teach students how to behave without communicating values. A character education curriculum is a means by which values and moral education can be formally addressed. Structured character education activities can facilitate young adolescents' ability and desire to think about who they are, who they want to be, and to form identities as self-respecting, career-minded persons (Davis, 1993).

❏ Implementation

The key ingredient in effectively implementing a school-wide discipline plan, is that of consistency (Burns, 1985; Gottfredson et al., 1989; Jones, 1984; Lane, 1989; Menacker et al., 1988). Consistency must be maintained in each offense with each student involved, with each teacher involved, and between administrators. Menacker et al. (1988) stated that a school-wide discipline plan should be based on the premise that rules must be consistently enforced. Consistent enforcement of school rules helps maintain students' respect for the school's discipline system (Gaustad,1992).

Other factors described as being necessary for a school-wide discipline plan to be implemented effectively include rules that are firm, but are administered and enforced fairly (Gottfredson et al., 1990; Greenlee & Ogletree, 1993; Menacker et al., 1988). In addition, enforcement of the plan is the responsibility of all, but for this shared responsibility to be effective, there must be strong administrative support (Burns, 1985). This responsibility also includes the parents. "Programs which involve parents in providing consequences in the home for student behavior in school have proven effective for reducing undesirable behavior" (Gottfredson et al., 1989). Finally, the school-wide discipline plan should be evaluated regularly. This evaluation should include investigation into the effectiveness of the elements of the plan, as well as inquiry as to how it is being used (Lane, 1989).

❏ Leadership

Hartzell and Petrie (1992) stated that the principal, as the school leader, is responsible for initiating an approach to address the issue of behavior management at the building level. In addition, the principal's role is to promote a positive organizational climate by developing a simple set of beliefs and expectations undergirding a supportive organizational structure. Burns (1985) referred to this development of beliefs and expectations as the principal's need to foster a common set of values. Without this common set of values, Burns (1985) stated that we cannot expect principals or teachers to take a stand on discipline.

A key principal behavior in well-disciplined schools is identified as visibility (MacNaughton & Johns, 1991; Short, 1988). Gaustad (1992) also stated that effective principals are liked and respected, rather than feared, and that teachers' satisfaction with school discipline policy was related to their relationship with the principal. The quality of support offered by the administration in handling discipline matters is also very important (Gaustad, 1992; Greenlee & Ogletree, 1993; Jones, 1984; Lasley & Wayson, 1982). This support includes the principal's being committed to the worth of the written rules and regulations in the school-wide discipline plan (Menacker et al., 1988). In addition, the principal must be an effective instructional leader in facilitating the problem-solving skills of teachers and students (Short, 1988) and in helping teachers to increase the connections between good instruction and good behavior (Hartzell & Petrie, 1992).

❏ Positive school climate

Unfortunately, the traditional views on school discipline are rooted in issues of authority and control. Generally, in this view, discipline is thought of as a set of regulatory and punitive actions directed towards students. Lipsitz (1984) stated that discipline should be seen as an integral part of a positive academic environment.

In a 1984 study, Lipsitz investigated discipline practices of successful middle level schools. These schools had a wide and differing array of specific disciplinary practices, but all of the schools shared the following characteristics: (1) clarity of mission; (2) close adult-student relationships; (3) an intimate and caring working environment for staff and students; (4) a rather high degree of student participation in the workings of the school; (5) high but flexible expectations for students; and (6) many diverse opportunities for achieving success. Lipsitz (1984) called this "indirect discipline," as these techniques help the students to be more self-directed and self-disciplined. She added that "direct discipline" emphasizes punishment and that "discipline and punishment should not be seen as synonymous" (p. 2).

Creating a positive climate in a middle school takes a unified effort by staff in providing a caring atmosphere for the students. "Better control and improved student self-discipline will come when there is teacher warmth and acceptance of the pupils" (Howard, 1968, p. 28). He also recommended provisions for activities and exploration, opportunities for creativity and for assuming real responsibilities, and teachers keeping in mind the characteristics of the preadolescent and adolescent. In their study, George and Oldaker (1985) found that all criteria relating to student discipline improved significantly when they used the practices prescribed in the middle school model. One fourth of the respondents reported that the interdisciplinary teaming approach assisted them in developing consistent procedures for handling disruptions.

Much of the value of middle school practices comes from the preventative nature of these elements. "Caring guidance is preventive discipline" (National Middle School Association, 1995, p. 50). "The general emphasis in the schools should be on the prevention of misconduct and the development of self-discipline" (Howard, 1968, p. 39). By developing self-control, self-direction, and good judgment in our students, we are enabling them to be, themselves, self-disciplined. Acquiring these skills not only assists in preparing our students for their futures in the adult world, it also frees up teachers to do what they desire most to do – teach. ℝ

References

Arhar, J. (1992). Interdisciplinary teaming and the social bonding of middle level students. In J.L. Irvin (Ed.), *Transforming middle level education: Perspectives and possibilities* (pp. 139-161). Boston, MA: Allyn and Bacon.

Berne, E. (1964). *Games people play: The psychology of human relations.* New York: Grove Press.

Blackham, G., & Silberman, A. (1975). *Modification of child and adolescent behavior.* Belmont, CA: Wadsworth Publishing.

Blendinger, J., Cornelious, L., McGrath, V., & Rose, L. (1993). *Win-win discipline* (Report No. ISBN-0-87367-353-0). Bloomington, IN: Phi Delta Kappa. (ERIC Document Reproduction Service No. DC 358 056)

Burns, J. (1985). Discipline: Why does it continue to be a problem? Solution is in changing school culture. *NASSP Bulletin, 77* (479), 1-5.

Canter, L., & Canter, M. (1976). *Assertive discipline: A take-charge approach for today's educator*. Seal Beach, CA: Canter and Associates.

Davis, G. (1993). Creative teaching of moral thinking: Fostering awareness and commitment. *Middle School Journal, 24* (4), 32-33.

DeMedio, D. & Mazur-Stewart, M. (1990). Attitudes toward middle grade certification: A national survey. *NASSP Bulletin, 74* (525), 64-71.

Dobson, J. (1970). *Dare to discipline.* Wheaton, IL: Prentice-Hall.

Dreikurs, R. (1968). *Psychology in the classroom: A manual for teachers.* (2nd ed.). New York: Harper & Row Publishers.

Emmer, E., & Evertson, C. (1981). Synthesis of research on classroom management. *Educational Leadership, 38* (4), 342-347.

Engleman, S. (1969). *Preventing failure in the primary grades.* New York: Simon and Schuster.

Evanac, D. (1993). *Developing and implementing a discipline plan for Hawthorne High School.* (Doctoral Dissertation, Alachua County, FL: Nova University, 1993). (ERIC Document Reproduction Service No. ED 364 984)

Furtwengler, W., & Konnert, W. (1982). *Improving school discipline: An administrators guide.* Boston: Allyn and Bacon.

Gaustad, J. (1992). *School discipline* (ERIC Digest Report No. 78). Eugene, OR: ERIC Clearinghouse on Educational Management. (ERIC Document Reproduction Service No. ED 350 727)

George, P., & Alexander, W. (1993). *The exemplary middle school.* (2nd ed.). Orlando, FL: Harcourt Brace Jovanovich College Publishers.

Gilchrist, R.S. (1989). *Effective schools: Three case studies of excellence.* Bloomington, IN: National Educational Service. (ERIC Document Reproduction Service No. 340 796)

Glasser, W. (1975). *Reality therapy: A new approach to psychiatry.* New York: Harper & Row Publishers.

Gordon, T. (1974). *T.E.T: Teacher effectiveness training.* New York: David McKay.

Gottfredson, D.G., Karweit, N.L., & Gottfredson, G.D. (1989) *Reducing disorderly behavior in middle schools* (Report No. 37). Baltimore, MD: The John Hopkins University, Center for Research on Elementary and Middle Schools. (ERIC Document Reproduction Service No. ED 320 654)

Gottfredson, D.C., Gottfredson, G.D., & Hybl, L.G. (1990). *Managing adolescent behavior: A multiyear, multi-school experiment* (Report No. 50). Baltimore, MD: The John Hopkins University, Center for Research on Elementary and Middle Schools. (ERIC Document Reproduction Service No. ED 333 549)

Greenlee, A., & Ogletree, E. (1993). *Teachers' attitudes toward student discipline problems and classroom management strategies* (Report No. 143). Chicago, IL: Chicago Public Schools IL. (ERIC Document Reproduction Service No. ED 364 330)

Harris, T. (1969). *I'm OK—you're OK: A practical guide to transactional analysis with gestalt experiments.* New York: Harper & Row Publishers.

Hartzell, G., & Petrie, T. (1992). The principal and discipline: Working with school structures, teachers, and students. *The Clearing House, 65* (6), 376-380.

Howard, A. (1968). *Teaching in middle school.* Scranton, PA: International Textbook Company.

Hutchins, W.J. (1917). *Children's Code of Morals for Elementary Schools.* Washington, DC: Character Education Institution.

Jones, V. (1984). An administrator's guide to developing and evaluating a building discipline program. *NASSP Bulletin, 68* (471), 60-73.

Lane, W.C., Jr. (1989, February). *The discipline of discipline*. Paper presented at the Annual Meeting of the National Association of Secondary School Principals, New Orleans, LA. (ERIC Document Reproduction Service No. ED 306 644)

Lasley, T.J., & Wayson, W.W. (1982). Characteristics of schools with good discipline. *Educational Leadership, 40* (3), 28-31.

Leming, J. (1993). In search of effective character education. *Educational Leadership, 51* (3), 63-71.

Lickona, T. (1991). *Educating for character: How our schools can teach respect and responsibility*. New York: Bantam.

Lipsitz, J. (1984). *Discipline and young adolescents: Issues in middle-grade education: Research & resources*. (National Institute of Education). Chapel Hill, NC: North Carolina University.

MacNaughton, R.H., & Johns, F.A. (1991). Developing a successful schoolwide discipline program. *NASSP Bulletin, 75* (536), 47-57.

Menacker, J., Hurwitz, E., & Weldon, W. (1988). Legislating school discipline: The application of a systemwide discipline code to schools in a large urban district. *Urban Education, 23* (1), 12-23.

National Middle School Association (1995). *This we believe: Developmentally responsive middle level schools*. Columbus, OH: Author.

Short, P. (1988). Effectively disciplined schools: Three themes from research. *NASSP Bulletin, 72* (504), 1-3.

Raths, L., Harmin, M., & Simon, S. (1966). *Values and teaching*. Columbus: Charles E. Merrill Publishing.

Stradley, W., & Aspinal, R. (1975). *Discipline in the junior high/middle school: A handbook for teachers, counselors, and administrators*. New York: The Center for Applied Research in Education.

Wolfgang, C. (1995). *Solving discipline problems: Methods and models for today's teachers*. Boston: Allyn and Bacon.

Youngblood, S. (1989). Middle level staff development needs: A survey of middle level educators. *NASSP Bulletin, 73* (515), 102-105.

Rebecca Mills

Grouping Students for Instruction: Issues of Equity and Effectiveness

Teachers and schools use a variety of ways to group students for instruction; most prevalent in middle level schools seems to be some form of ability grouping. *Turning Points,* the middle level reform document of the Carnegie Council on Adolescent Development (1989), recommended the elimination of all tracking that groups young adolescents with others of similar ability and referred to tracking as one of the most divisive and damaging school practices in existence. In 1990, Braddock wrote that "learning opportunities in middle grades remain highly stratified despite middle school philosophy that encourages heterogeneous classes" (p. 449). Oakes (1992), among others, reminded educators that detracking is central to reforming middle grades education. So, despite Braddock's lamentation, there is keen interest among educators in and a growing body of literature about seriously limiting or eliminating the practices of between-class ability grouping and homogeneous grouping of students.

Historically, grouping practices have been implemented in secondary schools despite the deleterious effects of ability grouping reported in numerous research studies. Fuligni, Eccles, and Barber (1995) reported that the "arguments for and against ability grouping remain essentially the same as they were at the beginning of the century" (p. 59). In fact, there is an obvious conflict between research and practice in middle level schools where students are tracked for instruction throughout all middle level grades despite considerable evidence of the importance of young adolescents' peer relationships, the harmful effects of tracking on self-esteem, and the perpetuation of class and racial inequities when students are tracked by ability. Research on young adolescents and their schooling reveals no known benefits of ability grouping. The one possible exception might be the benefits that can accrue from special academic programs for mathematically talented students. Arguments once considered persuasive for grouping students by ability for instruction are losing their influence in light of a growing body of evidence that the practice results in few achievement benefits and several negative effects. This chapter will include a summary of recent research on prevalent ability grouping practices, a review of recent research on ability grouping and tracking, and suggestions for further research.

Braddock (1990) reported that instructional grouping practices can do one of two things; either they can help schools meet the varying needs of students and create positive learning climates or they can exaggerate the differences among students, label some students as slow, and create poor climates for learning. He also reminded educators that, when students are assigned to classes, schools define their peer groups. Although students in tracked classes learn no more, on average, than peers of comparable ability in nontracked classes, many classroom teachers continue to defend the process of tracking. Proponents of tracking argue that the process helps schools meet the varying needs of students, provides low-achieving students with the attention and slower work pace that they require, allows high-achieving students to be sufficiently challenged by faster-paced, more demanding lessons, and permits teachers to provide different materials for high achievers and more support to low achievers.

Those who argue for the dissolution of the practice of tracking are concerned about the perceived psychological damage to low achievers, the slower pace and lower quality of instruction, the more inexperienced or sometimes less capable teachers assigned to teach lower ability students, the low expectations for student performance held by teachers, and the absence of strong behavioral peer role models in classes for low-ability students. Many middle level theorists believe that young adolescents cannot meet goals related to their personal development through tracking (Carnegie Council on Adolescent Development, 1989; Fuligni, Eccles, & Barber, 1995; Stevenson, 1992). They argue that young adolescents, naturally inclined toward learning from their peers, need to be grouped with individuals who are different. Additionally, young adolescents are vulnerable as they struggle to establish a sense of their own identity; tracking often creates negative perceptions of lower ability students that affect also the students' self-perceptions. Tracking, the literature says, has a negative effect on lower-tracked students' motivation and opportunities to learn as well as on their life chances. It also perpetuates class and racial inequities (Oakes, 1992).

Fuligni, Eccles, and Barber (1995) wrote that "academic group placement in junior high school acts as a punctuated event in the lives of early adolescents, placing them on particular developmental paths or trajectories that have important implications for their future academic and occupational achievement, as well as their overall psychological and behavioral development" (p. 59).

❑ Prevalent practices

Epstein and Mac Iver (1990), using data from Johns Hopkins Center for Research on Elementary and Middle Level Schools survey of 1,753 middle level schools, wrote that principals reported over 40% of the middle grade schools used some between-class grouping, and over 20% assigned students to all classes based on their ability. They found that the percentage increases proportionally from grades five through nine. Wheelock (1992) reported that there is great variation in grouping practices in all grade organizations of schools containing grade seven. Whole class ability grouping increases as students move from fifth through ninth grades (Epstein & Mac Iver, 1990; Lounsbury & Clark, 1990), and in grades five and six reading and mathematics are the subjects most often grouped by ability. In grades seven through nine, the subjects are mathematics and English; whereas, science and social studies are subjects that are least often grouped by ability at all middle grade levels.

A 1993 National Association of Secondary School Principals (NASSP) survey revealed that 82% of the responding middle level schools reported that they used some degree of ability grouping (Valentine, Clark, Irvin, Keefe, & Melton, 1993). Interestingly, the reported use of ability grouping had declined somewhat from an earlier survey. The 1981 NASSP survey found that 88% of schools practiced ability grouping; 59% grouped by ability at all grade levels in some subjects, and 9% grouped by ability in all subjects (Valentine, Clark, Nickerson, & Keefe, 1981). Braddock, (1990) reported similar findings.

Despite the continuing practice of ability grouping, 36% of the schools in the 1993 NASSP survey reported that they were considering eliminating ability grouping. George and Shewey (1994), in a survey to update evidence regarding the presence and effectiveness of middle school components in middle level schools, studied schools where serious attempts had been made to implement middle school concepts. Eighty-five percent of the respondents selected a "mostly yes" response to the statement that "flexible grouping strategies, primarily heterogeneous, have contributed to long-term effects of our middle school program (p. 75)."

❏ Recent research

Recently, research on ability grouping in the middle grades has shifted from that which reports only demographic data about how students are grouped and/or what principals report their schools are doing about grouping to studies that examine perceptions of teachers about ability grouping and focus over time on schools and teachers that are contending with detracking. In addition, a growing body of research exists concerning ability grouping in middle level mathematics.

In 1993, Slavin authored a review that summarizes what is known about the achievement effects of ability grouping in middle grades (6-9) and additional approaches to accommodating student diversity. He drew on his work in a 1990 best-evidence synthesis of research on ability grouping in secondary schools, and re-asserted that "if the effects of ability grouping on student achievement are zero, then there is little reason to maintain the practice" (p. 546). In much of his work, Slavin discussed instructional strategies, such as cooperative learning, that provide opportunities to group students for particular purposes for limited times.

In Spear's 1994 qualitative study he focused on understanding how and why teachers think the way they do about ability grouping and found that teachers who wish to retain ability grouping are more subject centered, and those who wish to eliminate ability grouping are more student centered; that teachers believe that teaching is easier in ability grouped classes; and that parents are important and powerful influences in decision making about ability grouping. He concluded that the "crucial issue is not whether we group students but how we group students" (p. 118).

Urdan, Midgley, and Wood (1995) worked collaboratively for three years with a middle school staff who wanted to examine and change their policies, procedures, and practices. The school previously had assigned students to ability-grouped classes despite repeated indications of the negative consequences of tracking. The staff and researchers concluded that "tracking affects the way teachers think about instruction" (p. 25) and realized that ability grouping makes the entire school schedule less flexible. They concluded that it was particularly important to provide inservice training for teachers in middle level schools to help them teach in new and challenging ways. Trimble and Sinclair (1987), in their study of the range of instructional activities used in classrooms, found a "numbing similarity of practices and content both within and across classes" (p. 20) and called for a change in grouping.

In a qualitative study, Roe and Radebaugh (1993) examined one middle school's elimination of tracking in mathematics, English, and reading classes. They found that shared decision making is important to a successful transition from tracking to de-tracking and that the teachers felt that heterogeneous grouping improves classroom culture. After the elimination of tracking, teachers reported positive social benefits, positive behavioral implications, and less parental competition. The teachers also felt that de-tracking had academic benefits due to the social nature of learning and the strong influence of the adolescent's peer group.

Hoffer (1992) examined whether ability grouping during middle level schooling does act as a "sorting" event with long-term consequences. Using mathematics class enrollment as an indicator that placement during junior high school affected the types of mathematics classes in which students enrolled in high school, Hoffer found that the main effects of ability level and ability grouping were significant; they also significantly interacted in affecting student performance. Hoffer found no positive long-term effects for low-ability students being placed in low-grouped mathematics classes. In fact, when compared to low-ability students in non-grouped classrooms those placed in low-grouped classrooms appeared to fare worse. "It appears that all students may gain if they receive the type of instruction typically found in higher ability grouped classes" (p. 84). In addition, Slavin (1993) cited a longitudinal study by Fuligni, Barber, Eccles, and Fingerman (1990) that examined the effects of seventh-grade ability grouping in mathematics and found strong negative tracking effects for low-achieving seventh graders on their tenth grade mathematics scores; however, Slavin reminded us that the authors did not report tracking practices for the students in grades eight through ten.

In one study (Mason, Schroeter, Combs, & Washington, 1992) focused specifically on the effects of tracking in mathematics, researchers placed thirty-four average-achieving eighth graders into high-track pre-algebra classes with their high-achieving peers. Several of the average-achieving students did better than their high-achieving classmates and took "substantially more advanced mathematics during high school and attained significantly higher grades in these classes than their cohort peers" (p. 597). Also the high-achieving students "suffered no decrease in computation or problem-solving achievement" (p. 595), and they scored higher in concepts than their cohort peer groups from previous years. The average-achieving students increased their achievement in concept development and did just as well in computation and problem solving as did their previous "average" classmates.

91

❏ Future research

One of the most compelling proponents of de-tracking America's schools is Oakes whose work with schools all over the country has led her to believe that educators need to rethink their fundamental educational beliefs and values in order to provide diverse groups of students with access to a common body of knowledge. Oakes (1992) reported she arrived at the "increasingly clear and consistent. . .conclusion that this common way of organizing students for instruction is, in most instances, neither equitable nor effective" (p. 12). She and her colleagues and students at UCLA have established a comprehensive research agenda that examines new ideas for research on the topic (see for example: Wells, Hirshberg, Lipton, & Oakes, 1995) and should yield additional information about this topic.

Theorists and researchers suggest the need for considerable further research on the topics of ability grouping and tracking. Specifically, we need long-term studies that consider the effects of ability grouping on children's development (Fuligni, Eccles, & Barber, 1995); give systematic accounts of particular schools' efforts to de-track and reorganize (Oakes, 1992; Slavin, 1993); provide documentation of promising alternatives to tracking (Roe & Radebaugh, 1993; Wheelock, 1992); discuss ways to help low achieving students keep up with more demanding content and higher expectations (Slavin, 1993). In short, we need to provide what Oakes (1992) called the "technology of tracking," useful guidance to establishing school cultures where tracking no longer makes sense. There is a strongly held belief among de-tracking proponents that if we provide for all students the type of instruction typically found in higher ability-grouped classes there will result a gain for all students. That assumption, also, needs to be studied. ⓡ

References

Braddock, J. M. (1990). Tracking in the middle grades: National patterns of grouping for instruction. *Phi Delta Kappan, 71* (6), 445-449.

Carnegie Council on Adolescent Development. (1989). *Turning points: Preparing American youth for the 21st century.* New York: Carnegie Corporation.

Epstein, J. L., & Mac Iver, D. J. (1990). *Education in the middle grades: National practices and trends.* Columbus OH: National Middle School Association.

Fuligni, A. J., Eccles, J. S., & Barber, B. L. (1995). The long-term effects of seventh-grade ability grouping in mathematics. *The Journal of Early Adolescence, 15* (1), 58-89.

Fuligni, A. J., Barber, B. L., Eccles, J. S., & Fingerman, K. L. (1990). *A longitudinal study of the effects of seventh-grade ability grouping in mathematics.* Paper presented at the annual meeting of the American Educational Research Association, Boston. As cited in Slavin, R. E. (1993), Ability grouping in the middle grades: Achievement effects and alternatives. *Elementary School Journal, 93* (5), 535-552.

George, P. S., & Shewey, K. (1994). *New evidence for the middle school.* Columbus, OH: National Middle School Association.

Hoffer, T. B. (1992). Middle school ability grouping and student achievement in science and mathematics. *Educational Evaluation and Policy Analysis, 14,* 205-227. As cited in Fuligni, A. J., Eccles, J. S., & Barber, B. L. (1995), The long-term effects of seventh- grade ability grouping in mathematics. *The Journal of Early Adolescence, 15* (1), 58-89.

Lounsbury, J. H., & Clark, D. C. (1990). *Inside grade eight: From apathy to excitement.* Reston, VA: National Association of Secondary School Principals.

Mason, D. A., Schroeter, D. D., Combs, R. K., and Washington, K. (1992). Assigning average-achieving eighth graders to advanced mathematics classes in urban junior high. *Elementary School Journal, 92* (5): 587-599.

Oakes, J. (1992). Can tracking research inform practice? Technical, normative, and political considerations. *Educational Researcher, 21* (4), 12-21.

Roe, M. F., & Radebaugh, M. (1993). One middle school's elimination of homogeneous grouping: A qualitative study. *Research in Middle Level Education, 17* (1), 47-62.

Slavin, R. E. (1993). Ability grouping in middle grades: Achievement effects and alternatives. *Elementary School Journal, 93* (5), 535-52.

Slavin, R. E. (1990). Ability grouping and student achievement in secondary schools: A best-evidence synthesis. *Review of Educational Research, 60* (3), 471-499.

Spear, R. C. (1994). Teacher perceptions of ability grouping practices in middle level schools. *Research in Middle Level Education, 18* (1), 117-130.

Stevenson, C. (1992). *Teaching ten to fourteen year olds.* New York: Longman.

Trimble, K. D., & Sinclair, R. L. (1987). On the wrong track: Ability groping and the threat to equity. *Equity and Excellence, 23* (1), 15-21.

Urdan, T., Midgley, C., & Wood, S. (1995). Special issues in reforming middle level schools. *Journal of Early Adolescence, 15* (1), 9-37.

Valentine, J., Clark, D. C., Irvin, J. L., Keefe, J. W., & Melton, G. (1993). *Leadership in middle level education: A national survey of middle level leaders and schools* (Vol. 1). Reston, VA: National Association of Secondary School Principals.

Valentine J., Clark, D. C., Nickerson, N. C., & Keefe, J. W. (1981). *The middle level principalship. A survey of middle level principals and programs* (Vol. 1). Reston, VA: National Association of Secondary School Principals.

Wells, A. S., Hirshberg, D., Lipton, M., & Oakes, J. (1995). Bounding the case within its context: A constructivist approach to studying detracking reform. *Educational Researcher, 24* (5), 18-24.

Wheelock, A. (1992). *Crossing the tracks: How 'untracking' can save America's schools.* New York: The New Press.

Hilda C. Rosselli

Differing Perspectives, Common Ground: The Middle School and Gifted Education Relationship

A curious relationship has evolved over the years between the fields of gifted education and middle grades education. On an initial glance, comparisons of beliefs held to be paramount by each field indicate an amazing overlap in philosophy with a weaker, but still substantial, agreement across practices (Rosselli, 1990). During the 1980s, middle grades philosophy positioned heterogeneous grouping as one of the pre-eminent guideposts for policies and practices endorsed by the field and the common ground between the two fields lessened, in some cases leading to the reduction and sometimes disappearance of appropriate educational services for students identified as gifted (Allan, 1991). Leaders in gifted education, unable to embrace a total abandonment of grouping, responded vehemently and expressed reservations regarding the ability of the middle school movement to meet the needs of high ability students (Gallagher, Coleman, & Nelson, 1995; Plucker & McIntire, 1996; Sicola, 1990; Tomlinson, 1992;1994). The resulting differences have reframed the relationship between experts from gifted education and middle grades education into what has sometimes become oppositional viewpoints and fueled lively debates on the moral and efficacious nature of ability grouping. However, one of the more positive outcomes of these debates has been a number of timely publications that have sought to re-examine the goodness of fit between the two movements by moving beyond the rhetoric of differences towards a healthier focus on programs and practices (Coleman, Gallagher, & Howard, 1993; Coleman & Gallagher, 1995; Mills & Durden, 1992; Rosselli, 1995). At the same time, with the advent of the National Research Center on the Gifted and Talented and several series of federally funded Javits grants, a more carefully defined national research agenda has evolved in the field examining areas such as outcomes and impact of gifted programs, underachievement, regular curriculum modifications, and identification/programming for special populations of gifted students (Renzulli, Reid, & Gubbins, n.d.). The resulting research has bolstered the field of gifted education and provided a rich source for examining implications for middle level education. This chapter provides a brief review of the literature that has historically framed the debates followed by a discussion of current research seeking solutions to the field's differences. A discussion of the evolving nature of giftedness and implications for both gifted and general education is also offered as a contextual backdrop. The chapter closes with a discussion of implications relative to middle school education policies and practices that hold promise for considering the unique needs of high ability students.

❑ Nature and Definition of Giftedness and Intelligence ❑

When Toepfer (1989) called for improved philosophical agreement about the terminology used to define giftedness, he probably could not have anticipated the continuing dialogue within the field of gifted education that still seeks to develop a predominant working definition. A growing interest in talent development, seemingly spurred by Gardner's theory of multiple intelligences (1983), has readdressed the use of traditional views of intelligence influencing the identification process as well as the development and implementation of gifted programs nationwide. On the heels of Gardner's work has followed a redefining of gifted education by well-renowned experts (Gagné, 1995; Feldhusen, 1992; Renzulli, 1994; & Treffinger, 1992) who believe that gifted educational practices often ignore the unique and individual talents of capable youth. In 1993, the first national report since the 1972 Marland Report was published titled *National Excellence: A Case for Developing America's Talent* (U. S. Department of Education). Significant in the title is the appearance of the term "talent" which appears liberally throughout the report and which serves as a cornerstone for encouraging more overlap between education reform and the development of individual gifts and talents.

❏ Characteristics of Gifted Students ❏

The literature regarding students who are gifted has consistently focused on the unique characteristics, concomitant problems, and resulting needs that can help define how this population of students is served. A number of developmental characteristics that apply to middle level adolescents apply to gifted adolescents as well, particularly: rapid physical growth, varying levels of cognitive operations, sporadic brain growth, affective ambivalence, and capacity for introspection. Like all adolescents, they must also cope with the achievement of independence, discovery of identity as a person, exploration and acceptance of sexuality, development of meaningful interpersonal relationships, and establishment of personal values and philosophy (Clark, 1988). According to Olszewski-Kubilius and Kulieke (1989), gifted adolescents seem to value a more cognitive approach to life than their non-gifted age peers and a greater desire for personal power. In addition, there are also several apparent gender differences in personality dimensions of gifted adolescents with girls being more sensitive and attentive to form and harmony and boys tending to be more dominant.

Clearly, being gifted places some additional twists on the already difficult tasks of adolescent maturation. Wallace (1985) described the gifted adolescent as a doubly marginal individual. The obvious move is away from the family, which is part of the adolescent experience, as well as a move away from the system that perhaps supported and nurtured a specific gift or talent. This new autonomy may cause an additional burden or responsibility for the gifted adolescent, just at a time when he/she has few appropriate peer role models to emulate. Manaster and Powell (1983) reported that gifted adolescents may feel "out of stage" due to their perfectionism and focus on success, causing them to be out of touch with their immediate environment. In addition, alienation from their age-peer group may be influenced by gifted students' awareness of their unusual abilities or interests, causing them to feel "out of phase." Lastly, these students may feel "out of sync" as though they do not, should not, or cannot fit in. Buescher (1985) also found that ownership, or the simultaneous owning and questioning of the abilities of these youngsters, may compete with the beliefs that a debt is owed towards parents, teachers, and society.

To be gifted and to be under-challenged in school creates another undesirable combination. High ability students have reported school work being too easy (Tomlinson, 1995), spending little or no time studying, and group work leading to gifted students doing all the work (Clinkenbeard, 1991). In one study of high ability middle level students, Plucker and McIntire (1996) found that students exhibited a variety of nonconstructive behaviors such as interacting with peers, selected attention, and reduced effort when the level of stimulation or challenge was inappropriate. In addition, teachers in the study did not always recognize when high ability students were trying to stimulate themselves intellectually and sometimes even allowed the students to pursue nonconstructive behaviors rather than adapt or modify instruction.

❏ Instructional implications

Middle school instruction is intended to respond to the recognized developmental needs of young adolescent students. Earlier research on brain periodicity fueled support for a movement away from abstract types of thinking. The resulting de-emphasis on academics also acknowledged that young adolescent students do not always prize school achievement and that over-challenging students at the middle school level could contribute to poor self-concept (NASSP, 1989). On an equity basis alone, Tomlinson (1992) questioned the implications of accepting findings that only 20% of 14-year-olds use even early formal operations. In her view, this finding still creates a need to explore viable options for these 20 percenters, many of whom might be identified as gifted students. In their study of talented teenagers, Csikszentmihalyi, Rathunde, & Whalen (1993) found that students seem to benefit more from a differentiated (more complex and even competitive) learning environment than an integrated (supportive and comfortable) environment. Beane and Lipka's (1986) finding that only 25% of an individual's academic school achievement is linked to IQ while 50% is related to self-concept has posed another anathema for researchers in gifted education who believe that for gifted students, academic success plays an important role in maintaining self-esteem. Furthermore this aspect of self-concept is supported by students' intellectual peers who act as "mental catalysts and who provide realistic perspective of their abilities" (Sicola, 1990). Many advocates for gifted education agree with Bloom (1985) who found in his study that "...exceptional levels of talent development require certain types of environmental support, special experiences, excellent teaching, and appropriate motivational encouragement at each stage of development" (p. 543).

To allow any student to underachieve continually is to impact negatively self-concept which then, in turn, will impact future performance. Ironically, it was the middle school movement that reminded educators that lockstep-graded practices "force[s] many students to compromise the integrity of their individual readiness" (NASSP, p. 7). In 1988, Chapman and McAlpine conducted a study to examine the academic self-concepts of mainstreamed intellectually gifted and average students over a two-year period. They measured perceptions of ability in the areas of math, reading/spelling, general ability, penmanship/neatness, and confidence/satisfaction at the beginning and the end of the sixth grade year and then again at the end of the seventh year. These researchers found that, with the exception of penmanship, the students identified as gifted had overall higher perceptions of general ability as well as specific academic areas. However, the gifted students showed lower perceptions of school satisfaction than the average students. Chapman and McAlpine felt that lack of challenge in a mainstreamed environment may cause boredom which could explain the lower scores.

In a qualitative study conducted in a sixth grade gifted class, Clinkenbeard (1991) found that students who were identified gifted felt that their general classroom teachers and peers held sometimes unrealistic expectations of them. Teachers expected them to achieve and behave at a gifted level consistently, sometimes failing to acknowledge that the students' achievements were linked to effort as well as ability. Students who participated in the study also felt that they were graded harder than were other students and their age peers were sometimes jealous and insulting. Gifted adolescents appear to develop a variety of coping strategies to deal with these types of pressures, including the use of one's abilities to help others in classes, making friends with other bright students, selecting programs and classes designed for gifted/talented students, and achieving in areas outside of academics/school. In their study of gifted adolescents' adjustment, Buescher and Higham (1989) found gender differences indicating girls to be more at risk for avoiding or walking away from their talents during early adolescence whereas boys more often select friends that provide support for their talent areas.

❑ Equity and excellence

The greatest philosophical difference that separates advocates of gifted and those of middle school concept does not lend itself to traditional research methodology. As Plowman (1988) stated, "Education of the gifted and talented is consistent with the philosophical principles and basic tenets of our educational and political systems which include: concern for individuals, individualized instruction, equal opportunity, and equal access" (p. 60). Yet, services that address the needs of high ability learners are sometimes suspect and equated with social discrimination (Johnston & Markle, 1986; McKay, 1995). Although the focus of Goals 2000 and many other national reform agendas is on academic excellence (Sicola, 1990), particularly on an international level, there appears to be a swing of the pendulum from excellence to equity resulting from economic and societal pressures (Gallagher, 1991; Tannenbaum, 1983). Within the field of gifted education, some of this criticism is well placed when considering the historically under-represented presence of students from culturally diverse backgrounds, low socioeconomic environments, and limited English proficiency. Fortunately, the 1990s have seen growth in a researchable knowledge base regarding the diversity rather than the homogencity within the gifted population (Betts & Neihart, 1988; Ford, 1993; Maker, 1996; Nielsen, Higgins, Hammond, & Williams, 1993). Salkind (1988) addressed two other types of equity which should be considered when examining issues of services for gifted and talented students. Horizontal equity involves the equal treatment of individuals who have similar needs while vertical equity exists when children who have different needs are treated differently; otherwise referred to as the "unequal treatment of unequals." These views have particularly been present at the heart of the most heated discussions between middle school proponents and advocates for gifted students when the issue of ability grouping is discussed.

❏ Ability Grouping ❏

In the middle school literature, the findings of George (1988a; 1988b) are among the most frequently cited research studies related to ability grouping. In the field of gifted education, Kulik and Kulik (1987, 1991) are considered the preeminent researchers examining the effects of ability grouping on gifted students. Kulik and Kulik's second meta-analysis (1987) coded 82 studies of between-class and 19 within-class programs and described the outcomes on a common scale. For inclusion, in their analysis, the studies had to be quantitative, involve both a control group and an experimental group with a similar aptitude, and be conducted in a classroom rather than a lab setting. In 49 studies of comprehensive between-class grouping, the effect sizes were .12 for high, .04 for middle, and .00 for low groups with the difference between the high and low groups statistically significant at $p < .05$. In 25 studies dealing with special classrooms only for talented students, a variation of effect size from -.27 to 1.25 led the Kuliks to believe that factors other than grouping played a role in the outcome. Two features showing significant relationships in an analysis of total class grouping within the classroom were instructor effects and flexibility/permanence of assignment. The authors did not explain why these features were able to be discerned, but they did conclude that because of the small number of studies analyzed, the findings were tentative. The Kuliks concluded that the strongest and clearest effects of grouping were in programs designed especially for talented students. They also concluded that programs designed for all students in a grade, rather than only for talented students, had significantly lower effects. The Kuliks noted that their results are, in some regards, similar to those of Slavin, particularly their findings that comprehensive grouping between classes has little or no effect, either positive or negative; and they reasserted that grouping can be a powerful tool in the education of gifted and talented students. They are cautious, however, about accepting Slavin's generalizations that grouping is most effective when done for only one or two subjects, when it substantially reduces student heterogeneity, and when group assignments are frequently reassessed. Still another review of both Slavin's and Kulik and Kulik's studies pointed out significant problems in both designs (Allan, 1990). The weighting of studies means that any study that met the adequacy criteria received equal weighting in the meta-analysis, and in the best evidence synthesis, selectivity is a problem. The commonly used argument against the use of standardized test scores with high ability and gifted students is also a flaw in both analyses, in that they may be too insensitive to pick up the effects of grouping. Allan also criticized Slavin for including studies in which no attempt was made to differentiate the content used in the regrouped classes. As the debates have ensued, Slavin has led a discussion on the practice of "regrouping" for select subjects as an alternative to ability grouping. To be instructionally effective, Slavin believes that regrouping plans must meet two conditions: 1) instructional level and pace must be completely adapted to student performance level, and 2) regrouping should only be done for one or two subjects so that students remain in a heterogeneous setting most of the day. The National Association for Gifted Children believes that this type of flexible use of grouping will help match students' advanced abilities and knowledge while still maintaining the important social goals of the middle school movement (NAGC, 1994).

❏ Revisiting Program Organization ❏

Over the years a wide variety of programs have been developed to meet the unique needs of gifted adolescents including: special classes, early admission or acceleration options, non-accelerative enrichment classes, special schools, mentorships, resource rooms, continuous progress, dual enrollment, and within-class individualization. As financial resources continue to shrink, the inclusion movement gains support, and the public debate regarding segregation continues, the field of gifted education has started to rally around options that move beyond the traditional pull-out and self-contained programs. As an alternative to formal grouping, Renzulli (1994) researched the use of Talent Pools which are composed of the top 15-20 percent of the general population using either general ability or one or more specific areas of ability. Students in these talent pools are then offered opportunities to learn subjects at a faster pace using "curriculum compacting"; thus, freeing up time for enrichment within the general education class. In addition, thousands of students now participate each year in Talent Searches during which seventh and eighth grade students take the SAT. The results of these talent searches can help districts identify able students who may be in need of more academic challenge. Many of these students may also qualify for accelerated summer programming offered at a number of universities around the country. The approach used by the Talent Searches is based on the research of Julian Stanley at Johns Hopkins who found that highly gifted students can progress through mathematics content in much less time than in traditional curriculums (Benbow & Stanley, 1983). As a result of Talent Searches, a number of middle schools have allowed students to take Algebra as early as 7th grade, thus allowing some students to be able to take math electives such as: Differential Equations, Real Analysis, Linear Algebra, or Theory of Numbers in their senior year of high school. Similar accelerative strands exist for science, foreign language, literature, writing, and oral discourse.

Although self-contained classes and pull-out programs have continued to be the most popular vehicles for serving gifted students, more and more districts are exploring alternative means of serving gifted students. Regardless of the delivery model employed, certain assumptions undergirding the philosophy of gifted services must be supported.

- All children progress through challenging material at their own pace. Gifted students often reach mastery in significantly less time than other learners.
- Achieving success for all students is not equated with achieving the same results for all students.
- Most students gain self-esteem and self-confidence from mastering work that initially seems slightly beyond their grasp.
- Program procedures should allow students to enter, exit, and reenter the gifted program as their profile of interests and abilities changes during their middle level school years.

- In addition to sometimes serving as peer role models, high ability students also need to spend time learning new material and stretching to their full potential.
- Flexible grouping of gifted learners should be offered for at least some specific areas based on students' abilities and talents in these areas.
- High ability students at the middle school level need access to a variety of challenging resources.
- Professionals working with gifted students require ongoing specialized training to support their ability to work with this population of students.
- Gifted students also benefit from associating with students of differing abilities and backgrounds.
- Gifted curriculum systems for gifted students should be aligned with the district's curriculum, instruction, and assessment.
- Gifted program delivery models should address practices such as flexible grouping, personnel, attention to social, emotional, and career needs, enhancement of study skills, and regular access to technology.
- Program strategies used with gifted students should address academic, social, and personal needs.

In 1995 Coleman and Gallagher conducted a study to identify schools where the middle school movement was blended with quality program services for students who are gifted. They found successful sites used some form of instructional grouping to offer challenges to students needing them as well as some form of enrichment. A variety of differentiation approaches were also utilized, including mentoring, flexible pacing, independent studies, interdisciplinary units, and thinking skills. In addition, each site also had at least one person on staff who was knowledgeable about the needs of gifted students. When schools move to embrace the practice of heterogeneity, they must be careful to avoid a one-size-fits-all instruction. Support must be provided to help teachers move along what Tomlinson (1995) found to be a continuum towards modifying instruction based on student need. Initially, teachers' objections to differentiation may be based on satisfaction with the status quo or a belief that "We already do that." Other barriers identified could be clustered under issues related to the administration, changing expectations, and professional support. Tomlinson also found that teachers' application of differentiation was often more reactive than proactive in that planning was still based on a single lesson format with minor modifications being made based upon need. However, there appears to be a profile of "early subscribers." They tend to be inquirers about students and believers that disequilibrium can be a catalyst for growth. The call for more

103

collaboration between gifted and the middle school movement will be enhanced if schools first explore the common ground existing between the two fields (Coleman & Gallagher, 1992), namely, that both are committed to meeting the unique developmental needs of students during early adolescence. As programs for the middle school gifted student continue to evolve, the following touchstones can be used to guide program decisions while assuring that differentiation is still provided:

1. Do the program services support excellence over mediocrity?
2. Will the program offerings help students see in themselves a strength, passion, or capability that can become a highly developed talent?
3. Do the program offerings support students' varying learning needs, e.g. pace, and style?
4. Do the program offerings eliminate an artificial ceiling for learning?
5. Do the program offerings promote depth of understanding rather than just access to quantity?
6. Do the program offerings promote the gifted student's capacities for creative and critical thinking skills?
7. Do the program offerings provide a balance of curricular and co-curricular offerings including appropriate exploratory activities?
8. Do the program offerings offer opportunities to develop an understanding for relationships within and between disciplines?

❏ Conclusion ❏

Joel Barker (1989) is fond of describing examples of corporations and industries that have suffered from paradigm paralysis. When rigid images and paradigms are retained, the opportunity to help define change is often ignored and potential agents remain as passive receptors. In the past, gifted programs have often served as lab settings for innovations in education that later have become part of the internalized system (e.g., thinking skills, mentorships, cooperative learning, independent study). Given the current situation, the challenge that presents itself now is for the fields of gifted education and middle school education to build upon their common philosophies and use their collective energies to create and refine innovative approaches that truly maximize the opportunity for the development of human potential, gifted or otherwise. ®

References

Allan, S. D. (1991). Ability-grouping research reviews: What do they say about grouping and the gifted? *Educational Leadership, 48* (6) 60-65.

Barker, J. (1989). *Discovering the future: The business of paradigms.* St. Paul, MN: ILI Press.

Beane, J., & Lipka, R. (1986). *Self-concept, self-esteem, and the curriculum.* New York: Teachers College Press.

Betts, G., & Neihart, M. (1988). Profiles of the gifted. *Gifted Child Quarterly, 32* (2) 248-253.

Benbow, C. P., & Stanley, J. C. (1983). An eight-year evaluation of SMPY: What was learned? In C. P. Benbow & J. C. Stanley (Eds.), *Academic precocity: Aspects of its development* (pp. 205-214). Baltimore, MD: Johns Hopkins University Press.

Bloom, B. (1985). Generalizations about talent development. In B. Bloom (Ed.), *Developing talent in young people* (pp. 507-549). New York: Ballantine Books.

Buescher, T. (1985). A framework for understanding the social and emotional development of gifted and talented adolescents. *Roeper Review, 8,* 10-15.

Buescher, T. M., & Higham, S.J. (1989). A developmental study of adjustment among gifted adolescents. In J. VanTassel-Baska & P. Olszewski-Kubilius (Eds.), *Patterns of influence on gifted learners: The home, the self, and the school* (pp.102-124). New York: Teachers College Press.

Chapman, J., & McAlpine, D. (1988). Students' perceptions of ability. *Gifted Child Quarterly, 32* (1) 222-225.

Clark, B. (1988). *Growing up gifted: Developing the potential of children at home and school* (3rd ed.). Columbus, OH: Charles E. Merrill.

Clinkenbeard, P. R. (1991). Unfair expectations: A pilot study of middle school students' comparisons of gifted and regular classes. *Journal for the Education of the Gifted, 15* (1) 56-63.

Coleman, M., & Gallagher, J. (1992). *Middle school suvey report: Impact on gifted students.* Chapel Hill, NC: Gifted Education Policy Studies Program, University of North Carolina at Chapel Hill.

Coleman, M. R., & Gallagher, J. J. (1995). The successful blending of gifted education with middle schools and cooperative learning: Two studies. *Journal for the Education of the Gifted, 18* (4), 362-384.

Coleman, M. R., Gallagher, J. J., & Howard, J. (1993). *Middle school site visit report: Five schools in profile.* Chapel Hill, NC: Gifted Education Policy Studies Program, University of North Carolina at Chapel Hill.

Csikszentmihalyi, M., Rathunde, K., & Whalen, S. (1993). *Talented teenagers: The roots of success and failure.* Cambridge, UK: Cambridge University Press.

Feldhusen, J. (1992). *TIDE: Talent identification and development in education.* Sarasota, FL: Center for Creative Learning.

Ford, D. (1993). An investigation of the paradox of underachievement among gifted black students. *Roeper Review, 16* (2), 78-84.

Gagné, F. (1995). From giftedness to talent: A developmental model and its impact on the language of the field. *Roeper Review, 18* (2), 103- 111.

Gallagher, J. (1991). Educational reform, values, and gifted students. *Gifted Child Quarterly, 35* (1), 12-19.

Gallagher, J. , Coleman, M. R. , & Nelson, S. (1995). Perceptions of educational reform by educators representing middle schools, cooperative learning, and gifted education. *Gifted Child Quarterly, 39* (2), 66-76.

Gardner, H. (1983). *Frames of mind.* New York: Basic Books.

George, P. (1988a). Tracking and ability grouping. *Middle School Journal, 20* (1), 21-28.

George, P. (1988b). *What's the truth about teaching and ability grouping really?* Gainsville, FL: Teacher Education Resources.

Griggs, S., & Price, G. (1980). A comparison between the learning styles of gifted versus average suburban junior high students. *Roeper Review, 3,* 7-9.

Johnston, J. H., & Markle, G. (1986). *What research says to the middle level practitioner.* Columbus, OH: National Middle School Association.

Kulik, J. A., & Kulik, C.-L. C.(1987). Effects of ability grouping on student achievement. *Equity and excellence, 23* (1&2) 22-30.

Kulik, J. A., & Kulik, C.-L. C. (1991). Ability grouping and gifted students. In N. Colangelo & G.A. Davis (Eds.), *Handbook of gifted education.* (pp 178-196). Boston: Allyn & Bacon.

Maker, C.J. (1996). Identification of gifted minority students: A national problem, needed changes, and a promising solution. *Gifted Child Quarterly, 40* (1), 41-50.

Manaster, G. J., & Powell, P. M. (1983). A framework for understanding gifted adolescents' psychological maladjustment. *Roeper Review, 6* (2) 70-73.

McKay, J. (1995). *Schools in the middle: Developing a middle-level orientation.* Thousand Oaks, CA: Corwin Press.

Mills, C. J., & Durden, W. G. (1992). Cooperative learning and ability grouping: An issue of choice. *Gifted Child Quarterly, 36* (1), 11-16. .

National Association of Secondary School Principals (1989). *Middle level education's responsibility for intellectual development.* Reston, VA: Author.

National Association for Gifted Children (1994). *Position Paper: Middle schools.* Washington, DC: Author.

Nielsen, E., Higgins, D., Hammond, A., & Williams, R. (1993). Gifted children with disabilities. *Gifted Child Today, 15* (5) p. 9-12.

Olszewski-Kubilius, P., & Kuliefe, M. (1989). Personality dimensions of gifted adolescents. In J. VanTassel-Baska & P. Olszewski-Kubilius (Eds.), *Patterns of influence on gifted learners: The home, the self, and the school.* (pp. 125-145) New York: Teachers College Press.

Plowman, P. (1988). Elitism. *Gifted Child Today, 56* (3) 60.

Plucker, J.A., & McIntire, J. (1996). Academic survivability in high-potential middle school students. *Gifted Child Quarterly, 40* (1), 7-14.

Renzulli, J. (1994). *Schools for talent development: A practical plan for total school improvement.* Mansfield Center, CT: Creative Learning Press.

Renzulli, J. S., Reid, B. D., & Gubbins, E.J. (n.d.). *Setting an agenda: Research priorities for the gifted and talented through the year 2000.* Storrs, CT: National Research Center on the Gifted and Talented.

Rosselli, H. (1995). Meeting gifted students halfway in the middle school. *Schools in the Middle, 5* (3) 12-17.

Rosselli, H. (1990). *Gifted education and the middle school movement: In pursuit of the heffalump of gifted education.* Unpublished manuscript.

Salkind, N. (1988). *Equity and excellence: The case for mandating services for the gifted child.* Unpublished document, University of Kansas.

Sicola, P. K. (1990). Where do gifted students fit? An examination of middle school philosophy as it relates to ability grouping and the gifted learner. *Journal for the Education of the Gifted, 14* (1), 37-49.

Slavin, R. E. (1987). Ability grouping and schoolachievement in elementary schools: A best-evidence synthesis. *Review of Educational Research, 57,* 293-336.

Slavin, R .E. (1990). Achievement effects of ability grouping in secondary schools: A best evidence synthesis. *Review of Educational Research, 60,* 471-499.

Tannenbaum, A. J. (1983). *Gifted children: Psychological and educational perspectives.* New York: Macmillan.

Toepfer, C. F. (1989). Planning gifted/talented middle level school programs: Issues and guidelines. *Schools in the Middle: A Report on Trends and Practices.* (pp.1-8) Reston, VA: National Association of Secondary School Principals.

Tomlinson, C. A. (1992). Gifted education and the middle school movement: Two voices on teaching the academically talented. *Journal for the Education of the Gifted, 15* (3) 206-238.

Tomlinson, C. A. (1994). Gifted learners: The boomerang kids of middle school? *Roeper Review, 16* (3), 177-182.

Tomlinson, C. A. (1995). Deciding to differentiate instruction in middle school: One school's journey. *Gifted Child Quarterly, 39* (2), 77-87.

Treffinger, D. (1992). Programming for giftedness: Needed directions. *INNOTECH Journal, 16* (1), 54-61.

U.S. Department of Education (1993). *National excellence: A case for developing America's talent.* Washington, DC: Author.

Wallace, D. (1985). Giftedness and the construction of a creative life. In F. Horowitz (Ed.), *The gifted and talented: Development perspectives.* Washington, DC: American Psychological Association.

Rebecca A. Hines and J. Howard Johnston

Inclusion

Inclusion has gained the attention of both the public schools and the media throughout this decade. *Time* and *Newsweek* as well as most major educational journals have featured articles on inclusion. School districts across the country have been challenged by supporters and legislation to find the most inclusive placement for students with special needs. In the wake of the attention, researchers have been left to consider the impact of this movement.

Sorting through results of research to determine inclusion's effectiveness is easier said than done. Inclusive programs vary greatly in definition, support provided, setting, and populations served. Currently most inclusive practices are idiosyncratic from school district to school district, and results of research appear to be based on the strength of the individual district's inclusive strategies. Specifically, contextual variables, particularly the amount and nature of the support provided to the classroom teacher, are almost always considered critical to the ability of the classroom teacher to maintain adequate attention to the needs of all children (Salisbury, Palombaro, & Hollowood, 1993). Since these variables are not easily controlled for research, it is difficult to deduce the true value of inclusion as an educational practice; quantitative research studies of the effects of inclusion are currently scarce in the literature (Baker, Wang, & Walberg, 1995; Lockledge & Wright, 1991; Straub & Peck, 1994).

Over the past several decades, mainstreaming (no direct special educator support) has been the primary way of including students with special needs, but teacher opposition has presented a strong barrier to the practice. In many cases, mainstreaming has called for students with varying disabilities to be placed in regular education classes with teachers who have not been trained to deal with the specialized needs of these students. The result has been that many teachers, even those who agree in principle with the practice of including special students, have found the practice to be disruptive (Hersh, 1990; O'Reilly & Duquette, 1988), and mainstreaming has been found to affect teacher job satisfaction negatively (Lobosco & Newman, 1992). In some cases, the curricular needs for handicapped students have been found to exceed the reasonable demands placed on the regular education teacher, and researchers have concluded that including these students presents too great a challenge for those not specifically trained for the task (Harris & Evans, 1994; Jenkins & Pious, 1991; Leyser & Abrams, 1986; Zigmond, Levin, & Laurie, 1985).

The current inclusion movement challenges schools to look beyond mainstreaming to find inclusive strategies. Specifically, it calls for a more complete merger of regular and special education. The movement has been gaining support since 1986 when Madeleine Will of the U.S. Department of Education called for the collaboration of special and regular education to contribute their collective skills and resources to carry out educational plans that benefit *all* students (Shumaker & Deshler, 1988; Will, 1986; Zigmond & Baker, 1994). In this chapter, the impact of inclusion on special education students, general education students, teachers, and schools is presented.

❏ Impact on students with special needs

Benefits to students with disabilities have been examined both in terms of social and academic results. In keeping with the controversial nature of the topic itself, research findings have varied. Some have argued that one of the rationales for inclusion – to eliminate the stigma of students who have to report to a "special ed" classroom – has actually backfired. Madge, Affleck, and Lowenbraun (1990) used peer ratings to assess the social status of students with and without learning disabilities in an integrated classroom model. They reported that the special education students had a significantly lower social status compared to their peers with no disabilities (but these authors did, however, conclude that the integrated classrooms provided better opportunities for special education students to blend in socially with their peers).

Clever, Bear, and Juvonen (1992) compared the self-perceptions of children with LD with those of their low-achieving or normally achieving peers in an integrated classroom. Their findings showed the lowest self-perceptions of scholastic achievement in the students with LD.

But these findings, as with so many of those in the area of inclusion, are countered with studies that show otherwise. Jenkins and Heinen (1989) surveyed elementary students' preferences about where and from whom they received instruction for learning difficulties. The authors concluded that regardless of the students' type (general, remedial, or special education), they preferred not to draw attention to their learning problems and would rather receive help from their classroom teacher than from a specialist.

In a meta-analyses of the effects of inclusion on students with special needs, Baker and Zigmond (1995) found a small to moderate positive effect of inclusive education on the academic and social outcomes of pupils. Academic benefits were measured through standard achievement tasks, and self, peer, teacher and observer ratings were used to evaluate social effects.

Staub and Peck (1995) examined studies using control groups to compare progress of children who are not disabled in classrooms said to be inclusive with those in classrooms that do not include children with disabilities. No significant differences in academic progress were found between the two groups of students. In addition, the presence of children with disabilities had no effect on either the time allocated to instruction or the levels of interruption.

Affleck, Madge, Adams, and Lowenbraun (1988) found no difference in the academic performance of students with learning disabilities and their "regular education" peers in integrated classrooms compared to more traditional settings. Reading, mathematics, and language achievement data of elementary students with learning disabilities served in a pull-out resource program was compared to an "integrated" program, and no significant differences among students with SLD served in the two settings were found. The researchers concluded that the integrated model is at least as effective as the resource model, thus supporting the concept of providing services in the least restrictive environment.

In an investigation of the collaborative teaching model, Walsh and Snyder (1994) compared ninth grade co-taught classes (that included special education students) to ninth grade regular classes in absences, discipline referrals, grades, and functional test results. Results indicated that high school classes with two teachers, a general educator and a special educator working collaboratively, can produce significantly better results than regular education classes alone in achieving academic requirements for graduation. A significantly greater percent of ninth grade students from co-taught classes passed statewide competency tests in three different areas. In the area of attendance and discipline referrals, however, there were no significant differences in classes that included a co-teacher.

In spite of the success reported by some studies, others have found that students with learning disabilities (the largest group of students receiving special services) do not fare well academically in the general education classroom where undifferentiated, large-group instruction is the norm (Schumm, Vaughn, Haager, McDowell, Rothlein, & Samuell, 1995). This lack of consensus in regard to benefits to students with special needs mirrors the findings of research on mainstreaming. Evidence exists both to support and refute inclusion's effectiveness with special needs students, and to date the research findings are inconclusive.

❏ Impact on general education students

Examining the practice of inclusion calls for researchers to consider the effect on the general student population. Although they are still scarce in the literature, studies have consistently found no deceleration of academic progress for nondisabled children enrolled in inclusive classrooms. Surveys conducted with parents and teachers who have been directly involved in inclusive settings generally show that both parties have positive views about inclusive programs and do not report any harm to the developmental progress of nondisabled children (Bailey & Winton 1989, Giangreco, Dennis, Coloninger, Edelman, & Schattman, 1993, Green & Stoneman, 1989; Peck, Carlson, & Helmstetter, 1992).

Staub and Peck (1995) specifically addressed the question, "Will nondisabled children lose teacher time and attention?" in a recent report, and found only one study, Hollowood, Salisbury, Rainforth, and Palombaro (1994), that investigated the topic. In the Hollowood study, allocated and actual instructional time were compared for six randomly selected nondisabled students in classrooms that included at least one student with severe disabilities. These students were compared to a group of non-disabled students in non-inclusive classrooms. Data were collected on the rate of interruptions to planned instruction. Findings indicated that the presence of students with severe disabilities had no effect on levels of allocated or engaged time. Further, time lost to interruptions of instruction was not significantly different in inclusive and noninclusive classrooms. In a related study, Helmstetter, Peck, and Giangreco (1994) surveyed a sample of 166 high school students who had been involved in inclusive classrooms in rural, suburban, and urban areas of Washington State. Seven categories of perceived positive outcomes of integration experiences resulted, such as increased responsiveness to needs of others, increased appreciation of human diversity, and development of personal values. The authors reported that positive outcomes were associated with more contact, receiving credit for the experience, and more substantive interaction. These students did not believe that their participation in inclusive classrooms had caused them to miss out on other valuable educational experiences.

Specifically examining inclusion in middle level schools, Hines (1995) used both qualitative and quantitative measures to study instructional time across inclusive and non-inclusive settings. Middle level teachers whose schedule included "regular," mainstreamed, and co-taught (inclusive) configurations were selected for the study. No statistical difference was found in the amount of time teachers engaged in instructional interactions across the three settings; but significantly more time was spent in managerial interactions in mainstream classrooms than in regular or co-taught settings.

Another research effort conducted follow-along case studies of non-disabled students in inclusive elementary and middle school classrooms (Staub & Peck, 1995). Interviews with parents and teachers as well as direct observational data collected over two successive school years indicated that non-disabled students do not acquire undesirable or maladjustive behavior from peers with disabilities.

While these studies provide the beginning of a research base on inclusion, most reports on the effectiveness of idiosyncratic programs reported with little empirical backing. Johnston, Proctor, and Corey (1995) reported positive results of a Team Approach to Mastery (TAM) model as an alternative to a pull-out system in Delaware. The approach includes seven basic elements for including students (at an average of two non-disabled students per child with a disability in the classroom): team (collaborative) teaching, learning centers, ego groups, direct instruction, positive approach, point cards, and teacher cadres. The authors reported that non-disabled third grade students in TAM achieved significantly higher scores than their non-disabled peers in general education classes based on the Comprehensive Test of Basic Skills.

The study of inclusion's impact on general education students will likely continue to be a priority as educators seek to assure equity in classrooms for all students, including the non-disabled. The literature base in this area continues to expand, and most reports have found that including special needs students does not produce negative effects for the regular education population in inclusive settings. As with all reports of inclusion's effectiveness, however, it appears that adequate support for the regular educator is a primary factor. Co-teaching, in particular, appears to offer direct support for the regular educator that in some cases has resulted in positive outcomes for both regular and special education students.

❏ Inclusion and the teacher

In spite of favorable reports, teachers still appear to favor a pull-out model for delivering special education services. In the Hines (1995) study, for example, teacher perceptions did not necessarily coincide with the empirical evidence gathered. Even though no significant statistical differences were found, half of the teachers studied felt they had the most time for instruction in the regular class. Survey results indicated that teachers felt their regular classes were, overall, more successful than either of the two classes (mainstream or co-taught) that included special students. In classes that did include special students, however, teachers in the study overwhelmingly preferred the co-teach model over mainstreaming (92%). Most teachers indicated that the co-teach model is beneficial to them (88%). Teachers also indicated that the co-teach model is beneficial to regular education students (84%) and to the special education students (92%). One respondent noted that success depends on the student. Mainstreaming emerged as the least preferred of the two methods for including special students, with 58% of the teachers in the study indicating that it is not beneficial to them. One teacher wrote in the survey margin: "Behavior suffers when you can't give them the individual instruction needed" (Hines, 1995).

This discrepancy between research findings and teacher perceptions are echoed in the literature. Semmel, Abernathy, Butera, and Lesar (1991) found in a survey of regular and special educators that they preferred their existing pull-out model even though they generally believed that students with mild disabilities have a basic right to an education in the general classroom.

In addition, Heffernan (1993) suggested that regular educators do not trust that the support offered initially for including special students will continue. He pointed to a "widespread belief that, despite what the system says it will provide in the way of support, ultimately, teachers will face the new challenges alone" (p. 100). Semmel, Abernathy, Butera, & Lesar's (1991) study reiterated this concern: "Our sample of teachers apparently also believed that currently mandated resources for the instruction of students with mild disabilities need to be protected" (p.19) and agreed that a redistribution of special education resources to regular classrooms would help decrease their instructional load.

And what of the role of the special educator? In many cases, it appears that, as Gerber (1995) described, "collaborate was a unidirectional mandate for special education teachers and had come to mean assist" (p.181). The nature of assistance in these schools more often than not has drifted to the lowest common denominators:

114

- physical presence in the classroom, and
- contingent response to children's immediate needs or teachers' directions. — Gerber, 1995

Gerber (1995) further concluded that "there is little evidence that substantial professional autonomy was accorded special education teachers and every evidence that their role was defined and accepted as subordinate. Power to make decisions regarding curriculum or methods was not equally shared. Special education teachers made recommendations and suggestions; classroom teachers made decisions. For special education teachers, teaching occurred in another teacher's workspace (classroom), not their own, with another teacher's students, not their own" (p.181).

The changing roles of teachers in inclusive classrooms may account in part for the discrepancy between teacher attitudes and research results. While inclusion may seem like a sound idea in theory and may even produce positive outcomes, teachers are, traditionally, resistant to change. Inclusion calls for teachers to not only open their classroom doors to a wide variety of students, but also in many cases to share their workspace with another adult. Perhaps for these reasons, middle school teachers may be well suited for an inclusive environment. Unlike elementary and high school teachers, these teachers have worked in team situations and may feel more comfortable negotiating time, space, and responsibilities. Currently research studies with a focus on middle schools are scarce, but may be critical to examining inclusion's effectiveness.

❏ The inclusive school

In a 1995 study by Baker and Zigmond, comparative descriptions of schools practicing inclusion and descriptions of the specific children or teachers experiencing it were presented. In these case studies, the authors provided a view of schools nominated as exemplary whose administrators and teachers think of themselves as engaged in inclusive practices. In each school studied, some form of collaboration occurred. The main element of this collaboration typically found special education teachers traveling to teach in general classrooms, sometimes for long periods, following co-planning, and sometimes for short periods without any significant planning. Gerber (1995) pointed out that "scheduling and allocation of instructional effort was determined primarily as a service to other teachers, and only indirectly, if at all, as a response to the defined needs of students themselves. In these schools, it was seen as both appropriate and efficacious for special education teachers to act as subordinates, often as passive instruments of their general class colleagues' plans, responsive to their policies, their schedules, lessons, and physical space" (p.183).

White, Swift, and Harmon (1992) reported more favorable opinions of the inclusive practices of the Cobb County, Georgia, school district. A collaborative pilot model was evaluated, and student progress was measured by report cards, IEPs, student attitude surveys, parent surveys, and observations. Eighty-six percent of the parents felt that their children made more academic progress in the co-teach model, and 62 percent stated that their child had improved behaviorally. Forty-two percent of the students claimed that they preferred the co-teach model, while 28 percent preferred the traditional pull-out resource model (White, Swift, & Harmon, 1992).

The system in Indian Prairie School district (outside Chicago) made a move in 1991 to educate all students, including those with special needs, in a unified setting. By the Fall of 1993, the district did not have any special education classes in any of its eleven elementary or three middle level schools, and all students with learning disabilities at the high school level were being served in regular classes. While no empirical data has been collected in the district, the Director of Student Services reports that the system has been beneficial to both regular and special needs students (Byrne, 1995).

The idiosyncratic nature of inclusive practices among schools and school districts makes results difficult to interpret. In many cases, reports are from those involved in the inclusive practices themselves, and therefore bias is difficult to eliminate. Results have generally taken the form of case studies and self-reports, which provide a valuable glimpse at inclusive practices but little empirical information.

❏ Conclusions

Finding data on inclusion remains elusive, since the methods used for including special needs students vary from setting to setting, and the nature of disabilities included spans the spectrum. The initial evidence that has emerged does appear, however, to support the claim that including special needs students poses no *worse* outcomes for either the special students themselves or their general education peers. Because of the difficulty in controlling for variables and finding adequate sample sizes and control groups, studies are often reported as case studies or loosely designed quasi-experimental studies.

Teacher perceptions appear to persistently favor the pull-out placement, even when research supports other practices. Favorable opinions are reported more in qualitative studies than in large-scale teacher surveys. It appears, also, that effective inclusive practices for students with disabilities occur more often when teachers are given adequate preparation and support as they strive to met the goals of inclusion. Ⓡ

References

Affleck, J. Q., Madge, S., Adams, A., & Lowenbraun, S. (1988). Integrated classroom versus resource model: Academic viability and effectiveness. *Exceptional Children, 54* (3): 339-348.

Baker, E.T., Wang, M.C., & Walberg, H.J. (1995). The effects of inclusion on learning. *Educational Leadership, 52* (4): 33-35.

Baker, J. M., & Zigmond, N. (1995). The meaning and practice of inclusion for students with learning disabilities: Themes and implications from the five case studies. *Journal of Special Education, 29* (2), 163-80.

Bailey, D., & Winton, P. (1989). Friendship and acquaintance among families in a mainstreamed day care center. *Education and Training of the Mentally Retarded, 24* (2), 107-113.

Byrne, M. (1995). Director of Student Services, Indiana Prairie School District. [Phone interview].

Clever, A., Bear, & Juvonen. (1992). Discrepancies between competence and importance in self-perceptions of children in integrated classes. *Journal of Special Education, 26* (2), 125-38.

Gerber, M. M. (1995). Inclusion at the high-water mark? Some thoughts on Zigmond and Baker's case studies of inclusive educational programs. *Journal of Special Education, 29* (2), 181-191.

Giangreco, M. F., Dennis, R., Cloninger, C., Edelman, S., & Schattman, R. (1993). "I've counted Jon": Transformational experiences of teachers educating students with disabilities. *Exceptional Children, 59* (4), 359-72.

Green, A., & Stoneman, Z.. (1989). Attitudes of mothers and fathers of nonhandicapped children. *Journal of Early Intervention, 13* (4), 292-304.

Harris, D.M., & Evans, D.W. (1994). Integrating school restructuring and special education reform. *Case in Point, 8* (2), 7-19.

Heffernan, R.N. (1993). *Serving students with disabilities in general education: The Partnership Program.* Unpublished doctoral dissertation. San Diego State University, San Diego, CA.

Helmstetter, E., Peck, C.A., & Giangreco, M.F. (1994). Outcomes of interactions with peers with moderate or severe disabilities: A statewide survey of high school students. *Journal of the Association for Persons with Severe Handicaps, 19* (2), 263-76.

Hersh, S.B. (1990, April). *Observing special and regular education classrooms.* Paper presented at the Annual Meeting of the American Educational Research Association. (ERIC Document No. ED 321 458).

Hines, R. A. (1995). *Instructional and non-instructional time in inclusive and non-inclusive classrooms.* Unpublished doctoral dissertation for the University of South Florida, Tampa, FL.

Hollowood, T. M., Salisbury, C. L., Rainforth, B., & Palombaro, M. M. (1994). Use of instructional time in classrooms serving students with and without severe disabilities. *Exceptional Children, 61* (3), 242-253.

Jenkins, J. R., & Heinen, A. (1989). Students' preferences for service delivery: Pullout, in-class or integrated models. *Exceptional Children, 55* (3), 516-523.

Jenkins, J.R., & Pious, C.G. (1991). Full inclusion and the REI: A reply to Thousand and Villa. *Exceptional Children, 57* (6), 562-64.

Johnston, D., Proctor, W., & Corey, S. (1995). Not a way out: A way in. *Educational Leadership, 56* (4), 46-48.

Leyser, Y., & Abrams, P.D. (1986). Perceived training needs of regular and special education student teachers in the are of mainstreaming. *The Exceptional Child, 33* (3),173-180.

Lobosco, A.F., & Newman, D.L. (1992). Teaching special needs populations and teacher job satisfaction. Implications for education and staff development. *Urban Education, 27* (1), 21-31.

Lockledge, A., & Wright, E.B. (1991). *Collaborative teaching and the mainstreamed student.* Research report, (ERIC Document Reproduction Service No. ED 358 100).

Madge, S., Affleck, J., & Lowenbraun, S. (1990). Social effects of integrated classrooms and resource room/regular class placements on elementary students with learning disabilities. *Journal of Learning Disabilities, 23* (7): 439-444.

O'Reilly, R.R., & Duquette, C.A. (1988). Experienced teachers look at mainstreaming: A study done in the Ottawa-Carelton area. *Education Canada, 28* (3), 9-13.

Peck, C. A., Carlson, P., & Helmstetter, E. (1992). Parent and teacher perceptions of outcomes for typically developing children enrolled in integrated early childhood programs: A stateside survey. *Journal of Early Intervention, 16* (1), 53-63.

Salisbury, C. L., Palombaro, M. M., & Hollowood, T. M. (1993). On the nature and change of an inclusive elementary school. *The Journal of the Association for Persons with Severe Handicaps,18* (2), 75-84.

Schumm, J.S., Vaughn, S., Haager, D., McDowell, J., Rothlein, L., & Samuell, L. (1995). General education teacher planning: What can students with learning disabilities expect? *General Education, 61* (4), 335-352.

Semmel, M.I., Abernathy, T.V., Butera, G., & Lesar, S. (1991). Teacher perceptions of the regular education initiative. *Exceptional Children, 58* (1), 9-22.

Shanker, A. (1994). Where We Stand. New York State United Teachers and the American Federation of Teachers. Column in the *New York Times*.

Shumaker, J. B., & Deshler, D. D. (1988). Secondary classes can be inclusive, too. *Educational Leadership, 56* (4), 50-51.

Straub, D., & Peck, C. (1995). What are the outcomes for nondisabled students? *Educational Leadership, 56* (4), 36-40.

Walsh, J., & Snyder, D. (1994). Cooperative teaching: An effective model for all students. *Case in Point, 8* (2), 7-19.

White, L., Swift, H., & Harmon, D. J. (1992). Collaborative teaching model in the elementary classroom. Unpublished raw data.

Will, M. C. (1986). Educating children with learning problems: A shared responsibility. *Exceptional Children, 52* (5), 411-415.

Zigmond, N., & Baker, J. (1994). Is the mainstream a more appropriate educational setting for Randy? A case study of one student with learning disabilities. *Learning Disabilities Research and Practice, 9* (2), 108-117.

Zigmond, N., Levin, E., & Laurie, T.L. (1985). Managing the mainstream: An analysis of teacher attitudes and student performance in mainstream high school programs. *Journal of Learning Disabilities, 18* (9), 535-541.

Jill VanNess and Elizabeth Platt

A Multifaceted Approach to Teaching Limited English Proficient Students

The ways in which the needs of linguistic minority students are addressed within middle level schools have become an important concern in American schools. A dramatic demographic shift in the school-age population during the past decade has caused an increase in limited English-proficient (LEP) students entering schools (U.S. Department of Education, 1994). To meet this challenge, program restructuring and staff development are being used to promote linguistic and cultural awareness (Burkart & Sheppard, 1995; LULAC v. Florida Department of Education 1989; Florida Department of Education, 1992). Educators must incorporate effective LEP program strategies within middle school programs. LEP student programming must address language and content learning needs simultaneously and within the social context of the classroom (Wilkins, 1976). "For limited English proficient (LEP) students success in school hinges upon gaining access to effective second language learning opportunities, and to a full educational program" (Council of Chief State School Officers, 1992, p. 4), and upon "continu(ing) to learn and expand their knowledge of new content, [thus not]. . . fall(ing) behind peers whose native language is English" (p. 6). These goals are particularly important during the middle grades where, facing five or six teachers rather than one, the needs of LEP students might easily be overlooked.

Although middle level educators may provide a positive climate for LEP students, it is often the case that specific needs go unaddressed. Hence, in this chapter we first present a discussion of the linguistic, cognitive, and social issues pertaining to learning languages. By understanding how a person learns a first language and understanding first language development one may become aware of how a second language is developed. We then discuss the theories and stages of second language development. When educators understand the stages of development, they can develop appropriate lessons and activities for LEP students. A review of how the native language and age of the student effects the learning of a second language follows. Next, the social, affective, and societal factors in second language acquisition (SLA) will be discussed. Finally, we will conclude the first section with differences between basic conversation and academic discourse and the rate it takes to learn both types of conversation.

The information about the variables involved in learning a second language is useful especially for specific teaching practices. However, at the site level, educators must design comprehensive programs for LEP students. Therefore in the second major section, we discuss various programmatic ways of addressing the needs of linguistic minority students in the middle school: bilingual, English as a Second Language (ESL) pull-out with content-based instruction, and inclusion. The three models presented are not exhaustive, but rather common program designs that are in place in many middle schools across the country.

❏ Linguistic, Cognitive, and Social Issues ❏

❏ First language acquisition (FLA)

The learning of a language by children is usually conceived as a process defined by stages of development (Brown, 1973). Most researchers now accept the notion that the process is a natural one, aided by an innate predispostion for language (Chomsky, 1965; Lenneberg, 1967), largely unaffected by specific input (Pine, 1994), and experienced by children across all cultures and in many different ways (Lieven, 1994). A child's first language, most agree, is not taught to children as Skinner (1957) claimed, but is instead acquired in a mostly unconscious manner (Brown, 1973; Chomsky, 1965; Gallaway & Richards; 1994; Hakuta, 1974). The stages have been well documented and described for first language acquisition (i. e. Bellugi, 1967; Clark & Clark, 1977; Major, 1974; Slobin, 1985), and are verified for second language learning as well. Despite differences in age, children and adults seem to pass through similar overall stages in their learning of a second language (Dulay & Burt, 1974).

❏ Theories and stages of second language development

Building on the idea that language learning is an innate, natural process, Krashen (1985) claims that comprehensible input (which means providing information that is understandable) and a positive affective environment (which is a warm, friendly atmosphere) are the necessary and sufficient conditions for second language acquisition. Despite the absence of substantive research support for this claim, Krashen has nonetheless been quite successful in promoting his ideas both in the United States and abroad. Few would argue that comprehensible input and a positive affective environment are necessary components for learning a second language; however, Long (1990) reported that in addition, learners need an opportunity to interact with others, negotiating meaning through conversation. Researchers arguing from a sociocultural perspective (Donato, 1994; Lantolf & Appel, 1994; Moll, 1990; Wertsch, 1979) also found evidence in support of environments where communication and interaction take place, though they also promote explicit assistance by the teacher. In a case study, Platt and Troudi (1997) found that although the teacher of the LEP student provided opportunities for interaction and communication, she failed to monitor the student's academic progress. The student appeared to be learning English and succeeding with classroom activities, but failed to be acquiring academic discourse and knowledge.

Just as FLA (first language acquisition) follows the unfolding of stages, SLA is also seen largely as a developmental process. The stages of second language learning by children from pre- to mid-puberty are briefly outlined in Table 1. Below each of the descriptions are indicators of the kind of tasks students at each of the four stages might be expected to perform. Given an adequate assessment of an incoming LEP student's language proficiency level, a content teacher is better informed regarding the optimal teaching activities for that student. This particular typology of stages (Florida Department of Education, 1992) presupposes that literacy is developing as language develops, an assumption that is problematic given the wide range of individual variation with respect to a student's prior literacy experiences. Nonetheless, it can be a helpful rule of thumb.

Krashen (1985), among others, presents a case for a silent period or delay of the onset of speech, similar to a period young children experience when they appear to be processing, but not producing, language (but see Gathercole, 1988, for evidence a silent period is not universal even in FLA). Young adolescents may need to listen to a great deal of language and make at least some sense of it before they are ready to attempt speech (Hakuta, 1974). For some, the learner's silent period lasts a very short time, while for others it can last for months. Non English-proficient beginners who listen but rarely speak in the new language may make just as much or more progress in second language development as their more talkative classmates by the end of the first year of exposure to English (Dulay, Burt, & Krashen, 1982; Saville-Troike, 1984; Wong Fillmore & Valadez, 1986). Heightened self-consciousness most teenagers experience with their peers, cultural socialization norms, or previous school background may also cause teens to remain silent in classrooms. Whatever the origins of silence, the teacher might devote more time and attention to listening activities at the beginning stages, not forcing LEP students to speak until they are ready to do so. Above all, teachers should not assume that a quiet LEP student understands the classroom talk and is learning from it, simply because s/he refrains from asking for help.

Table 1
Stages of second language acquisition
by early teens

Stage 1: **Preproduction** (minimal comprehension, no verbal production)
Listen, point, move, mime, draw, select, choose, act out, circle

Stage 2: **Early production** (limited comprehension, one/two word responses)
Name, label, group, respond, discriminate, list, categorize, tell, say, answer, count

Stage 3: **Speech emergence** (increased comprehension, simple sentences, basic errors in speech, reading largely limited to what has been learned by ear, writing limited to brief responses, little control)
Recall, retell, define, explain, compare, summarize, describe, role-play, restate, contrast

Stage 4: **Intermediate fluency** (very good comprehension, more complex sentences, fewer errors in speech, increased reading comprehension, developing cultural knowledge, errors in written language)
Analyze, create, defend, debate, predict, evaluate, justify, support, examine, hypothesize

---

❑ The effects native language and age have on second language learning

Despite general similarities, second language learning during the middle grades involves two important factors that make the task of SLA different than FLA: the effects of the native language and the age of the student. After early childhood the effects of the first language are prevalent and important to consider (Ellis, 1985; Selinker, 1992; White, 1989), especially at the early stages, and they also augment normal developmental processes (Zobl, 1980). Students may consistently use incorrect grammatical patterns while learning a second language. The inaccuracy may stem directly from the first or native language. It is important to determine the "root" of the incorrect patterns as they will have an influence on the student's abilities to speak, understand, read, and write in a second language, as well as to learn to function in the social and academic milieu of the American classroom.

Cognitive and academic development in the first language has an extremely important and positive effect on second language schooling (Collier, 1989, 1992; Cummins, 1991). Many academic skills, literacy development, concept formation, subject knowledge, and learning strategies developed in the first language transfer to second language learning in school. As LEP students expand their vocabulary and communicative skills in English, they can demonstrate the knowledge base that has already been developed in their first language (Collier, 1989, 1992; Cummins, 1991; Diaz & Klinger, 1991; Freeman & Freeman, 1994; McLaughlin, 1990; Tinajero & Ada, 1993; Wong Fillmore & Valadez, 1986). It should be mentioned however, that there are students entering middle school lacking first language literacy. Such students are at a strong disadvantage and, when possible, educators should make every attempt to teach literacy skills in the native language, while simultaneously teaching skills in the second language.

With respect to the age of the student learning a second language, ample evidence exists for the superiority of the preadolescent learner to acquire a second language to native-like proficiency (Krashen, Long, & Scarcella, 1982; Long, 1990; Scovel, 1981; Walsh & Diller, 1981). However, with the onset of puberty one's ability to sound like a native speaker and to use the morphology and syntax of the target language gradually diminishes through the teen years, leveling off after that (Johnson & Newport, 1989; Oyama, 1976). With respect to school learning, however, young adolescents have cognitive advantages such as greater concept development, memory capacity, and linked knowledge structures (Vosniadou & Brewer, 1985), so they may initially learn more quickly than the younger children (Snow & Hoefnagle-Höhle, 1978). Thus, they may move quickly through early stages of SLA because of transferrable literacy skills, but will nonetheless take a considerable amount of time to catch up to their native English-speaking peers, especially in such areas as American history and literature that depend on a considerable amount of exposure to American culture.

❑ Social, affective, and societal factors

Social and affective factors significantly influence second language in the young adolescent's second language learning (Wong Fillmore, 1991). Differences in learning have been found in studies on characteristics associated with personality traits such as introversion/extroversion, sociability, and conformity (Swain & Burnaby, 1976). Wong Fillmore (1991) concluded that the students who make the most progress are those predisposed to integrate socially with target language speakers (but, see Saville-Troike's [1984] study which revealed that such integration is not necessary). Moreover, Wong Fillmore has found little evidence that differences in achievement levels among the children could be attributed to intellectual ability. Despite findings that individual motivational, attitudinal, and personality factors can ameliorate or impede second language learning, however, Tollefson (1991), Pennycook (1989), and others have strongly criticized the field in general for overlooking the significance of issues of power, cultural dominance, and ideology underlying the circumstances under which any given student might be residing in the United States, as well as the effects of those issues on the programming in which the students are being served.

❑ Academic and communicative discourse

In examining the cognitive processes associated with SLA, Cummins (1979, 1981, 1989, 1991) has made a distinction between cognitive/academic language proficiency (CALP), the means through which students begin to understand subject matter (Collier, 1989, 1995; Cummins, 1979, 1981), and basic interpersonal communication skills (BICS) (Cummins, 1979, 1981), the social language used to communicate happenings throughout the day. Teachers should be aware even though students can speak well in social settings, they may not function well reading, writing, speaking, and understanding the academic language in the range of content domains. Literacy skills in the first language are transferable and are crucial to academic success in the second language (Bialystok, 1990; Cummins, 1989, 1991; Cummins & Swain, 1986; Freeman & Freeman, 1994; Hudelson,

1994; Lessow-Hurley, 1990; Tinajero & Ada, 1993; Wong Fillmore & Valdez, 1986). Thus, when middle level educators place LEP students, they must consider the student's academic background along with language ability.

❏ Rate of second language acquisition

In his analyses of Canadian immigrants' school performance on measures of social and academic language, Cummins (1981) reported that young adolescents acquiring ESL generally develop substantial proficiency in BICS within two to three years. In an extensive review of studies of language minority young adolescents in California, Wong Fillmore (1991) concluded that many young adolescents develop the oral system of vocabulary, grammar, phonology, semantics, and pragmatics of their second language for their age level over a two or three year period, although "differences of up to five years can be found in the time young adolescents take to get a working command of a new language" (p. 61). While developing social language may take up to five years, it may take up to seven or more years to develop proficiency in CALP (Collier 1995; Collier & Thomas, 1989; Cummins, 1981). In the teacher-centered, no-talking classroom where no interaction using the academic language takes place, cognitive academic language learning opportunities are limited for both native speakers of English and LEP students alike. In her extensive large scale studies of classrooms Collier (1989) found a decided advantage for language and content learning in highly interactive classrooms.

❏ Programs for Limited English Proficient Students ❏

Since SLA is a continuous process (Berko Gleason, 1993; Collier, 1992), and since academic language takes longer to learn than basic communication skills (Collier, 1995; Cummins, 1979, 1981; Wong Fillmore, 1991), optimum programming should maximize opportunities for language and content learning across the span of time the LEP student requires services or monitoring through the school years. Programs are of essentially two kinds: bilingual or English only.

❏ Bilingual programs

Bilingual instruction entails teaching in two languages, either by a teacher, aide, or peers. Often bilingual instruction is brought into the instructional mix in middle level schools. Paraprofessional staffing can be extremely diverse, representing the range of languages spoken by the student population of a given school (see Platt, 1992 for a discussion of different program models using two languages in instruction, counseling, and other program areas). Research by both Collier (1989,1992) and Wong Fillmore (1991) strongly supports bilingual education programs above all others in terms of overall LEP student progress. However, since bi- and multilingual programs no longer receive strong political support, and since most American teachers are monolingual English speakers, we turn to a discussion of other current instructional models for LEP students.

❏ ESL pull-out using content-based strategies

The pull-out model for LEP students has been used both within bilingual programs and as a stand-alone program. An ESL teacher works with LEP students in a different classroom where students may be grouped by proficiency level, or they may be placed according to grade level, regardless of how much English they know. Students may spend one or more class periods in the ESL classroom depending on their diagnosed needs. ESL may also be taught through the content areas to this group of students, either by an ESL teacher or by specially-trained teachers in the disciplines. Occasionally programs place ESL teachers as adjuncts in content classrooms where they collaborate with the content teacher. Although empirical research in the area of optimum ESL program design is limited, it is generally considered advantageous for teachers to use integrated language and content instruction to develop the academic skills in conjunction with the language skills (Crandall, 1987; Mohan, 1986; Short, 1991). Content topics, rather than grammar rules or vocabulary lists, form the core of instruction.

While typical ESL programs emphasize learning English apart from content (Crandall, 1987; Saville-Troike, 1984; Short, 1993), content area skills and academic language are taught together (Burkart & Sheppard, 1995; Kauffman, et al., 1995; Mancill, 1983), and teachers adjust their instruction to accommodate the various levels of proficiency (Kauffman, et al., 1995; Mohan, 1986). Over the past ten years, progress has been made in developing, implementing, and refining strategies that effectively integrate language and content instruction (Kauffman, 1995; Short, 1993). Higher order thinking skills such as inferencing, analysis, synthesis, evaluation, and hypothesis testing are also integrated into the curriculum (O'Malley & Chamot, 1989; Palinscar & Brown, 1988; Resnick, 1987). As Mohan (1986) suggested, the goal for both language and content teachers is to promote "understandable communication, cumulative language learning, and the development of academic thinking skills" (p. 4).

❏ Inclusion

Because of the various problems with ESL pull-out programs, such as (1) language learning objectives independent of the regular curriculum, (2) long periods of removal from non-LEP student environments, (3) lack of access to full programming in mainstream settings, and (4) generic English instruction in the absence of content. LEP students, like special needs students of all kinds, have increasingly found themselves in included classrooms. In this model services are brought into the classroom as opposed to pulling students out for special instruction. The inclusion model is in line with the least restrictive environment efforts made on behalf of special education students a decade ago (P.L. 94-142, 1975; Florida Department of Education, 1996). In a middle school, for example, LEP students would be placed in a mainstream, rather than in a self-contained ESL science class, and taught by the regular science teacher using ESL strategies.

Recently, educators have been searching for ways to address the challenges of inclusion and the diversity it brings to the classroom. The magnitude of challenges confronting teachers who try to meet the needs of students with a variety of special needs is often minimized or overlooked altogether. According to a survey of teachers who have completed an ESOL strategies course, however, full inclusion may be simply a polite term for the situation that obtained during the days when neither bilingual instruction nor ESL were mandated for LEP students, who may not even have been identified as having a special need (Harper, 1995). In discussing students with disabilities, Bricker (1995) argued that inclusion is a complex model that must be applied sensibly, not advocated unconditionally.

Well-supported inclusion requires planning, use of validated practices, collaboration, and a willingness to provide intensive and sometimes sustained instruction to meet students' needs. Educators must recognize the possibility that the placement of linguistic minority students in mainstream classrooms regardless of the willingness, ability, philosophical orientation, or certification qualifications of the teacher, is not in the best interest of the student (Harper & Platt, in preparation). The most unreasonable full inclusion scenario would have LEP students placed in regular language arts classes, which include no ESL skills or curricula. Educators promoting inclusion must therefore realize that this model does not adequately serve students with limited English or literacy skills (Harper & Platt, in preparation).

❏ Conclusion ❏

In sum, the scope of programs for linguistic minority students must be sufficiently broad to include a variety of learners who speak a variety of native languages, in a variety of settings (ESL and mainstream), a variety of academic and cognitive levels, and a variety of cultural differences that may help or hinder the learner's progress in the American classroom. Seliger (1984) stated that it is impossible to describe all the variables in SLA. Nonetheless, he noted: "In spite of such infinite diversity there exists the universal fact that human beings of all ages, attitudes, levels of intelligence, socioeconomic background, etc., succeed in acquiring L2s [second languages] in a wide variety of both naturalistic and formal settings" (p. 37). The task for middle level educators is to bring learners to grade level academically while they learn their second language. ℝ

References

Bellugi, U. (1967). *The acquisition of negation.* Unpublished doctoral dissertation, Harvard University, Boston, MA.

Berko Gleason, J. (1993). *The development of language* (3rd ed.). New York: Macmillian.

Bialystok, E. (1990). *Communication strategies.* Oxford: UK: Blackwell.

Bricker, D. (1995) . The challenge of inclusion. *Journal of Early Intervention, 19* (2), 179-194.

Brown, R. (1973). *A first language: The early stages.* Cambridge, MA: Harvard University Press.

Burkart, G., & Sheppard, K. (1995). *Content-ESL across the USA: Vol III, a training packet.* Washington, DC: Center for Applied Linguistics.

Chomsky, N. (1965). *Aspects of the theory of syntax.* Cambridge, MA: MIT Press.

Clark, H. H., & Clark, E. V. (1977). *Psychology and language.* New York: Harcourt Brace Jovanovich.

Collier, V. P. (1989). How Long? A synthesis of research on academic achievement in a second language. *TESOL Quarterly, 23* (3), 509-531.

Collier, V. P. (1992). The Canadian bilingual immersion debate: A synthesis of research findings. *Studies in Second Language Acquistion,14* (1), 87-97.

Collier, V. P. (1995). *Promoting academic success for ESL students: Understanding second language acquisition for school.* Elizabeth, NJ: New Jersey Teachers of English to Speakers of Other Languages-Bilingual Educators.

Collier, V. P., & Thomas, W. P. (1989). How quickly can immigrants become proficient in school English? *Journal of Educational Issues of Language Minority Students, 5* (1)26-38.

Council of Chief State School Officers (CCSSO). (1992). *Recommendations for improving the assessment and monitoring of students with limited English proficiency.* Washington, DC: Author.

Crandall, J. A. (Ed.) (1987). *ESL through content area instruction: Mathematics, science, social studies.* Englewood Cliffs, NJ: Prentice Hall Regents/Center for Applied Linguistics.

Cummins, J. (1979). Linguistic interdependence and the educational development of bilingual children. *Review of Educational Research, 49* (3),222-251.

Cummins, J. (1981). Age on arrival and immigrant second language learning in canada: a reassessment. *Applied Linguistics, 2* (1), 132-49.

Cummins, J. (1983). Language proficiency and academic achievement. In J. W. Oller, Jr. (Ed.), *Issues in language testing research* (pp. 108-129). Rowley, MA.: Newbury House.

Cummins, J. (1989). The sanitized curriculum: Educational disempowerment in a nation at risk. In D. M. Johnson & D. H. Roen (Eds.), *Richness in writing: Empowering ESL students* (pp. 19-38). New York: Longman.

Cummins, J. (1991). Interdependence of first-and second-language proficiency in bilingual children. In E. Bialystok (Ed.), *Language processing in bilingual children* (pp. 70-89). Cambridge UK: Cambridge University Press.

Cummins, J., & Swain, M. (1986). *Bilingualism in education.* New York: Longman.

Diaz, R. M. & Klinger C. (1991). Towards an explanatory model of the interaction between bilingualism and cognitive development. In E. Bialystok (Ed.), *Language processing in bilingual children* (pp. 167-192). Cambridge, UK: Cambridge University Press.

Donato, R. (1994). Collective scaffolding in second language learning. In Lautolf, J. P. & Appel, G. (Eds.) *Vygotskian approaches to second language research* (pp. 33-56). Norwood, NJ: Ablex.

Dulay, H. C., & Burt, M. K. (1974). Errors and strategies in child second language acquisition. *TESOL Quarterly, 8* (2), 129-136.

Dulay, H., Burt, M., & Krashen, S. (1982). *Language two.* Oxford, UK: Oxford University Press.

Ellis, R. (1985). *Understanding second language acquisition.* Oxford: Oxford University Press.

Florida Department of Education. (1990). *Agreement english for speakers of other languages* (ESOL). Tallahassee, FL. Author.

Florida Department of Education. (1992). *Empowering ESOL teachers: An overview. Vol I.* Division of Human Resource Development, Boca Raton: Florida Atlantic University, Multifunctional Resource Center.

Florida Department of Education. (1996). *Inclusion as an instructional model for LEP students* (technical assistance paper No. 019-ESOL-95). Tallahassee, FL: Office of Minority and Second Language Education.

Freeman, D., & Freeman, Y. (1994). *Between worlds: Access to second language acquisition.* Portsmouth, NH: Heinemann.

Gallaway, C., & Richards, B. J. (1994). *Input and interaction in language acquisition.* Cambridge, UK: Cambridge University Press.

Gathercole, V. C. (1988). Some myths you have heard about first language acquisition. *TESOL Quarterly, 22* (3), 407-436.

Hakuta, K. (1974). Prefabricated patterns and the emergence of structure in second language acquisition. *Language Learning, 24* (2) 287-297.

Harper, C. (1995). *An evaluation of ESOL inservice training in Florida.* (Technical report. 93120344). Gainesville, FL: University of Florida, Project LEEDS: US Department of Education.

Harper, C. & Platt, E. J. (in preparation). *Problems and possibilities with full inclusion of limited English proficient students in mainstream classrooms.*

Hudelson, S. (1994). Literacy development of second language children. In F. Genesee (Ed.), *Educating second language children* (pp. 129-158). Cambridge, UK: Cambridge University Press.

Johnson, J., & Newport, E. (1989). Critical period effects in second language learning: The influence of maturational state on the acquisition of English as a Second Language. *Cognitive Psychology, 21* (1), 60-99.

Kauffman, D., Burkart, G., Crandall, J., Johnson, D., Peyton, J., Sheppard, K., & Short, D. (1995). *Content-ESL across the USA: Vol. II, a practical guide.* Washington, DC: Center for Applied Linguistics.

Krashen, S. D. (1985). *The input hypothesis: Issues and implications.* New York: Longman Group Ltd.

Krashen, S. D., Long, M. H., & Scarcella, R. C. (1982). Age, rate and eventual attainment in second language acquisition. In S. Krashen, R. Scarcella, & M. Long (Eds.), *Child-adult differences in second language acquisition* (pp. 161-172). Rowley, MA: Newbury House.

Lantolf, J., & Appel, G. (1994). *Vygotskian approaches to second language research.* Norwood, NJ: Ablex.

Lenneberg, E. (1967). *Biological foundations of language.* New York: Wiley.

Lessow-Hurley, J. (1990). *The foundations of dual language instruction.* New York: Longman.

Lieven, E. V. M. (1994). Crosslinguistic and cross-cultural aspects of language addressed to children. In C Gallaway & B. J. Richards (Eds.) *Input and interaction in language acquisition* (pp. 56-73). Cambridge, UK: Cambridge University Press.

Long, M.H. (1990). Maturational constraints on language development. *Studies in Second Language Acquisition, 12* (3), 251-286.

Long, M. H., & Porter, P. A. (1985). Group work, interlanguage talk, and SLA. *TESOL Quarterly, 19* (207-227).

LULAC v. Florida Department of Education (1989). Tallahassee, FL.

Major, D. (1974). *The acquisition of modal auxiliaries in the language of children.* The Hague: Mouton.

Mancill, G. S. (1983). *A policymaker's guide to special language services for language minority students.* Alexandria, VA: National Association of State Boards of Education.

McLaughlin, B. (1990). "Conscious" versus "unconscious" learning. *TESOL Quarterly, 24* (4), 617-634.

Mohan, B. (1986). *Language and content.* Reading, MA: Addison-Wesley.

Moll, L. (1990). *Vygotsky and education: Instructional implications and applications of sociohistorical psychology.* Cambridge, UK: Cambridge University Press.

O'Malley, J. & Chamot, A. (1989). *Learning strategies in second language acquisition.* Cambridge, UK: Cambridge University Press.

Oyama, S. (1976). A sensitive period in the acquisition of a non-native phonological system. *Journal of Psycholinguistic Research, 5* (2), 261-285.

Palinscar, A. S., & Brown, A. (1988). Teaching and practicing thinking skills to promote comprehension in the context of group problem solving. *Remedial and Special Education, 9* (1), 53-59.

Pennycook, A. (1989). The concept of method, interested knowledge, and the politics of language teaching. *TESOL Quarterly, 23* (4), 589-618.

Pine, J. M. (1994). The language of primary caregivers. In R. Gallaway & C. Richards (Eds.) *Input and interaction in language acquisition* (pp. 15-37). London: Cambridge University Press.

P. L. 94-142. (1975). *Education for All Hancicapped Children Act* (EAHCA).

Platt, E. J. (1992). *Collaboration for instruction of LEP students in vocational education* (technical report). Berkeley, CA: University of California, Berkeley, National Center for Research in Vocational Education.

Platt, E.J., & Troudi, S. (in press). Mary and her teachers: A Grebo-speaking child's place in the mainstream classroom. *The Modern Language Journal, 81* (1).

Resnick, L. (1987). *Education and learning to think.* Washington, DC: National Academy Press.

Saville-Troike, M. (1984). What really matters in second language learning for academic achievement. *TESOL Quarterly, 18* (2), 199-219.

Scovel, T. (1981). The effects of neurological age on nonprimary language acquisition. In R. A. Andersen (Ed.), *New dimensions in second language acquisition research* (pp. 33-42). Rowley, MA: Newbury House.

Seliger, H. (1984). Processing universals in second language acquisition. In F. Eckman, L. Bell, and D. Nelson (Eds.) *Universals of second language acquisition* (pp. 36-47), Rowley, MA: Newbury House.

Selinker, L. (1992). *Rediscovering interlanguage*, London: Longmans.

Short, D. J. (1991). *How to integrate language and content instruction: A training manual*. Washington, DC: Center for Applied Linguistics.

Short, D. J. (1993). Assessing integrated language and content instruction. *TESOL Quarterly, 27* (4), 627-655.

Skinner, B. F. (1957). *Verbal behavior*. New York: Century Crofts.

Slobin, D. I. (1985). *The cross-linguistic study of language acquisition*. Hillsdale, NJ: Erlbaum.

Snow, C., & Hoefnagel-Hohle, M. (1978). The critical age for language acquisition: Evidence from second language learning. *Child Development, 49* (1), 114-28.

Swain, M., & Burnaby, B. (1976). Personality characteristics and second language learning in young children. *Working Papers on Bilingualism, 11* (2) 115-28.

Tinajero, J. V., & Ada, A.F. (Eds.). (1993). *The power of two languages: Literacy and biliteracy for Spanish-speaking students*. New York: Macmillan/ McGraw-Hill.

Tollefson, James. W. (1991.) *Planning language, planning inequality*. New York: Longman.

U. S. Department of Education. (1994). *Digest of education statistics*. Washington, DC: Author.

Vosniadou, S., & Brewer, W. F. (1985). *The problem of knowledge acquisition*. (Tech. rep. No. 348), Urbana-Champaign, IL: University of Illinois, Center for the Study of Reading.

Walsh, T. M., & Diller, K. C. (1981). Neurolinguistic considerations on the optimum age for second language learning. In K. C. Diller (Ed.), *Individual differences and universals in language learning and aptitude* (pp. 3-21). Rowley, MA: Newbury House.

Wertsch, J. (1979). From social interaction to higher psychological processes: An application of Vygotsky's theory. *Human Development, 22* (1)1-22.

White, L. (1989). *Universal grammar and second language acquisition*. Amsterdam: John Benjamins.

Wilkins, D. (1976). *Notional syllabuses.* London: Oxford University Press.

Wong Fillmore, L. (1991). Second language learning in children: A model of language learning in social context. In E. Bialystok (Ed.), *Language processing in bilingual children.* (pp. 49-69). Cambridge, UK: Cambridge University Press.

Wong Fillmore, L., & Valdez, C. (1986). Teaching bilingual learners. In M. C. Wittrock (Ed.) *Handbook of research on teaching* (3rd ed., pp. 648-685). New York: Macmillan.

Zobl, H. (1980). Developmental and transfer errors: Their common bases and (possibly) differential effects on subsequent learning. *TESOL Quarterly, 14* (4), 469-479.

Laura P. Stowell and Janet E. McDaniel

The Changing Face of Assessment

Many professional associations – National Council of Teachers of English, International Reading Association (1984), National Council of Teachers of Mathematics (1995) and the like – have called for sweeping reform in educational assessment. For a long time, test was used synonymously with assessment, as if that were the only way to gather information. "Test" no longer captures the kinds of measures currently being used in classrooms. In this chapter, we discuss the literature that links assessment to learning theory, how assessment information is collected and used, and issues of equity in assessment.

❏ Linking Assessment to Learning Theory ❏

Beyond knowing the language of assessment, most scholars recommend linking assessment to current thinking regarding how students learn. What we know about the nature of teaching and learning has changed. It once was possible to test the amount of knowledge that a student had gained and that was enough. But knowledge is expanding geometrically. Changes in the workplace and society at large suggest people need to be flexible and adaptable and apply rather than acquire knowledge. Assessment in school then, must be related to what a student knows, applies, and performs (Meyer, 1992; Zessoules & Gardner, 1991).

Assessment practices must also keep pace with what educators currently know about adolescent development. The National Center for Improving Science (1990) suggested that assessment should assist the learning process. Assessment that is responsive to the development of young adolescents is also in keeping with the recommendations of *Turning Points* (Carnegie Council on Adolescent Development, 1989), *This We Believe,* (NMSA, 1995), and other middle level reform documents.

The development of young adolescents takes place at different rates and unevenly across domains; they fluctuate between concrete operation and formal operations (Inhelder & Piaget, 1958). Thus, in any given middle grades classroom, there are likely to be wide variations and continuous change in the reasoning abilities of the students with regard to any particular subject matter. Therefore, good assessment measures are numerous and represent multiple perspectives – for example, all the teachers on an interdisciplinary team may contribute their input to the final evaluation of a major project. Students, as well, might have input on their grades through self-evaluation of their work. Frequent assessment measures that gauge both concrete and abstract thinking are also appropriate. Young adolescents need to be free to express their achievement without being constantly compared to all other students. Their individual achievement, especially when seen over time, is a better indicator of their learning than having all students expected to achieve the same mastery at the same time.

Young adolescents generally want to do well in school (Steinberg, 1993). Nonetheless, they sometimes exhibit frustration and lack of motivation in achieving the tasks established by their teachers. In the extreme, this frustration leads to dropping out of school (Wheelock & Dorman, 1988). Assessment can help rather than hinder students in expressing their thinking and in seeing their accomplishments. To help achieve this end teachers provide frequent opportunities for young adolescents to communicate their ideas and make explicit their own thinking about their achievements. Reflective writing, discussions, journals, logs, and portfolio assessment are means of helping students analyze their learning. When they see the progress they are making, being constantly compared with others in the class, they may take on a more optimistic view of their abilities and their likely continued success even as tasks become harder for them (Ames, 1990; Steinberg, 1993). Constructive feedback, ample opportunities for experiencing success, and tasks that are within the reach of young adolescents are keys to their continued positive attitude toward learning.

When young adolescents have mastered basic concepts such as reading, writing, computations, and map reading, they may become bored with repetitions of displaying those skills in drills. These students seek opportunities to apply their knowledge. Building into assessment the frequent use of application (as well as synthesis and evaluation) of previously gained knowledge will allow these students to grow and to demonstrate their thinking as well as their store of recall knowledge. In authentic assessment tasks, students are motivated to learn even while being assessed on what they have already learned. That is, students are constructing more knowledge while they are demonstrating that which they already have (Brooks & Brooks, 1993).

Young adolescents are changing not just in the intellectual domain, but also in their social and personal domains. A major challenge of young adolescents is identity formation (Erikson, 1981). Success in achieving a healthy adult identity begins with the young adolescent's weathering the conflicting demands of puberty, cultural expectations, and social pressures. Assessment can be supportive of middle school students by allowing them to express who they are and who they wish to become. Classrooms that support identity formation are safe environments in which young adolescents submit work that is an extension of who they are. Teachers respond to such work with sensitivity and understanding.

❏ Collecting Information ❏

Information about students from multiple sources, such as other teachers, peers, parents, self, and community members will provide the most complete picture of students' ability and growth. This information can also take many forms. What follows in the rest of this chapter are descriptions of formal and informal data sources, reporting mechanisms, and the use of authentic assessment, especially portfolios.

❏ Standardized tests

American educators, parents, and policy makers have come to rely heavily on standardized test scores. This reliance grew out of the early purpose of standardized tests to detect individual achievement among students (Stiggins, 1992). The emphasis on accountability and outcome-based education also contributed to this reliance on standardized tests. Even though standardized tests are consistently criticized by educators, sales continue to increase (Worthen, Borg, & White 1993). The 1990s have seen a move toward a broader array of assessment techniques and more alternative methods (Stiggins, 1992).

A growing body of work (Tierney, Carter, & Desai, 1991; Valencia & Pearson, 1990) points to the limitations regarding standardized test scores in making decisions about student achievement, student placement, and instruction. More specifically, standardized tests fail to view a content area, such as mathematics or literacy as an integrated whole, but rather as isolated pieces (Collins & Romberg, 1991; Hamayan, Kwait & Perlman, 1985; MSEB, 1993; Webb, 1992; Webb & Romberg, 1992). Romber, Wilson, and Khaketla (1992) assessed six of the most widely used standardized tests (such as the Comprehensive Test of Basic Skills and the Stanford Achievement Test) and compared them against NCTM's (National Council of Teachers of Mathematics) Curriculum and Evaluation Standards for School Mathematics to test for alignment. The results suggested that these tests do not assess the range of mathematics content, especially problem solving, do not adequately assess a student's process, and continue to emphasize procedures over content. Multiple choice tests do not capture the relationships among ideas and how students are thinking about a particular subject (Collins & Romberg, 1991). Valencia and Pearson (1986) found that assessment practices have also not kept pace with newer research in reading processes.

❏ Teacher-made tests

A national survey of elementary and secondary teachers in the United States (Valencia & Pearson, 1990) suggested that teachers administer an enormous number of teacher-developed tests. Middle school teachers use teacher-made tests more often than elementary teachers (Airasian, 1989). Despite the drive to challenge students to engage in higher level thinking, middle school teachers, more than elementary or high school teachers, rely almost exclusively on questions at the literal comprehension or knowledge level. Tests which require problem solving, critical thinking, and application of content knowledge are usually more valuable to teachers and students than low level comprehension tasks. If teacher-made tests are used, students can be very helpful with writing questions for them (Stevenson, 1992), especially when encouraged to stretch to higher levels of thinking.

❏ Observation/anecdotal records

While observation has been found to be a powerful assessment technique, teachers receive little training in using it effectively. Observation may be the most prevalent assessment tool used by classroom teachers. Elementary teachers rely on it more than high school teachers, and language arts teachers more than mathematics and science teachers (Stiggins, 1992). The best kind of observational instruments involve watching and systematically recording behavior – for example, counting how many times John speaks in a small group discussion. Carrying around a seating chart while leading a class discussion and recording who participates can provide a contrast to the small group record and give valuable information about participation in large and small groups or whether a student is more successful at verbal response than written. Observation is also a key to understanding what students learning English as a second language know about English (Genishi, 1989). The beginning of learning a second language, "the silent period" can go on for weeks or months (Krashen & Terrell, 1983). Students may also be silent at school and speaking English at home and so parents and extended family members become excellent sources of observational data for second language learners as well.

❏ Interviews, questionnaires, and conferences

Another means of obtaining information about students' attitudes, interests, and opinions is to ask them. Interviews, questionnaires, and conferences can be easily adapted to particular groups or individuals. Interviews and conferences can be structured or unstructured, provide immediate feedback, and give the teacher and student valuable one-on-one time. When students feel comfortable and free to talk, interviews and conferences, while time consuming, can be the most valuable time spent in assessment. These are very appropriate for middle school students as they are becoming more aware of their own identities, interests, attitudes, and thinking.

Nancie Atwell (1987), a well-known ethnographer of young adolescents' reading and writing, wrote at length on using conferences in the reading and writing classroom, which she calls the workshop. Since the publication of her groundbreaking book, *In the Middle: Writing, Reading and Learning with Adolescent*s, describing the reading and writing workshop, other disciplines (i.e. history, science, art) have adopted this structure and written about assessing through conferences, "status of the class" observation, and anecdotal record (see Brown, 1994; and Saul, Reardon, Schmidt, Pearce, Blackwook, & Bird,1993). Atwell (1987) provides a structure for on-line conferences as well as summative conferences. She also provided numerous examples of how she collects anecdotal records and provides ways for students to be data collectors and self-evaluators.

❏ Authentic assessment

Authentic assessment (also referred to as alternative assessment because it is an alternative to standardized, more formal assessment) is the process of gathering information about a student's progress and learning in a more authentic context on an authentic task. The student's work is compared to his or her past work rather than to other students' work. Almost every state is investigating or has implemented alternative assessment strategies which aim to measure how well students apply knowledge. This trend is due to dissatisfaction with norm-referenced, multiple choice tests and the inadequate information they give us. Great Britain and Canada have experimented successfully with authentic assessment. British schools have used a profiling technique which involves students and teachers in a continual dialogue about learning (Pole, 1993; Riding & Butterfield, 1990). Descriptions of successful uses of authentic assessment are appearing more regularly in the literature. However, there is very little rich description of how schools develop and use strategies like portfolios and performance-based assessment.

While portfolios are perhaps the most popular or well known form of authentic assessment, performance-based assessment and rubrics are also widely used. Performance assessment requires students to actively accomplish complex and significant tasks, while bringing to bear prior knowledge, recent learning and relevant skills to solve realistic problems (Herman, Aschbacher, & Winters, 1992). Drawing on his extensive experience, Wiggins (1993) has developed guidelines and criteria for designing authentic assessment. He calls for "authentic simulations," much like those a doctor, attorney, or pilot faces when confronted with situations that replicate challenges to be faced later.

❏ Rubrics

Rubrics have been widely used to score authentic assessments. A rubric is a scaled set of criteria that clearly defines for the student a range of what is acceptable and unacceptable performance. Rubrics let students know the criteria they will be judged upon prior to the task, and often students have participated in designing the rubric. The scores of a rubric are matched to an example of an appropriate response, and students (and parents) should have access to these examples. Two types of rubrics are used: analytic and holistic. A holistic rubric examines the quality of a student's work as a whole, not merely the collection of its parts and is an impressionistic evaluation. An analytic rubric measures specific aspects of the work. These two kinds of rubrics can be used together because they measure different things. Even numbered rubrics (four or six point scales) work better than odd numbered (especially five point scales) because scorers tend to choose the middle score in an odd numbered rubric and five point scale is too much like letter grades. Rubrics are good assessment tools as well as good teaching tools because they provide a clear target for students.

❏ Reporting Information ❏

One of the key purposes of assessment is to communicate with parents and students about a student's progress and achievement. Communication with parents and caregivers about student progress takes many forms. Following is a description of what the research has to say about reporting assessment information.

❏ Report cards

As schools and teachers examine ways to evaluate students authentically, they are also seeking ways to report that information in a meaningful manner. Report cards are being scrutinized in school districts looking for ways to reform them. However, they are still the most popular way (aside from standardized tests) to report assessment information. Almost all schools (99%) give students letter or number grades for academic performance. About a quarter of the middle schools surveyed (26%) give separate grades for effort and fewer (18%) give progress grades for student improvement (Epstein & Mac Iver, 1990). Half of the schools give students grades for conduct and half give written comments. Junior high and middle schools (30%) are more likely to use computer-generated comments than K-8 or K-12 schools who tend to give written comments (and are generally smaller schools). Other kinds of information found on report cards are attendance: absences and tardies (overall or by subject), citizenship, work habits, reading level, and requests for parent conferences. As students enter middle schools their report card grades tend to go down, "even as their overall competencies and knowledge go up" (Peterson, 1986). Schools that use student progress grades or handwritten comments on report cards are significantly associated with lower grade retention rates, lower projected dropout rates for males, and more successful middle school programs (Mac Iver, 1990).

Report cards are being re-examined and reformulated across the country. Educators are looking for ways to make a report card more meaningful and clear to students and parents. Wiggins (1994) has several suggestions for this including differentiating between norm-referenced and standard-referenced information, charting achievement against exit level standards (so a sixth grader knows how he or she is doing against a ninth grader), distinctions between the quality of a student's work and the sophistication, adding more "sub-grades" of performance (identifying strengths and weaknesses in more diverse areas), and an evaluation of the student's habits of mind and work (p. 29).

❑ Portfolios

Much of the recent research in assessment has been on portfolios. While portfolios have been a standard form of assessment in other professions, they are currently gaining popularity and credibility in classrooms as a way to create alternatives to norm referenced tests (Winograd & Paris, 1988; Wolf, 1989). Some classrooms are implementing portfolios for special purposes such as learning disabled students and English learners. A few states – Vermont, Michigan, and Kentucky – have adopted portfolios statewide.

Portfolio assessment is particularly appropriate for young adolescents, especially when utilized in a team or village setting. The use of portfolios also aligns nicely with current learning theory and middle level reform documents. First, portfolios provide a vehicle for collecting information about growth and improvement over time. Second, the teachers on the team (and the students themselves) can gain a full picture of a student's growth and ability across disciplines. Third, portfolios require students to reflect on their own knowledge and progress as they assess themselves. Fourth, portfolios can provide a vehicle for students to demonstrate other talents or interests outside of academic work.

Portfolios can contain anywhere from two to fifty artifacts, but generally contain ten to fifteen pieces. Below is a partial list of some of the artifacts that research has found students include in a portfolio (Kolanowski, 1993; Stowell & Tierney, 1991; Tierney, Carter, & Desai, 1991).

showcase pieces (most portfolios include this)
work in progress
work the student has learned from
evidence of thinking
goal statements/checklist of skills
work that shows growth
art work
journals
awards
interest and attitude surveys
collaborative work
explanations of work
things from outside of school
audio tapes
video tapes
photographs

144

Portfolios generally include a cover letter which explains the contents. Sometimes it is a metacognitive letter, in which the student not only explains what is in the portfolio, but reflects on why it is in the portfolio.

Two studies investigated teachers' use of portfolios in the classroom (Kolanowski,1993; Lamme and Hysmith 1991). These researchers found that teachers implemented portfolios on a small scale to begin with, usually beginning with showcase portfolios and simply collected the student work already taking place in the classroom, such as tests and writing assignments, and kept them in one folder (Kolanowski, 1993). As teachers become more comfortable and confident in using portfolios, their purposes enlarge. Teachers will collect and keep more in-depth records of what the student is doing, and the portfolio takes on a more centralized role in assessment in the classroom (Lamme & Hysmith, 1991). Eventually portfolios are used to inform instruction, assess student growth, and enable students to reflect on and evaluate their own work.

Student thinking about portfolios develops in similar ways to teachers' implementation. In most classrooms (Kolanowski, 1993) students make the decisions or if they make the decision with someone, their decision carries more weight. Rarely is the teacher the sole decision maker. Some teachers choose to relinquish control of more aspects of the portfolio to the students as the school year progresses. During the first semester the student might have one quarter of the input and the teacher three quarters, while during the second semester, the student would have three quarters of the input and the teacher one quarter (Stowell & Tierney, 1995).

Portfolios are generally a part of the final grade (Kolanowski, 1993). Some teachers tie the analysis to the report card and others revise the report card. Where the portfolio has taken the place of the report card, analysis occurred four or six times a year. Most portfolios are analyzed once a year. Some middle schools have a portfolio day at the end of the year in which they invite community members to listen to students present their portfolios.

❑ Student-led conferences

Students have been encouraged to take part in their own assessment and are now being asked to take part in sharing the information as well. Reflecting on one's performance can be a powerful learning experience as proved by portfolios. Young adolescents have sufficient metacognitive ability to realize what they do and do not understand (Flavell & Wellman, 1977). They also are more aware of their own perspectives when confronted with different perspectives. Therefore student-led conferences can offer a powerful learning experience as well as demonstrate to the student that his or her voice in valued in the assessment process.

Successful student-led conferences require a great deal of preparation on the part of students and teacher. Class meetings, journals, conferences with peers, self-evaluations, and portfolios can be used with students to prepare. One school (Denby, 1996) which implemented student-led conferences found that students felt more ownership of their work, were less interested in teacher approval and more interested in the pride derived from their own work, felt more accountable for their behavior and academic work, gave teachers feedback on their work, and even began to devise strategies for improvement during the conference. Parents also tried to help students develop strategies that they could do at home together (p. 379). Once a conference is complete, all parties may also be invited to reflect in writing on the experience.

❏ Assessment and equity

With an increasingly diverse population entering our schools, issues of equity cannot be overlooked. We know that the background knowledge and experiences children bring to the classroom are critical to their learning and the assessment of it. Current assessment practices are not providing all students the opportunity to demonstrate their knowledge (NCTM, 1995). Cultural biases do exist in achievement and IQ tests, and results must be interpreted with an awareness of these biases (Worthen &Spandel, 1991). While the tests are intended to give teachers information about a student's learning, they are generally used as sorting mechanisms (Nieto, 1992). Alternative means of assessment provide one answer. When assessing English learners it is important to distinguish between how well a student functions in social settings and academic settings (Schlam and Cafetz, 1997). Time is also a key factor in assessing students from different cultural and linguistic backgrounds and, as suggested before, portfolios can serve well in this capacity (Brandt, 1990).

❏ Conclusion ❏

Few issues in education get more attention (and more press) than assessment. Media reports inevitably leave out much of the complexity of assessing and reporting student achievement. It is up to educators to provide a more complete picture to students, parents, and the community they serve. Middle level teachers need to be clear about their purposes for using assessment tools, the right tool for the right task, assessment language, and communicating assessment information. Assessment guidelines which are linked to what we currently know about adolescent development will serve students and teachers most effectively. More research is needed on authentic assessment in middle school classrooms and its impact on teachers and students. Ⓡ

References

Airasian, P. W. (1989). Classroom assessment and educational improvement. In L. W. Anderson (Ed.), *The effective teacher* (pp. 333-342). New York: Random House.

Atwell, N. (1987) *In the middle*. Portsmouth, NH: Heinemann.

Brandt, R. (1990). On assessment in the arts: A conversation with Howard Gardner. *Educational Leadership, 47* (6), 24-29.

Brown, C.S. (1994) *Connecting with the past: History workshop in middle and high schools*. Portsmouth: Heinemann.

Carnegie Council on Adolescent Development (1989). *Turning points: Preparing American youth for the 21st century*. New York: Carnegie Corporation.

Charles, C.M. (1995) *Introduction to educational research*. White Plains, NY: Longman

Collins, K., & Romberg, T. A. (1991). Assessment of mathematical performance: An analysis of open ended test items. In M.C. Wittrock and E. Baker (Eds.), *Testing and cognition* (pp. 5-16). Englewood Cliffs: New Jersey: Prentice Hall.

Cooper, C.R., & Odell, L. (1977) *Evaluating writing*. Urbana, IL: NCTE.

Denby, J. (1996) Colegio Bolivar enters a new era in parent/teacher conferences. *Phi Delta Kappan, 77* (5), 378-379.

Epstein, J. L., & Mac Iver, D.J. (1990) *Education in the middle grades: National practices and trends*. Columbus, Ohio: National Middle School Association.

Erickson, E. (1968) *Youth, identity and crisis*. New York: Norton.

Flavell, J., & Wellman, H. (1997). Metamemory. In R.V. Kail & J. W. Hagen (Eds.), *Perspective on the development of memory and cognition*. Hillsdale, NJ: Lawrence Erlbaum.

Genishi, C. (1989) Observing the second language learner. An example of teachers' learning. *Language Arts, 66* (5), 509-515.

George, P.S., Stevenson, C., Thomason, J., Beane, J. (1992). *The middle school-and beyond*. Alexandria, VA: Association for Supervision and Curriculum Development.

George, P. S. & Alexander, W.M. (1993) *The exemplary middle school.* Fort Worth, TX: Harcourt Brace Jovanovich.

Hamayan, E., Kwait, J., & Perlman, R. (1985) *The identification and assessment of language minority students: A handbook for educators.* Arlington Heights, IL: Illinois Resource Center.

Kolanowski, K. (1993). *Use of portfolios in assessment of literature learning.* Albany, NY: Center for the Study of Literature.

Krashen, S., & Terrel, T. D. (1983) *The natural approach: Language acquisition in the classroom.* New York: Oxford/Alemany.

International Reading Association and National Council of Teachers of English. (1994) *Standards for the assessment of reading and writing.* Urbana, IL: NCTE: Author.

Lamme, L., & Hysmith, C. (1991). One school's adventure into portfolio assessment. *Language Arts, 68* (8). 620-629.

Mac Iver, D.J. (1990). *A national description of report card entries in the middle grades.* CDS Report 9. Baltimore: The John Hopkins University Center for Research on Effective Schooling for Disadvantaged Students.

Mathematical Sciences Educational Board. (1993). *Measuring what counts: A conceptual guide for mathematics assessment.* Washington, DC: Author.

Messick, R.G., & Reynolds, K.E.. (1992) *Middle level curriculum.* New York: Longman.

Meyer, C.A. (1992). What is the difference between authentic and performance assessment? *Educational Leadership, 49* (8), 39.

National Council on Teaching Mathematics. (1995). *Assessment standards for school mathematicians.* Reston, VA: Author.

National Middle School Association (1995). *This we believe: Developmentally responsive middle level schools.* Columbus, OH: Author.

National Center for Improving Science Education. (1990) *Assessment in science education: The middle years.* Washington, DC and Colorado Springs, CO: The Network and the Biological Sciences Curriculum Study.

Nieto, S. (1992) *Affirming diversity: The sociopolitical context of multicultural education.* New York: Longman.

Pate, P. E., Homestead, E., McGinnis, K. (1993). Designing rubrics for authentic assessment. *Middle School Journal, 25* (2), 25-27.

Paulson, L. F., Paulson, P.R., & Meyer, C.A. (1991). What makes a portfolio a portfolio? *Educational Leadership,* 60-65

Pole, C.J. (1993). *Assessing and recording achievement: Implementing a new approach in school.* New York: Routledge.

Riding, R. & Butterfield, S. (Eds.). (1990) *Assessment and examination in secondary schools.* New York: Routledge

Rhodes, L. K., & Shanklin, N. (1993). *Windows into literacy: Assessing learners K-8*. Portsmouth: Heinemann.

Romberg, T.A., Wilson, L., Khaketla, M., & Chavarria, S. (1992). Curriculum and test alignment. In T.A. Romber (Ed.), *Mathematics assessment and evaluation: Imperatives for mathematics educators*. (pp. 61-74) Albany, NY:SUNY.

Routman, R. (1991). *Invitations*. Portsmouth, NH: Heinemann.

Saul, W., Reardon, J., Schmidt, A., Pearce, C., Blackwook, D., & Bird, M. D. (1993) Science workshop. Portsmouth, NH: Heinemann.

Schlam, L., & Cafetz, S. (1997) Using portfolios with language minority students. In R. Weiner & J. Cohen (Eds.), *Literacy portfolios*. Englewood Cliffs, New Jersey: Prentice Hall.

Stevenson, C. (1992) *Teaching ten to fourteen year olds*. New York: Longman.

Stiggins, R. (1992). Facing the challenge of a new era of educational assessment. *Applied Measurement in Education, 4* (4), 263-274.

Stowell, L., & Tierney, R.J. (1995). Portfolios in the classroom: What happens when teachers and student negotiate assessment? In R. Allington & S. Walmsley (Eds.), *No quick fix* (pp.78-94). New York: Teachers College Press.

Stowell, L., & Tierney, R.J. (1991). *An ongoing examiniation of teacher shifts in thinking and practices in assessment: Portfolios across the disciplines in high school classrooms*. Columbus, Ohio: The Ohio State University, Technical Report for Apple, Inc.

Tierney, R.J. (1994). Learner-based assessment: Making evaluation fit with teaching and learning. In L.M. Morrow, J.K. Smith, & L.C. Wilkinson (Eds.), *Integrated language arts: Controversy to consensus* (pp. 231-240). Boston: Allyn & Bacon.

Tierney, R.J., Carter, M., & Desai, L.E.. (1991). *Portfolio assessment in the reading-writing classroom*. Christopher Gordon Publishers.

U.S. Congress, Office of Technology Assessment (1992). *Testing in American schools: Asking the right questions*, OTA-SET-519. Washington, DC: U.S Government Printing Office.

Valencia, S.W., & Pearson, P.D. (1990). *National survey of the use of test data for educational decision making*. Reading Research and Education Center Technical Report. Champaign, IL: University of Illinois at Champaign-Urbana.

Valencia, S.W., & Pearson, P.D. (1986) *New models for reading assessment*. Center for the Study of Reading Education, No. 71. Champaign, IL: University of Illinois at Champaign-Urbana.

Valencia, S. W., McGinley, W., & Pearson, P.D. (1990) Assessing reading and writing. In G. Duffy (Ed.), *Reading in the middle school* (pp. 124-153) Newark, DE: International Reading Association.

Webb, N. L. (1992). Assessment of students' knowledge of mathematics: Steps toward a theory. In D.A. Grouws (Ed.), *Handbook of research on mathematics teaching and learning* (pp. 661-683). New York: Macmillan.

Webb, N., & Romber, T.A. (1992). Implications of the NCTM standards for mathematics assessment. In T.A. Romber (Ed.), *Mathematics assessment and evaluation: Imperatives for mathematics educators* (pp. 37-60) Albany, NY: SUNY.

Wheelock, A., & Dornan, G. (1988). *Before its too late: Dropout prevention in the middle grades.* Carrboro, N.C.: Center for Early Adolescence; Boston: Massachusetts Advocacy Center.

Wiggins, G. (1991). Standards, not standardization: Evoking quality student work. *Educational Leadership, 48* (5), 18-26.

Wiggins, G. (1993). Assessment: Authenticity, context, and validity. *Phi Delta Kappan, 75* (3), 200-214.

Wiggins, G. (1994) Toward better report cards. *Educational Leadership, 52* (2), 28-37.

Winograd, P., & Paris, S. (1988) *Improving reading assessment.* The Heath Transcripts. Lexington, MA: D.C. Heath.

Wolf, D. (1989) Portfolio assessment: Sampling student work. *Educational Leadership, 46* (7), 35-39.

Worthen, B., Borg, W., & White, K. (1993) *Measurement and evalution in the schools.* New York: Longman.

Worthen , B. R., & Spandel, B. (1991). Putting the standardized test debate in perspective. *Educational Leadership.* 65-71.

Zessoules, R,. & Gardner, H. (1991). Authentic assessment: Beyond the buzzword and into the classroom. In V. Perone (Ed.), *Expanding student assessment* (pp. 47-71). Alexandria, VA: ASCD.

John H. Swaim and C. Kenneth McEwin

Competitive Sports Program

The agenda for middle level education is clear. Simply stated, middle level schools should focus on creating teaching and learning environments that are developmentally appropriate for young adolescents. Although much remains to be accomplished, significant gains have been made in the last 25 years toward accomplishing this goal. Increasingly, decisions regarding middle school programs and practices are being made based on the developmental needs and interests of young adolescents (McEwin, Dickinson, & Jenkins, 1996). Too often, however, these efforts have been centered primarily on the academic program, while co-curricular programs, such as competitive sports, continue to follow practices which revert back to those designed for older adolescents and adults.

Virtually all senior high schools, and approximately 80% of middle level schools offer organized competitive sports programs (Berryman, 1988; McEwin, Dickinson, & Jenkins, 1996). The belief that participation in these programs enhances social, psychological, physiological, and motor development is widely accepted. However, this belief has been increasingly questioned when trends in injury rates, psychological stress, and unqualified adult leadership are considered (Goldman, 1990; McEwin & Dickinson, 1996; Micheli, 1990; Micheli & Jenkins, 1990; Smith, Zane, Smoll & Coppol, 1983). These problem areas are diminishing the potential benefits that could come from such programs under appropriate circumstances (Seefeldt, Ewing, & Walk, 1993). What research says regarding these and related issues is reviewed below.

❏ Sports Injuries ❏

Due to the stage of physical development young adolescents are experiencing, they are predisposed to injuries (Micheli, 1990; Smith, 1986). The susceptibility of young adolescents to injuries is evident considering that one-third of all sports injuries occur in children and young adolescents ages 5 to 14 (Findley, 1987). An estimated 4,000,000 children and adolescents seek emergency room treatment for sports injuries each year with an additional 8,000,000 being treated by family physicians (Micheli, 1990). Significant numbers of these injuries occur in school-sponsored sports programs. Thirty percent of all injuries to children and youth which occur in and around schools result from participation in sports activities (Children's Safety Network, 1994).

According to estimates from the United States Consumer Product Safety Commission, sports injuries sustained by 5 to 14 year olds increased significantly from 1990 to 1994. The report shows that injuries in soccer increased by an estimated 10,000. During one year alone (1993), 38% (56,621) of soccer injuries occurred to young adolescents between the ages of 10 and 14. Also, during 1993, three fatalities of young adolescents were reported as a result of playing soccer. The report also found that football, the sport with the highest incidence of injuries in organized sports, increased by an estimated 15,000 between 1990 and 1994. However, baseball had the highest reported increase during this time period with 26,000 injuries (Carey, 1995; U. S. Consumer Product Safety Commission, 1990, 1995).

The statistics presented above are based on the number of sports injuries which were treated in hospital emergency rooms. For example, of the 460,000 baseball-related injuries treated in hospital emergency rooms during 1993, 28% (119,280) were to 10 to 14 year olds. Other sports such as wrestling, gymnastics, and basketball are also among the sports where the largest number of injuries to young adolescents occurred (Garrick, 1988; Goldburg, 1989; Herndon, 1988; Smith, 1986; Taft, 1991; U. S. Consumer Product Safety Commission, 1995).

Young adolescents participating in contact sports are particularly at risk for being injured because growth is still occurring in the long bones. The cartilage at the end of these bones is two to three times weaker than bones that are not growing. Thus injury to these vulnerable areas may cause one limb to grow longer than another and/or grow crooked, or stop growing altogether (Stark, 1993).

Injuries caused by contact in practices and games are not the only injuries resulting from participation in middle level organized sports programs. Overuse injuries, which are the result of repetitive microtramas (repeated small injuries), have become a serious problem in this age group. These injuries are frequently the result of young adolescents engaging in repetitive activities for which their muscles, tendons, ligaments, and bones are unprepared to withstand for long or intense periods of time. These kinds of injuries (e. g., stress fractures, tendonitis, shin splints) are intensified by factors such as overtraining, long playing seasons, and speciality sports camps. Damage caused by these injuries is often painful, and permanent and can lead to problems in later life (Fox, Jebson, & Orwin, 1995; Herndon, 1988; Poinsett, 1996; Rosenthal, 1993; Taft, 1991).

❏ Psychological Considerations ❏

There can be many positive psychological benefits for young adolescents as a result of participating in sports programs which enhance their self-esteem and increase their interest in sports. However, when young adolescent needs and interests become secondary to pressures and unreasonable expectations from coaches, parents, the community, and even themselves, sports often have the opposite effect. Young adolescents may begin to lose confidence in themselves as athletes which can lead to losing interest in participating in middle level sports. Even though psychological effects of sports are difficult to determine, young adolescents' psychological well-being should be a priority in developing middle level sports programs (Vaughan, 1984).

❏ Readiness to participate

Just as being aware of young adolescents' physical readiness to participate in organized competitive sports is crucial, so is their emotional readiness. It is common for organized sports competition to start as early as the preschool years with more than 20 million children ages 6 to 14 being involved in community-based, volunteer-directed youth sports programs (Boal, 1996; Smith, 1986). A problem with involving children and young adolescents in sports competition before they are physically or psychologically ready is that the play aspect is often eliminated, and regimented practices are substituted which instill the need to excel rather than have fun. Organized sports should not be overemphasized to the degree that the psychological readiness levels of young adolescents are overlooked.

❏ Cutting young adolescents from participation

Research indicates that being eliminated from participation has negative effects on many young adolescents. However, many middle schools include "cut policies" in their sports programs. When young adolescents are cut from sports, they not only lose the benefits of developing the physical skills needed to play that sport, but also opportunities for spending time with their peers and for gaining confidence in their ability to play a particular sport. It is common for students who have been cut not to try out again for a sports team because of the fear of being cut again (Ogilvie, 1988; Orlick & Broterill, 1978).

❏ Emphasis on winning

Competition is a reality in our society and, in fact, can be healthy when kept in proper perspective. Too often, however, the pressure to win permeates middle level competitive sports. The need to "win at all costs" is an all too common message given to young adolescents by peers, coaches, parents, and community members as well as collegiate and professional athletes and the press (Coop & Rotella, 1991). These messages are in direct conflict with the reasons most young adolescents participate in sports. These reasons frequently include having fun, being accepted as members of a group, the freedom of physical expression, and feeling successful, none of which requires highly stressful competition (Ogilvie, 1988). In fact, primarily focusing on winning negates many of the positive aspects which can be gained and fails to fulfill the purposes for which young adolescents go into sports in the first place.

❏ Expectations from adults

Parents who vicariously attempt to live their lives through the "sports careers" of their children, and coaches and others who have unrealistically high expectations which go beyond the physical and psychological capabilities of young adolescents are frequently the source of much of the stress associated with middle level sports (Fortanasce, 1995; Ogilvie, 1988). Parents and coaches might be the single most direct source of pressure placed on young adolescents in sports, but there is also a collective pressure that is brought to bear by the community. In comparison with community sponsored sports, school sports are usually more intense, instructional, competitive, and visible (e. g., number of practices/games, longer seasons, post season games) (Seefeldt, Ewing & Walk, 1993). These, and related factors, result in games being highly publicized and the outcomes being the subject of much discussion in communities. This discussion often focuses on which individual or team won, and as noted by Seefeldt "community patrons are seldom rational consumers of sport" (p. 25).

❏ Attrition in Sports ❏

The majority of youth drop out of sports programs by age 15. It has been estimated that 35% of youth drop out of sports each year and that 50% drop out by age 12 (Gould, 1987; Poinsett, 1996; Seefeldt, Ewing, & Walk, 1993). When it is considered that this represents only those who have chosen to participate in sports and does not include those who have never participated or were cut from sports programs, these figures become even more significant.

Today's young adolescents occupy their leisure time in a variety of ways other than sports. The emergence of new interests is one reason young adolescents drop out of sports. Other reasons include: (a) lack of playing time; (b) the way practices are conducted; (c) interactions with teammates; (d) dislike of coaches; (e) a feeling of unworthiness; (f) not having fun; and (g) needing additional time to study. These reasons apply to all sports, but the largest numbers of dropouts are in basketball, football, soccer, and track and field (Ewing & Seefelt, 1989; Gould, 1987; Holm, 1996; Rotella, Hanson, & Coop, 1991; Seefeldt, Ewing, & Walk, 1993).

Typically the type of young adolescents who are eliminated or drop out of sports are the ones who are poor performers (e.g., later maturing boys or those who do not show enough aggression). However, gifted athletes are also sometimes negatively effected when they are forced to specialize in one sport in which they have demonstrated talent or are placed under excessively high expectations by coaches, peers, and others (Lincoln, 1982; Stover, 1988). When these youth are continually pushed to be more competitive and to participate in intense practices, they begin to "burnout" and sometimes decide to leave sports.

❏ The Reality of Chances of Becoming ❏
College and/or Professional Athletes

Although it is appropriate to encourage young adolescents to be dedicated to realizing their potential in sports, it is clear that many youth have mistaken idealistic views of their chances of receiving college scholarships or making it to the professional sports league level. In reality, only a very small number of varsity high school players receive college sports scholarships. Although 59% of high school basketball and football players believe they will receive college scholarships, only about 1% do (Benedetto, 1990). Furthermore, of the approximately 150,000 high school seniors who play varsity basketball each year, only about 3% receive scholarships (Stacy, 1990).

The chances of becoming a professional athlete are almost nonexistent. For example, the odds against a high school football player, let alone a middle school football player, making it to the pros are 10,000 to 1 (.0001%) (Benedetto, 1990). The chances of receiving a professional sports contract in baseball are 5,000 to 1 (.0002%) (Dorsey, 1989), and the chances of playing professional basketball is 2,344 to 1 (.0004%) (Stacy, 1990).

The purpose of this kind of information should not be to discourage athletes with potential, but to help them have realistic expectations about their future in college and professional sports. The focus of middle level competitive sports should be on helping young adolescents set goals that reflect their current interests and abilities. This focus will make it easier for them to emphasize improvement rather than focus on the highly competitive aspects of sports which frequently pit one athlete against another.

❏ What Role Should Competitive Sports Play ❏ in the Lives of Young Adolescents?

Despite the many problems associated with organized sports programs for young adolescents, there are many potential benefits to be gained if competitive sports programs are based on developmentally responsive ideas and practices. Some of these potential benefits include: (a) enhanced fitness levels; (b) increased self-esteem; (c) appreciation for fitness; (d) the sense of belonging to a team or group; (e) enhanced social development; and, (f) providing community identity (Seefeldt, Ewing, & Walk, 1993).

Clearly competitive sports programs are popular with young adolescents with the most frequently offered middle school interscholastic sports for boys being basketball (82%), track (70%), football (56%), wrestling (41%), cross country (30%), and soccer (24%). Most frequently offered for girls are basketball (81%), track (70%), volleyball (57%), cross country (30%), softball (29%), and soccer (22%) (McEwin, Dickinson, & Jenkins, 1996). The popularity of a particular sport among young adolescents and the public, however, does not necessarily mean it is in the best interests of young adolescents to offer that sport at the middle school level (e. g., football, wrestling). Some difficult and courageous decisions regarding which sports should be played at the middle school level and what the rules and conditions for these sports should be need careful examination by those in decision-making positions.

Middle level sports programs which are developmentally inappropriate in many middle schools need and deserve immediate attention because the health and welfare of many thousands young adolescents are at stake. To turn away blindly from the problem areas associated with middle level competitive sports programs is irresponsible. Ethically, all school-sponsored activities are the responsibility of those decision makers who determine the nature of all school programs and practices. Changes such as the following can help assure that middle level competitive sports are safer and more developmentally appropriate for young adolescents: (a) improved coaching; (b) proper conditioning; (c) proper competitive environment; (d) rule changes; (e) improved supervision; (f) better matching of players; and, (g) proper equipment use (Goldberg, 1989).

Developmentally responsive middle level competitive sports programs can be an important part of the middle school curriculum. As with other middle school components (e. g., interdisciplinary team organization, teacher-based guidance programs, integrated curriculum), much study should precede changes, and implementation should be thoroughly planned and carefully implemented. The study process should directly address some of the issues discussed in this section and be extended to include other topics not included because of space limitations (e. g., use of unqualified coaches, legal liability issues, exclusion of youth with special needs). Only when these issues are resolved and middle level competitive sports programs are altered to become developmentally responsive will the many potential benefits of carefully planned sports programs be realized by large numbers of young adolescents. ®

References

Benedetto, W. (1990, December 10). Pro career just a dream for most kids. *USA Today,* 13A.

Berryman, J. (1988). The rise of highly organized sports for preadolescent boys. In F. Smoll, R. Magill, & M. Ash (Eds.), *Children in sport* (pp. 3-18). Champaign, IL: Human Kinetics Publishers.

Boal, J. (1996, August 12). To grow up right, we all must make time for playing: Even world's top athletes say they got into sports for fun. *Columbus Dispatch*, C3.

Carey, A. (1995, August 16). Doctor seeks to avert overuse injuries to children in sports. *Union Recorder,* pp. 1B-2B.

Children's Safety Network (1994). *Injuries in the environment: A resource packet.* Newton, MA: Author.

Coop, R. H., & Rotella, R. J. (1991). Sport and physical skill development in elementary schools: An overview. *The Elementary School Journal, 91* (5), 409-412.

Dorsey, V. L. (1989, August 3). If wood can't make bat grade, it might become "fishStunner." *USA Today,* 3C.

Ewing, M. E., & Seefeldt, V. (1989). *Participation and attrition patterns in American agency-sponsored and interscholastic sports: An executive summary.* North Palm Beach, FL: Sporting Goods Manufacturer's Association.

Findley, S. (1987, October 5). Breaks of the game. *U. S. News and World Report,* 75.

Fortanasce, V. M. (1995). *Life lessons from Little League: A guide for parents and coaches.* New York: Doubleday.

Fox, G. M., Jebson, J. L., & Orwin, J. F. (1995). Overuse injuries of the elbow. *The Physician and Sports Medicine, 23* (8), 58-66.

Garrick, J. G. (1988). Epidemiology of sports injuries in the pediatric athlete. In J. A. Sullivan, & W. A. Grana (Eds.), *The pediatric athlete* (pp. 123-132). Park Ridge, IL: American Academy of Orthopaedic surgeons.

Goldberg, B. (1989). Injury patterns in youth sports. *The Physician and Sportsmedicine, 89* (17), 175-184.

Goldman, J. (1990). Who's calling the plays? *The School Administrator, 90* (11), 8-16.

Gould, D. (1987). Understanding attrition in children's sport. In D. Gould & M. Weiss (Eds.), *Advances in pediatric sport sciences: Behavioral issues* (pp. 61-85). Champaign, IL: Human Kinetics.

Herndon, W. A. (1988). Injuries to the head, neck, and spine. *The pediatric athlete* (pp. 134-144). Park Ridge, IL: American Academy of Orthopaedic Surgeons.

Holm, H. L. (1996). Sport participation and withdrawal: A developmental motivational commentary. *Research in Middle Level Education Quarterly, 19* (3), 41-61.

Lincoln, C. E. (1982). The Nadia syndrome: Child athletes pushed into permanent injury. In T. G. George (Ed.), *American Health, 1* (2), 50-54.

McEwin, C. K., & Dickinson, T. S. (1996). Placing young adolescents at risk in interscholastic sports programs. *Clearing House, 69* (4), 217-221.

McEwin, C. K., Dickinson, T. S, & Jenkins, D. M. (1996). *America's middle schools: Practices and progress — A 25 year perspective.* Columbus, OH: National Middle School Association.

Micheli, L. (1990, October, 29). Children and sports. *Newsweek,* 12.

Micheli, L., & Jenkins, M. (1990). *Sportwise: An essential guide for young athletes, coaches, and parents.* Boston: Houghton Mifflin Company.

Ogilvie, B. C. (1988). The role of pediatric sports medicine specialist in youth sports. In J. A. Sullivan, & W. A. Grana (Eds.), *The pediatric athlete* (pp. 81-89). Park Ridge, IL: American Academy of Orthopaedic Surgeons.

Orlick, T., & Broterill, C. (1978). Why eliminate kids? In R. Martens (Ed.), *Joy and sadness in children's sports* (pp. 145-151). Champaign, IL: Human Kinetics.

Poinsett, A. (1996). *The role of sports in youth development.* New York: Carnegie Corporation.

Rosenthal, E. (1993, Summer). Sidelined. *Ladies' Home Journal Parents' Digest,* 51-53.

Rotella, J., Hanson, T., & Coop, R. H. (1991). Burnout in youth sports, *The Elementary School Journal, 91* (5), 421-428.

Seefeldt, V., Ewing, M., & Walk, S. (1993). *Overview of youth sports programs in the United States.* NY: Carnegie Council on Adolescent Development.

Smith, N. J. (1986). Is that child ready for competitive sports? *Contemporary Pediatrics, 86* (3), 30-54.

Smith, R., Zane, N., Smoll, F., & Coppol, D. (1983). Behavioral assessment in youth sports: Coaching behaviors and children's attitudes. *Medicine and Science in Sports and Exercise, 83* (15), 208-214.

Stacy, J. (1990, March 21). USA snapshots: Trying to beat the odds. *USA Today,* 3C.

Stark, E. (1983). Growing Pains. *Science, 83* (3), 88-89.

Stover, D. (1988). What to do when grown-ups want to spoil the fun of school sports, *The American School Board Journal, 175* (7), 10-22.

Taft, T. N. (1991). Sports injuries in children. *Elementary School Journal, 91* (5), 429-435.

United States Product Consumer Safety Commission (1991). *National electronic injury surveillance system product summary report: Injury estimates for the calendar year 1990.* Washington, DC: Author

United States Product Consumer Safety Commission (1995). *National electronic injury surveillance system product summary report: Injury estimates for the calendar year 1990.* Washington, DC: Author.

Vaughan, L. K. (1984). Psychological impact of organized sports on children. In L. J. Micheli (Ed.), *Pediatric and adolescent sports medicine* (pp.144-166) Boston: Little, Brown and Company.

Curriculum

Toepfer	Conrad F. Toepfer, Jr. State University of New York Buffalo, New York
Vars	Gordon F. Vars Kent State University Kent, Ohio
Brazee	Edward Brazee University of Maine Orono, Maine
Beane	James Beane National-Louis University Madison, Wisconsin
Powell	Richard R. Powell Texas Tech University Lubbock, Texas
Faircloth	C. Victoria Faircloth Western Carolina University Cullowhee, North Carolina

Conrad F. Toepfer, Jr.

Middle Level Curriculum's Serendipitous History

The establishment of junior high schools made the United States the first western nation with an intervening educational focus between elementary and high school. In this chapter, I review how curriculum specific to that level emerged. As with curriculum at all levels, middle level curriculum has had to cope with Alexander's (1973) concern.

> *So many educators know so little about curriculum planning but keep trying to reinvent the 'curriculum wheel.' These efforts by people poorly informed of the history and practice in the curriculum field really end up only rediscovering the same old ruts in the road.* — p. 3

Educators do, indeed, tend to be ambiguous about the definition of curriculum, often confusing curriculum content with approaches to its delivery. If the purpose of the school is learning, curriculum focuses the effort to carry out that purpose. Mamchur's (1990) definition is helpful in beginning that consideration.

> *Curriculum is the tool, the 'stuff' of education. Through the curriculum, students learn the skills, the attitudes, and the knowledge they need. Curriculum is a vehicle, a device.* — p. 634

❏ In the beginning

The events that led to the establishment of junior high schools did not focus on curricular needs. In the 1890s, Harvard University President Charles Eliot (1898) led the reorganization of the American elementary and secondary structure from an 8-4 to a 6-6 balance. Maintaining that seventh and eighth grade students were ready to study secondary school content, his goal was to shorten elementary school so that seventh and eighth grade students could study secondary school content in a high school environment. The Committee on College Entrance Requirements (National Education Association, 1899) endorsed this recommendation and concluded that:

> *In our opinion it is now important that the last two grades that now precede the high school course should be incorporated into it, and wherever practicable, the instruction in those two grades should be given under the supervision of the high school teacher.*
>
> — p. 659

By 1900, American school districts were shifting to six elementary and six secondary grades. However, at the beginning of the twentieth century, American education was delivered through a dual system of elementary and secondary schools. Educational purposes then were framed by the realities of the demands of life and opportunities for students when they left the school system. In 1900, approximately twenty percent of students completed high school.

Students lacking in intellectual ability and those with inadequate interest in study would leave school for the work force when they reached the appropriate age. Many others who possessed such intellectual ability and initiative but lacked financial resources also left school early. An early junior high school goal was to hold more students in school through grade nine.

The Committee on the Equal Division of the Twelve Years in the Public Schools Between the District and the High School (National Education Association, 1907) was concerned about the need to hold students in school longer. They recommended subdividing the six year high school into two equal school units, thus establishing the junior high school.

> *Change should be made in the present six-year high school. That is particularly important for students able to pursue their general education beyond the primary school. The high school ought to be subdivided into two administrative sections: (1) a junior high school of three years extending from the twelfth to the fifteenth year; and, (2) a senior high school also of three years, covering the period from the fifteenth year to the eighteenth year.*
>
> — p. 27

The administrative subdivision established the notion of junior high school as a "miniature high school." Thus, the initial junior high school lacked an educational identity separate from high school. This lack of identity hindered early efforts to identify and focus upon unique junior high student learning needs (Toepfer, 1962).

Douglass (1916) felt it important that junior high school curriculum make a shift in focus to the unique needs of young adolescents. Judd (1918) saw the evolution of the junior high school as a unique opportunity for the nation to develop more democratic schools. Van Denburg (1922) recommended that junior high schools "develop their own rationale and regimen rather than imitating or modifying high school practices" (p. 37). The need to define a clear middle level curriculum identity has persisted. Thirty-eight years later Tompkins (1960) again raised the central premise for the junior high school's existence.

> *Do early adolescents, 11 to 14, and later adolescents, 15-19, generally have systematic differences? If they do, then it is essential that schools serve the educational, social, and emotional needs of youth. If there is no difference (how anyone can credit that viewpoint psychologically is difficult to comprehend), then it really doesn't matter whether we have junior high schools or not.* — p. 44

Psychologist G. Stanley Hall (1905) initially noted the differences in educational needs of young adolescents from older students. In 1908, the Columbus, Ohio schools built a separate grade 7-9 school. Opening in September, 1909, the Indianola Junior High School became the nation's first junior high school (Shawan, 1910). In January, 1910, the Berkeley California schools introduced a similar program known as the Introductory High School.

The curriculum model in both programs was subject centered. The grades seven and eight curriculum offered English, history, geography, mathematics, drawing, music and chorus, beginning French or German foreign language, cooking and sewing (for girls), manual arts (for boys).

Berkeley also offered Spanish to students, and both schools allowed "advanced" students to take Latin instead of modern languages. Elementary science and principles of algebra were added in grade nine. Wide promulgation of the Columbus and Berkeley programs increased national efforts to develop junior high programs around those curriculum areas.

It is interesting that more than a decade before the subdivision of the six secondary grades into a junior and senior high school, that one community made the changes later heralded in Columbus and Berkeley. Bennett (1919) briefly noted that in 1896, Richmond, Indiana, had a three year school program separate from the local elementary and high school.

Toepfer (1962) searched Board of Education minutes and other primary sources in Richmond to find a program that had been instituted in 1896 (Study, 1897). More remarkably, in 1886 all of the city's grade seven and eight students were moved to Richmond's Garfield School. Garfield students had regular physical training classes (Study, 1891) in addition to a curriculum that included everything Columbus and Berkeley offered 12 and 13 years later.

The Garfield program also developed a unique curriculum function prior to the development of school guidance and counseling that today would be considered a teacher-advisory program. The principal coined the term "homeroom" to describe it (Heironimus, 1917).

> *The teacher of each room of the first period in the morning holds their pupils responsible for conduct, attendance, study, and general attitude throughout the day and out of class. The teacher is expected to be the guide, advisor, and friend to whom the pupil may come at any time on any pretext or need. While primarily a part of the disciplinary organization, the homeroom provides opportunity for the advisor to relate to those students in a non-instructional setting and it has become inspirational and directive.* — p. 91

Baker (1913) discussed the need for junior high schools "to bridge the gap between elementary and secondary education" (p. 27). To the contrary, Toepfer (1962) observed that the initial subdivision of the six secondary grades not only continued that separation but initiated a gap between junior and senior high school. This "bridging issue" continued to be a major curriculum articulation concern. Middle level curriculum must be much more than a conduit between elementary and high school. It is essential that curriculum codify and give life to middle level education's purposes and functions.

Glass (1923a) first recognized the critical role middle level schools must play in articulating programs across the district.

> *The primary role of the junior high school as a unit of transition is articulation. Until the junior high school ceases to be regarded exclusively as an isolated unit of organization and experimentation, there cannot be that unanimity of mutual understanding which alone can bring the united efforts of elementary and secondary education into focus as a concerted problem, not merely of junior high school problems, but of the greater problems of*

an articulated school system. — p. 519-520

The Roman God Janus with two faces looking in opposite directions, symbolizes middle level education's dilemma. In addition to accommodating the unique curriculum and learning instructional needs of young adolescents, its position between elementary and high schools makes middle level curriculum the critical link in district-wide curriculum articulation (Toepfer, 1986).

Unlike the focus of the college and university educators, most who studied and worked with junior high schools at that time were interested in curriculum/instruction rather than school administration/organization. A middle level curricular identity began to emerge and the junior high school gained acceptance by 1920 and spread rapidly (Briggs, 1920).

> *The junior school is accepted in theory, and its possibilities have proven so alluring that the movement for reorganization is well under way in both urban and rural districts. The physical redistribution of the grades seems assured; but if, having accomplished that, schoolmen rest content, they will have missed the one great educational opportunity of their generation for real educational reform. There is a demand for purposes so clear and cogent that they will result in new curricula, new courses of study, new methods of teaching, and new social relationships - in short, a new spirit which will make the intermediate years not only worth while in themselves, but also an intelligent inspiration for every child to continue, as long as profitable, the education for which he is by inheritance best fitted. In its essence the junior high school is a device of democracy whereby nurture may cooperate with nature to secure the best results possible for each individual adolescent as well as for society at large.*
>
> — p. 327

❏ Junior high curriculum functions emerge

The common curriculum areas anchored the junior high school's general education purpose. Calling English, mathematics, health, science, and social studies the "core of the curriculum" (p. 16), Glass (1924) reinforced the importance of maintaining the junior high school's general education role and resisted attempts to specialize education prior to the high school. Tryon, Smith, and Rood (1927) later noted:

> *The core curriculum is made up of those subjects which are important enough to be offered in every grade of the junior high*

school and which serve to give opportunity to the work done
throughout the system. — p.101

Briggs (1920) saw the purpose of exploratory experiences as allowing students to "try-out" specific areas and interests to see what their interests might be, particularly for students who might not move on to or complete high school. He viewed the curriculum purpose of exploratory experiences to:

> *...explore by means of material in itself worthwhile, the interests, aptitudes, and capacities of the pupils, and at the same time, to reveal by material otherwise justifiable, the possibilities of the major fields, both intellectual and academic.*
> — p. 41-42

Koos (1927) saw junior high learning experiences as helping students decide on areas of specialization they might select in high school.

> *There will be an opportunity for pupils to explore several fields to see where they fit; they will thus have a basis for making a selection when the time for specialization comes; in such a school it is possible in various ways to test each child and thereby find out what are his natural interests, his ambitions, and his capacities.* — p.51

Glass (1923b) had the most expansive junior high exploratory curriculum vision.

> *The junior high school has been variously entitled as the finding, the sorting, the trying out and testing period of the public school system. It is a probationary period before the vital question of educational or vocational choice is finally determined. Exploration of individual differences, the revelation of educational and vocational opportunities adaptable to individual differences, guidance of educational or vocational choice, equalization of opportunities, the adaptation of educational offerings to ascertained individual needs rather than conforming of all pupils to one educational pattern, and the stimulation of educational or vocational vision which conditions all progress in secondary education, all these and other purposes to adapt the educational program to the "individual" are objectives of the junior high school.* — p. 20-21

During the next two decades, other junior high school functions emerged. Gruhn & Douglas (1947) extensively discussed the curriculum implications of these six functions which they identified: articulation, differentiation, exploration, guidance, integration, and socialization.

❑ Moving away from subject-centered curriculum

Departmentalization is a vestige from the era when early secondary instructional procedures were modified later high school practices. It emphasizes in-depth study by organizing learning within separated subject areas. Departmentalization neither seeks to correlate or integrate learning among different content areas nor does it facilitate collaborative interaction teachers need to plan and integrate learning across content areas.

Feldlaufer, Midgley, and Eccles (1987) found departmentalization to be the least desirable pattern for organizing effective instruction in middle level grades. They identified that in grades 5 through 8, self-contained classrooms provide more correlation of learning and learning opportunities than departmentalization. In that regard, clear advantages of self-contained exist over departmentalized classrooms for young adolescents.

A number of junior high school curriculum options pioneered the emergence of broad-fields, social-problems, and emerging-needs curriculum approaches in American education. In the 1930s, junior high experience-centered learning options that combined aspects from broad-fields, social-problems, and emerging needs curriculum approaches led to the development of core curriculum approaches for delivering common learnings. Faunce and Bossing (1951) identified the following characteristics of core courses:

> *We have listed four characteristics of core courses that distinguish them from conventional subject-matter courses: (1) their freedom from subject-matter patterns and their emphasis upon vital problem situations; (2) their emphasis upon group problem-solving; (3) their use of a long block of time; and, (4) their emphasis on guidance by the classroom teacher.* — p. 86

In core curriculum options, Vars (1969) noted that block-time facilitated "a unification of structure in the disciplines without the discipline itself losing its identity" (p. 201). Block-time scheduling provided an ends-means continuum for effective implementation of core curriculum programs. Noar (1953) noted that:

> *The modern school is replacing the completely departmentalized program with one which permits a block of time within which units of work cut across subject matter lines.* — p. 5

As junior high instructional approaches other than departmentalization began to spread, Van Til, Vars, and Lounsbury (1967) observed the following:

> *Alternatives to departmentalized organization of instruction continued to grow in the 1950s. In the 1950s in the composite junior high school, the seventh grader found he had the same teacher longer than a single period and that he stayed with the same group of fellow students for the larger part of the day.* — p. 56

❏ The middle school concept emerges

By 1960, junior high developments suggested still further changes in schools serving young adolescents. Medical data that documented the increasingly earlier onset of puberty further supported that rubric. Eichhorn (1966) used those data to develop a curriculum model which became central in defining what became known as the middle school concept. The emergence of the middle school concept also initiated a nagging but meaningless "turf" confrontation between some junior high and middle school advocates. Lasting in varying degrees through the 1970s, these confrontations, unfortunately, distracted particular efforts to refine middle level educational initiatives. In 1981, Melton coined the term "middle level education" as a descriptor for all school programs between grades four and nine (Valentine, Clark, Nickerson, & Keefe, 1981).

Focused on young adolescent learning needs, the term succeeded in de-fusing the "junior high versus middle school" argument. Eichhorn's curriculum model (1966) was socio-analytically based in the physical, mental, social, and cultural characteristics of middle level school students. Language, mathematics, science, and social studies were organized under an analytical unifying center. A physical-cultural unifying center brought together cultural and fine arts with physical education. Eichhorn's model featured inter- and cross-disciplinary instructional approaches consistent with young adolescent developmental and learning characteristics. Several other middle school curriculum models followed the Eichhorn one. They were also based on the earlier onset of pubescence with more responsive curriculum options for young adolescent learners.

The Alexander model (Alexander, Williams, Compton, Hines, & Prescott, 1968) used three unifying centers. The first one, interrelated personal development, related curriculum issues to individual interests in values, health, and physical development. A skills for continued learning center dealt with curricular issues related to communication and problem-solving skills and an organized knowledge center dealt with the traditional range of middle level subject and content areas.

Moss (1969) developed a model based on a core curriculum approach. Traditional academic subject matter areas were centered on young adolescent problems of living. The arts center organized the areas of art, home economics, industrial arts, and music. The third center was organized around health, physical fitness, and recreational concerns.

Later, Lounsbury & Vars (1978) presented a middle level curriculum model featuring a core approach based on young adolescent personal-social problems relating student sequential skill needs to content areas. It had a variable component that included exploratory areas, elective opportunities, independent study options, enrichment opportunities, and student activity options.

Toepfer (1971) suggested three steps for differentiating middle level curriculum in such a manner.

1. *Identify and study the characteristics, needs, and developmental profiles of the emerging adolescent population in the local school-community setting.*

2. *Develop a curricular rationale which will implement and support those needs within the local setting.*

3. *Organize and implement an administrative vehicle to spell out an appropriate design for the community's total elementary, middle, and high school curriculum. — p. 3*

The middle school concept also extended concerns to refine earlier efforts to articulate curriculum horizontally among grade level subject areas. Team teaching developed from and extended earlier junior high school core curriculum approaches. As reported in the previous section, Faunce and Bossing (1951) noted that core curriculum "involves either a single teacher for two or more periods or teams of teachers who work together" (p. 9). Vars (1969) concurred that team teaching developed from core curriculum approaches as another means for delivering articulated teaching and learning among content areas.

In the 1970s and 1980s, attention moved beyond what should be taught to focus more on how that "what" might be taught. Unfortunately, some teaching teams focused on interdisciplinary units as the focus of instruction. All too often, the theme, rather than what it is the students want or need to learn in that unit, becomes the focus of the unit and teachers' planning. When that occurs the goals and objectives can become subordinate to the theme itself, especially if the theme and its content are selected and planned by teachers with little or no input from students. That kind of interdisciplinary planning achieves little real improvement over departmentalized, subject-centered approaches.

Properly defined and organized, teaming can reduce and overcome problems experienced in departmentalized subject isolation. It may facilitate the articulation and even integration of learning across subject areas (Toepfer, 1986). As in earlier successful core curriculum practice, the initial concern of teaming should be the collaborative planning and development of programs for those students whom team members commonly teach.

To get beyond simple correlation, teaming should be considered in content areas other than the so-called "academic" subjects. Middle level learning experiences in areas such as art, home economics, industrial arts/technology, and music can be powerful sources of personal and intellectual growth (Toepfer, 1992). All content areas are academic, and lesser importance or "second-class" citizenship for particular areas should be abandoned.

❏ Toward integration of learning

In itself, interdisciplinary teaming is not necessarily a first step to developing integrated curriculum options. Beane (1993) noted "interdisciplinary teaming does not necessarily lead to interdisciplinary curriculum organization" (p 33). Unfortunately, interdisciplinary planning has too frequently focused solely upon "how" to connect information in separated subject areas. Artificially forced connections make little sense to the learner. Meaningful curriculum articulation occurs when teachers use the interests and previous learning of students to define a context for further learning.

Jacobs (1989) developed a basic integrated curriculum format that further bridged earlier interdisciplinary efforts. Beane (1993) moved beyond that suggesting "the centerpiece of the curriculum would consist of thematic units whose organizing centers are drawn from the intersecting concerns of early adolescents and issues of the larger world" (p. 68). Pursuing the need to plan integrated learnings around learners' needs, interests, and concerns he stated:

Curriculum planning in an integrative context begins with collaborative discussion about young people's questions and concerns and identification of the themes they suggest. Once a theme and the related questions they suggest are clear, curriculum planning turns to identifying activities the group might use to answer the questions. It is after these "what" and "how" concerns are addressed that questions of knowledge, skill, and resources are appropriate. — p. 39

Integrated middle level curriculum should involve students in learning about aspects of real life issues. The increasing rapidity of change in the information society underscores the need for schools to update curriculum options and develop new ones. A regenerative, systemic capacity will be required for those efforts to succeed.

Beane (1995) suggested "coherent" curriculum as a broader frame for the development of integrated curriculum.

A 'coherent' curriculum is one that holds together, that makes sense as a whole; and its parts, whatever they are, are unified and connected by that sense of the whole. The idea of coherence begins with a view of the curriculum as a broadly conceived concept – as the curriculum - that is about 'something.' It is not simply a collection of disparate parts or pieces that accumulate in student experiences and on transcripts. A coherent curriculum has a sense of the forest as well as the trees, a sense of unity and connectedness, of relevance and pertinence. Parts or pieces are connected or integrated in ways that are visible and explicit. There is a sense of a larger, compelling purpose, and actions are tied to that purpose. — p. 3

From that perspective, integrated curriculum clearly seems prerequisite for achieving curriculum coherence. Beane (1995) offered two conditions such efforts need to address: "creating and maintaining visible connections between purposes and everyday learning experiences," and "creating contexts that organize and connect learning experiences" (p. 7).

❏ Conclusion

The middle level curriculum developments over the past hundred years sketched in this chapter have led educators to a watershed point. Broadening cultural heritage and rapidly occurring shifts in social, economic, and political life are shaping new challenges to our democratic way of living. As adults, current middle level students will have to deal with the intertwined dimensions of modern life from which those changing societal demands are emerging. To increase the learning success of all young adolescents, middle level curriculum must deal with a number of contextual issues including the conceptual separation and structural and sociocultural isolation of curriculum.

Cornbleth (1996), discussed the need to improve the conceptual integration of curriculum and its structural and sociocultural contextualization. In developing more coherent curriculum options, middle level schools need to deal with a range of critical questions Cornbleth raised.

- *What are the demographic, social, political, and economic conditions and trends that seem to shape the existing curriculum and seem likely to affect the desired changes?*

- *How is the desired curriculum change compatible with cultural traditions and prevailing ideologies? What influential groups are affected? (What are the potential sources of support and opposition?) What historical, recent, or continuing events are apt to influence the curriculum change effort?*

- *Which education system components or subsystems could mediate (supporting of oppositional) sociocultural influences. How are past experiences with curriculum change likely to influence the present effort?*

- *What system components are affected? (What roles, relationships, and patterns of activity? At what levels?) How is the desired curriculum change compatible or at odds with the prevailing culture of education systems? What are the bureaucratic operating procedures and challenges of formal and informal control of the affected system components? (Who controls what, to what extent, and how?) What and where are the tensions or contradictions within the system that might become loci for curriculum change?* — p. 160

To respond to the challenges young adolescents bring to school requires that middle level curriculum address and resolve these context concerns. In the position paper, *This We Believe: Developmentally Responsive Middle Level Schools* (NMSA, 1995) the authors noted:

> *The importance of achieving developmentally responsive middle level schools cannot be overemphasized. The nature of the educational programs young adolescents experience during this formative period of life will, in large measure, determine the future for all of us.* — p. 33

To do that, middle level curriculum must respond to the differences in both kind and degree of the learning needs young adolescents bring to school. Capelluti & Brazee (1992) identified our need to change existing middle level curricula.

Success at learning the old curriculum is no longer a guarantee of achievement in the adult world. Changing the curriculum is no longer a question of should we - it is a complex matter of when and how. — p. 1

Whether or not middle level curriculum prepares students to meet the demands of life in the next millennium depends on our willingness to accept that challenge. ®

References

Alexander, W. (1973). An imperative for the curriculum worker: An historical perspective. *Impact on instructional improvement, 8* (20), 3-8.

Alexander, W. M., Williams, E. L., Compton, M., Hines, V., & Prescott, D. (1968). *The middle school years.* New York: Holt, Rinehart, & Winston.

Baker, J. (Chairman) (1913). *Report of the committee of the national council of education on economy of time in education.* Bulletin 1913, No. 38. Washington, DC: Government Printing Office.

Beane, J. (1995). Introduction: What is a coherent curriculum? In J. Beane, (Ed.), *Toward a coherent curriculum* (pp. 1-14). Alexandria, VA: Association for Supervision and Curriculum Development

Beane, J. (1993). *A middle school curriculum: From rhetoric to reality* (2nd edition). Columbus, OH: National Middle School Association.

Bennett, G. (1919). *The junior high school.* Baltimore: Warwick & York.

Briggs, T. (1920). *The junior high school.* Boston: Houghton Mifflin.

Bunker, F. (1909). *Minutes of the November 30, 1909 meeting, Board of education minutes.*Berkeley, CA: Board of Education.

Capelluti, J., & Brazee, E. (1992). Middle level curriculum: Making sense. *Middle School Journal, 12* (5), 1-5.

Cornbleth, C. (1996). Curriculum in and out of context. In E. Hollins (Ed.), *Transforming curriculum for a culturally diverse society* (pp. 149-161). Mahwah, NJ: Lawrence Erlbaum Associates.

Douglass, A. (1916) *The junior high school plan.* Part III., The fifteenth yearbook of the National Society for the Study of Education. Bloomington, IN: Public School Publishing Company.

Eichhorn, D. (1966). *The middle school.* NY: Center for Applied Research in Education. (Jointly reissued in 1986 by the National Association of Secondary School Principals, Reston, VA, and the National Middle School Association, Columbus, OH.)

Eliot, C. (1898). *Educational reform: Essays and addresses.* New York: Century Company.

Faunce. R., & Bossing, N. (1951). *Developing the core curriculum.* Englewood Cliffs, NJ: Prentice-Hall.

Feldlaufer, H., Midgley, C., & Eccles, J. (1987). *Student, teacher, and observer perceptions of the classroom environment before and after the transition to junior high school.* Ann Arbor, MI: University of Michigan.

Glass, J. (1924). *Curriculum practices in the junior high school and grades five and six.* Supplementary Monographs, No, 25. Chicago: University of Chicago Press.

Glass. J. (1923a). The reorganization of the seventh, eighth, and ninth grades program of studies. *School Review, 30* (3), 518-532.

Glass. J. (1923b). The junior high school. *The New Republic, 30* (466), 20-24.

Gruhn, W. &. Douglas, H. (1947). *The modern junior high school.* NY: The Ronald Press.

Hall. G. S. (1905). *Adolescence, its psychology and its relations to physiology, anthropology, sociology, sex, crime, relition, and education.* Vol. II. NY: D. Appleton.

Heironimus, N. (1917) The teacher-advisor in the junior high school, *Educational Administration and Supervision, 3* (2), 91-94.

Jacobs, H. (1989). *Interdisciplinary curriculum: Design and implementation.* Alexandria, VA: Association for Supervision and Curriculum Development.

Judd, C. (1918). *The evolution of the democratic school system.* New York: Harcourt, Brace.

Koos, L. (1927). *The junior high school.* Boston: Ginn.

Lounsbury, J. H., & Vars, G. F. (1978). *A curriculum for the middle school years.* New York: Harper & Row.

Mamchur, C. (1990). But ... the curriculum. *Kappan, 71* (8), 634-638.

Melton G. (November 6, 1995). Personal conversation.

Moss, T. (1969). *The middle school.* Boston: Houghton-Mifflin.

National Education Association (1899). Report of the committee on college entrance requirements. *Journal of proceedings and addresses of the thirty-eighth meeting.* Chicago: University of Chicago Press.

National Education Association (1907). Report of the committee on the equal division of the twelve years in the public schools between the district and the high school. *Journal of proceedings and addresses of the forty-sixth annual meeting.* Chicago: University of Chicago Press.

National Middle School Association. (1995). *This we believe: Developmentally responsive middle level schools.* Columbus, OH: Author.

Noar, G. (1953). *The junior high school: Today and tomorrow.* New York: Prentice-Hall.

Shawan, J. (1910). *Annual report of the Board of Education of the city of Columbus for the year ending August 31, 1909.* Columbus, OH: Board of Education.

Study, J. (1891). *Biennial report of the public schools in Richmond, Indiana, for the years ending July 31, 1890 and July 31, 1891.* Richmond IN: M. Culliton.

Study, J. (1897). *Biennial report of the public schools in Richmond, Indiana, for the years the years ending July 31, 1896 and July 31, 1897.* Richmond, IN: Nicholson Publishing Company.

Toepfer, C., Jr. (1962). *Evolving curricular patterns in junior high schools: An historical study.* Unpublished Doctoral Dissertation, Buffalo, NY: The University of Buffalo.

Toepfer, C., Jr. (1971). Stone walls do not make nor iron bars a cage: Schools for emerging adolescents. *Association for Supervision and Curriculum Development News Exchange, 8* (5), 3-5.

Toepfer, C., Jr. (1986). Middle level transition and articulation issues. *Middle School Journal, 18* (1), 9-11.

Toepfer, C., Jr. (1992). Middle school curriculum: Defining the elusive. In J. Irvin (Ed.), *Transforming middle level education: Perspectives and possibilities* (pp. 205-243). Boston: Allyn & Bacon.

Tompkins, T. (1960). What's new at the National Association of Secondary School Principals? *National Association of Secondary School Principals Bulletin, 44* (2), 44-45.

Tryon, R., Smith, H., & Rood, A. (1927). The program of studies in the seventy-eight junior high school centers. *School Review, 35* (1) 96-107.

Valentine, J. W., Clark, D. C., Nickerson, N. C., & Keefe, J. W. (1981). *The middle level principalship, Volume 1: A survey of middle level principals and programs.* Reston, VA: National Association of Secondary School Principals.

Van Denburg, J. (1922). *The junior high school idea.* New York: Henry.

Van Til, W., Vars, G., & Lounsbury, J. (1967) *Modern education for the junior high school years.* Indianapolis: Bobbs-Merrill.

Vars, G. (1969). *Common learnings: Core and interdisciplinary team approaches.* Scranton, PA: International Textbook Company.

Gordon F. Vars

Effects of Integrative Curriculum and Instruction

The 1990s witnessed a virtual explosion of interest in integrative curriculum and instruction, especially among middle level educators. More than 30 books and monographs on that topic were published between 1990 and 1995. In countless articles, conferences, workshops, seminars, and inservice presentations, educators today are promoting a variety of integrative approaches. The integration movement is difficult to trace, because advocates often create their own terminology. As a result, more than a dozen terms may be found in the literature. Some of these reflect purpose, such as "holistic," whereas terms like "multidisciplinary" and "interdisciplinary" usually refer to a specific curriculum design (Vars, 1993, pp. 9-27).

The National Middle School Association (1995) used the term "integrative" in its position paper *This We Believe: Developmentally Responsive Middle Level Schools*. The association calls for "curriculum that is challenging, integrative, and exploratory" (p. 30). The meaning of "integrative" is explained as follows:

> *Curriculum is integrative when it helps students make sense out of their life experiences. This requires curriculum that is itself coherent, that helps students connect school experiences to their daily lives outside the school, and that encourages them to reflect on the totality of their experiences. — p. 30*

Despite assertions that integrative curriculum is a new phenomenon in education, efforts to bring about this kind of education span many decades and involve long-standing issues in educational decision making (Schubert, 1995; Vars, 1992; Wraga, 1996; and Chapter 14 in this volume).

This chapter deals with attempts to achieve coherence by combining or replacing courses or subject areas that ordinarily are taught separately. Such programs may be taught either by one teacher or by a team. More than 100 studies of such programs' effects on students were examined in preparing a research summary for the National Association of Secondary School Principals (Vars, 1996). This chapter draws heavily on a further synthesis of that research prepared for the Wisconsin Connecting the Curriculum Project (Vars, 1995).

❑ Cautions and complications

Analyzing research on combined programs is complicated, not only by the lack of common terminology, but also by the variety of curriculum designs employed and the differences attributable to whether the program is taught by one teacher or by a team. Moreover, no two teachers implement any curriculum design in exactly the same way. The research spans more than 60 years and employs many different research designs, making it even more difficult to summarize findings. Bias inevitably creeps into any research carried out in schools, too, because districts are understandably reluctant to publicize less-than-satisfactory results of any innovative program. All these limitations should be kept in mind when reading this or any other attempt to summarize research in such a complex field as education.

When combined courses are taught by one teacher, they usually occupy several periods in the daily schedule. Wright called these "block-time courses," since they show up as multiple-period blocks in the schedule (Wright, 1950, 1952, 1958; Wright & Greer, 1963). The different names given to block-time courses range from a simple hyphenated designation like "English-Social Studies" to more ambiguous terms like "Basic Education," "Unified Studies," "Common Learnings," or "Core."

The degree of curriculum integration within block-time classes also varies considerably, whatever the course is called. Even when each subject retains its separate identity, course sequences in several subjects may be rearranged so that content related to a particular theme or topic is taught at the same time; that is, courses are "correlated." Or the content of several courses may be combined or "fused" to make up a new course, such as "American Studies," which usually incorporates subject matter from English, social studies, art, and music.

Conventional subjects may even be replaced by courses or units jointly planned by students and teachers without regard to subject boundaries. Block-time courses that focus directly on student needs, problems, or concerns acquired the label "core" during the Eight-Year Study of the Progressive Education Association (Aikin, 1942), but the term often was applied to any block-time class. This student-centered "core curriculum" concept should not be confused with the term "core of the curriculum," referring to the courses required of all students.

A different way to promote curriculum coherence is to assign a group of students to an interdisciplinary team of teachers, typically made up of specialists in language arts, social studies, science, and mathematics. Interdisciplinary teams may operate within a block of time equivalent to the number of periods required for each of the subjects included. Here, too, the degree of curriculum integration achieved by interdisciplinary teams varies widely. Teams may plan and carry out interdisciplinary units from time to time, but few do much more than correlate subjects, since each team member continues to function as a specialist in one particular subject.

❏ Academic achievement

When any kind of integrative approach is considered, the first question raised is likely to be: "How will the new program affect student academic achievement?" Early research on block-time programs was summarized by Mickelson (1957), Alberty (1960), and Wright (1956, 1963). Recent studies, such as Lee and Smith (1992) confirm the earlier results. Research on the effects of interdisciplinary team teaching have been summarized by Armstrong (1977), Cotton (1982), Arhar, Johnston, and Markle (1992), and in Chapter 5 in the present volume.

Studies conducted over more than 60 years point to the same general conclusion: *Almost without exception, students in any type of combined curriculum do as well as, and often better than, students in a conventional departmentalized program.* These results hold regardless of whether the combined curriculum is taught by one teacher in a self-contained or block-time class or by an interdisciplinary team of teachers representing different subject areas (Vars, 1996; National Association for Core Curriculum, 1997). It should be noted that, for the most part, these results were obtained using standardized achievement tests designed for a conventional separate-subjects program.

❏ Other benefits

Advocates assert that integrative curriculum makes learning more meaningful for students, especially if, like a core class, it is student-centered and organized around issues or problems. This is expected to increase student motivation, foster higher order thinking, enhance interpersonal skills, and improve attitudes toward peers, teachers, and school (Vars, 1969).

Concrete evidence such as attendance rates and disciplinary referrals confirm that students usually do enjoy integrated classes. Measuring other less tangible results is exceedingly difficult, and the evidence tends to be anecdotal or based on personal opinions of students, teachers, and parents. Some studies have shown that students in integrated programs are better at critical thinking, get along better with their peers and teachers, and have more positive attitudes toward learning. However, most comparison studies have found few significant differences, mainly because teachers continue to use conventional, didactic methods, even when the curriculum is supposed to be integrated and student-centered.

❑ Effects due to type of curriculum

To date, few studies have attempted to distinguish among the effects of correlated, fused, and student-centered core approaches, whether taught by one teacher or by a team. Most of these found few significant differences. Programs proved to be very similar and were usually limited to the correlation of subjects, regardless of label. A few in-depth case studies of student-centered programs reveal many positive outcomes of curriculum integration when it is carefully-planned and executed (Alexander, Carr, & McAvoy, 1995; Pate, Homestead, & McGinnis, 1997; Springer, 1994; Stevenson & Carr, 1993).

❑ One teacher *versus* interdisciplinary team

Some evidence exists that student achievement is greater and interpersonal relationships are more positive in self-contained classes than in teamed programs, and that both are better than conventional separate-subjects arrangements (Lee & Smith, 1992). The differences between the effects of one-teacher and team approaches appear to vary according to subject matter and also student background factors such as socioeconomic status. Students predicted to make below-average success seem to do better under the closer teacher-student relations possible in a self-contained class, especially in verbal subjects like English, reading, and social studies. On the other hand, the teacher specialization in one or two subject areas that is possible in interdisciplinary teaming may bring about higher achievement with students at the upper end of the distribution (Becker, 1987; McPartland, 1992).

Some educators argue for a combination of both approaches, using teams of two teachers (Alexander, Carr, & McAvoy, 1995). Each would teach two or three subjects in an extended block of time. The time blocks would enable students and teachers to develop good rapport, and academic instruction would be sufficiently focused so that teachers could develop some expertise in their teaching fields. Additional research is needed to support this recommendation.

❏ Student success in later schooling

Studies carried out in the 1950s and 1960s indicated that students who complete combined courses in middle or junior high school nearly always make normal or better marks in high school. The Eight-Year Study, confirmed by some later research, concluded that graduates of integrative high school programs usually do better in college than those from conventional departmentalized programs, both in terms of academic performance and in participation in extracurricular activities. Moreover, graduates of the most experimental, student-centered programs made better progress in college than those from high schools that departed only slightly from the separate-subjects approach. More recent studies of this type are urgently needed.

❏ Maximizing the benefits of integrative curriculum

While the research is quite conclusive that there will be no loss of student academic achievement as a result of combining subjects, each school district should continuously monitor all student outcomes in any innovative program. Test scores, proficiency examination results, attendance, attitude surveys, and other kinds of data should be gathered before the new program is instituted, and at regular intervals thereafter. Data should be carefully interpreted, making due allowances for initial differences in student aptitude and other factors. Educators also may anticipate a temporary "implementation dip" that sometimes occurs whenever anything new is tried. The other less tangible benefits mentioned earlier will be realized only if the new program is carefully planned and executed, drawing on the decades of research and experience available on how it should be carried out (Van Zandt & Albright, 1996; Wraga, 1996). Above all, the new curriculum should not be sold as a panacea that will solve all problems, but rather as an approach that has proved its worth when properly implemented.

❏ Needed research

Although the research evidence on student achievement in integrative programs is substantial, many other aspects need further study. Consider, for example, the differential effects of correlated, fused, or student-centered core approaches on students' critical thinking, interpersonal skills, and commitment to further learning. All educators who are involved in integrating the curriculum can help by keeping careful records and using them in action-research on their own curriculum and instruction (Wisconsin Department of Public Instruction, 1997). Schools and school systems should budget for ongoing research on a wide variety of student outcomes. Districts might involve nearby colleges and universities in helping to assess the results of the new approach. Results should be shared carefully and honestly with students, teachers, parents, and the community, and disseminated to the education profession.

School patrons rightfully demand accountability, and schools have a professional obligation to report the full range of student outcomes, not just test scores. This is especially critical in as complex an undertaking as integrating curriculum and instruction, where many of the benefits are not easily measured but are, nevertheless, real and important. ℝ

References

Aikin, W. M. (1942). *The story of the eight-year study*. New York: Harper.

Alberty, H. B. (1960). Core programs. In C. W. Harris (Ed.), *Encyclopedia of educational research* (3rd ed.) (pp. 337-341). New York: Macmillan.

Alexander, W. M., Carr, D., & McAvoy, K. (1995). *Student-oriented curriculum: Asking the right questions*. Columbus, OH: National Middle School Association.

Arhar, J. M., Johnston, J. H., & Markle, G. E. (1992). The effects of teaming on students. In J. H. Lounsbury (Ed.), *Connecting the curriculum through interdisciplinary instruction* (pp. 23-35). Columbus, OH: National Middle School Association.

Armstrong, D. G. (1977). Team teaching and academic achievement. *Review of Educational Research, 47* (1), 65-86.

Becker, H. J. (1987). *Addressing the needs of different groups of early adolescents: Effects of varying school and classroom organizational practices on students from different social backgrounds and abilities*. Report # 16. Baltimore, MD: Center for Research on Elementary and Middle Schools, Johns Hopkins University.

Cotton, K. (1982). *Effects of interdisciplinary team teaching: Research synthesis*. Portland, OR: Northwest Regional Lab. ED 230 533.

Lee, V. E., & Smith, J. B. (1992). *Effects of school restructuring on achievement and engagement of middle grade students*. Madison, WI: Center on Organization and Restructuring of Schools. ED 346 617.

McPartland, J. M. (1992). *Staffing patterns and the social organization of schools*. Paper delivered at the 44th biennial meeting of the Society for Research on Adolescence.

Mickelson, J. M. (1957). What does research say about the effectiveness of the core curriculum? *School Review, 65* (2), 144-160.

National Association for Core Curriculum. (1997). *A bibliography of research on the effectiveness of block-time, core, & interdisciplinary team teaching programs*. Kent, OH: Author.

National Middle School Association. (1995). *This we believe: Developmentally responsive middle level schools*. Columbus, OH: Author.

Patc, P. E., Homestead, E. R., & McGinnis, K. L. (1997). *Making integrated curriculum work*. New York: Teachers College Press.

Schubert, W. H. (1995). Toward lives worth living and sharing: Historical perspectives on curriculum coherence. In J. A. Beane (Ed.), *Toward a coherent curriculum* (pp. 146-157). 1995 Yearbook of the Association for Supervision and Curriculum Development. Alexandria, VA: The Association.

Springer, M. (1994). *Watershed: A successful voyage into integrative learning*. Columbus, OH: National Middle School Association.

Stevenson, C., & Carr, J. F. (Eds.) (1993). *Integrated studies in the middle grades: Dancing through walls*. New York: Teachers College Press.

Van Zandt, L.M., & Albright, S.B. (1996).The implementation of interdisciplinary curriculum and instruction. In P.S. Hlebowitsh & W. G. Wraga (Eds.), *Annual review of research for school leaders* (pp. 165-201). Reston, VA: National Association of Secondary School Principals & Scholastic Publishing Company.

Vars, G. F. (1969), *Common learnings: Core and interdisciplinary team approaches*. Scranton, PA: Intext.

Vars, G. F. (1992). Integrative curriculum: A déja vu. *Current issues in middle level education, 1* (1), 66-78.

Vars, G. F. (1993). *Interdisciplinary teaching: Why and how.* (2d. ed.). Columbus, OH: National Middle School Association.

Vars, G. F. (1995). Synthesis of research. *CTC Briefing Papers.* Madison, WI: Connecting the Curriculum Project, WI Department of Public Instruction.

Vars, G. F. (1996). Effects of interdisciplinary curriculum and instruction. In P. S. Hlebowitsh & W. G. Wraga (Eds.), *Annual review of research for school leaders* (pp. 147-164). Reston, VA: National Association of Secondary School Principals & Scholastic Publishing Company.

Wisconsin Department of Public Instruction. (1997). *A guide to curriculum and action research*. Milwaukee, WI: Author

Wraga, W. G. (1996). A century of interdisciplinary curricula in American schools. In P. S. Hlebowitsh & W. G. Wraga (Eds.), *Annual review of research for school leaders* (pp. 117-145). Reston, VA: National Association of Secondary School Principals & Scholastic Publishing Company.

Wright, G. S. (1950). *Core curriculum in public high schools: An inquiry into practices, 1949*. Washington, DC: Government Printing Office.

Wright, G. S. (1952). *Core curriculum development: Problems and practices*. Washington, DC: Government Printing Office.

Wright, G. S. (1956). *The core program: Abstracts of unpublished research, 1946-1955*. Washington, DC: Government Printing Office.

Wright, G. S. (1958). *Block-time classes and the core program in the junior high school*. Washington, DC: Government Printing Office.

Wright, G. S. (1963). *The core program: Unpublished research, 1956-1962*. Washington, DC: Government Printing Office.

Wright, G. S. & Greer, E. S. (1963). *The junior high school: A survey of grades 7-8-9 in junior and junior-senior high schools, 1959-60*. Washington, DC: Government Printing Office.

Edward Brazee

Curriculum for Whom?

Who decides what is worthwhile to know and experience, in order that human beings might reach greater potential and develop a more just social order? — Schubert, 1993

The overarching purpose of all schooling in our society is to help students become good citizens, lifelong learners, and healthy, caring, ethical, and intellectually reflective individuals.— National Middle School Asssociation, 1995.

For whom is the curriculum? Is it for young adolescents or is it for adults, teachers, administrators, and parents? While it is logical that the curriculum should be designed with students as the primary benefactors, in actuality middle school curriculum rarely considers the questions and concerns of young adolescents. The problem with middle school curriculum is that we ask students to give answers to questions they do not ask (Arnold, 1993).

When adults make decisions about what young adolescents need to know and be able to do, the traditional curriculum has not been *for* young adolescents nor has it been designed *by* them either. Historically, curriculum has been developed by adults working with one agenda or another for such purposes as inculcating American culture, raising test scores, and teaching basic skills. Texts are written by adults, curriculum guides are written by adults, and adults serve on curriculum committees. Underlying the reality of this adult influence on the curriculum is the widespread belief that young adolescents do not know what is important to learn.

Beane (1993) reminded educators that, "a curriculum developed apart from the teachers and young people who must live it is grossly undemocratic in the ways it deprives them of their right to have a say in their own lives and to learn and apply the skills and understandings associated with making important decisions. In the area of curriculum planning and development, we ought to have learned this lesson by now: distance breeds contempt" (p.16). Perhaps this neglect has come from an older and more pessimistic view of young adolescents that does not capitalize on their positive possibilities. Scales (1991) noted that it is essential to base our actions on a more thorough understanding of what young adolescents developmentally need and who they are. What research says regarding the role of young adolescents in developmentally responsive curriculum planning is reviewed below.

❏ A misleading view of young adolescents

Misunderstanding, stereotypes, and misinformation about young adolescents pervade schools and the general public. All of these inhibit a curriculum that is both responsive and rigorous. Arnold (1993) reported the emphasis on younger children and older adolescents in the literature. For example, the chief stage theorists, Piaget, Kohlberg, and Erikson, have devoted relatively little research and description to 10-15 year olds, even when they included young adolescence in their frameworks; there is little coordination among various social service agencies serving this age group (Lipsitz, 1980). Historically, young adolescents have been neglected in the K-12 spectrum with little interest shown toward this age group, although this situation has improved dramatically in the past 15 years.

Myths of early adolescence do not reflect their true nature. In the past, adolescence has been characterized as a time of storm and stress, yet this concept which grew out of psychiatric literature (Hall, 1904) and has been popularized in the media is not accurate. More recent information (Hillman, 1991; Horowitz, 1989; Russell, 1990) has given us a broader view of development. Peterson (1987) found that a large majority of young adolescents are not strife ridden.

While the biological, social, emotional, and intellectual changes of early adolescence may certainly be upsetting to both children and their parents, approximately 80% of young adolescents make it through this period with only minor adjustments (Scales, 1991). Feldman and Elliott (1990) suggested that although the dominant characteristic of adolescence is change – change in physical, social, emotional, and intellectual functioning – there is scant evidence of unrelenting family conflict and dramatic, debilitating crises. Rather, most parents and adolescents enjoy considerable agreement on fundamental values concerning morality, marriage and sex, race, and religious and political orientations (Roberts, 1993). A realistic view of 10-15 year olds that recognizes who they are, their unique needs, and their aspirations for the future is a key element in providing the curriculum needed for all young adolescents (Lesko, 1994).

❏ A way of viewing young adolescents

What then are the normal needs, characteristics, and issues that distinguish this age group? Equally important, though addressed less frequently, what are the unique needs and conditions of young women and minority youth, especially those that may not be self-evident in larger discussions of early adolescence?

Understanding the period of early adolescence, the ages from 10-15 years, has been problematic for the lay-public, researchers, and practitioners. Because of the conjunction of biological, social, emotional, and intellectual needs and characteristics, and their attendant contexts – school, home, community – this period has often been overlooked (Hill, 1980). Yet, there is a growing consensus about the universal and essential requirements for healthy development for young adolescents.

> *This consensus can be simply stated. All adolescents, regardless of economic background, race and ethnicity, gender, and geographical region or country, have basic needs that must be satisfied: to experience secure relationships with a few human beings, to be a valued member of groups that provide mutual aid and caring relationships, to become a competent individual who can cope with the exigencies of everyday life, and to believe in a promising future in work, family, and citizenship.*
> — Takanishi, 1993

Based on this and other conceptions (Carnegie Council of Adolescent Development, 1989; NMSA, 1995; Steinberg, 1993) of early adolescence, the picture of not only what the curriculum should be, but for whom the curriculum should be becomes clearer. Breaking away from long-term stereotypes of the age group and building on positive and complex views of young adolescents is essential for understanding the curriculum needed for them (Arnold, 1993).

The central, underlying feature of middle level education, developmental responsiveness, is mentioned prominently in the literature, but has rarely been used as a base for curriculum development in schools (Brazee,

1995). Yet, the mismatch between developmental issues and middle level curriculum is seen as a major issue in advancing middle level education (Eccles & Midgley, 1989; Hillman, Wood, Becker, & Altier, 1990; Jackson & Hornbeck, 1989).

Perhaps the fact that applying information about young adolescent development has been more for show than for know, should not be surprising since middle level education has focused on climate and organizational change before curricular change (George, Stevenson, Thomason, & Beane, 1992; Lounsbury & Clark, 1990). While this is not a criticism of the excellent work done by middle level schools in the past, it acknowledges the need to apply knowledge about growth and development equally to all aspects of the middle level school – curriculum as well as schedule; assessment as well as advisor/advisee programs.

One promising framework for understanding the developmental needs of young adolescents is that developed by the former Center for Early Adolescence. Growing out of the issues recognized in most theories of adolescent development, and based on extensive research of successful schools and community-based programs, these seven needs focus on the positive goals for the healthy development of young people (Scales, 1991). Much of this work is based on Hill's (1980) model for understanding adolescence organized around three basic components: the fundamental changes of adolescence (biological, cognitive and social transitions), the contexts of adolescence (families, peer groups, schools, work, and leisure), and the psychosocial issues of adolescence (identity, autonomy, intimacy, sexuality, achievement). Scales (1991) acknowledged that the developmental needs framework does not show how those needs might vary in emphasis depending on a particular young adolescent's gender, race, or other important characteristics, so those areas will be examined in the section following.

This "working" framework will be used to illustrate several broad needs of young adolescents and subsequent implications for curriculum development in middle schools. Curriculum that meets these broad needs should be both developmentally responsive and answer the question "curriculum for whom?"

❏ Competence, achievement, and creative expression

Young adolescents need varied, legitimate opportunities to be successful and to have their accomplishments recognized by others. They want to be competent at something – doing mathematics, playing the tuba, building model planes, baking pies, or playing basketball. They also want to be competent in those subjects and skills taught at school. Yet, this need to be competent and achieve is often in conflict with a curriculum that is not developed with young adolescents in mind.

Opportunities for students to develop competence and to achieve at a high level are often limited in traditional subject areas. How often in language arts, science, mathematics, and social studies can students demonstrate competence beyond high scores on tests and essays or correctly answering questions at the end of the chapter?

Anecdotal accounts of integrated curriculum (Arnold, 1990; Brazee & Capelluti, 1995; Springer, 1995; Stevenson & Carr, 1993) demonstrated that young adolescents have a strong interest in intellectual pursuits, want to work at a high level, and want to be recognized as competent for their efforts. But, students must be allowed to pursue projects and answer questions of importance to them. While they may be totally indifferent to photosynthesis when it appears in a science textbook, they may be fascinated and ready to study it when it appears in a unit of ecology suggested by their own questions.

Several key elements have been identified which allow young adolescents to be competent and to achieve (Newmann, 1990; Resnick, 1986). Students need to be engaged with meaningful material where skills are needed to learn content or communicate understandings; acquiring isolated and fragmented content knowledge is nonproductive. Serious engagement with real problems has to occur in depth and over time. Students need experiences that lead to placing high value on critical thinking as a disposition, not isolated skill. Many of these elements occur most readily, and perhaps exclusively when students have the opportunity for real, ongoing discourse with teachers (Alexander, 1995; Feldman & Elliott, 1990).

Opportunities for students to be competent and to achieve in areas outside the conventional curriculum, through activity periods, exploratories, intramurals, and advisories, are prevalent in middle level schools (McEwin, Dickinson, & Jenkins, 1996). Young adolescents should not be limited and exposed only to typical ways of thinking and standard ways of responding to ideas. Gardner's (1983) theory of multiple intelligences and brain compatible theories (Caine & Caine, 1991) reminds us that the reading-writing-testing model is only one way to respond and is limiting if it is the only way. While it is certainly appropriate in some areas, young adolescents need multiple opportunities to learn a skill or concept and to express that learning to someone else. We seriously limit students' abilities if we expect them to learn only through reading and writing. Oral presentations, debates, position papers, technical writing, poetry, dance, drama, computer presentations are just a few of the many ways for students to respond creatively to the external world.

❏ Meaningful participation in families, schools, and communities

The middle school curriculum usually happens to, not with, young adolescents at a time when they are eager to contribute to life in meaningful ways. Middle schools continue to give young adolescents answers to questions they never asked or even care about. This at a time when we know they have compelling questions of their own.

McDonough (1991) reported the types of questions a sample of 500 young adolescents in rural, urban, and suburban school districts posed. When given opportunities to ask questions and pursue serious study of topics important to them students noted a concern for environmental problems; worries about their own reputation and the earth; and concerns for the inability of different countries to get along with each other.

Curriculum theorists (Beane, 1993; Brazee & Capelluti, 1995) suggest that young adolescents' questions should be the basis for middle school curriculum, one that allows meaningful participation in families, schools, and communities. A number of schools (Alexander, 1995; Powell & Skoog, 1995: Springer, 1994) are working toward an integrated curriculum where such activities are typical. Alexander described such a school where student questions form the base for the curriculum; many of their questions involve students in serious work with their schools, communities, and families. Arnold (1991) described middle schools where service learning is a major effort involving students in their communities.

Opportunities for service learning projects as part of the curriculum exist in other middle schools (Fertman, White, & White, 1996; Halsted, 1997). Boyer (1995) suggested that all students complete a community service project, working in day-care centers and retirement villages or tutoring other students at school as a way to create meaning in their lives.

❏ Opportunities for self-definition

Developing a sense of identity is a major developmental task of early adolescence. Researchers (Hillman, 1991; Steinberg, 1993) suggested different aspects of identity development including concern for physical appearance, developing an ethical system, and developing socially responsible behaviors. Young adolescents are concerned about how they appear to peers, parents, and other adults as they move from child to adolescent.

The curriculum must provide opportunities for young adolescents to explore such themes, both in themselves and for other young adolescents. Integrated curriculum projects that afford young adolescents opportunities to study other young adolescents in different times and different contexts are especially valuable. Risk-taking through opportunities to try out different ways of thinking and communicating is also critical in the changing young adolescent's sense of self-definition. Having time to work with adults who model and encourage a personal point of view yet retain an openness to other views is also critical (Harter, 1990).

Programs that involve students actively and allow them to explore their identity realistically through educational and occupational choices should also be used. On-the-job experience or job shadows from the school curriculum allow young adolescents to develop their identities by trying out new roles and developing new competencies. Finally, identifying the sources of self-esteem, those areas of competence important to young adolescents, is the key in changing attitudes about self (Harter, 1986).

❑ Positive social interaction with adults and peers

A common myth about young adolescents is that they neither want nor desire adult companionship or help. Young adolescents, however, still count on their parents and other significant adults for assistance with crucial decisions and issues. They want to know that their parents and teachers are nearby, close enough to offer assistance when needed, but not too close. Ongoing, consistent, and caring relationships between students and adults in the school setting are critical components of middle level classrooms.

Perhaps the best way to visualize the positive possibilities of such close relationships with adults is to consider something different. Some middle schools recognizing the developmental needs of young adolescents have replaced the current system of short duration, random, formal teacher-student contacts, those that usually result in only a superficial and formal working relationship, with a different organization (McEwin, et al., 1996).

Looping, the practice of keeping a team of teachers and students together for at least two grade levels (for example, grades 5 and 6 or grades 6 and 7) is an increasingly popular practice because it achieves longer-term relationships. A block schedule which gives teachers a longer class period with a group of students is also gaining popularity as a means of keeping students together for longer periods of time.

❑ Physical activity

Given the dramatic and compelling physical changes that occur during early adolescence, it is not surprising that physical activity has a high priority for young adolescents. Furthermore, physical activity is a symbol of the larger health-promoting behaviors with which middle schools are concerned.

Steinberg (1993) reminded us of the paradox of adolescent physical health: on the one hand, adolescence is one of the healthiest periods in the life span with low incidences of disabling or chronic illnesses; while, on the other hand, it is a period of relatively great physical risk due to unhealthy behaviors (such as drug use), violence, and risky behavior (such as unprotected sexual intercourse).

It is critical for middle level schools to become health-promoting environments. The Carnegie Council on Adolescent Development (1996), recommended three broad-based approaches that are more powerful when combined: a life sciences curriculum with human biology; life-skills training; and social support programs offering a range of human services.

❏ Structure and clear limits

Young adolescents need assistance setting boundaries in many aspects of their lives, but they do not need to be told what to do. They need authoritative adults who provide clear guidance, but who also know when to "back-off" and allow young adolescents space to try things on their own (Baumrind, 1967). Even those young adolescents who appear older and more mature may have difficulty setting the limits they need.

Young adolescents need frequent assistance and instruction when developing these skills. For example, setting realistic time limits for a task, deciding with whom to collaborate, determining what materials are needed, defining the purpose of the task, responding to the audience, and demonstrating mastery of the learning in question, are all examples of structures needed.

Declining opportunities for autonomy and choice, in combination with increased levels of teacher control, can undermine students' academic interest and motivation (Eccles, Midgley, & Adler, 1984). Young adolescents' involvement in decision making is crucial. We cannot expect them to know how to make decisions if we have not given them opportunities to do so. Because so many areas of their lives are changing rapidly, young adolescents need to know that they can count on consistency from parents and other adults. Parenting that is characterized by parental warmth, democratic parent-child interaction, and parental demandingness is consistently associated with positive developmental outcomes in young people (Steinberg, 1990).

❏ Self-identity for all students

The emphasis middle school educators place on attending to the personal and developmental needs of young adolescents and the imperative to help them develop a secure, clarified, self-identity are applicable to all students. These concerns have some additional dimensions for African American, Hispanic, Asian-American, and Native American youth because of factors of race and ethnicity, as well. — Gay, 1994

Fortunately, a body of research addressing young women and minority students as they achieve a sense of identity has become more prevalent.

Older views of development interpreted the differences in achievement and self-concept measures between girls and boys as stemming from deficiencies in females, or did not differentiate girls' and boys' development at all. More recent work by researchers on female development (Gilligan, 1982; Gilligan, Lyons, Hanmer, 1990; Hancock, 1989; Mee, 1997) suggested that females approach knowledge, events, and experiences from a set of goals very different from those of boys.

Boys are socialized to excel in the individuating activities of competition (in sports, making grades, argumentation), and therefore, find personal self-worth in activities our culture associates with the rugged individual. These researchers find that girls locate their identities in the nurturing atmosphere of relationships and their connection as individuals to the needs of others (Butler & Sperry, 1991; Mee, 1997)

Researchers (Gilligan et al., 1990; Orenstein, 1994) found that early maturing females who score lower on measures of self-esteem than do their early maturing male counterparts, indicate the need for addressing gender role socialization at a time when young women discover the disparity in power and prestige associated with options for females and males. Complicating the picture of girls' development further, other researchers (Belenky, Clinchy, Goldberger, & Tarule, 1986) have described a very different developmental paradigm of intellectual development that primarily characterizes women's growth.

Thus research suggests that, due to differences in the way boys and girls are socialized in our society, different developmental paths as well as different development concerns (moral, social, and intellectual) are created by the time of the middle level school years for females and males. This significant body of research suggests that girls respond differently to the classroom environment than boys and that educators, especially middle level edu-

cators, whose claim is that their very curriculum arises from the
nature of young adolescent development, cannot afford to ig-
nore these findings.   — Butler & Sperry, 1991, p.21

Gay (1994) suggested that teachers need to know how "to translate the theoretical edict of developmentally appropriate and responsive pedagogy into effective instructional practices for early adolescents of color" (p. 149). Researchers (Atkinson, Morten & Sue, 1983; Cross, 1991; Phinney, 1989, 1992; Phinney & Traver, 1988) found that the processes of personal and ego identity development for adolescents of color working to achieve a clarified ethnic identity are similar to those proposed by Erikson (1968). It is necessary for young adolescents of color to negotiate what Du Bois (1969) called a "double-consciousness" while others (Darder, 1991; Ramirez & Castaneda, 1974) described it as the "bi-culturality" of their ethnic-racial identity and their American-ness.

While some variations exist by ethnic groups and age, the general pattern of ethnic identity development begins with self-ethnic unawareness, denial or disaffiliation, and unconscious and unquestioning dependence upon Eurocentric, mainstream cultural values and standards of self-definition. It then progresses through increasing levels of consciousness, pride, affirmation, and acceptance of the validity and worth of one's own ethnic culture and heritage (Gay, 1994). Ethnic identity development must be regarded as part of the natural "coming of age" process of each young adolescent.

Cross (1995) delineated several advantages of teaching diverse cultures including children's seeing themselves in the curriculum and children's benefitting from seeing people of diverse cultures in the curriculum, Viewing curriculum as singular and standardized endangers curriculum equality for all children, while structuring curriculum around culture has implications for children's life in classrooms, for what children will learn, and for what they want for their future and the future of others.

❏ For whom should the middle school curriculum be?

Developmental responsiveness has provided the rationale for such common middle level practices as advisory programs, teams, exploratory programs and many more. Yet, the same standard of developmental responsiveness has had less influence on curriculum development. Only in the last few years has the curriculum become a focal point of study as reformers recognized the limitations of concentrating on school climate and school organizational issues to change the middle school.

This recent interest in middle school curriculum has spurred new roles and new questions for everyone involved – teachers, parents, students, and community members. Determining what curricula is responsive to young adolescents' needs, projecting what students will need to know and be able to do in the future, as well as staying current with community expectations and changing disciplines, all are critical aspects of the curriculum development process. As a part of this process, significant student input, involvement, and planning in all aspects of the curriculum development process is critical. Ultimately, middle school students must be engaged in developing the curriculum, by posing questions about themselves and their world, as well as answering questions the world poses for them.

Emphasis on developmentally responsive curricula will become an increasingly important aspect of middle level development. The role young adolescents play in curriculum development will be strengthened as more teachers recognize that their students have significant concerns and interests in skills, content, and attitudes that are studied within a context of critical issues. ℝ

References

Alexander, W. (1995). *Student-oriented curriculum: Asking the right questions.* Columbus, OH: National Middle School Association.

Arnold, J. (1990). *Visions of teaching and learning: 80 innovative middle level projects.* Columbus, OH: National Middle School Association.

Arnold, J. (1991). Towards a middle level curriculum rich in meaning. *Middle School Journal, 23* (2), 8-12.

Arnold, J. (1993). A curriculum to empower young adolescents. *Midpoints 4:1.* Columbus, OH: National Midle School Association.

Atkinson, D.R., Morten, G., & Sue, D.W. (1983). Proposed minority identity development model. In D.R. Atkinson, et al. (Eds.), *Counseling American minorities: A cross-cultural perspective.* (pp. 191-200). Dubuque, IA: William C. Brown.

Baumrind, D. (1967). Child care practices anteceding three patterns of preschool behavior. *Genetic Psychology Monographs, 75,* 43-88.

Beane, J.A. (1993). *The middle school curriculum: From rhetoric to reality* (2nd ed.), Columbus, OH: National Middle School Association.

Belenky, M.F., Clinchy, B.M., Goldberger, N.R., & Tarule, J.M. (1986). *Women's ways of knowing: The development of self, voice, and mind.* New York: Basic Books.

Boyer, E. (1995). The educated person. In J. Beane (Ed.), *Toward a coherent curriculum* (pp. 16-25). Alexandria, VA: Association for Supervision and Curriculum Development.

Brazee, E.N. (1995). An integrated curriculum supports young adolescent development. In Y. Siu-Runyan & V. Faircloth (Eds.), *Beyond separate subjects: Integrative learning at the middle level.* Norwood, MA: Christopher-Gordon Publishers, Inc.

Brazee, E.N., & Capelluti, J. (1995). *Dissolving boundaries: Toward an integrative curriculum.* Columbus, OH: National Middle School Association.

Butler, D., & Sperry, S. (1991). Gender issues and the middle school curriculum. *Middle School Journal, 23* (2), 18-23.

Caine, R.N., & Caine, J. (1991). *Making connections: Teaching and the human brain.* Alexandria, VA: Association for Supervision and Curriculum Development.

Carnegie Council on Adolescent Development. (1989). *Turning points: Preparing American youth for the 21st century.* New York: Carnegie Corporation.

Carnegie Council on Adolescent Development. (1996). *Great transitions: Preparing adolescents for a new century.* New York: Carnegie Corporation.

Cross, B. (1995). The case for a culturally coherent curriculum. In J. Beane (Ed.), *Toward a coherent curriculum* (pp. 71-86). Alexandria, VA: Association for Supervision and Curriculum Development.

Cross, W. E. (1991). *Shades of black: Diversity in African American identity.* Philadelphia: Temple University Press.

Darder, A. (1991). *Culture and power in the classroom: A critical foundation of bicultural education.* New York: Bergin & Garvey.

Du Bois, W.E.B. (1969). *The souls of Black folks.* New York: New American Library.

Eccles, J.S., & Midgley, C. (1989). Stage environment fit: Developmentally appropriate classrooms for young adolescents. In C. Ames & R. Ames (Eds.), *Research on motivation in education* (pp. 139-186). New York: Academic Press.

Eccles, J, Midgley, C., & Adler, T. F. (1984). Grade-related changes in the school environment: Effects on achievement motivation. In J. G. Nicholls (Ed.), *Advances in motivation and achievement* (pp. 283-331). Greenwich, CT: JAI Press.

Erikson, E.H. (1968). *Identity: Youth and crisis.* New York: Norton.

Feldman, S.S., & Elliott, G.R. (Eds.).(1990). *At the threshold: The developing adolescent.* Cambridge, MA: Harvard University Press.

Fertman, C, White, G, & White, L. (1996). *Service learning in the middle school: Building a culture of service.* Columbus, OH: National Middle School Association.

Gardner, H. (1983). *Frames of mind: The theory of multiple intelligences.* New York: Basic Books.

Gay, G. (1994). Coming of age ethnically: Teaching young adolescents of color. *Theory Into Practice, 33* (3), 149-156.

George, P., Stevenson, C., Thomason, J., & Beane, J. (1992). *The middle school and beyond.* Alexandria, VA: Association for Supervision & Curriculum Development.

Gilligan, C. (1982). *In a different voice.* Cambridge, MA: Harvard.

Gilligan, C., Lyons, N. P., & Hanmer, T. J. (1990). Making connections: *The relational worlds of adolescent girls at Emma Willard School.* Cambridge, MA: Harvard University Press.

Hall, S. (1904). *Adolescence.* New York: Appleton.

Halstead, A. (1997). A bridge to adulthood: Service learning at the middle level. *Midpoints 7* (1).

Hancock, E. (1989). *The girl within.* New York: Random House.

Harter, S. (1986). Processes underlying the construction, maintenance, and enhancement of the self-concept in children. In J. Suls & A. Greenwald (Eds.), *Psychological perspectives on the self* (Vol 3, pp.137-138). Hillsdale, N.J.: Erlbaum.

Harter, S. (1990). Self and identity development. In S. Feldman & G. Elliott (Eds.), *At the threshold: The developing adolescent* (pp. 352-382). Cambridge, MA.: Harvard University Press.

Hill, J. P. (1980). *Understanding early adolescence - a framework.* Carrboro, NC: The Center for Early Adolescence.

Hillman, S.B. (1991). What developmental psychology has to say about early adolescence. *Middle School Journal, 23* (1), 3-8.

Hillman, S.B., Wood, P. C., Becker, M.J., & Altier, D.T. (1990). Young adolescent risk-taking behavior: Theory, research and implications for middle level schools. In J.L. Irvin (Ed.), *Research in middle level education: Selected studies* (pp. 39-50). Columbus, OH: National Middle School Association.

Horowitz, F.D. (1989). Children and their development: Knowledge base, research agenda, and social policy application. *American Psychologist,44* (5) 441-445.

Jackson, A. W., & Hornbeck, D.W. (1989). Educating young adolescents: Why we must restructure middle grade schools. *American Psychologist, 44* (5) 180-187.

Lesko, N. (1994). Back to the future: Middle schools and the Turning Points Report. *Theory Into Practice 33* (3), 139-148.

Lipsitz, J. (1980). *Growing up forgotten.* New Brunswick, NJ: Transaction Books.

Lounsbury, J., & Clark, D. C. (1990). *From apathy to excitement: Inside grade eight.* Reston, VA: National Association of Secondary School Principals.

McDonough, L. (1991). Middle level curriculum: The search for self and social meaning. *Middle School Journal, 23* (2), 29-35.

McEwin, K, Dickinson, T.S., & Jenkins, D.M. (1996). *America's middle schools: Practices and progress—A 25 year perspective.* Columbus, OH: National Middle School Association.

Mee, C. (1997). *2,000 voices: Young adolescents' perceptions and curriculum implications.* Columbus, OH: National Middle School Association.

National Middle School Association. (1995). *This we believe: Developmentally responsive middle level schools.* Columbus, OH: Author.

Newmann, F. M. (1990). Higher order thinking in the teaching of social studies: Connections between theory and practice. In D. Perkins, J. Segal, & J. Voss (Eds.), *Informal reasoning and education* (pp. 381-400). Hillsdale, N.J.: Erlbaum.

Orenstein, P. (1994). *School girls: Young women's self-esteem and the confidence gap.* New York: Doubleday.

Peterson, A. (1987). Those gangly years. *Psychology Today, 21* (9), 28-34.

Phinney, J. S., & Traver, S. (1988). Ethnic identity search and commitment in black and white eighth graders. *Journal of Early Adolescence 8* (3), 265-277.

Phinney, J.S. (1989). Stages of ethnic identity development in minority group adolescents. *Journal of Early Adolescence 9* (1), 34-49.

Phinney, J.S. (1992). The multigroup ethnic identity measure: A new scale for use with diverse groups. *Journal of Adolescent Research, 7* (2), 156-176.

Powell, R., & Skoog, G. (1995). Students' perspectives on integrative curricula: The case of Brown Barge Middle School. *Research in Middle Level Education Quarterly, 19* (1), 85-115.

Ramirez, M., & Castaneda, A. (1974). *Cultural democracy, biocognitive development, and education.* New York: Academic Press.

Resnick, L. B. (1986). *Education and learning to think.* Washington, DC: National Research Council.

Roberts, D. F. (1993). Adolescents and the mass media: From "Leave It to Beaver" to "Beverly Hills 90210." In R. Takashani (Ed.), *Adolescence in the 1990s: Risk and opportunity* (pp. 171-186). New York: Teachers College Press.

Russell, A. (Ed.). (1990). Exploring territory west of childhood: The early teens. *Carnegie Quarterly, 35* (1-2), 3-13.

Scales, P. (1991). *A portrait of young adolescents in the 1990s: Implications for promoting healthy growth and development.* Carrboro, NC: Center for Early Adolescence.

Schubert, W. (1993). Curriculum reform. In G. Cawelti (Ed.), *Challenges and achievements of American education: The 1993 ASCD Yearbook.* Alexandria, VA: The Association for Supervision and Curriculum Development.

Springer, M. (1994). *Watershed: A successful voyage into integrative learning.* Columbus, OH: National Middle School Association.

Stevenson, C., & Carr, J. F. (Eds.). (1993). *Integrated studies in the middle grades:'Dancing through walls.'* New York:Teachers College Press.

Steinberg, L. (1990). Autonomy, conflict, and harmony in the family relationship. In S. Feldman & G. Elliott (Eds.), *At the threshold: The developing adolescent* (pp. 255-276)). Cambridge, MA.: Harvard University Press.

Steinberg, L. (1993). *Adolescence.* 3rd Edition. New York: McGraw-Hill.

Takanishi, R. (Ed.). (1993). *Adolescence in the 1990s: Risk and opportunity.* NY: Teachers College Press.

James A. Beane

Curriculum for What?

In the past few years, middle level educators have given increased attention to the question, "What should be the middle school curriculum?" (Beane, 1990, 1993). This question has proven to be a very difficult one for several reasons, not the least of which is that it involves a prior question, "What is the purpose of the middle school curriculum?"

Educational historians point to the beginnings of the junior high school as one instance where a school reform movement was supported by several groups whose interests often competed under other circumstances (Cremin, 1961; Cuban, 1992; Kliebard, 1986; Lounsbury, 1960). Among these groups were the Committee of Ten (National Education Association, 1985) that included the concept of a junior high school among its recommendations for accelerating college preparation, child labor activists anxious to keep young people in schools, vocational educators desiring guidance for school dropouts, and developmentalists interested in making the schools more responsive to what they claimed were the characteristics of young adolescents.

While such widespread support was instrumental in the implementation of the early junior high school, it also created an ambiguous and, at times, contradictory set of purposes as each group was a source of both demands and criticism. Moreover, all of those expectations were complicated by the contentious issue of whether the junior high school curriculum ought to emphasize a general or "common" educational program for young people or one that would begin the process of differentiation with regard to career paths after formal schooling.

This mix of curriculum purposes was nowhere better captured than in one of the earliest broad-scope volumes on this level, Briggs's (1920) *The* lum was asked to take on such purposes as promoting social integration, addressing personal concerns of young adolescents, exploring interests, surveying the traditional subjects, and investigating career possibilities.

Some educators, like Koos (1927), sought to assuage this ambiguity with a curriculum consisting of "constants" and "variables." That view resulted in a fairly standard collection of academic subjects supplemented by vocational and academic selections and a homeroom guidance program, such as that detailed by Bruner (1925). Other educators, however, chose to push for one or two purposes rather than the whole array. For example, Thomas-Tindal and Myers (1924) called for a curriculum developed for "the child of junior high school age, the adolescent, [who] is in particular need of physical, mental, and moral guidance in those all-important transition years..." (p. 10). The curriculum they described followed the " Cardinal Principles of Education" (National Education Association, 1918) report by providing "guidance" in physical, academic, social, vocational, civic, aesthetic, and ethical areas. And Cox (1929) described a "core-curriculum" in which subject distinctions broke down as emphasis was placed less on specific content and skills and more on "what they (students) shall want to know, to do, and to be" (p. 13).

In the 1930s the curriculum purposes already sketched out were expanded to include the concept of "democratic education" as that was revitalized in the midst of economic depression and social discontent (e.g. Faunce & Bossing, 1951; Rugg, 1936). The junior high schools were a focal point for this effort, especially in the form of problem-centered "core" programs that emerged during and after the Eight Year Study (Aikin, 1942). Though these programs were implemented by a relative minority of junior high schools (Wright, 1958), many leaders in the junior high school movement used the "core" emphasis on personal and social/democratic education in a renewed attempt to define the general education portion of the curriculum (Gruhn & Douglass, 1948; Hock & Hill, 1960; Lounsbury & Vars, 1978; Noar, 1953; Van Til, Vars, & Lounsbury, 1961).

As the middle school movement has unfolded, relatively little has changed regarding the ambiguity of purposes for the curriculum. This is not surprising since, as Kliebard (1986) argued, the story of curriculum is one of continuous struggle among various positions rather than ascendance of one position or another. For example, the widely read Carnegie Council report, *Turning Points* (1989), sounds practically the same litany of purposes as Briggs (1920) or Gruhn and Douglass (1948).

The official position statement of the National Middle School Association (1995) argued again the case of the developmentalist, as do Stevenson and Carr (1993). Practically any document prepared under the regime of federal or state standards continues the Perennialist and Essentialist purposes of subject and skill mastery. And the contemporary work around progressive curriculum integration carries forward the theme of democratic education and the "core" curriculum (Alexander with Carr & McAvoy, 1995; Beane, 1990; Brazee & Capelluti, 1995; Brodhagen, 1995; Middle Level Curriculum Project, 1993; Pace, 1995; Pate, McGinnis, & Homestead, 1995; Siu-Runyan and Faircloth, 1995).

Clearly the definition of purpose for the middle level curriculum is as problematic today as it was in the early junior high school. If anything, it is even more complicated with the addition of references to "preparation for the future" in popular media and professional sources (Brazee & Capelluti, 1994; National Middle School Association, 1995). Tensions continue over whether the curriculum ought to emphasize general or specialized education, academic or life-centered purposes, concerns of young adolescents or desires of adults, mastery of discipline-based knowledge or thematic-based problem-solving, or preparation for future education or responsiveness to present situations. And within these, even more tensions simmer as, for example, in the question of whether the curriculum ought to encourage young adolescents to adjust to the present society or critically examine the need for social change (Beane, 1990).

In the current public scrutiny of schools in general, the ambiguity of purposes for the middle school curriculum has made this level particularly vulnerable to criticism. Today's descendants of the original junior high school advocates - classical humanists, developmentalists, vocationalists, and social reformers - are no less invested in the middle school movement and have the same expectations that their interests will be accommodated. For this reason, the curriculum of middle level schools will probably continue to serve multiple purposes at the same time that it is a site for struggle over whether one or a few ought to be emphasized over others. ℝ

References

Aikin, W. M. (1942). *The story of the eight year study.* New York: Harper and Brothers.

Alexander, W. M., with Carr, D., & McAvoy, K. (1995). *Student-oriented curriculum: Asking the right questions.* Columbus, OH: National Middle School Association.

Beane, J. A. (1990). *A middle school curriculum: From rhetoric to reality.* Columbus, OH: National Middle School Association.

Brazee, E. N., & Capelutti, J. (1994). *Second generation curriculum: What and how we teach at the middle level.* Topsfield, MA: New England League of Middle Schools.

Brazee, E. N., & Capelutti, J. (1995). *Dissolving boundaries: Toward an integrative curriculum.* Columbus, OH: National Middle School Association.

Briggs, T. H. (1920). *The junior high school.* New York: Houghton Mifflin.

Brodhagen, B. L. (1995). The situation made us special. In M. Apple & J. Beane (Eds.) *Democratic schools* (pp.83-100). Alexandria, VA: Association for Supervision and Curriculum Development.

Bruner, Herbert B. (1925). *The junior high school at work.* New York: Teachers College, Columbia University.

Carnegie Council on Adolescent Development. (1989). *Turning points: Preparing American youth for the 21st century.* New York: Carnegie Corporation.

Cox, P. (1929). *The junior high school and its curriculum.* New York: Charles Scribner's Sons.

Cremin, L. A. (1961). *The transformation of the school: Progressivism in American education, 1876-1957.* New York: Alfred A. Knopf.

Cuban, L. (1992). What happens to reforms that last: The case of the junior high school. *American Educational Research Journal, 29* (Summer), 227-251.

Faunce, R., & Bossing, N. (1951). *Developing the core curriculum.* New York: Prentice-Hall.

Gruhn, W. T., & Douglass, H. R. (1948). *The modern junior high school.* New York: Ronald.

Hock, L., & Hill, T. (1960). *The general education class in the secondary school.* New York: Holt-Rinehart.

Kliebard, H. M. (1986). *The struggle for the American curriculum, 1893-1958.* Boston: Routledge and Kegan Paul.

Koos, L. V. (1927). *The junior high school.* Boston: Ginn and Co.

Lounsbury, J.H. (1960). How the junior high school came to be. *Educational Leadership, XVIII,* 147-148, 198.

Lounsbury, J. H., & Vars, G. F. (1978). *A curriculum for the middle school years.* New York: Harper and Row.

Middle Level Curriculum Project (1993). Middle level curriculum: The search for self and social meaning. In T. Dickinson (Ed.), *Readings in middle school curriculum* (pp. 105 -118). Columbus, OH: National Middle School Association.

National Education Association. (1895). *Report of the Committee of Ten.* Washington, DC: US Government Printing Office.

National Education Association (1918). *Cardinal principles of secondary education: A report of the Commission on the Reorganization of Secondary Education.* Washington, DC: US Government Printing Office.

National Middle School Association (1995). *This we believe: Developmentally responsive middle level schools.* Columbus, OH: Author.

Noar, G. (1953). *The junior high school.* New York: Prentice-Hall.

Pace, G. (Ed.). (1995). *Whole learning in the middle school.* Norwood, MA: Christopher-Gordon.

Pate, P. E., McGinnis, K., & Homestead, E. (1995). Creating Coherence Through Curriculum Integration. In J. A. Beane (Ed.) *Toward a coherent curriculum* (pp.62-70). 1995 Yearbook of the Association for Supervision and Curriculum Development. Alexandria, VA: ASCD.

Rugg, H. (1936). *American life and the school curriculum.* Boston, Ginn and Co.

Siu-Runyan, Y., & Faircloth, C. V. (Eds.). (1995). *Beyond separate subjects: Integrative learning at the middle level.* Norwood, MA: Christopher-Gordon.

Stevenson, C., & Carr, J. F. (1993). *Integrated studies in the middle grades: 'Dancing through walls.'* New York: Teachers College Press.

Thomas-Tindal, E. V., & Myers, J. D. (1924). *Junior high school life.* New York: Macmillan.

Van Til, W., Vars, G. F., & Lounsbury, J. H. (1961). *Modern education for the junior high school years.* Indianapolis, IN: Bobbs-Merrill.

Wright, G. S. (1958). *Block time classes and the core program.* Washington, DC: U.S. Government Printing Office.

Richard R. Powell and C. Victoria Faircloth

Current Issues and Research in Middle Level Curriculum: On Conversations, Semantics, and Roots

❏ Critiquing Conversations ❏

The number of books written about middle level curriculum has increased dramatically over the last few years. Educators have sought new ways of engaging students in school-based curriculum and instruction. As a result, a curriculum reform movement for young adolescents has surfaced (e.g., Irvin, 1992). This movement has given rise to alternative school structures which involve, for example, reworking relationships among teachers (Powell & Mills, 1995), creating smaller interdisciplinary communities of learners within larger schools (Vars, 1993), rethinking the organization of content to be taught (Powell, Skoog, & Troutman, in press), and so on.

The notion of *conversation* has been a guiding metaphor for curriculum reform in general (Applebee, 1996; Goodlad & Su, 1992), and for current discourse in middle level curriculum reform in particular (e.g., Dickinson, 1993). The metaphor of conversation suggests that curriculum may be viewed from several levels or viewpoints. At one level the dialogue centers on the kinds of school and classroom curricula that are best suited for young adolescents. On another level, the issue at stake is students, specifically at giving students an important *voice* in not only what is taught, but how teaching and learning unfold. (Boomer, Lester, Onore, & Cook, 1992; Oldfather & McLaughlin, 1993). On yet another level the notion of conversation is used more broadly as a means to successfully and equitably help young learners ultimately take part in the greater conversation of humanity (Greene, 1993). Each level shares one important attribute: each is linked directly and intimately to a school's curriculum, that is, to "the form and substance of middle level learning" (Dickinson, 1993, p. ix).

These levels of curricular conversations, coupled with the diverse voices of stakeholders, have created a proliferation of middle level curriculum designs and definitions (Apple & Beane, 1995; Fogarty, 1993; George & Alexander, 1993; Jacobs, 1989; Schumacher, 1995; Siu-Runyan & Faircloth, 1995; Vars, 1993; Vars & Rakow, 1993; for broader discussions of curriculum designs and definitions, see for example Applebee, 1996; Doll, 1993; Jackson, 1992; Schubert, 1986; Tanner and Tanner, 1990.) This proliferation has arguably caused a splintering of curriculum reform in middle level education and confusion in two key areas of middle level curriculum reform. These areas of confusion pertain to kinds of knowledge, arrangement of knowledge, and ways of knowing that are embodied in specific curriculum designs (e.g., conventional subject-centered, interdisciplinary subject-centered, integrative), and that are best suited to preparing young learners for becoming socially aware individuals who are capable of making important decisions about social, cultural, political, and environmental issues.

Our purpose for this chapter is to consider more closely, within a framework of middle level curriculum theory and related research, the areas of confusion noted above. We discuss three issues in middle level curriculum reform. First, we discuss the issue of *semantics*, or curriculum meaning, as related to the proliferation of middle level curriculum designs. Second, we discuss the *roots* of middle level curriculum designs. Using the idea of root, we consider the need to clarify the philosophical and historical bases for curriculum reform efforts, and for conducting research in middle level environments. Third, we discuss issues pertaining to collaborative and action research. Drawing from our discussion of these three issues, we suggest a possible avenue for moving toward a conceptually rich and more meaningful curriculum theory for middle level practitioners and researchers.

❏ The Issues of Semantics and Clarity ❏

❏ On semantics

The proliferation of curriculum designs over the past two decades has raised the issue of curriculum semantics. This is because the same kind of curriculum can have different meanings for differing individuals, and because different kinds of curricula can have the same meanings for differing individuals (see the discussion of curriculum terminology offered by Drake, 1993; Hough & St. Clair, 1995; Vars, 1993;). Moreover, the proliferation of curriculum designs has been embedded in three agendas, which further conflates the problem of middle level curriculum semantics. First, there are political and emancipatory agendas that are related to contextualized learning, what Applebee (1996) called *knowledge-in-action,* and what Anderson, Reder, and Simon (1996) called *situated learning.* This first agenda, which is represented by curriculum theorists such as Beane (1993), pertains to theme-based non-linear instruction, and causes educators to re-think what to teach, and how to best engage students in content germane to specific themes. The second agenda pertains to behavioral and decontextualized learning. Applebee (1996) gave the name, *knowledge-out-of-context,* to the information associated with this kind of learning. This second agenda reflects traditional subject-centered curricula of junior high schools, and tends to privilege the structure of the content over the needs of students. The third agenda pertains to developmental and cognitive orientations, which are related to the social, personal, and academic needs of young adolescents (Carnegie Council on Adolescent Development, 1989; Irvin, 1995; Vars, 1993). This agenda relates to developmental restructuring of interpersonal relationships of teachers and students (e.g., interdisciplinary teams) but not necessarily restructuring the content to be taught.

For each of the three agendas above, there exists a specific definition for curriculum and a set of corresponding values for learning content in a designated manner. There might appear to be little need for concern over the semantics related to these three agendas for middle level reform. However, a closer look reveals the confusion that can occur when educators at both university and precollege levels use educational terms loosely when discussing middle level curriculum.

Perhaps the most striking semantical problems associated with middle level curriculum are those associated with what some educators call integrative curricula. For example, consider the question: What does it mean to be a teacher in an integrative school? If we ask teachers at Brown Barge Middle School (BBMS) (Pensacola, Florida) and Carver Academy (Waco, Texas) this question, we will get different responses than those given, for example, by teachers at Thurman White Middle School (TWMS) (Henderson, Nevada) (see Powell, 1997; Powell, Skoog, Troutman, & Jones, 1996). This is because curricula at BBMS and Carver Academy are non-linear and theme-based, following the work of Beane (1993). At TWMS, on the other hand, the curriculum is interdisciplinary, and consequently subject-centered. Learning for students at TWMS is linear and hierarchical, although teachers at the school still develop some interdisciplinary units; teaching and learning at BBMS is nonlinear and holistic. Living the educative experience of a non-linear, holistic curriculum, as demonstrated at schools such as BBMS and Carver Academy, is vastly different for both teachers and learners than living the educative experience of a linear curriculum (Powell & Skoog, 1995).

On philosophical, cultural, social, and academic levels, education at BBMS and Carver Academy, two schools richly embedded in integrative curriculum theory, differs notably from education at TWMS, a school richly embedded in interdisciplinary curriculum theory. Yet teachers in interdisciplinary contexts such as TWMS may very well claim that they, too, are integrative in their orientation. The questions then surface: What really is an integrative curriculum? Can the notions of integrative and interdisciplinary, two curriculum practices that are grounded in radically different philosophical and theoretical assumptions, be used interchangeably on any level, as suggested by Hough and St. Clair (1995)? Are the differences between these two curriculum designs important enough to draw distinction between them in the literature? We believe that the differences are important enough, and the designs vary enough, that clarity in meaning, and thus in practice, is now needed.

❏ On clarity

Ask a middle school teacher to define or explain what is meant by curriculum that is developmentally appropriate for young adolescents and expect to hear conflicting, and sometimes ambiguous responses. This is particularly unsettling in light of the fact that the middle school movement has grown rapidly in the last few decades. Educators frequently use terms like *interdisciplinary* and *integrated* interchangeably. Inservice workshops for teachers frequently draw upon the works of writers who contradict one another about what the curriculum should be. Therefore, it is imperative that the work of educational researchers in middle level contexts move toward clarity in definition, and toward clarity in educational goals and practices of middle level curriculum. This kind of clarity will properly contextualize research momentum, thus permitting readers to more easily, and more accurately, make sense of empirical reports.

In our work in various middle school contexts, we have discovered that middle level practitioners working within curriculum contexts that are radically different from traditional contexts and from interdisciplinary contexts have clearer ideas about the nature of their school curriculum. This reflects the work of Quartz (1995, 1996), who suggested that true reform, if it is to be long-lasting, requires clarity of purpose, of definition, and of mission. This same reform, Quartz argued, requires that teachers in a school where such reform is happening must be willing to live out, in a collective and collaborative fashion, the purpose, definition, and mission of the reform effort. Turning again to our example of BBMS above, we discovered that most teachers at this school were very clear about the definition of their integrative curriculum, and were aware of the kind of learning, which was integrative, holistic, and emancipatory in nature, that the school had adopted for students (Powell, Skoog, Troutman, & Jones, 1996). The study by Powell and associates (1996) revealed that teachers at BBMS had a collective consciousness for their educational mission; this consciousness enabled them to work together, along with their students, as a strongly cohesive group. The kind of clarity demonstrated by BBMS educators is the kind of clarity we suggest that school-based educators and university workers both need if the current conversation about middle level curriculum reform is to be meaningful.

❏ The Issue of Roots ❏

Explicating the roots, what we more formally call *etymology,* of curriculum designs, movements, and traditions is an essential process in cleaning up middle level semantics. In this section we argue that conversations about middle level curriculum reform, whether these conversations occur in school classrooms, in scholarly journals, or ethnographic accounts of middle school life, mostly overlook the connection of the conversation to its historical roots, thus leaving educators to draw their own conclusions about what curriculum design is being explored, discussed, or reformed.

We shall draw from two recently published ethnographic works to demonstrate what we have described in the foregoing paragraph. First, in an important study on the influence of student transitioning from a progressive middle school to a conventional high school, Wells (1996) provided an account of the gradual deconstruction of literacy skills in five students. Wells carefully and somewhat painstakingly documented how one school culture, namely a conventional high school, gradually eroded the literacy skills that a selected group of students acquired in their "progressive" middle school. Wells' valuable study, while serving to raise many important and certainly pressing questions about learning in progressive and traditional schools, assumed that readers understand the curriculum assumptions underlying the schools described in the study, although a discussion of the historical antecedents of the schools' curricula was mostly lacking from Wells' report.

The second study we briefly highlight here is that reported by Roe (1994), who conducted a microethnography of a social studies seventh grade classroom. The study provided a needed and useful account of the relationship between textbooks and learning in a middle school classroom. The research setting, as described by Roe in this study, was "a seventh grade classroom in a small town in central Illinois" (p. 23). Few other details are offered in the report about the curriculum orientation of the school, about how the use of textbooks in the school was a function of the school's overarching assumptions for learning and teaching, or about the general tradition of the school's curriculum. Textbook usage has long been linked to conventional subject-centered curriculum designs, but has not been linked to unconventional integrative curriculum designs. Knowing whether the school was conventional or integrative clearly has an impact on the perspective from which readers can interpret Roe's findings.

Reporting the curriculum traditions and linking these traditions to earlier curriculum work would have been important additions to the two studies above. For example, in Wells' study of a progressive middle school, was this school part of the progressive educational movement in America, thus linking it to the earlier writings of Dewey (e.g., 1916)? Was the school more integrative in nature, thus linking it to the earlier writings of Hopkins (1937) and more recently to Beane (1993)? These questions, while important in helping us understand more fully the place of Wells' study in the greater curriculum conversation, remain unanswered. The same questions remain unanswered for the study reported by Roe. Thus, in a theoretical sense, both studies mentioned above are decontextualized from the middle level curriculum conversation. That is, while Wells' study has added significantly to our understanding of transitioning from one school design to another school design, we are unsure how all of this fits into the greater scheme of middle level curriculum reform, both past and present, because we are not aware of the curriculum assumptions that framed the schools that were reported in the study.

❏ The Issue of Site-based Collaborative ❏
and Action Research

Throughout this chapter we have discussed issues of semantics, clarity, and etymology as they pertain to the middle level curriculum conversation. One means for approaching these issues is through site-based collaborative and action research. Clearly, these forms of research will not provide answers for all of the questions related to these issues, but this research will help middle level educators address questions related to semantics, clarity, and etymology, as we have discussed them here.

The value of collaborative and action research, two related forms of inquiry, is that teachers and university professors tend to work together, collegially, to explore questions of common concern. As Mclaughlin, Hall, Earle, Miller, and Wheeler (1995) noted, "Whatever the research question, action research in K-12 classrooms begins with teachers' questions, not the questions and hypotheses of researchers" (p. 7). This approach to exploring middle level learning environments can be an important vehicle to begin asking questions about the meaning of curriculum, about the assumptions underlying daily practice, and about the historical and philosophical antecedents to middle level curriculum designs.

An example of such a site-based research endeavor is provided by Burnaford, Beane, and Brodhagen (1994). Burnaford and colleagues demonstrated how teachers and university workers can work together to explore semantical and etymological dimensions of middle level curriculum, thus bringing clarity of purpose to the teaching moment. In this report, the authors provided an overview of action research. In the second part of the report, Beane provided an overview of the central tenets of integrative curriculum. In the third section of the report, Brodhagen builds on the central tenets described by Beane to explore her classroom practice. The kind of action research described by Burnaford and associates reflects the kind of clarity we discuss above, and contributes meaningfully to the middle level conversation on curriculum.

❏ Toward Conceptually Rich Middle Level ❏ Curriculum Conversation

In this paper we have raised issues pertaining to the middle level curriculum conversation that has been unfolding for the past few decades. We raised issues of ambiguity in the conversation, of a lack of clear semantics for curriculum theory, of the need to gain clarity when discussing curriculum issues, and the proper place of theoretical and philosophical antecedents to modern day curriculum initiatives. If we are to move to an era in our curriculum conversation that is meaningful and purposeful, and that is conceptually rich and useful, then we, as middle level educators, must become curriculum theorists in the truest sense (see Powell & Skoog, 1995). To move toward a conceptually rich curriculum conversation, and consequently to a conceptually rich curriculum theory that guides our daily practices, then we must also move toward:

- clarity of definition of developmentally appropriate curriculum for young adolescents,
- clarity of curriculum semantics,
- clarity of curriculum definition,
- clarity of curriculum etymology in daily discourse and in scholarly reports,
- theoretically rich site-based collaborative and action research,
- meaningful dialogue filled with critical perspectives and pressing questions pertaining to efficacy of curriculum design.

❏ Conclusion ❏

We agree with Van Zandt & Totten (1995) that for too long, the middle level community has implemented designs of curriculum and instruction in a wholesale, superficial fashion without necessarily grounding this implementation in conceptually rich, historically accurate, and philosophically consistent ways. The issues we have reported in this chapter, which have emerged from recent research and practice in middle level contexts, are pressing and immediate. Moving toward a conceptually rich and meaningful curriculum conversation means moving toward addressing these pressing issues. While we agree with Beane (1993) that there is no recipe in doing this kind of curriculum work, we cannot move forward in this arena with these pressing issues confusing the research agendas and resulting educational practices. ℝ

References

Anderson, J. R., Reder, L. M., & Simon, H. A. (1996). Situated learning and education. *Educational Researcher, 25* (4), 5-11.

Apple, M. W., & Beane, J. A. (Eds.). (1995). *Democratic schools.* Alexandria, VA: Association for Supervision and Curriculum Development.

Applebee, A. N. (1996). *Curriculum as conversation.* Columbia: NY: Teachers College Press.

Beane, J. A. (1993). *A middle school curriculum: From rhetoric to reality.* (2nd. ed.) Columbus, OH: National Middle School Association.

Boomer, G., Lester, N., Onore, C., and Cook, J. (1992). *Negotiating the curriculum.* London: The Falmer Press.

Burnaford, G., Beane, J., & Brodhagen, B. (1994). Teacher action research: Inside an integrative curriculum. *Middle School Journal, 26* (2), 5-13.

Carnegie Council on Adolescent Development. (1989). *Turning points: Preparing American youth for the 21st century.* New York: Carnegie Corporation.

Dewey, J. (1916). *Democracy and education.* New York: Macmillan.

Dickinson, T. (Ed.). (1993). *Readings in middle school curriculum: A continuing conversation.* Columbus, OH: National Middle School Association.

Doll, W. (1993). *A post-modern perspective on curriculum.* New York: Teachers College Press.

Drake, S. (1993). *Planning integrated curriculum. The call to adventure.* Alexandria, VA: Association for Supervision and Curriculum Development.

George, P., & Alexander, W. (1993). *The exemplary middle school.* (2nd. ed.) Fort Worth, TX: Harcourt, Brace Jovanovich College Publishers.

Goodlad, J. I, & Su, Z. (1992). Organization of the curriculum. In P. Jackson (Ed.), *Handbook of research on curriculum,* (pp. 327-346). New York: Macmillan.

Greene, M. (1993). The passions of pluralism: Multiculturalism and the expanding community. *Educational Researcher, 22* (1), 13-18.

Hopkins, L. T. (1937). *Integration, its meaning and application.* New York: Appleton-Century.

Fogarty, R. (1993). *The mindful school: How to integrate the curricula.* Palatine, IL: IRI/Skylight Publishing.

Hough, D., & St. Clair, B. (1995). The effects of integrated curricula on young adolescent problems solving. *Research in Middle Level Education Quarterly, 19* (1), 1-26.

Irvin, J. (Ed.). (1992). *Transforming middle level education: Prospectives and possibilities.* Needham Heights, MA: Allyn and Bacon.

Irvin, J. (1995). Cognitive growth during early adolescence: The regulator of developmental tasks. *Middle School Journal, 27* (1), 54-55.

Jackson, P. (Ed.). (1992). *Handbook of research on curriculum.* New York: Macmillan.

Jacobs, H. (1989). *Interdisciplinary curriculum: Design and implementation.* Alexandria, VA: Association for Supervision and Curriculum Development.

McLaughlin, H. J., Earle, K., Hall, M., Miller, V., & Wheeler, M. (1995). Hearing from our students: Team action research in a middle school. *Middle School Journal, 26* (3), 7-12.

Oldfather, P., & McLaughlin, H. J. (1993). Gaining and losing voice: A longitudinal study of students' continuing impulse to learn across elementary and middle level contexts. *Research in Middle Level Education, 17* (1), 1-25.

Powell, R. (1997). Teams and the affirmation of middle level students' voices: The case of Jimmie and related thoughts of a concerned educator. In T. Dickinson & T. Erb (Eds.), *We gain more than we give: Teaming in middle schools.* Columbus, OH: National Middle School Association.

Powell, R., & Mills, R. (1995). Professional knowledge sharing among interdisciplinary team teachers: A study of intra-team mentoring. *Research in Middle Level Education, 18* (3), 27-40.

Powell, R., & Skoog, G. (1995). Students' perspectives on integrative curricula: The case of Brown Barge Middle School. *Research in Middle Level Education Quarterly, 19* (1), 85-115.

Powell, R., Skoog, G., & Troutman, P. (in press). On streams and odysseys: Reflections on reform and research in middle level integrative learning environments. *Research in Middle Level Education Quarterly.*

Powell, R., Skoog, G., Troutman, P., & Jones, C. (1996, April). *Standing on the edge of middle level curriculum reform: Factors influencing the sustainability of a non-linear integrative learning environment.* Paper presented at the annual meeting of the American Educational Research Association, New York.

Quartz, K. (1996, April). *Becoming better: The struggle to create a new culture of school reform.* Paper presented at the annual meeting of the American Educational Research Association, New York.

Quartz, K. (1995). Normative, technical, and political dimensions of creating new educational communities. In J. Oakes & K. H. Quartz (Eds.), *Creating new educational communities: Ninety-fourth yearbook of the National Society for the Study of Education* (pp. 240-252). Chicago: University of Chicago Press.

Roe, M. F. (1994). A microethnography of a seventh grade social studies classroom. *Research in Middle Level Education, 18* (1), 21-38.

Schubert, W. H. (1986). *Curriculum: Perspective, paradigm, and possibility.* New York: Macmillan Publishing Co.

Schumacher, D. H. (1995). Five levels of curriculum integration defined, refined, and described. *Research in Middle Level Education, 18* (3), 73-93.

Siu-Runyan, Y., & Faircloth, C. V. (1995). *Beyond separate subjects: Integrative learning at the middle level.* Norwood: MA. Christopher Gordon Publishers.

Tanner, D., & Tanner, L. (1990). *History of the school curriculum.* New York: Macmillan.

Van Zandt, L., & Totten, S. (1995). The current status of middle level education research: A critical review. *Research in Middle Level Education, 18* (3), 1-26.

Vars, G. F. (1993). *Interdisciplinary teaching: Why and how.* Columbus, OH: National Middle School Association.

Vars, G. F., & Rakow, S. R. (1993). Making connections: Integrative curriculum and the gifted student. *Roeper Review, 16* (1), 48-53.

Wells, M. C. (1996). *Literacies lost: When students move from a progressive middle school to a traditional high school.* New York: Teachers College Press.

Teacher Education

McEwin C. Kenneth McEwin
  Appalachian State University
  Boone, North Carolina

Dickinson Thomas S. Dickinson
  Indiana State University
  Terre Haute, Indiana

Hart Laurie E. Hart
  University of Georgia
  Athens, Georgia

C. Kenneth McEwin and Thomas S. Dickinson

Middle Level Teacher Preparation and Licensure

The continuing absence of sufficient numbers of middle level teachers who have the specialized knowledge, skills, and dispositions needed to be highly successful teachers of young adolescents has served as a major barrier to the full implementation of developmentally responsive middle level schooling since at least the turn of the century (McEwin & Dickinson, 1995, 1996). Although the need for specially prepared middle level teachers has been recognized in the literature for over 70 years (Douglas, 1920), the majority of young adolescents continue to be taught by teachers whose initial professional preparation and interests rest with teaching other developmental age groups, or who were interested in a middle level teaching career but found specialized middle level teacher preparation programs unavailable.

In many states, teacher preparation institutions, state departments of education, and the teaching profession have ignored the importance of such specialized programs and the middle level licensure which sustains them (Valentine & Mogar, 1992). One result of this neglect and malpractice is that thousands of young adolescents are being taught by teachers who are, at least initially, inadequately prepared to be highly successful (McEwin, 1992; McEwin, Dickinson, Erb, & Scales, 1995; Scales & McEwin, 1994, 1996). For example, a 1991 eight-state survey of middle level teachers revealed that only 17% had received specialized professional preparation to teach young adolescents (Scales, 1992). Additionally, 62% of respondents to a study of 1,798 middle level schools estimated that less than 25% of teachers at those schools had specialized middle level professional preparation (McEwin, Dickinson, & Jenkins, 1996).

❏ Barriers to special middle level teacher preparation

A complex set of reasons have caused and perpetuated the lack of universal implementation of specialized middle level teacher preparation and licensure. It is important that these roadblocks be recognized and planned for so that future efforts to establish and maintain specialized middle level teacher preparation and licensure can be highly successful. Some of the major barriers are: (a) the unavailability of specially prepared middle level teachers; (b) the negative stereotyped image of young adolescents; (c) the presence of too few advocates at teacher preparation institutions and state agencies; (d) the desire for flexibility in assignment of middle level teachers; (e) the public's lack of knowledge about appropriate middle level schooling; (f) the lack of program comprehensiveness; (g) teacher resistance to change; (h) problems, real or perceived, with other teacher preparation programs; and, (i) the limited number of instructors in teacher preparation programs with the depth of middle level knowledge and experience needed. These barriers should not discourage those advocating specialized middle level teacher preparation and licensure for they have been overcome in several states (McEwin & Dickinson, 1995, 1996).

❏ The status of middle level teacher preparation

Results from research studies investigating the extent of specialized middle level teacher preparation programs have shown that the number of these programs is increasing, but at a slow pace when compared with the growth of middle level schools (Alexander & McEwin, 1988; McEwin, 1992; McEwin & Dickinson, 1995). For the first time in history, however, the majority of teacher preparation programs in the nation offer specialized middle level teacher preparation programs. In the 1995/96 academic year, 51% of the nation's teacher preparation institutions reported offering specialized middle level programs at some degree level, with these programs ranging from major specializations to a series of special middle level courses and field experiences (McEwin, Dickinson, & Swaim, in press). This percentage compares with 34% in 1991 (McEwin & Dickinson, 1995).

❏ Essential program elements

A growing consensus regarding the need for the specialized professional preparation of middle level teachers and the licensure creates and supports that preparation (Carnegie Council on Adolescent Development, 1989; DeMedio & Mazur-Stewart, 1990; Jenkins & Jenkins, 1991; McEwin & Dickinson, 1996; National Middle School Association, 1991). A strong consensus also exists about the essential programmatic components that should be included in specialized middle level teacher preparation (Alexander & McEwin, 1988; Arth, Lounsbury, Swaim, & McEwin, 1995; Dickinson & Butler, 1994; Hart, Smith, Grynkewich, Primm, Mizell, Jackson, & Mahaffey, 1994; Lawton, 1993; McEwin & Dickinson, 1996; National Board for Professional Teaching Standards, 1994; National Middle School Association, 1996; Page, Page, Dickinson, Warkentin, Tibbles, 1992). The components listed below include only those that are unique and/or need special focus in middle level teacher preparation. They do not include other elements that are essential to any type of teacher preparation (e. g., diversity issues, effective use of instructional technology). They are: (a) a thorough study of early adolescence and the needs of young adolescents; (b) a comprehensive study of middle level philosophy and organization; (c) a thorough study of middle level curriculum; (d) an intensive focus on planning, teaching, and assessment using developmentally and culturally responsive practices; (e) early and continuing middle level field experiences in a variety of good middle level settings; (f) study and practice in the collaborative role of middle level teachers in working with colleagues, families, and community members; (g) preparation in two or more broad teaching fields; and, (h) a collaborative teacher preparation partnership between faculty at middle level schools and university-based middle level teacher educators that is responsible for all aspects of a site-based middle level teacher preparation program (McEwin & Dickinson, 1996).

It is important to recognize that these elements are not experimental in nature nor based solely on theory. They have been programmatic components of many highly successful middle level teacher preparation programs for many years (McEwin & Dickinson, 1995; Swaim & Stefanich, 1996). What is really needed is significant numbers of persons willing to take the steps necessary to make these specialized programs a universal reality in teacher preparation.

❏ Middle level licensure

A major reason that specialized middle level teacher preparation programs are not more prevalent is the lack of special mandatory licensure for middle level teachers. Approximately 33 states now have some type of specific middle level license, but requirements in many of these states are rendered largely ineffective by problems such as the overlapping of grade levels with elementary and/or secondary licenses (e. g., K-8, 6-12) (McEwin & Dickinson, 1995; Valentine & Mogar, 1992). This situation exists despite the fact that specialized middle level licensure directly influences the establishment of middle level teacher preparation programs and signifi-

225

cantly shapes their curriculum (McEwin & Scales, 1995). Stated another way, specialized middle level teacher preparation follows specialized middle level licensure requirements. This is an important lesson that should be learned by those making decisions about the nature of licensure requirements.

The majority of prospective and practicing middle level teachers are unlikely to pursue specialized middle level professional preparation if this commitment is not rewarded nor required to practice their profession (McEwin, Dickinson, Erb & Scales, 1995). Altruism alone is seldom sufficient motivation for middle level teachers to seek out specialized professional preparation when there is no recognition of their efforts to acquire specialized middle level knowledge and skills (Alexander & McEwin, 1988). Experience also clearly demonstrates that most teacher preparation institutions are unlikely to develop middle level teacher preparation programs when there is no specialized license required for middle level teaching (McEwin, Dickinson, Erb, & Scales, 1995).

❏ The expanding knowledge base on specialized middle level professional preparation

The knowledge base on middle level teacher preparation has expanded significantly in the past few years. For example, results from a national survey of 2,139 practicing middle level teachers revealed that specialized middle level teacher preparation is highly valued by middle level teachers. Teachers who were prepared in "mixed" professional preparation programs (e. g., elementary/middle/secondary) did not rate the quality of their preparation highly, while those who graduated from programs that focused specifically and extensively on middle level teaching rated their programs much more positively. Respondents were also more likely to have seven program components that are considered essential for successful middle level teacher preparation programs: young adolescent development, curriculum and organization of the middle school, middle level teaching methods, middle level reading, two academic concentrations, middle level field experiences, and middle level student teaching (Scales & McEwin, 1994).

Results from the study further revealed that the more middle level courses preservice teachers had taken, the more likely they were to report that their program was highly comprehensive, and that the greater the number of courses devoted to the middle level, the more favorably they rated their middle level teacher preparation programs on each of the topic investigated. A major finding from this study was that add-on courses and endorsements, while bureaucratic shortcuts, are a less effective form of preparation than a major comprehensive program (McEwin & Scales, 1995; Scales & McEwin, 1996).

A recent empirical research study also offers support for the importance of specialized middle level teacher preparation (Stahler, 1995). This study examined the knowledge base of two groups of middle level student teachers, one group with specialized middle level teacher preparation and the other with elementary (1-8) or secondary (7-12) rather than middle level preparation. Results showed specially prepared teachers made significantly more favorable scores on knowledge, planning, videotaped teaching performance, and attitude toward middle level teaching than generally prepared preservice teachers. Further, the specially prepared teachers possessed strong beliefs about the middle school movement and appropriate teaching for young adolescents. More studies of this nature are needed to strengthen the move to improve teaching and learning significantly in middle level schools through improving teacher preparation programs.

❏ Conclusion

Only when middle level licensure becomes universally required will young adolescents have some assurance of being taught by teachers who have the specialized knowledge, skills, and dispositions to be highly successful. Widespread consensus that spans several decades has been reached by teacher educators, middle level professional personnel, and other stakeholders regarding the importance of such programs. This consensus also includes other important issues including the programmatic components needed and other related factors.

History has taught a major lesson that needs to be recognized by all those responsible for the education and welfare of young adolescents and their teachers. Without distinctive, mandatory licensure requirements too many middle level classrooms will continue to be staffed by teachers who have no specialized preparation for their assignments. The false hope of "endorsements" which rely on prospective and practicing middle level teachers to "add a course or two" to elementary or secondary licenses and magically become successful teachers of young adolescents is a delusion.

Young adolescents are the ones who ultimately "pay the price" for the unwillingness of those responsible for their education to take courageous stands that will guarantee them access to teachers who have the specialized knowledge, skills, and dispositions to help them realize their full potentials. While stopping short of full mandatory middle level teacher preparation and licensure may make staffing and employment "easier," it clearly compromises the education and welfare of young adolescents. As noted by the authors, "A wide range of individuals and groups now realize that to neglect teachers of young adolescents is to neglect the education and welfare of young adolescents themselves. Efforts to improve one without the other would be misguided and unsuccessful" (McEwin & Dickinson, 1996, p. 39). ℝ

References

Alexander, W. M. & McEwin, C. K. (1988). *Preparing to teach at the middle level*. Columbus, OH: National Middle School Association.

Arth, A. A., Lounsbury, J. H., McEwin, C. K., & Swaim, J. H. (1995). *Middle level teachers: Portraits of excellence*. Columbus, OH: National Middle School Association, and National Association of Secondary School Principals.

Carnegie Council on Adolescent Development (1989). *Turning points: Preparing American youth for the 21st century*. New York: Carnegie Corporation.

DeMedio, D., & Mazur-Stewart, M. (1990). Attitudes toward middle grades certification: A national survey. *NASSP Bulletin, 74* (525), 64-71.

Dickinson, T. S., & Butler, D. (1994). The journey to the other side of the desk: The education of middle school teachers. In F. M. Smith & C. O. Hausafus (Eds.), *The education of early adolescents: Home economics in the middle school, Yearbook of the American Home Economics Association* (pp. 183-191). Peoria, IL: Macmillan/McGraw-Hill.

Douglas, A (1920). *The junior high school*. Bloomington, IL: National Study of Education.

Hart, L. E., Smith, D. W., Grynkewich, L. C., Primm, S., Mizelle, N. B., Jackson, D. F., & Mahaffey, M. L. (1994). *Principles of educating teachers: Middle grades mathematics and science*. Georgia Initiative in Mathematics and Science. Athens, GA: University of Georgia.

Jenkins, D. M., & Jenkins, K. D. (1991). The NMSA Delphi report: Roadmap to the future. *Middle School Journal, 22* (4), 27-36.

Lawton, E. (1993). *The effective middle level teacher*. Reston, VA: National Association of Secondary School Principals.

McEwin, C. K. (1992). Middle level teacher education and certification. In J. L. Irvin (Ed.), *Transforming middle level education: Perspectives and possibilities* (pp. 369-380). Boston: Allyn and Bacon.

McEwin, C. K., & Dickinson, T. S. (1995). *The professional preparation of middle level teachers: Profiles of successful programs*. Columbus, OH: National Middle School Association.

McEwin, C. K., & Dickinson, T. S. (1996). *Forgotten youth, forgotten teachers: Transformation of the professional preparation of teachers of young adolescents*. Middle Grade School State Policy Initiative, Carnegie Corporation of New York.

228

McEwin, C. K., Dickinson, T. S., Erb, T. O., & Scales, P. C. (1995). *A vision of excellence: Organizing principles for middle grades teacher preparation.* Columbus, OH: National Middle School Association.

McEwin, C. K., Dickinson, T. S., & Jenkins, D. M. (1996). *America's middle schools: Practices and progress — A 25 Year Perspective.* Columbus, OH: National Middle School Association.

McEwin, C. K., Dickinson, T. S., & Swaim, J. H. (in press). *Specialized middle level teacher preparation programs in the United States: A status report.* Boone, NC: Appalachian State University.

McEwin, C. K., & Scales, P. S. (1995). Middle school teachers' views of specialized professional preparation. *Quality Teaching, 5* (1), 6-7.

National Board for Professional Teaching Standards (1994). *Early adolescence/generalist standards for national board certification.* Washington, DC: Author

National Middle School Association (1991). *Professional certification and preparation for the middle level: A position paper of National Middle School Association.* Columbus, OH: Author.

National Middle School Association. (1996). *National Middle School Association/NCATE-Approved Teacher Preparation Curriculum Guidelines* Columbus, OH: Author.

Page, F., Page, J., Dickinson, T. S., Warkentin, R., &, Tibbles, A. (1992). 4000 voices. *Middle School Journal, 24* (1), Insert.

Scales, P. C. (1992). *Windows of opportunity: Improving middle grades teacher preparation.* Carrboro, NC: Center for Early Adolescence.

Scales, P. C., & McEwin, C. K. (1994). *Growing pains: The making of America's middle school teachers.* Columbus, OH: National Middle School Association.

Scales, P. C., & McEwin, C. K. (1996). The effects of comprehensive middle level teacher preparation programs. *Research in Middle Level Education Quarterly, 19* (2), 1-21.

Stahler, T. (1995). A comparative analysis of specifically prepared and generally prepared middle school preservice teachers. *Action in Teacher Education, 17* (3), 23-32.

Swaim, J. H., & Stefanich, G. P. (1996). *Meeting the standards: Middle level teacher education.* Columbus, OH: National Middle School Association.

Valentine, J. W., & Mogar, D. (1992). Middle level certification: An encouraging evolution. *Middle School Journal, 24* (2), 36-43.

Laurie E. Hart

Multicultural Issues in Middle Level Teacher Education

Middle level teacher education is a relatively new field with origins in the 1960s and 1970s movement to establish middle schools throughout the United States. The roots of middle level teacher education come mainly from concerns about the intellectual, physical, social, and emotional development of young adolescents. So much emphasis has been placed on these developmental needs of young adolescents that some other important characteristics of middle level students and teachers have received too little attention. A crucial area that needs more attention from middle level educators is the great and growing cultural diversity of the student population in schools at the same time the teaching force is becoming less diverse. Multicultural education can help middle level teacher educators better address issues of cultural diversity for both students and teachers. This can help improve teachers' understanding and ability to teach *all* students and, therefore, the quality of school experiences for young adolescents.

The purpose of this chapter is to examine the contributions research and theory on multicultural education can make to enhance middle level teacher education. In this chapter as I draw from scholarship on multicultural education, the intent is not to lessen the current emphasis on the nature of the young adolescent as a basis for designing middle level schools and middle level teacher education. Rather, the intent is to deepen our understanding of who young adolescents are and how best to help them learn by paying attention to their widely diverse cultural characteristics in addition to the great variability in their physical, intellectual, social, and emotional development.

❏ Multicultural education

A review of literature indicates that many different approaches to multicultural education have been proposed by authors (Banks, 1995). At the same time, however, there is a "developing consensus about the nature, aims, and scope" (Banks, 1995, p. 3) of multicultural education. One part of this consensus is agreement that "a major goal of multicultural education . . . is to reform the school and other educational institutions so that students from diverse racial, ethnic, and social-class groups will experience educational equality" (Banks, 1995, p. 3). Further, agreement exists that gender equity is a major goal of multicultural education (Banks, 1995). For the purposes of this chapter, multicultural education is defined as education to provide female and male students from diverse groups an equitable education of high quality to prepare them well for their present and future lives.

❏ Demographic characteristics of students, teachers, and teacher educators

The United States is a society of great cultural diversity. The composition of the school population in the United States is becoming more diverse while the teaching force is becoming less diverse (Banks, 1991). Teachers of color are underrepresented in the teaching force in general and particularly in mathematics and science, and the percentage of African American and Hispanic college students preparing to teach declined steadily from 1972 to 1987 (Darling-Hammond & Sclan, 1996). It is projected that in the year 2000, teachers of color will comprise only 5% of the United States teaching force and that "85% of the nation's teachers will . . . be white, mainstream, and largely female" (Banks, 1991, p. 136). This teaching force that is largely white and middle class will work with "students who differ from them racially, culturally, and in social class status" (Banks, 1991, p. 136). These contrasting profiles for teachers and students make it crucial for teacher education to both recruit more people of color into the teaching profession and help *all* teachers gain the knowledge, skills, and dispositions to work effectively with students from diverse racial, cultural, and social class groups (Banks, 1991; Boyer & Baptiste, 1996; Darling-Hammond, 1995; Ladson-Billings, 1995). The demographic profile of the teacher education professoriate makes it especially critical for teacher education to accomplish these important tasks. Approximately 93% of teacher educators are white, 3% are African American, 3% are Hispanic, and 1% are American Indians, Alaskan natives, and other people of color combined (American Association of Colleges for Teacher Education [AACTE],

1987). There is no indication that these figures have changed markedly in the last decade.

❑ Need for multicultural education

Ample evidence exists that the quality of education differs for students of differing race, ethnicity, and social class in the United States (e.g., Larkin & Sleeter, 1995; Rios, 1993). African American, Hispanic American, and Native American students score lower on standardized tests and drop out of school at higher rates than European American students (e.g., Garcia, 1995; Lomawaima, 1995; Snipp, 1995). According to Darling-Hammond (1995):

> *As a consequence of structural inequalities in access to knowledge and resources, students from racial and ethnic 'minority' groups in the United States face persistent and profound barriers to educational opportunity....Documentation of and serious policy attention to these ongoing systematic inequalities are critical for improving the quality and outcomes of education for all students. Without acknowledgment that students experience very different educational realities, policies will continue to be based on the presumption that it is students, not their schools or classroom circumstances, that are the sources of unequal educational attainment. — p. 465*

Changes in teacher education are needed to meet the challenges of unequal educational opportunities and differing cultural backgrounds of teachers and students. Too often we assume that teachers will learn strategies to work with students from diverse cultural backgrounds without receiving specific, careful instruction. Often prospective teachers assume that they will teach in middle level schools like they attended when they were students and that their students will come from backgrounds similar to their own. What is most likely is that in the course of their careers, the majority of teachers will work with students who are from different racial and social class backgrounds than their own. Further, the typical race and social class backgrounds of teacher educators make it unlikely that adequate knowledge, skills, and dispositions for working with students from diverse cultural groups will be provided in teacher education programs unless multicultural issues become a specific focus.

❑ NCATE and multicultural education

The National Council for Accreditation of Teacher Education

(NCATE) is responsible for setting standards for teacher education programs in the United States. Since 1979, NCATE has required institutions applying for accreditation to "show evidence of planning for multicultural education in their curricula" (Gollnick, 1991, p. 226). NCATE has steadily expanded the requirements for multicultural education over the past 15 years (Gollnick, 1995). The 1992 NCATE standards included the following requirements:

- *The initial teacher preparation program must provide knowledge about and appropriate skills in...cultural influences on learning....Courses and experiences ensure the development of ...[and] knowledge of different learning styles.*

- *The unit [i.e., the school, college, or department of education] provides for study and experiences that help education students understand and apply appropriate strategies for individual learning needs, especially for culturally diverse ....populations.*

- *The curriculum for professional studies component(s) incorporates multicultural and global perspectives.* —p. 50

Further, the 1992 NCATE standards require that "education students participate in field-based and/or clinical experiences with culturally diverse and exceptional populations" (p. 51) and that both the student body and faculty in teacher eduction programs be culturally diverse. The National Middle School Association/NCATE-Approved Teacher Education Curriculum Guidelines do not directly address multicultural issues since institutions submitting their middle level teacher preparation programs for review by NMSA must also meet the above NCATE multicultural standards.

❏ Middle level teacher education and multicultural education

There is a growing acknowledgment among middle level educators of the importance of multicultural education. In a major review of literature on middle level teacher education, Williamson (1996) included a discussion of multicultural education. He encouraged us to view multicultural education not "as the study of others, but as the study of us" (p. 388). Williamson concluded that as the student population becomes increasingly diverse, "the role of all schools is to accept those students, to work with them and their families in order to address their needs, and to ensure that all students are provided with the knowledge and skills to be successful contributing members of society" (Williamson, 1996, p. 388).

In addition, the work of Beane (1993) on middle school curriculum has emphasized the importance of not only curriculum integration and students' involvement in curriculum decisions but also issues of equity and social justice in education. In California, a strong example of a middle level teacher education program that integrates multicultural education into initial teacher preparation can be found at California State University San Marcos (McDaniel, Stowell, Rios, & Christopher, 1994; Stowell, McDaniel, & Rios, 1995). CSU San Marcos is a new university located in North San Diego County; its middle level teacher education program was developed by a group of five university and seven public school faculty members during the 1991-1992 academic year. The CSU San Marcos middle level program models curriculum integration in each of the two semesters of the post-baccalaureate program. Multicultural education is a theme that runs throughout the program. In the second semester a course on multicultural education is integrated throughout course and field work for prospective teachers. Stowell, McDaniel, and Rios (1995) provided a detailed description of the program's thematic units, including sample topics and activities and the major theoretical foundations on which the program is based.

❏ Effective multicultural teacher education

Ladson-Billings (1995) and Zeichner (1992) described key elements of effective multicultural teacher education. These elements include procedures for admission to teacher education programs, exploration of prospective teachers' attitudes and identities concerning their own and other ethnic and cultural groups, topics and instructional strategies to include in teacher education courses, and design of field experiences in communities and schools. One aspect of an effective multicultural teacher education program is helping prospective teachers develop a clearer conception of their own ethnic and cultural identities. This can be important in understanding the cultural perspective of others. Multicultural education for prospective and practicing teachers must help teachers understand the histories and contributions of various cultural groups, the characteristics and learning styles of various groups and individuals, and ways to identify and deal with prejudice, racism, and sexism in the classroom. In addition, multicultural teacher education should help teachers learn about the specific communities from which their students come. This information helps teachers gain a clearer understanding of who their students are and improve their ability to communicate successfully with both students and families. Effective multicultural teacher education helps teachers understand the relationship between particular teaching methods and the preferred interaction and learning styles students may be familiar with at home and in their communities. Further, it is important for teacher education to include teaching strategies and assessment techniques that are sensitive to students' cultural and linguistic characteristics and methods of instruction and assessment that can be adapted to build upon students' cultural resources.

The elements of field experiences Ladson-Billings (1995) and Zeichner (1992) presented are essential to effective multicultural teacher education. They advocate:

> ...*exposure [of prospective teachers] to examples of successful teaching of ethnic- and language-minority students, opportunities [to] complete community field experiences with adults and/ or children of other ethnocultural groups with guided reflections, and opportunities for practicum and/or student teaching experiences in schools serving ethnic- and language-minority students.* — p. 753

Field experiences in diverse classroom settings are crucial. However, some studies indicate that experiences of white middle class prospective teachers in diverse field experiences can reinforce the teachers' initial negative preconceptions about poor students and students or color (Ladson-Billings, 1995). Careful selection of field placements, good quality supervision, and opportunities for debriefings and guided reflections can help prevent such reinforcement of prospective teachers' initial prejudices.

❏ Multicultural teacher education strategies

Many approaches to multicultural education can be found in the literature that are appropriate for middle level teacher education even though they have not been used exclusively in middle level schools. Several approaches to multicultural teacher education are described in the book edited by Larkin and Sleeter (1995). For example, Sleeter (1995) described assignments and activities she has used with European American prospective teachers to help them understand the significance of culture in teaching. Another book (Ladson-Billings, 1994) described the instruction of several teachers who have been successful teachers of African American children. An excellent approach to improving education through multicultural processes is presented by Jacob (1995). She described a process to help teachers use concepts from anthropology to examine their own practice and to identify and solve problems where particular teaching practices may have inhibited the learning or performance of students.

Two programs developed at the Lawrence Hall of Science at the University of California, Berkeley are excellent for mathematics multicultural education: EQUALS is designed to help teachers, counselors, and administrators encourage girls and students of color to participate in mathematics courses and activities (Kreinberg, 1989) and Family Math helps increase mathematics participation through programs in which parents and children learn mathematics together (Kreinberg, 1989; Stenmark, Thompson, & Cossey, 1986). Clewell, Anderson, and Thorpe (1992) described many programs to help female and minority students succeed in mathematics and science. In reading, the Kamehameha Early Education Program (KEEP) was designed to improve the reading achievement of native Hawaiian children (Au & Jordan, 1981; D'Amato, 1993). These are a small fraction of the many strategies that have been published to improve education for classrooms with diverse cultural groups.

❏ Conclusion

Many middle level teacher preparation programs come from what Zeichner and Liston (1990) termed a *developmentalist* tradition of teacher education practice, stressing instruction based on teachers' understanding of their students, the students' developmental readiness, and the content under study. A potential weakness of teacher education programs that fit within a developmentalist tradition is that too little attention may be directed at issues of equity and justice. In this time of increasing ethnic, racial, and economic diversity in the nation as a whole, middle level teacher education can ill afford to assume that the current level of attention to multicultural issues in teacher education programs is sufficient. Although many teachers and teacher educators within middle level education have worked to create equal educational opportunities for all students, much more must be done. A large and quickly growing base of research and theory from multicultural education can help us continue our quest to improve the education of young adolescents. ℝ

References

American Association of Colleges for Teacher Education (AACTE). (1987). *Teaching teachers: Facts and figures*. Washington, DC: Author.

Au, K. H., & Jordan, C. (1981). Teaching reading to Hawaiian children: Finding a culturally appropriate solution. In H. Trueba, G. P. Guthrie, & K. H. Au (Eds.), *Culture and the bilingual classroom* (pp. 139-152). Rowley, MA: Newberry House.

Banks, J. A. (1991). Teaching multicultural literacy to teachers. *Teaching Education, 4* (1), 135-144.

Banks, J. A. (1995). Multicultural education: Historical development, dimensions, and practice. In J. A. Banks & C. A. M. Banks (Eds.), *Handbook of research on multicultural education* (pp. 3-24). New York: Macmillan.

Beane, J. (1993). *A middle school curriculum: From rhetoric to reality* (2nd ed.). Columbus, OH: National Middle School Association.

Boyer, J. B., & Baptiste, H. P., Jr. (1996). The crisis in teacher education in America: Issues of recruitment and retention of culturally different (minority) teachers). In J. Sikula, T. J. Buttery, & E. Guyton (Eds.), *Handbook of research on teacher education* (2nd ed., pp. 779-794). New York: Macmillan.

Clewell, B. C., Anderson, B. T., & Thorpe, M. E. (1992). *Breaking the barriers: Helping female and minority students succeed in mathematics and science.* San Francisco, CA: Jossey-Bass.

D'Amato, J. (1993). Resistance and compliance in minority classrooms. In E. Jacob & C. Jordan (Eds.), *Minority education: Anthropological perspectives* (pp. 181-207). Norwood, NJ: Ablex.

Darling-Hammond, L. (1995). Inequality and access to knowledge. In J. A. Banks & C. A. M. Banks (Eds.), *Handbook of research on multicultural education* (pp. 465-483). New York: Macmillan.

Darling-Hammond, L., & Sclan, E. M. (1996). Who teaches and why: Dilemmas of building a profession for twenty-first century schools. In J. Sikula, T. J. Buttery, & E. Guyton (Eds.), *Handbook of research on teacher education* (2nd ed., pp. 67-101). New York: Macmillan.

Garcia, E. E. (1995). Educating Mexican American students: Past treatment and recent developments in theory, research, policy, and practice. In J. A. Banks & C. A. M. Banks (Eds.), *Handbook of research on multicultural education* (pp. 372-387). New York: Macmillan.

Gollnick, D. (1991). Multicultural education: Policies and practices in teacher education. In C. Grant (Ed.), *Research and multicultural education: From the margins to the mainstream* (pp. 218-239). London: Falmer Press.

Gollnick, D. M. (1995). National and state initiatives for multicultural education. In J. A. Banks & C. A. M. Banks (Eds.), *Handbook of research on multicultural education* (pp. 44-64). New York: Macmillan.

Jacob, E. (1995). Reflective practice and anthropology in culturally diverse classrooms. *Elementary School Journal, 95* (5), 451-463.

Kreinberg, N. (1989). The practice of equity. *Peabody Journal of Education, 66* (2), 127-146.

Ladson-Billings, G. (1994). *The dreamkeepers: Successful teachers of African American children*. San Francisco: Jossey-Bass.

Ladson-Billings, G. (1995). Multicultural teacher education: Research, practice, and policy. In J. A. Banks & C. A. M. Banks (Eds.), *Handbook of research on multicultural education* (pp. 747-759). New York: Macmillan.

Larkin, J. M., & Sleeter, C. E. (1995). Introduction. In J. M. Larkin & C. E. Sleeter (Eds.), *Developing multicultural teacher education curricula* (pp. 1-16). Albany: State University of New York Press.

Lomawaima, K. T. (1995). Educating Native Americans. In J. A. Banks & C. A. M. Banks (Eds.), *Handbook of research on multicultural education* (pp. 331-347). New York: Macmillan.

McDaniel, J. E., Stowell, L. P., Rios, F. A., & Christopher, P. A. (1994). Do as we do and as we say: Modeling curriculum integration in teacher education. *Middle School Journal, 26* (2), 14-20.

National Council for Accreditation of Teacher Education (NCATE). (1992). *Standards, procedures, and policies for the accreditation of professional education units*. Washington, DC: Author.

Rios, F. A. (1993). Thinking in urban, multicultural classrooms: Four teachers' perspectives. *Urban Education, 28* (3), 245-266.

Sleeter, C. E. (1995). White preservice students and multicultural education coursework. In J. M. Larkin & C. E. Sleeter (Eds.), *Developing multicultural teacher education curricula* (pp. 17-29). Albany, NY: State University of New York Press.

Snipp, C. M. (1995). American Indian studies. In J. A. Banks & C. A. M. Banks (Eds.), *Handbook of research on multicultural education* (pp. 245-258). New York: Macmillan.

Stenmark, J. K., Thompson, V., & Cossey, R. (1986). *Family math*. Berkeley, CA: Lawrence Hall of Science, University of California.

Stowell, L. P., McDaniel, J. E., & Rios, F. A. (1995). Fostering change for democratic middle schools through teacher education. *Middle School Journal, 26* (5), 3-10.

Williamson, R. D. (1996). Middle level education. In J. Sikula, T. J. Buttery, & E. Guyton (Eds.), *Handbook of research on teacher education* (2nd ed., pp. 378-391). New York: Macmillan.

Zeichner, K. (1992). *Educating teachers for cultural diversity* (Special Report). East Lansing, MI: National Center for Research on Teacher Learning.

Zeichner, K., & Liston, D. (1990). Traditions of reform in U.S. teacher education. *Journal of Teacher Education, 41* (2), 3-20.

Social Context

Mac Iver Douglas J. Mac Iver
The Johns Hopkins University
Baltimore, Maryland

Plank Stephen B. Plank
The Johns Hopkins University
Baltimore, Maryland

Schine Joan Schine
City University of New York
New York, New York

Brough Judith A. Brough
Gettysburg College
Gettysburg, Pennsylvania

Douglas J. Mac Iver and Stephen B. Plank

Improving Urban Schools: Developing the Talents of Students Placed at Risk

Many of America's urban middle school students have been placed at risk of falling far short of their academic potential. Among the most often-cited factors that place youth in danger of school failure are poverty, unstable or abusive home situations, peers and role models who provide anti-academic or antisocial pathways, feelings of distrust or alienation toward school personnel, limited English skills, and mismatches between students' developmental needs and the services, curriculum, and instruction provided by schools. The presence of even one serious risk factor jeopardizes a child's likelihood of persisting and succeeding in school, and as risk factors become multiple so do the threats to academic success.

Whether one considers students placed at risk or those enjoying more advantaged and supportive environments, all middle school students exhibit some common traits and needs during the tumultuous developmental stage of early adolescence. Young adolescents have definite physical, social, cognitive, and emotional needs as they begin their initiation into adulthood (Irvin, 1992). Bodies are changing rapidly and dramatically, often threatening individuals' feelings of self-esteem (Wavering, 1995). The desire for peer interaction and peer acceptance is great as individuals are forming identifies and ideas about appropriate attitudes and behaviors (Spear, 1992). The transition from purely concrete thinking to abstract and reflective reasoning is taking place but will be strong and smooth only with nurturance and guidance (Irvin, 1992; Spear, 1992). Feelings of confidence, optimism, and motivation can emerge in certain settings, but uncertainty, pessimism, and resignation can emerge in other circumstances (Davies, 1995; Thomason and Thompson, 1992).

243

Although these physical, social, cognitive, and emotional traits and needs characterize all young adolescents, some are especially salient for students placed at risk, and schools can play especially important roles in helping at-risk students navigate the turbulent waters of early adolescence. The scarcity of (1) resources, (2) positive role models, (3) high-quality learning opportunities, and (4) guidance and emotional support that often characterizes the lives of at-risk students increases the danger that these young people will have great troubles as they encounter the challenges and self-doubt of the adolescent years. If left unaided, their troubles can become so great that these individuals never develop (1) proficiency in reading, writing, mathematics, and science, (2) confidence to explore and to take intellectual or social risks, (3) motivation to work hard for success, (4) feelings of worth and efficacy, and (5) aspirations and expectations for long-term educational, occupational, and personal accomplishment. By offering the proper educational and guidance opportunities and communally organized learning environments, middle schools can do much to prevent this tragic sequence. Schools cannot remove all of the obstacles and uncertainty of adolescence. They cannot ameliorate all of the societal and personal factors that place so many children at risk. But they can provide appropriate learning opportunities and school organization, as well as systematic and pervasive guidance, nurturance, and support to help students through these challenges and uncertainties.

As researchers and practitioners have come to understand the unique traits and needs of middle school students more fully, they have also attempted to customize school organization, curriculum, and pedagogy to suit students' traits and needs. In the remainder of this chapter, we describe some of these aspects of organization, curriculum, and pedagogy, explaining the ways in which they are responsive to the needs of urban middle school students. We then describe our own efforts in incorporating these aspects into a model which we call the Talent Development Middle School. Finally, we highlight some of the early findings of the Talent Development Middle School's effects on student motivation and achievement.

❏ Promising Practices for Urban Middle Schools: ❏ School Organization, Curriculum, and Pedagogy

The 1990s have been filled with promising efforts aimed at nurturing and educating middle school students that are of particular relevance to urban schools serving large numbers of students placed at risk. A first set of efforts includes the development and use of cooperative learning methods that embed peer tutoring into the daily routine of classroom life and that create positive peer pressure and peer support for achievement. A second set includes detracking and an awareness of the course sequences and gateways that historically have been somewhat covert but highly influential in sorting students and determining future opportunities. A third set includes semi-departmentalization and interdisciplinary teams of teachers. While the world of educational theory and practice is filled with fads, it seems likely that these three sets of efforts will display some real effectiveness and staying power because they·are firmly rooted in an increasingly nuanced understanding of the psychology and sociology of urban education.

❏ Cooperative learning

Cooperative learning refers to a variety of teaching methods in which students work in small groups to help each other master subject matter content and skills. Effective cooperative learning methods incorporate group goals and individual accountability (Cohen, 1994; Slavin, 1995). In contrast to traditional pedagogy in which only the teacher supervises and instructs, cooperative learning involves a shifting of authority from the teacher to the students, who become largely responsible for their teammates' effort and understanding during team study periods. The methods are responsive to the needs of middle school students, as they allow for peer interaction and offer opportunities for self-direction and autonomy. These methods shift the focus of the inevitable peer pressures and interpersonal comparisons of adolescence in positive directions which support effort and academic achievement.

Cooperative learning methods that incorporate group goals and individual accountability consistently increase student achievement and self-esteem, and they improve intergroup relations, acceptance of traditionally low status students, and peer support for achievement (Mac Iver & Reuman, 1993; Slavin, 1995). As researchers have begun to examine the conditions under which cooperative learning works best, it has been shown that the effectiveness of cooperative learning is related to the time and effort dedicated to preparing students for the cooperative experience and for their roles as peer tutors to the other members of their teams. Although middle school students usually respond favorably to opportunities to interact with peers during learning activities, they often lack social skills and strategies for resolving conflicts, staying on task, and involving all teammates (Williams, Harris, & Hayakawa, 1995). To realize the greatest possible benefits of cooperative learning, it is important to work explicitly with students in

developing skills for basic communication, conflict resolution, peer tutoring, and task completion (Fuchs, Fuchs, Bentz, Phillips, & Hamlett, 1994;
Meloth & Deering, 1994; Webb & Farivar, 1994).

❏ Detracking and an awareness of course sequences and gateways

Tracking refers to the practice of assigning students to instructional
groups or course sequences on the basis of prior achievement or perceived
ability. Several decades of research have documented the prevalence of
tracking in American middle and high schools, and have investigated both
the determinants of track placements and the effects of tracking. As Hallinan
(1994a) summarized, a combination of survey research and case studies
support the following conclusions about tracking:

1. In practice, track placements are usually based not only on academic
   considerations (such as grades, test scores, teachers' and counselors'
   recommendations, and course prerequisites) but also on nonacademic
   considerations (such as course conflicts, extracurricular schedules,
   and teacher and curricular resources). As a result, track levels are rarely
   homogeneous with respect to achievement and the distribution of
   achievement in any one track overlaps considerably with the distribution in adjacent tracks.

2. Schools vary in the set of factors which guide track placements. Thus,
   track assignments depend, in part, on the schools that students attend.

3. A greater proportion of minority and low-income students are assigned
   to the lower tracks, as compared to white and higher-income students.
   When academic achievement is controlled, these tendencies decrease,
   but do not disappear.

4. Quality and quantity of instruction increases with the level of the track,
   resulting in gross inequalities in students' access to knowledge, instructional resources, and well-qualified teaching.

5. Students in higher tracks learn more and at a faster pace than do those
   in lower tracks.

6. Tracking provides no learning advantages over heterogeneous grouping for students in the middle of the achievement range.

The cumulative body of research is fairly unified in stating that tracking as it usually has been implemented is inequitable, and harmful at least
to students placed in the lowest tracks. Related research has shown that
opportunities for taking some key courses during middle school - such as
eighth grade algebra - have strong consequences for enrollment opportunities and trajectories in high school and beyond (Catsambis, 1994; Dauber,

Alexander, & Entwisle, 1996; Stevenson, Schiller, & Schneider, 1994). In general, the past decade has brought a greater awareness among researchers and educators about how certain middle school courses and course sequences function as gateways for students' future opportunities.

Opinions differ regarding whether an appropriate solution is to alter and fine-tune the way tracking is practiced (Gamoran, 1993; Gamoran, Nystrand, Berends, and LePore, 1995; Hallinan, 1994a, 1994b) or to abandon the practice completely by detracking schools, thereby organizing students into classrooms that are heterogeneous with regard to prior achievement and other characteristics which have generally been associated with tracking (Oakes, 1994a, 1994b). A moral argument can be made for detracking if one views separate as inherently unequal and if one believes that all students deserve exposure to the same high quality curriculum, instruction, and opportunities to learn.

❏ Semi-departmentalization and interdisciplinary teams of teachers

Middle school research and reform efforts have generated increasing excitement about the potential benefits of semi-departmentalization and interdisciplinary teaming. Efforts in these directions aim to change middle school organizational structures fundamentally, just as detracking efforts do. Semi-departmentalization is a faculty organization in which most teachers reduce their student load by 60% or 50% by teaching two or three subject areas during the course of a school day rather than specializing in just one "department." Interdisciplinary teaming is the assignment of common students and planning time to two or more teachers who teach different subjects so that they can coordinate content, schedules, special events, and parent conferences.

Semi-departmentalization. By seventh grade, most students in the U.S. are taught each of their academic subjects by a different (usually secondary-certified) specialist in that subject (Epstein & Mac Iver, 1990). As a result, most teachers of seventh graders instruct five different sections of students every day. Unfortunately, when students have a different teacher for each of their academic subjects and when teachers are responsible for five different sections of students, teacher-student relations suffer compared to the closer and more positive relations found in schools with semi-departmentalized staffing (McPartland, 1987, 1990, 1992). The reason for this negative impact of departmentalization is clear. Compared to teachers who teach only two or three different sections of students, teachers who teach five different sections of students cannot easily maintain close personal contacts with, and detailed knowledge of, each student. The heavy load of students in departmentalized schools makes it less likely that teachers:

> *...will come to know their students well, to feel that they are trustworthy, and to grant them autonomy ... [In departmentalized settings], teachers may feel that it is difficult to affect the achievement of a large number of students, especially since they see them for a relatively small proportion of the school day, making it difficult to sustain feelings of efficacy.*
>
> — Eccles & Midgley, 1988, p.13; see also Eccles, Midgley,
> Wigfield, Buchanan, Reuman, Flanagan, & Mac Iver, 1993

Departmentalization and its concomitants may be partly responsible for the consistent finding that middle level teachers' attitudes and beliefs are typically more negative than those held by upper elementary level teachers (Eccles & Midgley, 1989; Eccles, Midgley, & Adler, 1984). For example, Midgley, Feldlaufer, and Eccles (1989) compared the beliefs of the teachers that students had for mathematics the year before and the year after the transition to junior high school. The junior high teachers rated students as less trustworthy than did the elementary teachers. Similarly, the junior high teachers believed that students needed to be controlled and disciplined more strictly than did the elementary teachers. Finally, the junior high teachers felt significantly less efficacious than did the elementary school teachers. For example, they were less likely to endorse items such as " I am certain I am making a difference in the lives of my students" (Midgley, Feldlaufer, & Eccles, 1989).

The classroom climate in departmentalized schools is affected by the increased negativity of teachers' beliefs and attitudes. When students enter a departmentalized middle level school, both students and classroom observers perceive the teachers to be less supportive, friendly, and fair than the elementary school teachers that the students had just a year earlier (Feldlaufer, Midgley, & Eccles, 1988).

On the other hand, because departmentalized staffing permits teachers to concentrate their energies on one subject, they are better able to focus on creating outstanding learning experiences and keeping up with the latest approaches in that subject area. This may result in higher quality instruction in departmentalized schools. In turn, the increases in instructional quality that accompany departmentalization may lead to increases in student achievement unless the positive impact of departmentalization on instructional quality is outweighed by the negative effects of departmentalization on teacher-student relations and on other factors that influence student motivation and achievement.

The positive effects of departmentalization on student achievement have been more persuasively documented (using the National Assessment of Educational Progress and the national NELS:88 survey) for seventh- and eighth-graders and for middle-class and upper-class students than for sixth-graders and economically-disadvantaged students (McPartland, 1987, 1990, 1992). In fact, data on sixth-graders from the Pennsylvania Educational Quality Assessment (EQA) and from eighth-graders in the lowest SES quartile of NELS:88 demonstrates that a departmentalized structure is not always associated with higher student achievement (Becker, 1987; McPartland, 1987, 1992). For example, although McPartland found that sixth-graders' perceptions of the quality of instruction in science and social studies were higher when departmentalization was used, there was a negative relation between the degree of departmentalization and the students' average test scores in science and social studies (McPartland, 1987). Becker's (1987) analyses of the EQA data suggested that the achievement of most sixth-grade students in most subjects is greater when they have fewer teachers (less departmentalization). He found that the detrimental effects of departmentalization on achievement are strongest for students from low and low-middle social backgrounds. Similarly, McPartland (1992) found no evidence of a significant positive impact of departmentalization on the achievement of eighth-graders from the lowest SES quartile in the NELS:88 sample.

Interdisciplinary teams of teachers. Proponents of the middle school philosophy have long advocated organizing teachers into interdisciplinary teams. Alexander and George (1981) defined an interdisciplinary team organization as "a way of organizing the faculty so that a group of teachers share (1) the responsibility for planning, teaching, and evaluating curriculum and instruction in more than one academic area; (2) the same group of students; (3) the same schedule; and (4) the same area of the building" (p. 115). An interdisciplinary team organization is hypothesized to increase the student orientation of teachers: "Teachers talk about what they have in common, and when the teachers share the same students rather than the same academic discipline, the students are at the center of discussion and program planning" (p. 133). Because they teach the same group of students, team members can share student information and develop common strategies for meeting individual student needs or for dealing with problems. Furthermore, they can prepare for and conduct parent conferences as a team.

Interdisciplinary teaming has been shown to increase students' feelings of attachment to teachers, peers, and the school and to partially ameliorate the negative effects of departmentalization and heavy student loads on student-teacher relations (Arhar, 1992; Arhar & Kromrey, 1995, McPartland, 1992). Finally, data from a national sample of middle level schools indicate that when a school implements interdisciplinary teaming, teachers gain social support and understanding from their team members and students' problems are more quickly identified and resolved (Mac Iver & Epstein, 1991) .

❏ The Talent Development Middle School ❏

We, the authors of this chapter, are involved in a school improvement effort and research project which incorporates cooperative learning, detracking, interdisciplinary teaming, and semi-departmentalization into middle school education. The project is called the Talent Development Middle School. The first site is being operated and evaluated at Central East Middle School in Philadelphia. All efforts in the Talent Development Middle School are guided by a belief that all students can learn challenging academic material if the right types of support are given (Madhere & Mac Iver, 1996).

Nine fundamental components define Talent Development Middle Schools. 1) A demanding standards-based core curriculum aimed at active student learning is provided for all students in heterogeneously-grouped classes. 2) Opportunities for extra help and enrichment are expanded through the use of cooperative learning and "extra dose" elective classes in mathematics and reading. 3) A communal organization of the school is established that includes semi-departmentalization, two- or three-person interdisciplinary teams, and small learning communities that endure for two or three years. 4) Students are assisted every year in setting goals, planning for the future, and systematically exploring educational and career options through a Career Exploration and Educational Decision-Making course that meets weekly. 5) An intensive transition program (involving eighth graders as "older partners") ensures a good start for students who are new to the school. 6) Growth-oriented evaluation practices are used that recognize individual improvement and progress towards high standards in addition to giving students realistic, unambiguous feedback concerning how their performance compares to national norms and performance standards. 7)

Students are assisted with personal problems and concerns such as substance abuse, teenage parenthood, home difficulties, or poor attendance habits by integrating professional services at the school and through coordinated efforts by each student's small learning community. 8) School-family-community partnerships are established. 9) Instruction is attentive to cultural patterns and norms, promotes cultural literacy, and helps students connect to and interpret cultural traditions.

Cooperative learning is central to the way academic subjects and career exploration are taught in Talent Development schools. And within the cooperative learning activities, there is a focus on higher order competencies, attention to literature and lessons from a wide range of cultures, an attempt to generate strong and achievement-oriented norms and bonds, and evaluation that rewards progress as well as excellence. A detracked demanding curriculum is made to work well for all students by the expanded opportunities for extra help and enrichment. Finally, the use of interdisciplinary teams, semi-departmentalization, and multi-year small learning communities creates a communal organization within the school which supports strong teacher-student bonds and addresses adolescents' needs for affiliation.

❏ Early Findings From (and the Ongoing Evaluation of) ❏ the Talent Development Middle School Initiative

The effects of implementing the nine Talent Development Middle School components are being carefully evaluated at Central East Middle School by comparing student outcomes there to those obtained in a closely matched control school. Similar evaluations will be conducted at other schools when they fully implement the Talent Development Middle School model . Early implementation and outcome data have already been collected to examine the beginning effects of the Talent Development Reading\English\Language Arts (RELA) program at Central East. In this program, there is a total detracking of instruction, and Student Team Reading (STR) is used in RELA to focus the curriculum and instruction on excellent novels, many of which are award winners (e.g., Newberry, American Book Award, Coretta Scott King, American Library Association). Student Team Reading changes both the instructional processes and the curriculum in RELA to create a motivational climate that is conducive to high achievement. Similarly, Student Team Writing is used in the Talent Development Program to get students to write often and to work cooperatively when planning, revising, and editing their writing as they learn to give feedback to one another and use feedback that has been given. Large-scale middle school studies (Stevens & Durkin, 1992) found that Student Team Reading and Student Team Writing programs significantly improved the achievement of urban middle school students on standardized tests of reading comprehension, reading vocabulary, and language expression.

Our initial implementation data from February, 1996 indicated that the teachers at Central East Middle School are well on their way to a strong implementation of Student Team Reading. Further, our February 1996 assessment of motivational outcomes indicates that STR implementation has produced RELA classrooms where peer support for achievement is high, where student-teacher relations are positive, where students give their best and work hard to master the content and meet adults' standards, and where students are confident both in their ability to learn and in the future utility of what they are learning (Mac Iver & Plank, 1996). We have also found strong positive effects of STR at Central East on student achievement (Mac Iver, Plank, & Balfanz, 1997), and evaluations of the extra help (Mac Iver, Balfanz, & Plank, 1997); and career exploration (Mac Iver & Plank, 1997) components of the Talent Development model have also yielded encouraging initial findings. ⓡ

References

Alexander, W., & George, P. (1981). *The exemplary middle school*. New York, Wiley.

Arhar, J.M. (1992). Interdisciplinary teaming and the social bonding of middle level students. In J.L. Irvin (Ed.), *Transforming Middle Level Education: Perspectives and Possibilities* (pp. 139-161). Boston: Allyn and Bacon.

Arhar, J.M., & Kromrey, J.D. (1995). Interdisciplinary teaming and the demographics of membership: A comparison of student belonging in high SES and low SES middle level schools. *Research in Middle Level Education 18* (2), 71-88.

Becker, H. (1987). *Addressing the needs of different groups of young adolescents: Effects of varying school and classroom organizational practices on students from different social backgrounds and abilities*. (CREMS Report No. 16). Baltimore, MD: Johns Hopkins University, Center for Research on Elementary and Middle Schools. (Available from Publications Dept., Attn: Diane Diggs, CREMS, Johns Hopkins University, 3505 N. Charles Street, Baltimore, MD 21218).

Catsambis, S. (1994). The path to math: Gender and racial-ethnic differences in mathematics participation from middle school to high school, *Sociology of Education 67* (3), 199-215.

Cohen, E.G. (1994). *Designing groupwork: Strategies for the heterogeneous classroom* (Second Edition). New York: Teachers College Press.

Dauber, S.L., Alexander, K.L., & Entwisle, D.R. (1996). Tracking and transitions through the middle grades: Channeling educational trajectories. *Sociology of Education, 69* (4), 290-307.

Davies, M.A. (1995). Age-appropriate teaching strategies. In M.J. Wavering (Ed.), *Educating young adolescents: Life in the middle* (pp. 307-352). New York, Garland Publishing.

Eccles, J. S., & Midgley, C. (1988). *Understanding motivation: A developmental approach to person-environment fit. Unpublished maunuscript.* (Available from Jacquelynne Eccles, 5271 Institute for Social Rescarch, PO Box 1248, Ann Arbor, MI 48106-1248.)

Eccles, J. S., & Midgley, C. (1989). Stage/environment fit: Developmentally appropriate classrooms for young adolescents. In R. E. Ames & C. Ames (Eds.), *Research on motivation in education* (Vol. 3, pp. 139-186). San Diego, CA: Academic Press.

Eccles, J. S., Midgley, C., & Adler, T. (1984). Grade-related changes in the school environment: Effects on achievement motivation. In J. G. Nicholls (Ed.), *The development of achievement motivation* (pp. 283-331). Greenwich, CT: JAI Press.

Eccles, J. S., Midgley, C., Wigfield, A., Buchanan, C.M., Reuman, D., Flanagan, C., & Mac Iver, D. (1993). Development during adolescence: The impact of stage-environment fit on young adolescents' experiences in schools and in families. *American Psychologist, 48* (2), 90-101.

Epstein, J. L., & Mac Iver, D. J. (1990). *Education in the middle grades: National practices and trends.* Columbus, OH: National Middle School Association.

Feldlaufer, H., Midgley, C., & Eccles, J. S. (1988). Student, teacher, and observer perceptions of the classroom environment before and after the transition to junior high school. *Journal of Early Adolescence, 8* (2), 133-156.

Fuchs, L.S., Fuchs, D., Bentz, J., Phillips, N.B., & Hamlett, C.L. (1994). The nature of student interactions during peer tutoring with and without prior training and experience, *American Educational Research Journal, 31* (1), 75-103.

Gamoran, A. (1993). Alternative uses of ability grouping in secondary schools: Can we bring high-quality instruction to low-ability classes? *American Journal of Education, 102* (1), 1-22.

Gamoran, A., Nystrand, M., Berends, M., & LePore, P.C. (1995). An organizational analysis of the effects of ability grouping. *American Educational Research Journal, 32* (4), 687-715.

Hallinan, M.T. (1994a). Tracking: From theory to practice. *Sociology of Education, 67* (2), 79-84.

Hallinan, M.T. (1994b). Further thoughts on tracking, *Sociology of Education, 67* (2), 89-91.

Irvin, J.L. (1992). Developmentally appropriate instruction: The heart of the middle school. In J.L. Irvin (Ed.), *Transforming middle level education: Perspectives and possibilities* (pp. 295-313). Boston: Allyn and Bacon.

Mac Iver, D.J., Balfanz, R., & Plank, S.B. (1997). *An 'elective replacement' approach to providing extra help and enrichment in mathematics in the Talent Development Middle School: Effects of the Computer- and Team-Assisted Mathematics Acceleration Program. Center for Research on the Education of Students Placed At Risk.* (Available in December, 1997, from Publications Dept., Attn: Diane Diggs, CRESPAR, Johns Hopkins University, 3505 N. Charles Street, Baltimore, MD 21218)

Mac Iver, D.J., & Epstein, J.L. (1991). Responsive practices in the middle grades: Teacher teams, advisory groups, remedial instruction, and school transition programs. *American Journal of Education, 99* (4), 587-622.

Mac Iver, D.J., & Plank, S.B. (1996). *The talent development middle school: Implementation and effects of student team reading. Report No. 4.* Center for Research on the Education of Students Placed At Risk. (Available from Publications Dept., Attn: Dian Diggs, CRESPAR, Johns Hopkins University, 3505 N. Charles Street, Baltimore, MD 21218)

Mac Iver, D.J., & Plank, S.B. (1997, March). *From "at risk" to "on target": Effects of a career exploration and educational decision-making course on urban middle school students.* Paper presented at the Annual Meeting of the American Educational Research Association.

Mac Iver, D.J., Plank, S.B., & Balfanz, R. (1997). *Working together to become proficient readers: Early impact of the Talent Development Middle School's Student Team Literature Program.* (Report 15). Baltimore, MD and Washington, DC: Center for Research on the Education of Students Placed at Risk.

Mac Iver, D.J., & Reuman, D.A. (1993). Giving their best: Grading and recognition practices that motivate students to work hard, *American Educator, 17* (4), 24-31.

Madhere, S., & Mac Iver, D.J. (1996). *The talent development middle school: Essential components.* Report No. 3., Center for Research on the Education of Students Placed At Risk. (Available from Publications Dept., Attn: Diane Diggs, CRESPAR, Johns Hopkins University, 3505 N. Charles Street, Baltimore, MD 21218).

McPartland, J.M. (1987). *Balancing high quality subject-matter instruction with positive teacher-student relations in the middle grades: Effects of departmentalization, tracking, and block scheduling on learning environments.* (CREMS Report No. 25). Baltimore, MD: Johns Hopkins University, Center for Research on Elementary and Middle Schools. (ERIC Document Reproduction Service No. ED 291 704.)

McPartland, J.M. (1990). Staffing decisions in the middle grades. *Phi Delta Kappan, 71* (6), 438-444.

McPartland, J.M. (1992, February). *Staffing patterns and the social organization of schools for young adolescents.* Paper presented at the fourth biennial meeting of the Society for Research on Adolescence, Washington, DC.

Meloth, M.S., & Deering, P.D. (1994). Task talk and task awareness under different cooperative learning conditions, *American Educational Research Journal 31,* (1), 138-165.

Midgley, C., Feldlaufer, H., & Eccles, J. S. (1989). Change in teacher efficacy and student self- and task-related beliefs during the transition to junior high school. *Journal of Educational Psychology, 81* (2), 247-258.

Oakes, J. (1994a). More than misapplied technology: A normative and political response to Hallinan on tracking, *Sociology of Education, 67* (2), 84-89.

Oakes, J. (1994b). One more thought. *Sociology of Education, 67* (2), 91.

Slavin, R.E. (1995). *Cooperative learning: Theory, research, and practice* (Second Edition). Boston: Allyn and Bacon.

Spear, R.C. (1992). Appropriate grouping practices for middle level students, In J.L. Irvin (Ed.), *Transforming middle level education: Perspectives and possibilities* (pp.244-274). Boston: Allyn and Bacon.

Stevens, R. J. & Durkin, S. (1992). *Using student team reading and student team writing in middle schools.* (CDS Report No. 36). Baltimore, MD: Johns Hopkins University, Center for Research on Effective Schooling for Disadvantaged Students. (Available from Publications Dept., Attn: Diane Diggs, CDS, Johns Hopkins University, 3505 N. Charles Street, Baltimore, MD 21218)

Stevenson, D.L., Schiller, K.S., &Schneider, B. (1994). Sequences of opportunities for learning. *Sociology of Education, 67* (3), 184-198.

Thomason, J., &Thompson, M. (1992). Motivation: Moving, learning, mastering, and sharing. In J.L. Irvin (Ed.), *Transforming middle level education: Perspectives and possibilities* (pp.275-294) Boston: Allyn and Bacon.

Wavering, M.J. (1995). Cognitive development of young adolescents. In M.J. Wavering (Ed.), *Educating young adolescents: Life in the middle* (pp. 111-130). New York, Garland Publishing.

Webb, N.M. & Farivar, S. (1994). Promoting helping behavior in cooperative small groups in middle school mathematics. *American Educational Research Journal, 31* (2), 369-395.

Williams, D.R., Harris, J., & Hayakawa, C. (1995). Cooperative learning and conflict resolution: Perspectives of urban middle school adolescents. *Research in Middle Level Education, 18* (2), 23-47.

Service Learning and Young Adolescents: A Good Fit

From the perspective of the middle school practitioner concerned with service learning, perhaps the most significant research of the last twenty years deals, not with service learning or experiential education, but with young adolescent development. As more has been learned about the developmental characteristics of early adolescence, it has become evident that experiential learning, and in particular service learning, can respond to many of the developmental needs of this stage.

In 1982, when the Early Adolescent Helper Program[1] was introduced in three New York City junior high and middle schools, service learning at the high school level was still far from common, and service learning initiatives in the middle grades were scarcer still. Early adolescence had only recently been "discovered" as a discrete developmental stage; Joan Lipsitz's (1977) influential book, *Growing Up Forgotten,* was published five years earlier, and the middle school movement had begun to grow. Researchers, practitioners, and policy makers were taking a fresh look at adolescence, and had begun to recognize that adolescence cannot be viewed as a single developmental stage, and that differentiating between early, middle, and late adolescence would increase our capacity to respond to the needs of this critical period. "Considerable insight is gained when we recognize that growth unfolds in a mildly predictable manner, and as a consequence, early adolescents are considerably different in temperament and ability from late adolescents" (Mitchell, 1986, p.91).

---

[1] A service learning program designed for the middle grades, the Helper Program is now the action arm of the National Helpers Network, based in New York City.

In 1983, the Center for Early Adolescence (CEA) compiled an inventory of eleven characteristics of the young adolescent, pairing each trait with a related developmental need. More recently, the Carnegie Council on Adolescent Development (1989), in its influential report, *Turning Points: Preparing American Youth for the 21st Century,* called attention to "the volatile mismatch between the organization and curriculum of middle grade schools and the intellectual and emotional needs of young adolescents" (p. 8). A review of several of the items in the CEA's (1983) list argued for the "fit" between service learning and the middle school program:

Young adolescents...	*Therefore they need...*
... undergo rapid physical, social, emotional, and intellectual changes.	... to explore who they are and what they can become.
... can be painfully self-conscious and critical. They are defining themselves, and they vary widely in maturity and ability.	... many opportunities to achieve and have their competence recognized by others.
... identify with the peer group; they want to belong, and they are developing deepening friendships.	... opportunities to form positive relationships and experiences with peers.
... identify more maturely with their race, gender, and potential for employment.	... relationships with diverse adult role models.
... are idealistic about social and religious issues.	... to participate meaningfully in their communities.

—p. 2

While some middle school educators initially had doubts about the suitability of service learning for their students, others recognized in service learning a way to provide new opportunities for growth. This latter group found affirmation in the research of the Center for Early Adolescence and of the pioneers of the middle school movement, who were advocating a school structure that would take into account the curiosity, the restlessness, and the volatility of this time of transition.

Although existing research on adolescent development suggested that service learning is indeed an appropriate undertaking for the middle school students, more information was needed. Parents, teachers, community members, decision makers at every level, ask about the short- and long-term effects of these programs, about the impact on the community, and about taking students away from the traditional classroom. Researchers, educators, and program planners sought answers to these questions and means to discover whether there were significant differences in outcome depending upon the **kind** of service in which youngsters engaged, and on whether the service learning was elective or required. This chapter will examine the limited research to date on service learning reporting first the incidence and nature of service learning programs and then information on the outcomes of service learning.

❏ Incidence and nature of service learning programs

In a national survey (Hodgkinson & Weitzman, 1992), the authors found that 61% of teenagers (young people between the ages of 12 and 17) volunteered an average of 3.2 hours per week in 1991. Of these, however, only 25% reported that their service was school-related. What has been lacking until relatively recently is the kind of systematic research that is essential for program improvement – research that is often a critical factor in determining whether innovations are incorporated into our schools or remain disposable "add-ons." Scant research and evaluation exist specifically focused on service learning in the middle grades. As Switzer, Simmons, Dew, Regalski, and Nang (1995) pointed out, "there is an extensive literature on prosocial behavior in general, and on altruism specifically. However, much of the research has been conducted on adults or college students; fewer studies have involved young adolescents" (p. 429). Needed, too, are studies that compare the impact of service *learning* (here defined as hands-on service, combined with provision for structured preparation and ongoing reflection) with community service experiences that do not include the reflective component.

Much of what we know or believe at the present time about service learning in the middle grades is based on anecdotal data or self-reporting by participants and adult leaders. For some time there has been an abundance of anecdotal information confirming the value of service learning, as well as a body of teacher and parent observations that suggest positive changes resulting from participation in service. Pre- and post-tests have been administered in numerous programs, and they provide some evidence that attitudinal change occurs, stereotyping is reduced, and self-efficacy is enhanced (Schine & Campbell, 1987; Search Institute, 1991; Shumer & Belbas, 1996).

❑ Outcomes of service learning

Concern for the growing number of "at-risk" youth, and what many perceive as a fraying social fabric, combined with renewed interest in "a youth development approach," has led to exploration of the power of service learning as a protective factor. Some indication that participation in service may indeed contribute to a reduction of risk factors can be found in Search Institute's study of 46,000 young people titled *The Troubled Journey,* supported by the Lutheran Brotherhood through its RespecTeen program. Researchers found that youth who serve others are less likely to be involved in at-risk behaviors. Out of twenty at-risk indicators, boys who serve one or more hours per week average 2.9 indicators, compared to 3.4 indicators for boys who spend no time serving. Girls who serve average 2.2 indicators, compared to 2.9 indicators for non-servers. It is not clear, however, whether those who engaged in service were a self-selected population.

Several studies currently under way are intended to explore the short- and long-term effects of service learning.[2] Some preliminary findings indicate that service learning does indeed produce positive outcomes. Criteria for success vary across programs, and it is safe to say that there is a need for more data and for rigorous research.

Pressure is growing for information about the relationship of academic achievement to participation in service learning. In a review of research articles and books Robert Shumer and Brad Belbas (1996) of the National Service-Learning Clearinghouse concluded that "we know much more than people usually describe when they talk about service programs...We know service learning has a rich history of evaluation and research. Tied to other areas, such as vocational education or community-based learning, we know it contributes significantly to development of self-esteem, to career awareness, and to academic connections between classroom and community" (p. 221). But, they acknowledged that "Although we know a lot about service learning, there is still much more to learn about service and its effect on learning" (p. 221).

Spurred in part by the proliferation of service learning initiatives following the passage of the National and Community Service Trust Act of 1993, and the need to evaluate Learn and Serve America programs, funded by the Corporation for National Service, a number of studies are now under way. Richard Kraft (1996) cautioned:

---

[2] For a fairly comprehensive listing of current research and evaluation in service learning, see **Search Institute:** *Proceedings from the Service Learning Summit, September 9-10, 1995.* Search Institute, Minneapolis, MN.

One of the major difficulties in evaluating or researching ser-vice-learning programs is the lack of agreement on what is meant by the term service learning and exactly what it is meant to ac-complish. Whereas some programs emphasize social growth, character development, or civic responsibility, others attempt to study psychological development and effects of programs on self-concept. Moral judgment studies have sought to evaluate the effects of service on moral and ego development, and other studies have attempted to measure the effects of service on the broader community. Perhaps the most difficult arena has been in the area of intellectual, cognitive, and academic effects. It has been difficult to design tight experiments to isolate the ef-fects of service on specific academic achievements.
— pp. 142-143

The Early Adolescent Helper Program, founded in 1982, and based until 1994 at the City University of New York's Graduate Center, was the subject of a study by Galen Switzer and colleagues at the University of Pittsburgh in the 1992-93 school year. The study was limited to a seventh grade class in a single urban junior high school, but included students who were required to serve as tutors for younger children or students with lim-ited English proficiency or as helpers in a senior center, as well as a larger number who selected their own service projects from a list provided by the school.

It was hypothesized that Helper Program participants (n=85) relative to nonparticipants (n=86), and especially boys, would show improvement in 4 domains: self-image, commitment to school and community, problem behavior, and commitment to altruism. The results were gender specific: Participating boys showed positive changes in self-esteem, depressive affect, in-volvement, and problem behavior relative to other groups. The findings indicate that, with program modifications to augment potential benefits to girls, Helper programs might become an important mechanism in producing positive life changes for ado-lescents. — Switzer, et al., 1995, p.429

Middle school educators who work with service learning programs, and those who contemplate initiating service learning, may find it useful to take their cue from these findings, and examine strategies to augment the positive effects of participation for girls. These findings suggest, too, that planners will do well to consider how boys are enrolled in service learning when the program is elective; although more systematic information is needed, it appears, from teacher reports, that in settings where participation is voluntary – neither integrated into the academic curriculum nor required as a separate activity – boys are customarily under-represented.

Other lessons of interest to the middle school practitioner have begun to emerge from recent or ongoing research projects. Rahima Wade (1995), in a study of the experience of ten teachers in integrating service into the academic curriculum, found that "the rewarding aspects of teachers' service-learning experiences included: student enthusiasm, motivation, caring, and learning; recognition from others (i.e. administrators, colleagues, parents, the media); and perceived benefits for the community" (p. 1). Wade found, too, that "the most problematic aspect is time: for planning projects and fitting service into the school day" (p. 1). Other problems cited echoed those mentioned in informal teacher reports from a variety of service learning programs: difficulties in communicating with community agency representatives, limited finances and transportation, and lack of collegial and administrative support.

At this writing, Search Institute, with a grant from the W.K. Kellogg Foundation, is leading an effort to coordinate service learning research, and has developed an open network of a dozen or more organizations and scholars. Search Institute's emphasis is on K-12, but the network includes researchers in university and college-based service learning. In addition, Brandeis University's Center for Human Resources has undertaken a comprehensive study of Learn and Serve America, the K-12 program of the Corporation for National Service. With this growth in systematic study of the rich variety of service learning efforts, practitioners can look forward to expanding their knowledge of effective programs.

References   Ⓡ

Carnegie Council on Adolescent Development. (1989). *Turning points: Preparing American youth for the 21st century.* New York: Carnegie Corporation.

Center for Early Adolescence. (1983) *Common Focus: An exchange of information about early adolescence, 5* (2), 1-4.

Hodgkinson, V.A., & Weitzman, M.S. (1992). *Giving and volunteering 1992; Findings from a national survey.* Washington, DC: The Gallup Organization .

Kraft, R. C. (1996). Service learning: An introduction to its theory, practice, and effects. *Education and Urban Society, 2* (2), 131-159.

Lipsitz, J. (1977). *Growing up forgotten: A review of research and programs concerning early adolescence.* Lexington, MA: Lexington Books.

Mitchell, J. (1986). *The nature of adolescence*. Calgary, Alberta, Canada: Detselig Enterprises Ltd.

Schine, J., & Campbell, P. (1987). *Helping to success: Early adolescents and young children*. NY: Bruner Foundation.

Search Institute of Minneapolis. (1991). *Source, 7* (3).

Shumer, R., & Belbas, B. (1996). What we know about service learning. Education and Urban Society, Special issue: *Learning by serving and doing, 28* (2), 208-223.

Switzer, G. E., Simmons, R. G., Dew, M., Regalski, J., & Wang, C. (1995). The effect of a school-based helper program on adolescent self-image, attitutdes, and behavior. *Journal of Early Adolescence, 15* (4), 429-455.

Wade, R.C. (1995, April) Contextual influences on teachers' experiences with community service-learning. Paper presented at the annual meeting of the American Educational Research Association, San Francisco.

Judith A. Brough

Home-School Partnerships:
A Critical Link

Many educators agree that parental involvement in schools is desirable and has positive impact on students' levels of achievement and behavior in school. What is less understood are the depths of benefits and the roles educators can play in influencing levels of family involvement in specific middle level school programs.

Education Secretary Richard Riley (1996) said, "Thirty years of research shows that when family and community members are directly involved in education, children achieve better grades and higher test scores, have much higher reading comprehension, graduate at higher rates, are more likely to enroll in higher education, and are better behaved" (p. 1). As educators, we tend to agree with Secretary Riley's statement, but throw our hands up in resignation when parents neglect to show up for conferences and workshops. It would seem more productive to analyze why the parents are not involved and build a partnership program which will be appealing to a wide range of family structures and backgrounds. This article presents the best thinking concerning reasons for noninvolvement as well as the research findings of specific benefits which can be experienced through high levels of parent involvement. Successful parental involvement programs are described and key elements and practices are listed.

❏ Barriers to involvement

Reasons for noninvolvement are as many and varied as there are families. Some parents, quite simply, do not understand how vital their involvement is to the academic success of their children. They want what is best for their children, but may not understand the level of involvement and support that is necessary. Other parents probably were not particularly enamored with schooling as adolescents themselves, and they may find it distasteful to return to the school as adults. The school system and its educators may intimidate parents with more expensive clothes, different vocabularies, or different language and customs. Parents may be distrustful of professionals who have never experienced life as they know it. Additionally, some parents just do not have the time or energy to become active in school functions. The Carnegie Council on Adolescent Development (1996) described the difficulties:

> *...job and career demands, the rigid boundaries between work and home life, and the frequent claims on their time and resources from aging parents or younger children, among other constraints. Existing school policies and teacher attitudes, in addition, have long discouraged the involvement or accepted the absence of parents in school activities beyond the elementary school years.* – pp. 21-22

In their study of parent involvement barriers, Leitch and Tangri (1988) found that parents cited such reasons as "health problems, economic differences between themselves and teachers, and work responsibilities. Parents also said they felt that teachers looked down on them for not being as successful as teachers" (p. 74). One third of reporting parents said that they had not been asked to do anything for or with the school.

It is especially difficult for single and working parents to become involved. As more mothers have joined the work force, the traditional means of school-home communication have become less effective and successful. The Educational Testing Service (ETS) (1992) reported that "one in five children live in a single-parent family, . . . more than double the proportion in 1965" (p. 2). Gough (1991) found that 60% of students live in homes where the lone parent or both parents work. Yet, test results examined by ETS showed that students with two parents in the home scored considerably higher on achievement tests than those with one parent. The difference remained even after considering the fact that single-parent families, on average, have lower income and less education (ETS, 1992).

Unfortunately, parent involvement enjoyed by elementary schools tends to decrease as students move from elementary to middle level schools (Carnegie Council on Adolescent Development, 1989; Epstein, 1987). Parents feel less able to help with their middle level student's school work and express a desire for more leadership and guidance from teachers (Dauber & Epstein, 1989). Many parents also become intimidated by conferences where they are faced by four or five teaching team members. The very structure of most middle level schools discourages many parents from remaining involved in their children's educations (Berla, 1991).

These changes in school, family, and society make it even more vital that parents and schools collaborate, but make it more difficult to do so (Coleman, 1987; Comer, 1986; Johnston, 1990; Takanishi, 1993). It, therefore, is imperative that middle level educators develop alternate means for enhancing home-school partnerships in their school communities.

❑ Benefits from parent involvement

All students seem to benefit from parental involvement in the school, but the effects are more significant and longer lasting for children of the involved parents. Students whose parents are involved report increased motivation and understand school as being important to them. These students experience higher levels of achievement, are less likely to drop out, have fewer absences from school, and maintain better relationships with their parent(s). Epstein and Herrick (1991) found that students who worked with their parents on Summer Home Learning Packets completed more learning activities and achieved better than expected in school the following fall.

Parent involvement makes a difference in the academic achievement of middle level students. As a matter of fact, Henderson (1991) went so far as to say that "the single most important determinant of a child's success in school, and ultimately throughout life, is not family status, education level, income or IQ. It is whether that child's parents are involved in his or her education" (p. 6). In elementary schools with high levels of parent involvement, children did better in reading comprehension. The average reading scores of fourth graders were 26 points below the national average where involvement was low, but 17 points above the national average where parent involvement was high (National Center for Education Statistics, 1996).

According to the 1992 National Assessment of Education Progress, 90% of the differences in math achievement were attributable to factors which can be controlled in the home: student absences, reading materials available in the home, reading aloud with children, and the amount of television watching (Lewis, 1995). The National Education Longitudinal Study (NELS:88) showed that proficiency scores of eighth graders in reading and math were related to parental involvement (Horn & West, 1992). Parent and community involvement indisputably improves student motivation and achievement and reduces dropout rates and delinquency (see, for example, Coleman, 1987; Comer, 1986; Henderson, 1988; Henderson & Berla, 1994; Moles, 1994). Henderson and Berla (1994) stated that "the most accurate predictor of a student's achievement in school is not income or social status, but the extent to which that student's family is able to: 1) create a home environment that encourages learning, 2) express high (but not unrealistic) expectations for their children's achievement and future careers, and 3) become involved in their children's education at school and in the community" (p.1).

Involved parents feel more comfortable with teachers and the school program. Their children do better academically and they get more accurate and frequent information from the school. Involved parents more likely know how to help their middle school children at home, understand curricular requirements, and are more apt to attend school functions and meetings.

Schools with strong parent involvement programs report receiving more information and backing from the home. Teachers who form parent partnerships benefit from higher student achievement gains and stronger home support. Students are then more likely to do homework and to perceive school as being important. Parents are more apt to believe teachers and schools to be effective and to support school reform initiatives (Rutherford & Billig, 1995; Tracy, 1995).

❑ **Programs and models**

Over the past fifteen years, several effective programs and models for building and maintaining home-school partnerships have been developed, implemented, and evaluated. Two of the more notable specific models of parent involvement were designed by Joyce Epstein (1987) and Janet Chrispeels (1992). Both authors acknowledged that family involvement does and should include various roles and responsibilities on the parts of family members and school personnel.

Epstein's model (Epstein & Connors, 1992) included the following components:

1. Basic obligations of parents – responsibilities of parents to ensure their children's health and safety; supervision, discipline and guidance of the children; and building of an environment which supports school learning and appropriate behavior.
2. Basic obligations of schools – the school's responsibilities of communicating about school programs and student progress
3. Parent involvement in school – parent support of and attendance at performances, events, workshops and other programs offered by the school. It also includes parent volunteers in the school.
4. Parent involvement at home – parent monitoring and assistance with learning activities at home which coordinate with class work.

5. Parent involvement in school governance and advocacy – parent involvement in school advisory committees, PTO/PTA organizations, and/or groups which monitor school improvement programs.
6. Collaborations and exchanges with the community – community members and young adolescents building working relationships.

Chrispeels (1992) described parental involvement in terms of an hierarchical configuration. Implementation of lower levels would foster participation at the higher levels. She described the following involvement roles:

1. Co-communicators – communications between home and school.
2. Co-supporters – parents and educators working together to support learning at home and school.
3. Co-learners – educators and parents attending or presenting workshops to promote understanding.
4. Co-teachers – educators provide parents and students with home learning activities and strategies.
5. Co-decision-makers – school personnel and parent collaborate on educational decisions.

Many middle level schools report involvement on the first two levels of both models, but few enjoy more complex home-school partnerships (Dietz, 1992; Leiderman, 1996).

Various other models for involvement are described in *Educational Leadership*, April 1996; *Schools in the Middle*, Winter, 1992; *Phi Delta Kappan*, January 1991; For Our Children: Parents and Families in Education, Results of the National Parent Involvement Summit, April 1992, National PTA; *International Journal of the W.K. Kellogg Foundation*, Volume 3, number 2 (to order the publication write to W.K. Kellogg Foundation, Media Resources Division, P.O.Box 5196, Battle Creek, MI 49016. No date is given for the publication). Several models are described in sources listed in the references. Factors consistent among the models are that schools assess the effectiveness of their own efforts at developing home-school partnerships, determine why uninvolved parents are not assuming a role in school activities, build a rationale and commitment for getting the parents and families involved, and make a concerted and unflagging effort to reach all families.

❏ Key elements and practices

While parent involvement begins with reading at home, it expands as childhood gives way to adolescence. Information regarding effective parenting, characteristics of young adolescents, study skills, and new curricular demands is necessary for families of middle level students. Young adolescents seem to dislike parental interference, but the adolescent stage is precisely when the need for parental roles is amplified. Although many young adolescents voice a distaste for parent involvement, the majority cherish it.

Researchers (see, for example, Becker & Epstein, 1982; Berla, 1992; Carnegie Council on Adolescent Development, 1996; Chrispeels, 1991; Epstein & Herrick, 1991; Foster-Harrison & Peel 1995; Leiderman, 1996; Rutherford & Billig, 1995; Rutherford, Billig & Kettering, 1995; Tracy, 1995) recommended the following practices to enhance home-school partnerships:

1. Schools actively work to involve parents and keep them informed about school policies and events. Goals and policies regarding parent involvement should be needs-driven, and legitimized by being clearly written, easily understood, evaluated often, and administratively supported.

2. Parents are actually recruited for involvement in programs through various means. In addition to newsletters, brochures, and phone calls, educators employ home visits, personal invitations, media blitzes, agency referrals, clergy and community participation, and family learning centers to solicit family involvement. Parent recognition programs are developed with the support of local businesses and other organizations.

3. Communications such as conferences, orientations, newsletters, personal notes, and phone calls are frequent and supported by school policy, procedure, leadership, and allocated resources. Telecommunications and video tapes are used effectively. Homework, calendar, and bilingual hot lines are used. Educators acknowledge various family structures, work schedules, and ethnic and cultural backgrounds. Translators are provided if needed. Transportation for non-mobile parents is provided as is child care for students and siblings.

4. Middle level schools establish practices and staffing patterns that encourage and support home-school partnerships. Practices are open, friendly, and welcoming. Schools establish a parent liaison position. Parents are familiar with and understand the various roles they can play in the home-school partnership. Parents feel comfortable in the school and benefit from a place in the school where they can work (i.e. a parents' center or resource room). Educators analyze the cul-

ture of the school to determine how welcoming they really are to parents and community members. Conferences are held with collaborative rather than confrontational attitudes and procedures. Round tables, for example, are more conducive to collaborative efforts than rectangular tables where teachers sit on one side and parents on the other.

5. Educators market the importance of middle level education and build opportunities for businesses and community groups to interact meaningfully with young adolescents. Schools develop means for community, business, and agency representatives to support the school program.

6. Schools provide parents with information and strategies to enhance their youngsters' academic success. Parents learn how to support their children's learning at home, even when the work becomes difficult. They learn why their support is so crucial and how to support their children's learning within their own constraints. They learn about young adolescent growth and development, signs of physical and mental distress, ways of promoting healthful life-styles, and means of preventing risky behaviors and relationships.

7. Parents, community members, and students are included in decisions about curriculum and instruction.

8. Staff development about family involvement practices is provided for teachers. Training for parent/community volunteers and leaders is recommended. Teachers understand the importance of home-school relationships and can articulate rationale and effective practices to parents. Teachers develop and maintain attitudes and behaviors that welcome and encourage family involvement.

❏ Conclusions

Educators frequently complain that "it's always the parents who are involved who don't need to be, and the parents who aren't involved who need to be." This dilemma is not a coincidence. Parent involvement itself affects student achievement. In the past, though, we have tended to blame student lack of ambition, motivation, or achievement on the neglectful parent and assume there was nothing we could do. Research has shown otherwise. With a sincere commitment to increasing parent involvement and an acceptance of the changes in family structures, schools can create home-school partnerships which meet the needs and constraints of all involved. We cannot afford NOT to have family involvement. Middle level educators must find ways and means to build strong partnerships, thus insuring our own success in helping our students to reach their potentials. We cannot do it alone. It is time to admit to ourselves that "Trying to educate the young without help and support from the home is akin to trying to rake leaves in a high wind" (Gough, 1991, p. 339). Ⓡ

Selected Bibliography

Becker, H., & Epstein, J. (1982) *Influence on teachers' use of parent involvement at home.* Baltimore, MD: The Johns Hopkins University, Center for Social Organization of Schools (Report No. 324).

Berla, N. (1991). Parent involvement at the middle school level. *The Eric Review, 1* (3), 16-20.

Berla, N. (1992). Getting parents involved. *Education Digest, 58* (2), 118-119.

Carnegie Council on Adolescent Development (1989). *Turning points: Preparing American youth for the 21st century.* New York: Carnegie Corporation.

Carnegie Council on Adolescent Development (1996). *Great transitions: Preparing adolescents for a new century.* New York: Carnegie Corporation.

Chrispeels, J.H. (1991). District leadership in parent involvement. *Phi Delta Kappan, 72* (5), 367-371.

Chrispeels, J.H. (1992). *School restructuring to facilitate parent and community involvement in the middle grades.* Paper presented at A Working Conference: Parent and Community Involvement in the Middle Grades, Crystal City, VA.

Coleman, J.S. (1987). Families and schools. *Educational Researcher, 16* (6), 32-38.

Comer, J.P. (1986). Parent participation in the schools. *Phi Delta Kappan, 67* (6), 442-446.

Dauber, S., & Epstein, J. (1989). *Parent attitudes and practices of parent involvement in inner-city elementary and middle schools* (Report No. 32). Baltimore: Center for Research in Elementary and Middle Schools, Johns Hopkins University. (ERIC ED 314152)

Dietz, M. (1992). *Principals and parent involvement in Wisconsin middle level public schools.* Unpublished doctoral dissertation, University of Wisconsin, Madison.

Educational Testing Service (1992). *America's smallest school: The family.* Princeton, NJ: Policy Information Center.

Epstein, J. (1987). Parent involvement: What research says to administrators. *Educational and Urban Society, 19* (2), 119-136.

Epstein, J. (1987). What principals should know about parent involvement. *Principal, 66* (3), 6-9.

Epstein, J., & Dauber, S. (1991). School programs and teacher practices of parent involvement in inner-city elementary and middle schools. *The Elementary School Journal, 91* (3), 289-305.

Epstein, J., & Herrick, S. (1991). *Implementation and effects of summer home learning packets in the middle grades* (Report No. 21). Baltimore: Center for Research on Effective Schooling for Disadvantaged Students.

Epstein, J., & Connors, L. (1992). School and family partnerships. *Practitioner, 28* (4), 1-4.

Foster-Harrison, E.S., & Peel, H.A. (1995). Parents in the middle: Initiatives for success. *Schools in the Middle, 5* (2), 45-47.

Gough, P. (1991). Tapping parent power. *Phi Delta Kappan, 72* (5) 339.

Henderson, A. (1988). Parents are a school's best friends. *Phi Delta Kappan, 70* (2), 148-153.

Henderson, A. (1991). Why parent involvement? In Wisconsin Department of Public Instruction, *Families and education: An educator's resource for family involvement* (pp. 6-7) Madison, WI: Wisconsin Department of Public Instruction.

Henderson, A., & Berla, N. (1994). *A new generation of evidence: The family is critical to student achievement.* Washington, DC: National Committee for Citizens in Education.

Horn, L., & West, J. (1992). *National educational longitudinal study of 1988: A profile of parents of eighth graders.* Washington, DC: National Center for Educational Statistics. (NCES 92-488).

Johnston, J.H. (1990). *The new American family and the school.* Columbus, OH: National Middle School Association.

Kellogg Foundation (n.d.). Families and neighborhoods: Building blocks for a prosperous future. An issue of *International Journal of the W.K. Kellogg Foundation, 3* (2).

Leiderman, J. (1996). *Factors associated with parent involvement in the middle grades.* Unpublished doctoral dissertation, Lehigh University.

Leitch, M. L.,& Tangri, S. (1988). Barriers to home-school collaboration. *Educational Horizons, 66* (2), 70-74.

Lewis, A.C. (1995). Changing views of parent involvement. *Phi Delta Kappan, 76* (6), 430-431.

Moles, O., Project Director (1994). *Home learning recipes.* Washington, DC: Office of Educational Research and Improvement, U.S. Department of Education.

National PTA (1992). *For our children: Parents and families in education.* Chicago: Author.

National Center for Education Statistics (1996). *Reading literacy in the United States: Findings from the IEA Reading Literacy Study.* U.S. Department of Education, NCES 96-258.

Riley, R. (1996). Secretary Riley urges Americans to get involved in education, *Community Update, (No. 38)*. U.S. Department of Education, Washington, DC.

Rutherford, B., & Billig, S. (1995). Eight lessons of parent, family, and community involvement in the middle grades. *Phi Delta Kappan, 77* (1), 64-68.

Rutherford, B., Billig, S., & Kettering, J. (1995). A review of the research and practice literature on parent and community involvement. In B. Rutherford (Ed.), *Creating family/school partnerships* (pp. 3 73). Columbus, OH: National Middle School Association.

Takanishi, R. (1993). Changing views of adolescence in contemporary society. In R. Takanishi (Ed.), *Adolescence in the 1990's: Risk and opportunity* (pp. 1-7). NY: Teachers College Press.

Tracy, J. (1995). Family... involving families in student achievement. *Schools in the Middle, 5* (2), 31-37.

Organization

Valentine	*Jerry Valentine* *University of Missouri* *Columbia, Missouri*
Whitaker	*Todd Whitaker* *Indiana State University* *Terre Haute, Indiana*
Hough	*David Hough* *Southwest Missouri State* *University* *Springfield, Missouri*
Trimble	*Susan B. Trimble* *Georgia Southern University* *Statesboro, Georgia*
Mizelle	*Nancy B. Mizelle* *University of Georgia* *Athens, Georgia*
Mullins	*Emmett Mullins* *Harbins Elementary School* *Gwinnett County, Georgia*

Jerry Valentine and Todd Whitaker

Organizational Trends and Practices in Middle Level Schools

Historians are quick to remind us that the value of history lies not in the documentation of the past per se, but in the manner with which an understanding of the past informs the future. Therein lies the goal of this chapter – What significant organizational trends in middle level education inform future practice? The importance of understanding the past and present to prepare for the future is evident. Contemporary futurist Joel Barker even described this ability as a key leadership skill. He said that a role of the school leader is to "visit" the future and report what you have observed (Barker, 1992).

This chapter provides a research summary of three middle level organizational trends and offers thoughts about the implications of those trends for current practice. The organizational trends selected for this chapter include schools' organizational grade patterns, enrollment, and schedules. The chapter also suggests three research reports for the professional library – reports that provide more detail about trends discussed in this chapter and other issues frequently faced by middle level practitioners.

❏ Organizational grade patterns

Our analysis of critical information that informs the current era of middle level education begins with the general issue of organizational grade patterns, in other words, what grades should be grouped together for optimum effectiveness. We begin our analysis of grade patterns with data from William Alexander's seminal study of middle schools. In 1967-68 Alexander (1968) identified 1,101 middle schools across the United States. These numbers did not include schools with grades 7-8 and 7-8-9. However, the study has been recognized as the first major national analysis of middle schools.

Since 1967, the number of middle schools has grown steadily. In 1981, Valentine, Clark, Nickerson, and Keefe (1981) reported 4,094 schools with grade patterns 5-8 or 6-8. Fifteen years later, McEwin, Dickinson, and Jenkins (1996) reported data from 7,378 schools. During the same time span, the 7-8-9 junior high organizational pattern declined dramatically, dropping from a high of 67% of the approximately 7000 schools in 1965 (Rock &Hemphill, 1966) to 33% of the 12,226 schools in 1981 (Valentine, Clark, Nickerson, & Keefe, 1981) and then to 19% of 12,100 schools in 1992 (Valentine et al., 1993). Simply stated, the past three decades have been a meteoric rise of the "middle school" organizational pattern of 5-8 and 6-8 and the demise of the 7-9 "junior high" pattern. In the most recent national study McEwin and associates (1996) reported 7,378 schools of 6-8 or 5-8 grade patterns and only 1,425 schools of 7-9 grade patterns, a thirty year drop from approximately 4,700 to 1,425.

With such a drastic grade pattern shift, researchers commonly asked school leaders why their schools transitioned to a 5-8 or 6-8 grade pattern. Alexander (1968) noted that the most common reason was to "adjust to enrollment needs." However, by 1981 (Valentine et al., 1981) the most common response was "to provide a program best suited to the needs of the middle level age student." That response continued as the most common through the eighties and nineties (Alexander & McEwin, 1989; Valentine et al., 1993; McEwin et al., 1996). Such data support the notion that middle level education of the nineties is more focused on programs designed to meet the needs of young adolescents than was the case three decades ago.

Is a particular grade pattern viewed by educators as more appropriate for young adolescents than other grade patterns? That question was asked of principals in a 1966 national study (Rock & Hemphill, 1966) and has been repeated in each of the major national studies since that time. In 1966, a majority of principals believed that the 7-9 grade pattern was most appropriate for young adolescents. By 1981, that belief shifted significantly, with 54% favoring the 6-8 configuration (Valentine et al., 1981). The shift continued into the nineties, with 72% favoring 6-8 by 1992 (Valentine et al., 1993).

❑ Implications

As McEwin et al. (1996) concluded, "increasing numbers of school districts across the nation are moving to the three-tier school organization which usually includes separately organized middle schools with grades 5-8 or 6-8. Decisions regarding grade organization are increasingly being made based on what is best for young adolescents rather than on expediency and tradition" (p. 131). Clearly, most middle level educators believe that a middle school organizational pattern is more appropriate for students than a junior high pattern. Therefore, if the overwhelming majority of school leaders from across the country who work with young adolescents is convinced that students are better served in this organizational structure, policy makers evaluating school effectiveness or considering reorganization should take note of this collective wisdom.

❏ School enrollment trends

Trends in student enrollment in middle level schools also provide insight for current policy makers. In 1966, Rock and Hemphill reported that 43% of middle level schools served between 500 and 1,000 students, with 23% serving more than 1,000. In 1981, 49% of middle level schools enrolled between 400 and 800 students, with 13% having more than 1,000 students (Valentine et al., 1981). By 1992 the numbers were 50% between 400 and 800 and 16% above 1,000 (Valentine et al., 1993). McEwin et al. (1996) noted a similar increase between 1988 and 1993 of schools with very large enrollments. If this pattern continues, it has significant implications for school programs. As McEwin et al. (1996) noted, "the trend toward larger middle schools raises concerns among those who question the ability of these larger schools to be developmentally responsive to the needs of young adolescents" (p. 17).

During this time of increasing enrollment, school leaders' opinions about appropriate school size moved toward smaller enrollments. For example, in 1981 (Valentine et al.. 1981) 36% of principals favored school sizes between 600 and 800 students and 27% believed optimum size was between 400 and 600. By 1993 (Valentine et al., 1993) 27% favored the 600-800 range and 41% favored the 400 to 600 range. Such beliefs are consistent with the general educational literature which supports downsizing schools for effectiveness.

❏ Implications

From the practical perspective of administering a school system, selecting optimal enrollment in a given school is difficult to manage. Shifting enrollment patterns, financial issues, facilities, and community values directly affect school enrollment possibilities. However, efforts to down-size may be an issue worth pursuing. Middle level leaders support in unison the notion that "smaller is better." Policy makers should consider both school enrollment as well as grade patterns when planning district reorganization or construction.

❏ School schedule trends

The school's schedule should support instructional practices most appropriate for middle level students. The flexible, interdisciplinary block schedule commonly described in middle level literature can easily be confused with the "high school alternating-day block schedule" or 4 by 4 plans currently in vogue in secondary school reform. While those alternating blocks may be appropriate as a transition between a traditional departmentalized schedule and a flexible interdisciplinary block schedule, little research or literature supports that type of schedule in lieu of the flexible-block schedule so long espoused by middle level educators. While variations of the flexible block schedule are described in recent literature (Williamson, 1993), the flexible, interdisciplinary block schedule has become a trademark of middle level education. Our purpose in this chapter is not to argue for or against the worth of a particular schedule, but to address evident scheduling trends.

Though strongly advocated for many years as the most appropriate instructional delivery system for middle level students, flexible block schedules are not the most common type of schedules in middle level schools across the country. In 1993, Valentine and associates reported traditional period-by-period schedules as most common. In 1966, McEwin and colleagues were able to clarify just how pervasive daily periods of uniform length were. They were present in more than 85% of 6-7-8 middle schools. They found flexible block schedules present in approximately 40% of the sixth and seventh grades and 27% of the eighth grades of 6-7-8 schools.

While it is easy to be pessimistic about school schedules and point to the relatively low percentage of schools using a flexible block schedule, the trend has clearly been toward that schedule. In 1993, Valentine and colleagues summarized data from three national studies which documented the continued growth of interdisciplinary teaming, the instructional process often associated with a flexible block schedule. The number of schools reporting interdisciplinary teaming increased from 33% in 1989 (Alexander & McEwin) to 42% in 1990 (Epstein & Mac Iver) to 57% in 1992 (Valentine et al.) in1993. As the emphasis on interdisciplinary instruction continues, so too must the changes to more flexible, block-type schedules to effectively facilitate this instructional process.

❏ Implications

McEwin and associates (1996) concluded, as had researchers before them, that "all middle schools should implement flexible scheduling so that developmentally responsive curriculum and instruction can occur" (p.

137). All middle level educators and policy makers have a responsibility to provide a schooling experience that is developmentally responsive. The instructional schedule is the organizational heart of this responsibility.

❏ Recommended readings

Knowing where to obtain critical information about middle level trends can be as valuable as having specific information about a limited number of trends. We have chosen to address three significant organizational trends in this chapter. Limitations of space prevent the inclusion of trends about other issues such as organizational leadership, organizational staff, and instructional programs. For insight about many of the trends in middle level education, three recent national research reports are recommended. Copies of each can be obtained from the professional organization that published the study.

Education in the Middle Grades: National Practices and Trends. In 1988, the Center for Research on Elementary and Middle Schools at The Johns Hopkins University surveyed 2,400 public schools from some 25,000 schools with grade seven in the grade pattern. Joyce L. Epstein and Douglas J. Mac Iver wrote the report published in 1990 by the National Middle School Association. This study is worthy of note because the data are reported for the traditional middle level grades and for schools that serve the needs of young adolescents outside the traditional grade configurations, e.g. K-8, K-12, and 7-12.

Leadership in Middle Level Education, Volume I: A National Survey of Middle Level Leaders and Schools. From 1991 through 1993, the National Association of Secondary School Principals sponsored an extensive study of middle level programs and leadership. The first volume of the study provided detailed information about educational practices in middle level schools across the nation. The researchers and authors of the 1993 report were Jerry W. Valentine, Donald C. Clark, Judith L. Irvin, James W. Keefe, and George Melton. The study was published in 1993 by National Association of Secondary School Principals.

America's Middle Schools: Practices and Progress — A 25 Year Perspective. The most recent national data of significance comes from C. Kenneth McEwin, Thomas Dickinson, and Doris Jenkins. Their 1993 national survey of middle level schools used the 1988 Alexander and McEwin definition of middle level which included schools with grade patterns 5-6-7-8, 6-7-8, 7-8, and 7-8-9. Their report was published by National Middle School Association in 1996. Chapter 14, Conclusions and Recommendations, would be of particular value to any middle level educator seeking to understand the trends and practices of middle level education over the past three decades.

❏ Concluding thoughts

As we conclude this chapter, we return to the historical concept posed in the opening paragraph: What can we learn from the trends of the past that will inform us for the future? Many will argue that grade organizational patterns are insignificant compared to the developmental appropriateness of the program for students at a given maturational stage. While this may be sound theoretically, in practice it is evident that differences exist between the educational practices found in schools of varying grade patterns. McEwin and associates (1996) concluded that "Those believing that grade organization is not a key factor in the success levels of middle schools need only to reflect on the findings of this and other recent studies to see the fallacy of this assumption" (p. 131). They recommend that "grade organization decisions should be driven by the developmental characteristics, needs, and interests of young adolescents" (p. 131). Middle level education has moved at a deliberate speed toward embracing the middle school grade level patterns. Every expectation exists that research will continue to support the value of smaller school enrollments and flexible block schedules, two trends discussed in this chapter. Perhaps educators should move with more haste to implement those trends as well. A study of the three research reports recommended in this chapter will provide additional insight about specific issues prevalent in specific schools. "Beam me up Scotty, for I have some insight into the future and I want to discuss with the crew how to apply it to the present." Ⓡ

References

Alexander, W. (1968). *A survey of organizational patterns of reorganized middle schools.* Research Project No. 7-D-026. Washington, DC: United States Department of Health, Education, and Welfare.

Alexander, W. M., & McEwin, C. K. (1989). *Schools in the middle: Status and progress.* Columbus, OH: National Middle School Association.

Barker, J. (1992). *Paradigms: The business of discovering the future.* New York: Harper Collins.

Epstein, J. L., & Mac Iver, D. J. (1990). *Education in the middle grades: National practices and trends.* Columbus, OH: National Middle School Association.

McEwin, C. K., Dickinson, T. S., Jenkins, D. M. (1996). *America's middle schools: Practices, and progress — A 25 year perspective.* Columbus, OH: National Middle School Association.

Rock, D. A., and Hemphill, J. K. (1966). *The junior high school principalship.* Washington, DC: National Association of Secondary School Principals.

Valentine, J. W., Clark, D. C., Nickerson, N. C., & Keefe, J. W. (1981). *The middle level principalship, Volume I: A survey of middle level principals and programs.* Reston, VA: National Association of Secondary School Principals.

Valentine, J. W., Clark, D. C., Irvin, J. L., Keefe, J. W., & Melton, G. (1993). *Leadership in middle level education, Volume I: A national survey of middle level leaders and schools.* Reston, VA: National Association of Secondary School Principals.

Williamson, R. (1993). *Scheduling the middle level school to meet early adolescent needs.* Reston, VA: National Association of Secondary School Principals.

David Hough

A Bona Fide Middle School: Programs, Policy, Practice, and Grade Span Configurations

F ive important findings can be drawn from the research literature accompanying middle school programs, policies, and practice (i.e., components) and grade span: (1) components are generally conceptualized in a similar, agreed-upon fashion by most middle school scholars, (2) these same components do enhance student achievement, (3) grade span does make a difference in student achievement, (4) the number of schools in the United States implementing middle school components around a 6,7,8 grade span continues to grow, and (5) research is just now beginning to provide necessary data to help researchers ask the "right" questions leading to definitive answers for the first time ever.

Middle school components are most often conceptualized as *teams of teachers* meeting during a *common planning time* to (among other things) develop *integrated curricula* and teach within the structure of a *flexible schedule* that allows for more in-depth study and experiential learning. *Advisory* programs are provided in an effort to establish positive relationships between young adolescents and adults, ensuring that students are known well by at least one adult. Students are encouraged to participate in *intramural* activities to build self-esteem and promote healthy life-styles. *Exploratory* classes or enrichment experiences are provided to allow students a chance to experiment with novel subject matter and interest areas without fear of being penalized by a letter grade. And all of the above are accomplished within *small heterogeneous* learning *communities* that emphasize *cooperative* teaching strategies that capitalize on the social dimension of teaching and learning.

❑ Background

Discussions surrounding middle level programs, policies, practice, and grade span configurations spawn some of the most frequently asked questions about middle level education. Chief among these (and underlying the entire middle level education movement) are questions associated with the impact of middle school components and grade span on student outcomes, especially academic achievement. While research on middle level education programs, policies, and practice (i.e. components) has increased over the past two-and-a-half decades, virtually all studies have focused on the following: (a) ways to design and implement middle school components effectively, (b) the impact of this change process on teachers, teaching, and overall school organization, (c) student affect and/or teacher/principal perceptions of outcomes (Hough, 1991a; 1991b; 1991c; 1991d; Irvin, 1992).

Before 1996, not enough empirical data had been collected to show conclusive evidence that any given combination of middle school components implemented within any given grade span configuration impacted student achievement (Hough, 1991d; Van Zant & Totten, 1995). This is not to say that middle school components have no relationship to grade span. They do. However, until recent efforts guided by comprehensive empirical data, too much past research had been based on only a few studies that had concentrated on a single program, policy, or practice (Hough, 1991a; 1991b; 1991c; 1991d; Irvin, 1992; Mac Iver & Epstein, 1993; Melton, 1984), leaving too much to speculative theory and incipient understandings instead of scientific fact – the latter of which is now the central focus (Felner, 1996).

Bona fide "middle schools" can and do differ greatly in the number and type of components operationalized at varying degrees; however, all should exhibit specific programs, policies, and practice that meet the diverse physical, social, emotional, moral, cognitive needs of young adolescents. These learners ranging roughly between 10 and 14 years of age are most often, but not always, found in grades six, seven, and eight; some may be found in the fifth grade, while others may be in the ninth grade, due to differing rates of maturation. This wide range of diverse development adds to the component/grade span-outcomes conundrum.

Relationships among and between components and grade span to student achievement is measurable; however, the direct, indirect, and interactive paths of these relationships are just now being understood by researchers. Preliminary findings indicate that the paths are seldom direct, but that they almost always interact with one or more other variables and in concert do favorably impact student achievement when implemented conscien-

286

tiously over time (Felner, 1996). The plausibility of middle level education, then, necessitates broad definitions of a variety of far-ranging components and outcomes.

❑ Rationale

A bona fide middle school is not an organizational structure consisting of a specific grade level configuration, set of components, and name that includes the word *middle*. It is, however, any organizational structure consisting of developmentally appropriate programs, policies, and practice tailored to maximize young adolescent learning while nurturing affect (Clark & Clark, 1993; Cuban, 1993; Epstein, 1990; Hough, 1989; Johnston, 1984; Romano & Georgiady, 1994). A number of demographic variables peculiar to a specific school community make an impact on middle level organizational structures (Becker, 1987; Epstein, 1990; Hough, 1995a; 1995b; Hough & Irvin, 1995), and these factors do influence types, degrees and levels of implementation that make a difference in learning outcomes, including achievement and socialization (Epstein, 1990; Hough, 1995b; Hough & Sills-Briegel, in press).

While middle school components most often refer to programs, policies, and practice perceived to hold promise as effective ways to facilitate learning and affect, not unlike other innovations in education or any other field, many of the effects or outcomes have yet to be fully substantiated through empirical research (Hough, 1995a; 1995b; Mac Iver & Epstein, 1993; Van Zant & Totten, 1995). Even though lack of data regarding the effects of change prior to full implementation over time is not uncommon in any field of study, some have misconstrued incipient or incomplete data and used same as grounds for opposing middle level education ideals. Too often, well-meaning groups use "ipso facto" logic to challenge the efficacy of new approaches. In an effort to ensure the highest quality education possible for their children, parents and school boards sometimes associate declining test scores, for example, with what they may perceive to be a "warm-fuzzy" curriculum infused with advisory and exploratory classes that detract from time that could be devoted to more rigorous "basics." In an extreme example, some have been led to believe that middle level education has caused schools in rural communities to consolidate and believe, further, that consolidation is detrimental to children (see, e.g., DeYoung, Howley, & Theobald, 1995). In reality, while varied, middle level education programs, policies, and practice have more often been viewed as reform initiatives to be implemented after consolidation had already taken place. And many of these initiatives share basic philosophical and operational similarities with middle school components that are grounded in research theory and composed of equally varied orientations, approaches, and methodologies (Cuban, 1993; Hough, 1995a; Mac Iver & Epstein, 1993).

In addition to descriptive data used to identify middle school components, two premises undergird the research/theory used to determine grade levels most often found to be appropriate for inclusion in middle schools. The first premise holds that early adolescence is a separate developmental stage situated between childhood and adolescence. The second premise holds that appropriate programs, policies, and practice designed to meet young adolescent needs are difficult to generalize to grade levels because differing rates of maturation are highly individual between childhood and adolescence. Therefore, it would follow that the most prudent approach to the grade configuration issue is to develop a bona fide middle school first, then determine which children are at the young adolescent stage before assigning them to grades in that organizational structure. Too often in the past, the reverse has been tried, i.e., grouping students by grade level (vertical articulation) and then trying to manufacture solutions to fit whatever resulting grade span configuration emerges – usually as a result of administrative expediency in reaction to facilities utilization (e.g., Alexander, 1988; Johnston, 1984). This latter approach has not met with high levels of success (e.g., Hough, 1989; Van Zant & Totten, 1995). The former, however, is just now being tried in enough locales nationally to allow for empirical research to be conducted among truly different school types (Hough & Irvin, 1995).

❏ Programs, policies, practice = components

Middle school components can be conceptualized in a variety of ways. One very general rubric classifies all components as either curricular, co-curricular, or extramural programs. More often, middle level researchers, scholars, and practitioners refer to a list of programs, policies, and practice that often vary in number from six to twelve (e.g., Epstein & Mac Iver, 1990; McEwin, Dickinson, Erb, & Scales, 1995; Romano & Georgiady, 1994). Among the most common are advisory, intramurals, teaching teams with common planning time, flexible (usually block) scheduling, integrated curricula (multidisciplinary or interdisciplinary), and exploratory classes. Each of these, as well as additional "components," are discussed in some depth throughout this volume.

Since 1989, *Turning Points: Preparing American Youth for the 21st Century* (Carnegie Council on Adolescent Development, 1989) has been the catalyst for development of both components and blueprints for designing and implementing bona fide middle schools throughout the United States (e.g., Oakes, Serna, & Guiton, 1996). Using *Turning Points* as a blueprint, many schools have developed and implemented a variety of programs, policies, and practices that focus on the following: creating small communities for learning in which every student is known well by at least one adult; designing and teaching a common core of academics that centers around literacy, the sciences, critical thinking, healthy life-styles, ethical behavior, and citizenship in a pluralistic society; ensuring success for all students by eliminating tracking by achievement while promoting cooperative learning and flexible instructional time; empowering teachers and administrators; exerting more centralized control over instruction leading to high levels of measurable performance; staffing middle grades with teachers who have been specially prepared to teach young adolescents; improving academic performance through fostering health and fitness; reengaging families through meaningful roles and school governance; and connecting school with communities by forming partnerships that are mutually responsible for students' success (Carnegie Council on Adolescent Development, 1989).

In addition, a new blueprint, *Great Transitions* (Carnegie Council on Adolescent Development, 1996), published as the fourth and concluding report of the Carnegie Task Force on Education and Young Adolescence, along with a new position paper from National Middle School Association (NMSA), *This We Believe: Developmentally Responsive Middle Level Schools* (1995), may very well become the next catalysts for middle level school improvement by providing innovative ways of viewing the components of a middle school. Using *This We Believe* as a guide, middle schools would design programs, policies, and practice addressing the following: curriculum that is challenging, integrative, and exploratory; varied teaching and learning approaches; assessment and evaluation that promote learning; flexible organizational structures; health, wellness, and safety; comprehensive guidance and support services (NMSA, 1995).

An encouraging facet of the NMSA rubric of reform is that, regardless of how programs, policies, and practices are fashioned, the middle school components become *descriptive* rather than *prescriptive* in nature. This is a marked departure from earlier efforts to replicate components across schools. The descriptive nature of these middle school components guards against proselytizing or attempts to routinize charismatic reform initiatives. Instead, the NMSA recommendations concentrate on customized components to meet individual school improvement plans in conjunction with community needs and preference. While site-based initiatives are welcome, "customization" adds to the methodological complexities presented researchers studying the effect of components and grade span on student outcomes, including achievement.

❏ The relationship between components and grade span

Before the mid 1980s, designing a "middle school" had traditionally involved grouping students by grade level (e.g., 7-8, 6-8, 7-9) and changing the name of the school from *junior high* to *middle school*. Numerous descriptive studies have documented this reorganization movement and have examined changing demographics by grade level configuration, usually noting decreases in the number of 7-9 and K-6 schools coupled with increases in the number of K-5 and 6-8 schools (Alexander & McEwin, 1989; Hough 1991a; 1991b; 1991c; McEwin, Dickinson, & Jenkins, 1996; Valentine, Clark, Nickerson, & Keefe, 1981; Valentine, Clark, Irvin, Keefe, & Melton, 1993). According to the National Center for Education Statistics (1995) and verified by McEwin, Dickinson, & Jenkins (1995), the following data were identified for the most common grade spans housing a seventh-grade in 1993:

Number and Percent of Middle Level Schools in 1993 by Grade Span			
Grade Span	Number of Schools	Percent of Total	Past 20 Years % of Change
5-8	1,223	11%	+ 53%
6-8	6,115	55%	+293%
7-8	2,412	22%	+ 5%
7-9	1,424	13%	- 91%

If one begins by examining the seventh grade and then expands the examination in a direction either toward higher grade levels included in the school's overall configuration or toward lower grade levels, a clear pattern emerges. As higher grades are included, say the 8th and 9th, programs, policies, and practices tend to be more subject centered. Fewer components are operational and at lower levels. As lower grades are included, say the 6th and 5th, programs, policies, and practices tend to be more student-centered. More components are generally operational and at a higher level in schools with these lower grades including K-8 schools (Hough, 1995a). In short, there is a relationship between components and grade span.

The above is an important finding whenever one considers how most young adolescent students are grouped for instruction. More than 35 different grade span configurations contain a seventh grade. Of these, seven are common enough to warrant attention (PK/K/1 - 8, 4-8, 5-8, 6-8, 7-8, 7-9, 7-12), and four grade spans (5-8, 6-8, 7-8, 7-9) house almost 90% of all seventh-grade students (Hough, 1995b).

Most recently, attention has focused on programmatic and policy changes that seek to effect changes in practice. As a result, young adolescent teaching-learning dimensions have been determined to be more closely aligned to elementary schooling than to secondary schooling (Epstein, 1990; Hough 1995a; Mac Iver, 1990; Melton, 1984; Scales & McEwin, 1994). Many states have changed their teaching certification requirements to reflect this shift. Instead of being an "add-on" to the secondary certificate, middle level teaching certification is becoming more closely aligned to the elementary program, or it is a stand-alone program (McEwin, Dickinson, Erb, & Scales, 1995; Swaim & Stefanich, 1996). These developments have led to closer scrutiny of appropriate grade level configurations, especially placement of fifth, sixth, and ninth grade students.

Regardless of their grade span placement, young adolescents should not be thrust into an inappropriate learning environment. The most prudent approach is to develop appropriate programs, policies, and practices for young adolescents first, then place students into the resulting organizational structure. ℝ

References

Alexander, W. M. (1988). Schools in the middle: Rhetoric and reality. *Social Education, 52* (2), 107-121.

Alexander, W. M., & McEwin, C. K. (1989). *Schools in the middle: Status and progress.* Columbus, OH: National Middle School Association.

Becker, H.J. (1987). *Addressing the needs of different groups of early adolescents: Effects of varying school and classroom organizational practices on students from different social backgrounds and abilities.* (Report No. 16, June). Baltimore: VSP Industries

Carnegie Council on Adolescent Development. (1989). *Turning points: Preparing American youth for the twenty-first century.* New York: Carnegie Corporation.

Carnegie Council on Adolescent Development. (1996). *Great transitions: Preparing adolescents for a new century*. New York: Carnegie Corporation.

Clark, S.N., & Clark, D.C. (1993). Middle level school reforms: The rhetoric and the reality. *The Elementary School Journal, 139* (5), 447 - 460.

Cuban, L. (1993). What happens to reforms that last? The case of the junior high school. *American Education Research Journal, 29* (1), 227-251.

DeYoung A.J., Howley, C., & Theobald, P. (1995). The cultural contradictions of middle schooling for rural community survival. *Journal of Research in Rural Education, 11* (2), 24-35.

Epstein, J.L. (1990). What matters in the middle grades—grade span or practices? *Phi Delta Kappan, 71* (6), 438-444.

Epstein, J.L., & Mac Iver, D.J. (1990). *Education in the middle grades: National practices and trends*. Columbus, OH: National Middle School Association.

Felner, R. (November, 1996). *Most frequently asked questions about middle level education*. Presentation made to the National Middle School Association National Conference, Baltimore, MD.

Hough, D. (1995a). The elemiddle school: A model for middle grades reform. *Principal, 74* (3), 6-9.

Hough, D. (November, 1995b). *The effect of grade-span configuration on student outcomes*. Research Symposium, presented to the Annual Conference of the National Middle School Association. New Orleans, LA.

Hough, D. (April, 1991a). *A review of middle level organization*. Paper presented to the American Educational Research Association, Annual Conference, Chicago, IL.

Hough, D. (1991b). *A review of middle level organization. Resources in Education*. Eugene, OR: ERIC Clearinghouse on Educational Management.

Hough, D. (February, 1991c). *Middle level organization: A curriculum policy analysis*. Paper presented to the National Association of Secondary School Principal National Convention; Orlando, FL.

Hough, D. (1991d). Setting a research agenda for middle level education. *Crossroads, 1* (1), 3-11.

Hough, D. (1989) *Vertical articulation for the middle grades*. Riverside, CA: California Educational Research Cooperative, University of California (ERIC Document Reproduction Number ED 315 8e).

Hough, D., & Sills-Briegel, T. (in press). Student achievement and middle level programs, policies, and practices in rural America: The case of community-based v. consolidated organizations. *Journal of Research in Rural Education.*

Irvin, J. (1992). A research agenda for middle level education: An idea whose time has come. *Current Issues in Middle Level Education, 1* (1), 21-29.

Johnston, J. H. (1984). A synthesis of research findings on middle level education. In J.H. Lounsbury (Ed.), *Perspectives: Middle school education, 1964-1984* (pp. 134-156). Columbus, OH: National Middle School Association.

Mac Iver, D.J. (1990). Meeting the needs of young adolescents: Advisory groups, interdisciplinary teaching teams, and school transition programs. *Phi Delta Kappan, 71* (6), 458-464.

Mac Iver, D.J., & Epstein, J.L. (1993). Middle grades research: Not yet mature, but no longer a child. *The Elementary School Journal, 93* (5), 519-533.

McEwin, C.K., Dickinson, T.S., Erb, T.O., & Scales, P.C. (1995). *A vision of excellence: Organizing principles for middle grades teacher preparation.* Columbus, OH: National Middle School Association.

McEwin, C. K., Dickinson, T. S., & Jenkins, D. (1996). *America's middle schools: Practices and programs—A 25 year perspective.* Columbus, OH: National Middle School Association.

Melton, G.E. (1984). The junior high school: Successes and failures. In J.H. Lounsbury (Ed.), *Perspectives: Middle school education, 1964-1984* (pp.5-13). Columbus, OH: National Middle School Association.

National Center for Education Statistics (1995). *Digest of education statistics: Common core data.* Washington, DC: Department of Education Statistics.

National Middle School Association. (1995). *This we believe: Developmentally responsive middle level schools.* Columbus, OH: Author.

Oakes, J., Serna, I., & Guiton, G. (1996). Introduction. *Research in Middle Level Education Quarterly, 20* (1), 1-10.

Romano, L.G., and Georgiady, N.P. (1994). Building an effective middle school. Madison, WI: WCB Brown & Benchmark.

Scales, P. C., & McEwin, C. K. (1994). *Growing pains: The making of America's middle school teachers.* Columbus, OH: National Middle School Association.

Swaim, J.H., & Stefanich, G.P. (1996). *Meeting the standards: Improving middle level teacher education.* Columbus, OH: National Middle School Association.

Valentine, J. W., Clark, D., Irvin, J., Keefe, J., & Melton, G. (1993). *Leadership in middle level education, Volume I: A national survey of middle level leaders and schools.* Reston, VA: National Association of Secondary School Principals.

Valentine, J. W., Clark, D. C., Nickerson, N. C., & Keefe, J. W. (1981). *The middle level principalship: A survey of middle level principals and programs.* Reston, VA: National Association of Secondary School Principals.

VanZant, L.M., & Totten, S. (1995). The current status of middle level education research: A critical review. *Research in Middle Level Education, 18* (3), 1-25.

26

Susan B. Trimble

Components of Effective Teams

Throughout the literature about restructuring schools are references to the use of teams (Maeroff, 1993) and teacher collaboration (Lieberman, 1990; Little, 1982). The increasing use and variety of educational teams stretch from interdisciplinary teacher teams to school-based improvement/advisory or faculty teams and at district levels consortiums connecting schools and districts. Little work, however, as been done in the area of educational team effectiveness, mainly due to the difficulty of studying groups outside of the laboratory setting and the complexity of team work. We do, however, know key components of effective group work from research in sociology, business, and psychology from the 1950s to the present. These key components provide a framework for organizing what we know about interdisciplinary teams at the middle level.

❏ Section I: Effective Teams in General ❏

Several themes of effective groups/teams emerge across non-education disciplines. From group/team analysis in the literature and from business, psychology, and sociology, there is consensus that group performance and organizational phenomenon can be described in terms of four factors: *task, people, process,* and *interactions with the environment* (Morgan, 1986).

Factor 1: Effective teams accomplish their tasks in a superior fashion. Common sense argues that successful sports teams win their matches. Although it seems obvious to point out such teams are considered effective because they accomplish their purpose more efficiently in terms of process or more effectively in terms of outputs, the observation focuses attention on the central purpose of each team. Effective teams link purpose and performance.

Factor 2: Effective teams satisfy the human needs of the participants. The human dimensions of teams may be most evident in dysfunctional groups. By contrast, effective teams appear free of problematic relationships (Napier & Gershenfeld, 1993). Team members are secure psychosocially and socially, freely express feelings and ideas, and willingly grapple with the team's work. These feelings generate connectedness with other team members and result in heightened group experience and shared meaning (Serge, 1990).

Factor 3: Effective teams develop suitable procedures and skills for being productive while sustaining involvement and energy. Members of effective teams exhibit group-orientated behaviors, resulting in cooperation, commitment, and participation of team members. Team members also exhibit flexibility to adjust to new developments and to each other's personalities and talents. They easily change roles and can assume leadership responsibilities when needed. Other skills include decision-making, formulating group goals, determining strategies to provide service to the clients, and networking with experts (Peters, 1993). One can correctly argue that a team member's personal skills coupled with his/her value system influences the development of any team's procedures for group work.

Factor 4: Effective teams maintain interactions with the environments. Effective teams are responsive to changes in the environment (Conner, 1992; Peters, 1993) in two fundamental ways that may appear contradictory, but which, in reality, pivot on the team's ability to evaluate the impact of an event on the team's functioning. In certain instances, effective teams filter out elements from the environment that distract their focus from performance. In other cases, they adapt quickly to changes in resources, demographics, market demands, societal interests, and legal decisions. Overall, they know the necessity of maintaining open communication with people outside the team while tapping resources.

❏ Section II: Effective Interdisciplinary Teams ❏

Empirical data for research related to teaming began with the ten studies associated with the Pontoon Transitional Design (Clark and Clark 1992). By the 1990s, a growing research base about teaming was emerging (Irvin & Arhar, 1995; Trimble & Irvin, 1996) with the findings providing guidelines for creating and sustaining effective teams (Trimble & Miller, 1996). For middle school practitioners, three comprehensive teaming handbooks address implementation of teaming, team functioning, and maintenance: Merenbloom's (1991, 3rd ed.) *The Team Process* and Erb and Doda's (1989) *Team Organization: Promise, Practices and Possibilities* have been available for several years. The most comprehensive work about middle school teaming is Dickinson and Erb's (1997) book *We Gain More Than We Give: Teaming In Middle Schools*. The text is a compilation of team stories from a variety of perspectives (students, teachers, administrators, rural schools, mature, and new teams) and a variety of knowledge bases (historical, organizational, research, and sports).

Using the key components of successful teams gleaned from these research studies and publications, what we know about successful interdisciplinary teams can be grouped by the four factors of effective groups/teams in general.

Factor 1: Effective interdisciplinary teams accomplish their tasks in a superior fashion. Interdisciplinary team tasks are divided into the three main areas: (1) teaching, (2) advising, and (3) managing the logistics of record-keeping, scheduling, and grouping students. We know that effective teams accomplish their purposes with a variety of skills and strategies despite the barriers of additional responsibilities, time restraints, and inconveniences that seem to hinder other teams' performance.

In the area of teaching, teachers are experts in their subject area; they design and implement thematic units and integrated studies; they use a variety of grouping arrangements including heterogeneous groups of students both within the classroom as cooperative learning groups and among classes and, in some cases, between grade levels. Many teams use flexible scheduling for rearranging time to match and support learning activities. Effective teams coordinate activities with exploratory teachers, incorporate service and civic programs, and use community resources (Stevenson & Carr, 1993). Assessment combines holistic measures such as portfolio assessment and advisory time for conferences and student peer reviews, with careful attention to record-keeping of student progress.

Effective teams manage other team responsibilities efficiently to allow time for development of thematic learning and integrated studies. Unfortunately, the task of managing students, their records, placement, and special education students' needs can dominate team meeting time and discussion (Cooper-Straw, 1993; McQuaide, 1992). Effective teams establish procedures to overcome these pressures. They may delegate among themselves the responsibilities and chores associated with discipline, student assignments, scheduling, and supervision of students in the halls, bus areas, and around the school. They usually develop a systematic method of record-keeping of parent and student forms, attendance and disciplinary referrals, curriculum manuals, textbook orders, schedules, and other pertinent information.

In the area of advising, many teams use advisory time, project time, field trips, and sports events for strengthening student ties to each other and to teachers, conduct face-to-face parent conferences, coordinate test days and homework assignments. Goals for integrated study in the middle grades offered by Stevenson and Carr (1993) integrate two tasks of teams and may provide a framework for reflective assessment by team members and researchers in these areas. The goals are (1) students will grow more confident, (2) students will work together cooperatively, (3) students will develop social-ethical consciousness, (4) students will think, think, and think.

The integration of advising and teaching elements of team functioning is exemplified in the activities of an eighth grade two-person team at Shoreham-Wading River Middle School as described by Burkhardt (1997). For example, expectations for the team's behavior and attitude are termed The Distinctions and are frequently discussed and taken seriously; the Inquiry Project targets students producing a researched individual magazine of a topic that integrates math, science, foreign language, English and social studies plus the writing process; the three day trip to the Pocono Environmental Education Center complete with canoeing, square dancing, and sunrise hikes provides the setting for teaming bonding.

Factor 2: Effective teams satisfy the human needs of the participants.

Effective teams interact easily, professionally, and socially on the job. Members of nominated high performing teams in a study of team functioning commented, "we get along great!" "We consider ourselves like a family," and "Not only are we co-workers, but good friends, too! We love teaming. We can't imagine ever working alone again" (Trimble, 1995, p. 178).

The personal needs and preferences of team teachers are reinforced and successfully interact with those of other teachers on successful teams. George & Stevenson (1988) surveyed 154 middle school principals for their perceptions of highly effective interdisciplinary teams. They distilled characteristics of the "best" teams in the "best" schools: team teachers' personal characteristics of noncompetitiveness, high "work ethic," and expertise in their subject areas; commitment to students' success, attention to record-keeping of their progress; and attitudes toward teammates of "diverse but united," combined with a spirit of cooperation. Effective teams are those where the personal characteristics and values of the teachers are aligned with the purposes of teams.

George and Alexander (1993) touched upon the essence of teams centered around people when they wrote, "Educators, like corporate managers, must find ways to organize relatively large institutions so that authentic person-centered communities exist within them" (p. 73). When teams become "real" teams, they supply the professional satisfaction and opportunities for professional growth for teachers and, simultaneously help to build teams that meet student needs more effectively (Johnston, Markle, & Arhar, 1988).

Factor 3: Effective teams develop suitable procedures and skills for being productive while sustaining involvement and energy. Effective teams have passed through the beginning stages of group development of "forming," "storming," and "norming" (Tuckman, 1965) and through the first two phases George (1982) proposed as "organization" and "community." Within these stages, team teachers grow to understand, value, and integrate the personalities and styles of one another. Personality issues do not dominate in effective teams because the team has moved into focusing on students or projects, while using group processes that sustain relationships and communication.

Specific team procedures to maintain communication and facilitate the work of the team include (1) regular team meetings with all team members present and on time, guided by an informal or formal agenda, (2) the participation of all team members in decision-making process, (3) goal-setting for the school year, (4) the use of team meeting time to concentrate on instructional planning and evaluation.

Factor 4: Effective teams interact with their environment according to their purposes. Effective teams tap the rich array of resources within their own schools and communities. They may create design integrated studies around local rivers or mountains (Stevenson & Carr, 1993), initiate partnerships with businesses, offer open-houses for parents and "munchies-for-mothers," do presentations at workshops and conferences, write articles for newsletters, or become involved in action research with universities. George and Stevenson (1989) called it "outreach" in their article about the best teams in the best schools.

Continual and successful adjustments to changing youth culture can stem from team members keeping a pulse on student interests, community events, and trends in the media. The current growth of gang-related behaviors, the offering of beepers by Pepsi Company ("Take Note," 1996), rings in noses and eyebrows, and the drooping pants fashion can result in additional stresses for some teachers and administrators. Understanding the underlying causes and being prepared through dialogue of the issues and in some cases, staff development, increase the ability of team members to interact with students. Effective teams keep current.

Cited as the main determinant of the implementation of school reform, principals have a major effect on team functioning, although initial investigations of principal/team relations show less attachment by nominated high-performing teams to principals than nominated average performing teams (Trimble, 1995). A principal's participatory leadership style increases the sense of ownership, boosts moral and self-esteem, and saves time after decision making (Spindler and George, 1984). In answer to the question, "What principal behaviors increase team performance?" Spindler (1994) described the following behaviors: modeling shared decision making, providing training, clearly defining areas of responsibilities for teams and honoring team decisions in those areas, grooming future team leaders, providing resources, receiving input from teams through describing school problems to teams (not solutions) and asking for input, and adjusting his/her style of leadership to the team's level of development. Principals help to develop and sustain effective teams (Trimble & Miller, 1996).

All of us have worked on teams and known the work of teams is not easy. On the other hand, we know the benefits of effective teams and are making headway in understanding their components. As teams are positioned between the students and teachers on one hand and the larger organization on the other, our efforts to build effective teams will be richly rewarded in both contexts. ℝ

References

Arhar, J. M., & Irvin, J. L. (1995). Interdisciplinary team organization: A growing research base. *Middle School Journal, 26* (5), 65-67

Burkhardt, R. (1997). Teaming: Sharing the experience. In T. S. Dickinson and T. O. Erb (Eds.), *We gain more than we give: Teaming in middle schools* (pp. 163-184). Columbus, OH: National Middle School Association..

Clark, S. N., & Clark, D. C. (1992). The Pontoon Transitional Design: A missing link in the research on interdisciplinary teaming. *Research in Middle Level Education, 15* (2), 57-81.

Conner, D. R. (1992). *Managing at the speed of change.* New York: Villard Books.

Cooper-Shaw, C. (1993). A content analysis of teacher talk during middle school team meetings. *Research in Middle Level Education, 17* (1), 27-45.

Dickinson, T. S., & Erb, T. O. (1997) *We gain more than we give: Teaming in middle schools.* Columbus, OH: National Middle School Association

Erb, T. O., & Doda, N. (1989). *Team organization: Promise, practices and possibilities.* Washington, DC: National Education Association.

George, P. S., & Stevenson, C. (1989). *Highly effective interdisciplinary teams: Perceptions of exemplary middle school principals.* (ERIC Reproduction Service No. ED 303 866).

George, P. S. (1982). Interdisciplinary team organization. *Middle School Journal, 13* (3), 10-13.

George, P. S., & Alexander, W. M. (1993). *The exemplary middle school* (2nd ed.). New York: Harcourt Brace Jovanovich College Publishers.

Goodman, P. S., & Associates (1986). *Designing effective work groups.* San Francisco: Jossey-Bass.

Johnston, J. H., Markle, G. C., & Arhar, J. M. (1988). Cooperation, collaboration, and the professional development of teachers. *Middle School Journal, 19* (3), 28-32.

Lieberman, A. (Ed.). (1990). *Schools as collaborative cultures: Creating the future now.* New York: The Falmer Press, 325-340.

Little, J. W. (1982). Norms of collegiality and experimentation: Workplace conditions of school success. *American Educational Research Journal, 19* (3), 325-340.

Lytle, J. H. (1996). The inquiring manager: Developing new leadership structures to support reform. *Phi Delta Kappan, 77* (10), 664-670.

Maeroff, G. I. (1993). Building teams to rebuild schools. *Phi Delta Kappan, 74* (7), 512-519.

McQuaide, J. (1992). Implementation of team planning time. *Research in Middle Level Education, 17* (2), 27-45.

Merenbloom, E. Y. (1991). *The team process in the middle school: A handbook for teachers* (2nd ed.). Columbus, OH: National Middle School Association.

Morgan, G. (1986). *Images of organizations*. Beverly Hills, CA: Sage.

Napier, R. W., & Gershenfeld, M. K. (1993). Groups: Theory and experience. Boston: Houghton Mifflin Company.

Peters,T. (1992). *Liberation management*. New York: Fawcett Columbine.

Senge, P. M. (1990). *The fifth discipline: The art and practice of the learning organization*. New York: Doubleday Currency.

Spindler, J. P. (1994). Personal communication. Atlanta, GA.

Spindler, J. P., & George, P.S. (1984). Participatory leadership in the middle school. *The Clearing House, 57* (7), 293-295.

Stevenson, C., & Carr, J. F. (Eds.). (1993). *Integrated studies in the middle grades: 'Dancing through walls.'* New York: Teachers College Press, Columbia University.

Take note. (1996, May 29). *Education Week*, p. 3.

Trimble, S. B., & Miller, J. W. (1996). Creating, invigorating, and sustaining effective teams. *NASSP Bulletin, 80* (584).

Trimble, S. B. (1995). *A theoretical framework for the analysis of high performing interdisciplinary team functioning in selected middle schools*. Unpublished doctoral dissertation, Florida State University, Tallahassee.

Trimble, S. B., & Irvin, J. L. (1996). Emerging from the mists: The field of teaming. *Middle School Journal, 27* (5), 53-56.

Tuckman, B. W. (1965). Developmental sequence in small groups. *Psychological Bulletin, 63* (6), 384-399.

Nancy B. Mizelle and Emmett Mullins

Transition Into and Out of Middle School

T ransition or change from one school to another is an exciting yet apprehensive process, particularly when the transition is from elementary to middle school or from middle to high school. Though a student's social status may increase with each of these normative school changes, within the school context his or her status diminishes. The "top dogs" at the end of elementary and middle schools become the students with the least status in their new school. Young adolescents entering middle school express concern about failure, drugs, giving class presentations, being sent to an administrator's office, being picked on, unkind teachers, and keeping up with assignments. Similarly, young adolescents entering high school are concerned about being picked on and teased by older students, having harder work, making lower grades, and getting lost in a larger, unfamiliar school (Maute, 1991; Mizelle, 1995; Phelan, Yu, & Davidson, 1994; Wells, 1996).

Most middle level educators recognize these student concerns and seek to ease the transition of their incoming and outgoing students to their new school. According to Epstein and Mac Iver's (1990) report of the survey, *Education in the Middle Grades,* the average middle level school used four to five practices to bridge young adolescents' transition into middle school and three to four (significantly fewer) practices to ease their students' transition into high school. Furthermore, those schools that reported the most extensive transition programs were 6-7-8 and 7-8 schools. The most commonly used practices at both levels included students' visiting their new school and administrators and counselors from both schools meeting together to discuss their respective programs. The challenge remains, however, for middle grades educators to do more because students continue to experience difficulty in transition (e.g., Barone, Aguirre-Deandreis, & Trickett, 1991; Hertzog, Morgan, Diamond, & Walker, 1996) and because "school transition programs that use numerous and diverse articulation activities were seen to help students succeed in their first year following a school transition," (Mac Iver, 1990, p. 464). Various ways to meet this challenge are outlined in the remainder of this chapter.

❏ Transition Into Middle School ❏

Among the first to document possible problems at transition were Simmons, Rosenberg, and Rosenberg (1973). In their cross-sectional study of students in grades three through twelve, the researchers noted that at the transition to a middle level school, students experienced significant declines in several areas of self-image. Among the disturbances to self-image were an increased level of self-consciousness, unstable self-image, a decline in global self-esteem, and a reduced sense that others held positive opinions of them. The researchers noted that the disturbances cited were linked to the change in grade level more than age. Thus, the physiological effects of puberty were determined to be less influential in the decline than grade level. Of particular significance was that the disturbances seemed to continue into later adolescence and were not simply the short-term effects of changing schools.

Simmons, Burgeson, Carlton-Ford, and Blyth (1987) examined the impact of multiple life changes and found that children experiencing many changes in coincidence were at a greater risk of failing to cope successfully with the changes. Making the transition to a new school level was one of the major stressors indicated for children along with onset of puberty, early dating, geographic mobility, and changes in parents' marital status. Although boys and girls suffered loss of self-esteem when multiple changes occurred, girls seemed to be particularly vulnerable and had a more difficult time coping as the number of life changes increased.

Eccles and Midgley (1989) suggested that declines in motivation and behavior they documented in students at transition resulted from a mismatch between the psychological needs of young adolescents and the characteristics of the social environment of the school. These researchers asserted that structures and conditions in place in middle level schools facilitated the problems experienced by students. Such structures and conditions included increases in: student population, departmentalization, ability grouping, competitive motivational strategies, grading stringency, and teacher control. Students may at the same time experience decreases in: close relationships with teachers, time to develop a peer network, opportunities to make decisions, and teachers' sense of their own effectiveness.

More recently, researchers have begun to suggest that the disturbances students face at transition are the result of both multiple life changes and the social context that the students are entering (Eccles, Lord, & Midgley, 1991). These researchers documented declines in academic performance, intrinsic motivation, and school attachment after the transition to a middle level school. For example, at a time when students are experiencing a heightened sense of self-focus, middle level teachers often emphasize competition and comparisons between students. Middle level students often have decreased opportunities for decision making at a time when they cognitively and emotionally desire more control. Entering larger middle level schools tends to disrupt students' social networks at a time when peer relationships are of particular importance. Although higher levels of cognitive ability are emerging in young adolescents, middle level teachers often use lower level strategies. Finally, at a time when positive adult relationships may be especially needed, schools do not often plan for or facilitate these relationships.

Fenzel (1989) and Mullins (1997) examined students' transition from elementary to middle school. In both studies, the deleterious effects on students' self-perceptions identified in other studies seemed mitigated by the schools' structures. Specifically, both studies were conducted in middle schools where the sixth graders were on interdisciplinary teams and other aspects of a "middle school philosophy" were implemented.

❏ What Can Middle School Educators Do to Ease ❏ Students' Transition into Middle School?

Middle school educators may have little or no control over the previously cited major life changes that are potentially experienced by their incoming students, but they do have control over the environment created within the school. They can facilitate smooth transition into middle school. Strategies to promote young adolescents' successful transition into middle school can be broken down into two categories: easily implemented events and programs and larger and possibly more formidable changes in curriculum and instruction. The degree of difficulty in implementing programs will likely depend on the status of the individual schools involved. Some schools already have many developmentally attentive programs in place for young adolescents while others may require extensive restructuring.

The first task to undertake to help students make successful school transitions is to organize articulation and planning programs that involve not only administrators and counselors from the various schools, but teachers as well. In his studies of over 1,000 classrooms, Goodlad (1984) concluded that elementary schools and post-elementary schools existed independently from each other, and continuity from one to another was not assured. Even schools in close proximity to one another "might as well have been in different towns, given the lack of communication and articulation between them" (Goodlad, 1984, p. 304). Gaps and overlaps in instruction often occur without a well-articulated curriculum plan. How can students be expected to be prepared for entry into each grade level if their teachers have had little or no communication or knowledge about the grade levels before and after their own? Many authors have suggested "shadow days" in which students from one school "shadow" another student from their new school. In theory, this gives rising middle schoolers an opportunity to feel comfortable with such things as changing classes, instruction, exploratories, and electives with which they may not be familiar. We propose that such "shadow" experiences could be valuable for teachers, as well. This experience would allow teachers at both the "exit" and "entry" level grades to gain a better understanding of the environment where students have been and where they are going. Debriefing opportunities would allow educators to discuss their experiences and focus on ways that instructional programs and academic expectations could be better aligned. Some districts (Weldy, 1991) have adopted the concept of articulation committees to study all aspects of students' transition. Shadow experiences for educators might be a critical factor in the success of such committees.

Epstein and Mac Iver (1990) advocated the adoption of numerous and varied transition programs to help alleviate the short-term stress of school transition. As previously mentioned, a program which allows students from one level to visit the next can be much more powerful than a simple visitation or assembly. By participating in actual classes, students are able to see what goes on in the school firsthand and come away with the understanding that they will be able to do what is expected of them (Epstein & Mac Iver, 1990).

While parents often feel left out and unwanted at middle schools, they should not. Mac Iver (1990) reported that parents that were involved in transition programs were more likely to become active participants in the school and the child's education. Middle school articulation or transition committees should challenge themselves to find ways to involve parents in their child's school from the beginning. Multiple practices may be needed for a successful strategy to emerge.

Finally, middle schools should pay particular attention to students who may be experiencing multiple major life stressors during the transition phase. As a part of some articulation plans, counselors complete forms for students who are at risk for problems at transition to send to the counselors at the next level. Counselors at the new school then provide students individual or small group counseling as needed. A contrasting strategy, and one that demonstrates the need for elementary and middle school educators to work together to facilitate students' transition, is to provide a coping skills curriculum for all students in the year before transition. Snow, Gilchrist, Schilling, Schinke, and Kelso (1986), in support of this strategy, argue that skills for promoting young adolescents' positive mental health are better effected in the year prior to transition than in the year after transition.

❏ Transition Out of Middle School ❏

Larger, more formal and impersonal; a greater variety of teachers and peers; more curriculum choices and extracurricular activities; competitive and grade-oriented – this is the high school environment most young adolescents experience as they make the transition from middle school to high school (Eccles, Midgley, & Adler, 1984). Faced with this transition, young adolescents look forward to more freedom, more choice, the opportunity to participate in more extracurricular activities, and the opportunity to develop friendships; but they also admit to being "nervous" and "scared" about the older students, a larger, unfamiliar school, and harder work (Mizelle, 1995; Wells, 1996).

Research indicates that as young adolescents make the transition into high school many experience a decline in grades and attendance (Barone et al., 1991; Reyes, Gillock, & Kobus, 1994); they view themselves more negatively and experience an increased need for friendships (Hertzog et al., 1996); and by the end of tenth grade, as many as six percent drop out of school (Owings & Peng, 1992). For middle school students including those who have been labeled "gifted" or "high-achieving" the transition into high school can be an unpleasant experience (Mizelle, 1995; Phelan et al., 1994; Wells, 1996)).

❏ What Can Middle School Educators Do to ❏ Ease Students' Transition into High School?

Facilitating young adolescents' transition from middle school to high school seems to require programs that specifically address the transition period (Felner, Ginter, & Primavera, 1982; Hertzog et al., 1996; Mac Iver, 1990) as well as middle school programs that challenge and support students (Belcher & Hatley, 1994; Mac Iver & Epstein, 1991; Mizelle, 1995). Mac Iver (1990) found that when middle school students experienced a high school transition program with several diverse articulation activities, fewer students were retained in the transition grade. Furthermore, middle school principals indicated that they expected fewer of their students to dropout before graduation when the school provided supportive advisory group activities or responsive remediation programs (Mac Iver & Epstein, 1991). When asked at the end of eighth grade and then again in ninth grade "what their middle school teachers could have done to help them get ready for high school," one group of young adolescents responded that teachers should have told them more about high school and that during middle school teachers should have given them more challenging work and taught them more about how to learn on their own (Mizelle, 1995).

❏ Transition-specific program

According to Mac Iver (1990), a high school transition program includes a variety of activities that (a) provide students and parents with information about the new school, (b) provide students with social support during the transition, and (c) bring middle school and high school personnel together to learn about one another's curriculum and requirements. Designing and implementing appropriate activities for a particular high school transition program involves middle school and high school educators working together. It is not the sole responsibility of the middle school or the high school educators but the mutual responsibility of the middle school and high school administrators, counselors, and teachers involved. Ultimately, we believe, it includes input from students and parents at both levels.

Middle school students want to know what high school is going to be like (Mizelle, 1995) and they and their parents need to know about and understand high school programs and procedures (Mac Iver, 1990; Phelan et al., 1994; Sansone & Baker, 1990). "Will I really have classes all over the building?" "What happens if I don't make it to class on time?" "What is a vocational class?" "Should I take College Prep Algebra I or General Algebra I?" " How should I know?" and "What can I do if I get in the wrong class?" Providing students and parents the answer to these and many other questions should be a central component of a high school transition program. In particular, parents need to understand and be actively involved in the decisions their eighth graders are asked to make about classes they will take in ninth grade (Baker & Stevenson, 1986; Paulson, 1994). Parents need to understand students' options and the long-term effects of the course decisions.

Some of the ways students can learn about high school include visiting the high school in the spring, perhaps to "shadow" a high school student; attending a presentation by a high school student; visiting the high school in the fall for schedule information; attending a fall orientation assembly; and discussing high school regulations and procedures with eighth grade teachers. As middle school educators, we need to be able to discuss and answer questions about high school; we also need to encourage students to participate in transition activities.

When parents are involved in students' transition to high school, they tend to stay involved in their child's school experiences (Mac Iver, 1990). When parents are involved in their child's school experiences, students also have higher achievement in high school (Paulson, 1994) and are less likely to drop out of school (Horn & West, 1992). Parents may be invited to participate in conferences with their child and the high school counselor to discuss course work and schedules; they may be invited to visit the high school with their child in the spring and/or in the fall. At the middle school, our responsibility is to inform parents about these opportunities and to encourage them to participate. Perhaps, more importantly, our responsibility is to work to keep parents involved in their child's education and school activities during the middle school years so that they are comfortable "coming to school" and confident that their involvement makes a difference in their child's academic success.

At a time when friendships and social interaction are particularly important for young adolescents, the normative transition into high school often serves to disrupt friendship networks. It is important for a high school transition program to include activities that will provide incoming students social support, activities that give students the opportunity to get to know and develop positive relationships with older students and other incoming students (Hertzog et al., 1996; Mac Iver, 1990). A "Big Sister/Brother" Program, a spring social event for current and incoming high school students, writing programs where eighth and ninth graders correspond with each other (Rosa & Vowels, 1988; Sportsman, 1987), and Freshmen Awareness Groups where students spend time discussing common problems (Deck & Saddler, 1983) are just a few ways that transition programs can provide students social support.

Underlying a successful high school transition program are activities that bring middle school and high school administrators, counselors, and *teachers* together to learn about the programs, courses, and requirements of their respective schools (George, Stevenson, Thomason, & Beane, 1992; Hertzog et al., 1996; Mac Iver, 1990). Activities that create a mutual understanding of curriculum requirements at both levels and of the young adolescent learner will enable middle school educators to better prepare students for high school and will help educators at both levels to develop a high school transition program to meet the particular needs of their students. In addition to the more typical committee or team meetings with representatives from each level, these activities may include K-12 curriculum planning meetings, and teacher and/or administrator visitations, observations, and teaching exchanges that involve both middle and high school educators.

❏ Transition-support program

Providing young adolescents with activities that relate directly to their transition into high school certainly is important. It seems also that providing young adolescents with a challenging and supportive middle school experience is an important factor in their making a successful transition into high school (Belcher & Hatley, 1994; Bry & George, 1980; Mizelle, 1995). For example, Mizelle (1995) found that students (the Delta students) who stayed together with the same teachers through sixth, seventh, and eighth grade and experienced more hands-on, life-related learning activities, integrated instruction, and cooperative learning groups (the Delta Project) were more successful in their transition to high school than were students (the Non-Delta students) from the same school who had a more traditional middle school experience. In ninth grade, the Delta students had higher language arts, science, and social science grades and were more likely to enroll in higher level mathematics courses than the Non-Delta students. More importantly, the Delta students said that being involved in the Delta Project helped them make the transition into high school because it helped them feel more confident about learning and it helped them learn how to get along with their peers.

At the same time, the Delta and Non-Delta students recognized that they were stressed about their grades because the high school teachers expected them to learn more and faster and to do more learning on their own.

In reflection, these young adolescents indicated that their middle school program would have eased their transition into high school if it had provided them with an even more challenging curriculum and if teachers had held students more responsible for their learning and had taught them more strategies for learning on their own.

❏ Conclusion ❏

At first glance, it may seem we are placing sole responsibility for young adolescents' successful transitions into and out of middle school on middle school educators; we are not. Rather, we believe middle school teachers, administrators, and counselors should be actively involved, along with their elementary and high school counterparts, in planning specific transition activities for their students. Additionally, they should be aware that the structure of their middle school program and curriculum may have a long-term influence on their students' success beyond the point of transition. In particular, middle school educators need to seek ways to involve families in their student's education and to challenge *all* young adolescents to be thinking, responsible students. ®

References

Baker, D. P., & Stevenson, D. L. (1986). Mothers' strategies for children's school achievement: Managing the transition to high school. *Sociology of Education, 59* (3), 156-166.

Barone, C., Aguirre-Deandreis, A. I., Trickett, E. J. (1991). Mean-ends problem-solving skills, life stress, and social support as mediators of adjustment in the normative transition to high school. *American Journal of Community Psychology, 19* (2), 207-225.

Belcher, D. C., & Hatley, R. V. (1994). A dropout prediction model that highlights middle level variables. *Research in Middle Level Education, 18* (1), 67-78.

Bry, B. H., & George, F. E. (1980). The preventive effects of early intervention on the attendance and grades of urban adolescents. *Professional Psychology, 11* (2), 252-260.

Deck, M. D., & Saddler, D. L. (1983). Freshmen awareness groups: A viable option for high school counselors. *The School Counselor, 30* (5), 392-397.

Eccles, J. S., Lord, S., & Midgley, C. (1991). What are we doing to early adolescents? The impact of educational contexts on early adolescents. *American Journal of Education, 99* (4), 521-543.

Eccles, J. S., & Midgley, C. (1989). Stage/environment fit: Developmentally appropriate classrooms for early adolescents. In C. Ames & R. Ames (Eds.), *Research on motivation in education: Goals and cognitions* (Vol, 3, pp. 139-186). New York: Academic Press.

Eccles (Parsons), J., Midgley, C., & Adler, T. F. (1984). Grade related changes in the school environment: Effects on achievement motivation. In J. G. Nicholls (Ed.), *Advances in motivation and achievement* (Vol. 3, pp. 283-331). Greenwich, CT: JAI Press.

Epstein, J. L., & Mac Iver, D. J. (1990). *Education in the middle grades: National practices and trends.* Columbus, OH: National Middle School Association.

Felner, R. D., Ginter, M., & Primavera, J. (1982). Primary prevention during school transitions: Social support and environmental structure. *American Journal of Community Psychology, 10* (3), 277-290.

Fenzel, L. M. (1989). Role strains and the transition to middle school: Longitudinal trends and sex differences. *Journal of Early Adolescence, 9* (3), 211-226.

George, P. S., Stevenson, C., Thomason, J., & Beane, J. (1992). *The middle school — and beyond.* Alexandria, VA: Association for Supervision and Curriculum Development.

Goodlad, J. I. (1984). *A place called school.* New York: McGraw-Hill.

Hertzog, C. J., Morgan, P. L., Diamond, P. A., & Walker, M. J. (1996). Transition to high school: A look at student perceptions. *Becoming, 7* (2), 6-8.

Horn, L., & West J. (1992). *National education longitudinal study of 1988: A profile of parents of eighth graders.* Washington, DC: U.S. Government Printing Office.

Mac Iver, D. J. (1990). Meeting the needs of young adolescents: Advisory groups, interdisciplinary teaching teams, and school transition programs. *Phi Delta Kappan, 71* (6), 458-464.

Mac Iver, D. J,. & Epstein, J. L. (1991). Responsive practices in the middle grades: Teacher teams, advisory groups, remedial instruction, and school transition programs. *American Journal of Education, 99* (4), 587-622.

Maute, J. K. (1991). *Transition concerns of eighth-grade students in six Illinois schools as they prepare for high school.* Unpublished doctoral dissertation, National-Louis University, Evanston, IL.

Mizelle, N. B. (1995, April). *Transition from middle school into high school: The student perspective.* Paper presented at the Annual Meeting of the American Educational Research Association, San Francisco.

Mullins, E. R. (1997). *Changes in young adolescents' self-perceptions across the transition from elementary to middle school.* Unpublished doctoral dissertation, University of Georgia, Athens.

Owings, J., & Peng, S. (1992). *Transitions experienced by 1988 eighth graders.* Washington, DC: U.S. Department of Education, Office of Educational Research and Improvement.

Paulson, S. E. (1994). Relations of parenting style and parental involvement with ninth-grade students' achievement. *Journal of Early Adolescence, 14* (2), 250-267.

Phelan, P., Yu, H. C., & Davidson, A. L. (1994). Navigating the psychosocial pressures of adolescence: The voices and experiences of high school youth. *American Educational Research Journal, 31* (2), 415-447.

Reyes, O., Gillock, K., & Kobus, K. (1994). A longitudinal study of school adjustment in urban, minority adolescents: Effects of a high school transition program. *American Journal of Community Psychology, 22* (3), 341-369.

Rosa, A., & Vowels, M. (1988). Helping 8th graders make a "smooth move." *Educational Leadership, 47* (6), 58.

Sansone, J., & Baker, J. (1990). Ninth grade for students at risk for dropping out of high school. *The High School Journal, 73* (3), 218-231.

Simmons, R. G., Burgeson, R., Carlton-Ford, S., & Blyth, D. (1987). The impact of cumulative change in early adolescence. *Child Development, 58* (5), 1220-1234.

Simmons, R. G., Rosenberg, F., & Rosenberg, M. (1973). Disturbance in the self-image at adolescence. *American Sociological Review, 38* (5),553-568.

Snow, W. H., Gilchrist, L., Schilling, R. F., Schinke, S. P., & Kelso, C. (1986). Preparing students for the junior high school. *Journal of Early Adolescence, 6* (2), 127-137.

Sportsman, S. J. (1987). What worries kids about the next level. *Middle School Journal, 18* (3), 34-35.

Weldy, G. R. (Ed.). (1991). *Stronger school transitions improve student achievement.* Bloomington, IN: Indiana University, School of Education.

Wells, M. C. (1996). *Literacies lost: When students move from a progressive middle school to a traditional high school.* New York: Teachers College Press.

Leadership

Clark	*Sally N. Clark* *University of Arizona* *Tuscon, Arizona*
Clark	*Donald C. Clark* *University of Arizona* *Tuscon, Arizona*
Valentine	*Jerry Valentine* *University of Missouri* *Columbia, Missouri*
Trimble	*Susan B. Trimble* *Georgia Southern University* *Statesboro, Georgia*
Whitaker	*Todd Whitaker* *Indiana State University* *Terre Haute, Indiana*

Sally N. Clark and Donald C. Clark

Collaborations and Teacher Empowerment: Implications for School Leaders

Collaboration extends the opportunity for making significant decisions or for influencing decisions about the school and its programs to the various school stakeholder groups. While in middle level schools collaboration takes place in a variety of ways (e.g. teaching teams, advisory groups, task forces, partnerships), the focus of this chapter will be on collaborative or participatory decision making. This form of collaboration is most commonly organized around school/site-based management/leadership teams, organizational development, school improvement teams, and quality circles (Clark & Clark, 1996). While the focus of each of these collaborative approaches may vary slightly, Carlson (1996) contended that each approach provides a process for teachers to "play a significant role in identifying needs or problems, generating alternative strategies, and implementing promising interventions. The key is to recognize the legitimacy of various members playing a significant role in enhancing the quality of life at their school" (p. 267). This recognition through inclusion in collaborative decision-making groups empowers teachers to become actively involved in the life of their schools.

Little doubt exists that American middle level schools have embraced the concept of collaboration. In the National Association of Secondary School Principals' (NASSP) National Survey of Middle Level Leaders and Schools (Valentine, Clark, Irvin, Keefe, & Melton, 1993), 68% of the principals reported the existence of leadership teams in their schools. In their study of effective middle level schools, George and Shewey (1994) also found strong support for shared decision making. Almost three-quarters of the respondents agreed that "a shared decision-making model which is formal, systematic, and provides authentic collaboration between and among teachers, administrators, parents, and students has contributed to the long-term effectiveness of our middle school program" (p. 99). With the strong degree of support for collaborative decision making in middle level schools, it is instructive to examine the following questions:

1. What are the benefits of collaborative decision making to schools and to classroom instruction?
2. What is nature of teacher involvement in collaborative decision making?
3. What are the implications of research on collaborative decision making for school leaders?

Drawing from the current research on collaborative decision making, the remaining part of this chapter will address these three questions.

❏ Benefits of collaboration

The benefits of collaborative decision making are well documented. Collaboration, with its emphasis on collaborative planning, collegial relationships, and sense of community provides middle level teachers and administrators with a viable approach to school restructuring. Research shows that involvement clearly enhances the ability of the school to respond to problems and opportunities and increases effectiveness, efficiency, and productivity (Shedd & Bacharach, 1991). Involvement also leads to better decision making, enhanced relationships between teachers and administrators, and higher employee satisfaction (Smith & Scott, 1990). In addition, collaboration facilitates better decisions by eliciting more viewpoints and improves communication by opening more channels. Human resources are also used more effectively in collaborative environments, and the distance between decisions and implementation is reduced (Lindelow, Coursen, Massarella, Heynderickz, & Smith, 1989). It is evident from the research that collaborative environments increase job satisfaction, help reduce conflict, reduce stress and burnout, and raise morale and trust for school leaders (Shedd & Bacharach, 1991).

Other benefits of teacher and administrator collaboration, as identified by researchers (Little, 1982; Purkey & Smith, 1982; Rosenholtz, 1985; Rosenholtz, 1989; Shedd & Bacharach, 1991; Smith & Scott, 1990) are:

1. Teachers in collaborative schools share ideas about instruction.
2. Schools where teachers talk to each other, design their instruction together, and teach each other have higher achievement scores than schools where teachers work in isolation.
3. Collegial relationships fostered by collaboration break down barriers between departments and among teachers and administrators. Colle-

giality also encourages intellectual discourse that leads to consensus and promotes feelings of unity and commonality among the staff.

4.   Collaboration supports professional development and contributes to improved teaching and learning.

5.   Collaborative environments are particularly helpful to beginning teachers.

6.   Teacher participation is critical to the success of any change effort.

Smylie (1994) reviewed studies dealing with participative decision making and found that collaboration increases teacher commitment, satisfaction, and morale. He suggested, however, that these collaborative efforts usually have little impact on the way teachers teach. In her study of school-based decision making, Hannaway (1993) found very little evidence of positive change in the classroom. In fact, her analysis suggested that high level involvement in school-based management, because of the time and energy it takes, may actually have detrimental effects on classroom instruction. Elmore (1993) suggested that school/site-based management clearly threatens established power relationships and that "Debates about centralization and decentralization in American education, then, are mainly debates about who should have access to and influence over decisions, not about what the content and practice of teaching and learning should be or how to change those things" (p. 40).

Some research, however, supports positive classroom effects of collaboration. For example, teachers who participate in district-level curricular and instructional program decision making reported substantial gains in their own understanding of student learning and the instructional processes that influenced the work of their students (Smylie, Brownlee-Conyers, & Crowson 1991). In addition, Smylie (1994) found that school-site collaborative decision making "prompted teachers to share ideas and experiment with different instructional strategies" (p. 140). Strong relationships between participative decision making and systemic curriculum and instructional changes were found in Chicago schools with democratic politics and strong professional cultures (Bryk, Easton, Kerbow, Rollow, & Sebring, 1993).

The research on collaborative decision making suggests that teacher participation does positively affect the school. Higher morale and teacher satisfaction, positive school climate, better communication, and increased involvement and empowerment are consistently reported. On the other hand, with a few exceptions, there appears to be little evidence that collaboration brings about changes in classroom practice.

❏ Teacher involvement in decision making

The extent to which teachers are empowered to make decisions is an area that has been examined by several studies. The NASSP Study of Leadership in Middle Level Schools (Valentine et al., 1993) investigated the degree of involvement of leadership teams in decision making. The findings do not reflect a high degree of active involvement in decision making on the part of leadership teams or staff committees. The level of involvement was most typically focused on making recommendations or holding discussions. Real power to make decisions was infrequent. When compared to data from the NASSP 1981 Study (Valentine, Clark, Nickerson, & Keefe, 1981) the "degree of change in the 12 years and the level of impact of shared decision making in middle level schools across the nation is modest at best" (Valentine et al. 1993, p. 39).

The low degree of participation in collaborative decision making may be indicative of differing perceptions of teachers and administrators about participative decision making. In a study conducted by Shedd and Bacharach (1991), 93 percent of the principals queried reported that decision making in their schools was a collaborative process. Only 32 percent of the teachers in these same schools characterized the decision-making process as being collaborative. Shedd and Bacharach (1991) attributed the differences in perception to the principals' belief that giving teachers opportunities to share opinions was collaborative decision making. Teachers, however, "dismissed mere consultation, particularly if it involved a handpicked group of teachers" (p. 141).

Is the low degree of teacher participation in decision making primarily an issue of differing perceptions between administrators and principals? Probably not. Other factors may also come into play. For example, principals may be uncomfortable with or unwilling to share decision making or to give up their consolidated power (Bryk, Easton, Kerbow, Rollow, & Sebring, 1993). Teachers may not be willing to become involved in decision making, particularly if they perceive it to be based on external compliance models or district, school board, or state mandates (Smylie, 1994). In addition, teachers and administrators may not be willing to or able to find the time to collaborate (Bird & Little, 1986; Clark & Clark, 1994; Dawson, 1984).

Drawing from their research, Levine and Eubanks (1992) identified the following as major obstacles in implementing site (school)-based management, a comprehensive form of collaborative decision making:

- Inadequate time, professional development, and technical assistance.

- Difficulties in stimulating consideration and acceptance of inconvenient changes.
- Unresolved issues involving administrative leadership and enhanced power among other participants.
- Constraints on teacher participation in decision making.
- Reluctance of administrators at all levels to give up traditional prerogatives.
- Restrictions imposed by school board, state, and federal regulations and by contracts with teacher organizations.

Bailey (1991) and Carlson (1996) identified additional potential problems in collaborative decision making. These problems included : (1) change takes time and teachers are often too busy to spend much time on school decision making; (2) collaborative decision making can raise unrealistic expectations of what can or should be accomplished through collaborative efforts as many of the problems facing schools lie outside the control of teachers, parents, and administrators; (3) the uncertainty surrounding schools about the issues of effectiveness and the processes of becoming effective creates a climate of ambiguity that makes school decision making a difficult task.

❏ Collaboration: Implications for school leaders

The organization, development, and implementation of successful collaboration requires that principals assume a variety of important roles. These roles draw heavily from the research and literature on transformational leadership. Burns' notion that "transforming leadership is elevating" and as a result "leaders and followers raise one another to high levels of motivation and morality" (Rost, 1991, p. 83) serves as a foundation for successful collaboration. In addition, the following concepts of transformational leadership as identified by Louis, Kruse, and Raywid (1996), Louis and Murphy (1994), Leithwood and Steinbach (1995), Sergiovanni (1990), Rost (1991), and others provide the structure critical for bringing about meaningful school change through collaborative decision making.

Leading from the Center (delegating leadership responsibilities; developing collaborative decision-making processes; bringing shared authority to life)

Enabling and Supporting Teacher Success (helping formulate a shared vision; cultivating a network of relationships; allocating resources consistent with vision; providing information; promoting teacher development)

Managing Reform (ensuring that resources align with goals; bringing teachers into the information loop; managing relationships between school and community)

321

Extending the School Community (promoting the school; working with the governing board)

The desirability of the transformational approach to leadership in bringing about school change is well documented. The research findings of Hall and Hord (1987), Smith and Andrews (1989), and Wilson and Corcoran (1989) suggested that effective leaders are those who inspire followers to a higher purpose while at the same time taking specific actions that enable the process to move forward toward some expressed or articulated goal or objective. These findings were reinforced by Leithwood and Jantzi (1990) who found that principals who were successful in school improvement:

- Used a variety of bureaucratic mechanisms to stimulate and reinforce cultural change;
- Fostered staff development;
- Engaged in direct and frequent communication about cultural norms, values, and beliefs;
- Shared power and responsibility with others; and
- Used symbols to express cultural values.

The findings of Leithwood and Jantzi (1990) and others support Carlson when he stated "there is a consensus view that the organizations of the future . . . will need leaders and followers invested in a transformational process" (1996, p. 137). Such a process, according to Bryman (1992), includes visionary leadership, communicating the vision, empowerment, organizational culture, and trust.

School leaders who practice the principles of transformational leadership will facilitate collaborative decision making by (Leithwood & Jantzi, 1990; Louis, Kruse, & Raywid, 1996):

- Providing time for collaborative decision making;
- Assuming the role of intellectual leader and stimulating intellectual growth of all stakeholders;
- Empowering and trusting others to make good decisions;
- Allowing others to assume leadership positions;
- Creating, supporting, and nurturing a community of learners;
- Focusing collaborative efforts on the improvement of educational experiences of the students.

❏ Summary

Building involvement in decision making presents some major challenges for middle level leaders. These challenges, which focus around issues of influence, authority, and direction raise some interesting questions: How can authority be shared while still meeting the demands for administrator accountability expected by superintendents, school boards, and state legislatures? How can schools be organized to facilitate broadly based participation in decision making? How can collaborative decision making be focused to foster positive climate and empowerment while at the same time improve the quality of educational experiences? Answers to these questions lie in the various forms adopted for collaboration and the attitudes and willingness of middle level leaders to share decision making in ways that are meaningful and significant. ℝ

References

Bailey, W. (1991). *School-site management applied*. Lancaster, PA: Technomic.

Bird, T., & Little, J. (1986). How schools organize the teaching occupation. *The Elementary School Journal, 86* (4), 493-511.

Bryk, A., Easton, J., Krebow, D., Rollow, S., & Sebring, P. (1993). *A view from the schools: The state of reform in Chicago*. Chicago: University of Chicago, Consortium on Chicago School Research.

Bryman, A. (1992). *Charisma and leadership in organizations*. Newbury Park, CA: Sage.

Carlson, R. (1996). *Reframing and reform: Perspectives on organization, leadership, and school change*. White Plains, NY: Longman Publishers.

Clark, S., & Clark, D. (1996). Building collaborative environments for successful middle level restructuring. *NASSP Bulletin, 80* (578), 1-16.

Clark, S. & Clark, D. (1994). *Restructuring the middle level school: Implications for school leaders*. Albany, NY: State University of New York Press.

Elmore, R. (1993). School decentralization: Who gains? Who loses? In J. Hannaway & M. Carnoy (Eds.), *Decentralization and school improvement* (pp. 33-54). San Francisco: Jossey-Bass.

Dawson, J. (1984). *The principal's role in facilitating teacher participation. Mediating the influence of school context*. Philadelphia, PA: Research for Better Schools.

George, P., & Shewey, K. (1994). *New evidence for the middle school*. Columbus, OH: National Middle School Association.

Hall, G., & Hord, S. (1987). *Change in schools: Facilitating the process*. Albany, NY: State University of New York.

Hannaway, J. (1993). Decentralization in two school districts: Challenging the standard paradigm. In J. Hannaway & M. Carnoy (Eds.), *Decentralization and school improvement* (pp. 135-162). San Francisco: Jossey-Bass.

Leithwood, K., & Jantzi, D. (1990, April). *Transformational leadership: How principals can help reform school culture.* Paper presented at American Educational Research Association annual meeting, Boston.

Leithwood, K., & Steinbach, R. (1995). *Expert problem solving: Evidence from school and district leaders.* Albany, NY: State University of New York Press.

Levine, D., & Eubanks, E. (1992). Site-based management: Engine for reform or pipedream? Problems, prospects, pitfalls, and prerequisites for success. In J .J. Lane & E. E. Epps (Eds.), *Restructuring the schools: Problems and prospects* (pp. 61-82). Berkeley, CA: McCutchan.

Lindelow, J., Coursen, D., Mazzarella, J., Heynderickz, J., & Smith, S. (1989). Participative decision making. In S. Smith, & P. Piele (Eds.), *School leadership: Handbook for excellence* (pp. 152-167). Eugene, OR: ERIC Clearinghouse on Educational Management, University of Oregon.

Little, J. (1982). Norms of collegiality and experimentation: Workplace conditions of school success. *American Educational Research Journal, 19* (3), 325-340.

Louis, K., Kruse, S., & Raywid, M. (1996). Putting teachers at the center of reform: Learning schools and professional communities. *NASSP Bulletin, 80* (580), 9-21.

Louis, K., & Murphy, J. (1994). The evolving role of the principal. In J. Murphy and K. Louis (Eds.), *Reshaping the principalship: Insights from transformational reform efforts* (pp. 265-279). Thousand Oaks. CA: Corwin Press, Inc.

Purkey, S., & Smith, M. (1982). *Effective schools: A review.* Madison, WI: Wisconsin Center for Educational Research, University of Wisconsin.

Rosenholtz, S. (1985). Political myths about educational reform: Lessons from research on teaching. *Phi Delta Kappan, 66* (5), 349-355.

Rosenholtz, S. (1989). *Teachers' workplace: The social organization of schools.* New York: Longman.

Rost, J. (1991). *Leadership for the twenty-first century.* New York: Praeger.

Sergiovanni, T. (1990). *Value-added leadership: How to get extraordinary performance in schools.* San Diego: Harcourt Brace Jovanovich.

Shedd, J. & Bacharach, S. (1991). *Tangled hierarchies: Teachers as professionals and the management of schools.* San Francisco, CA: Jossey-Bass Publishers.

Smith, S., & Scott, J. (1990). *The collaborative school: A work environment for effective instruction.* Eugene, OR: ERIC Clearinghouse on Educational Management/National Association of Secondary School Principals.

Smith, W., & Andrews, R. (1989). *Instructional leadership: How principals make a difference.* Alexandria, VA: Association for Supervision and Curriculum Development.

Smylie, M., (1994). Redesigning teachers' work: Connections to the classroom. In L. Darling-Hammond (Ed.), *Review of research in education,* No. 20 (pp. 129-169), Washington, DC: American Educational Research Association.

Smylie, M., Brownlee-Conyer, J., & Crowson, R. (1991, April). *When teachers make district-level decisions: A case study.* Paper presented at the annual meeting of the American Educational Research Association, Chicago.

Valentine, J., Clark, D., Irvin, J., Keefe, J., & Melton, G. (1993). *Leadership in middle level education, Vol. I: A national survey of middle level leaders and schools.* Reston, VA: National Association of Secondary School Principals.

Valentine, J., Clark, D., Nickerson, N., Jr., & Keefe, J. (1981). *The middle level principalship: A survey of middle level principals and programs,* Vol. I., Reston, VA: National Association of Secondary School Principals.

White, P. (1992). Teacher empowerment under "ideal" school-site autonomy. *Educational Evaluation and Policy Analysis, 14* (1), 69-82.

Wilson, B. & Corcoran, T. (1988). *Successful secondary schools: Visions of excellence in American education.* Philadelphia: Falmer Press.

Sally N. Clark and Donald C. Clark

Women in Leadership Roles

In spite of the increased involvement of women in a variety of school leadership roles over the past decade, little of the past leadership literature has focused on women leaders in education. Noddings (1990), for example, lamented the absence of feminist scholarship from educational administration as a field of study. Throughout the 1970s and 1980s, the theoretical bases that emerged for educational leadership were predominantly centered around research conducted by white males studying white male leaders (Dunlap, 1995; Hill & Ragland, 1995). In fact, this research has largely shaped the standards of success for school administrators, standards of success that are built around male models of discipline and power (Kempner, 1991).

Women leaders, however, are redefining leadership on their own terms and devising ways of leading that make sense to them (Helgeson, 1995). They are achieving success in implementing appropriate programs in middle level schools (Valentine, Clark, Irvin, Keefe, & Melton, 1993), and they are overrepresented in principalships of schools identified as being highly successful (Shakeshaft, 1987). This success of women leaders should not be surprising, for over the past ten years numerous research studies have suggested that: (a) the new vision of the effective school principal is of one who is collaborative in decision making and skilled at instructional leadership (Andrews & Basom, 1990; Kanthak, 1991), (b) the traditional female approaches to schooling look like the prescriptions for administrative behavior in effective schools (Rutherford, 1985), (c) successful women leaders demonstrate high levels of skill in communication, problem solving, organizational savvy, team building, and instruction and curriculum

(Andrews & Basom, 1990; Gardenswartz & Rowe, 1987; Hill & Ragland, 1995; Marshall, 1988; Shakeshaft, 1987), and (d) as a group women are more likely to evidence behavior associated with effective leadership (Smith & Andrews, 1989).

In this chapter, we will examine the evolution of research on women in leadership positions, offer a profile of women leaders in education, and describe the qualities that women bring to their leadership positions. The chapter will conclude with the implications of the research for women desiring to obtain leadership positions.

❏ Perspectives on Research on Women Leaders ❏

In examining the unique role of women in leadership, Shakeshaft (1987) suggested that research on women in administration began to appear in the early 1970s and by the mid 1980s the literature and research had become substantial and progressed through the following six stages:

1. Documentation of the lack of women in leadership positions (How many women in school administration? What kinds of positions do they hold?)
2. Identification of famous or exceptional women in the history of school leadership (Is there a history of women in school leadership? Have women done the same things men have done? Do women's achievements meet male standards?)
3. Investigation of women's place in schools from the framework as disadvantaged or subordinate (Why are there so few women leaders?)
4. Examination of women leaders - women studied on their own terms and the female world of leadership is documented (How do women leaders describe their experiences and lives?)
5. Confrontation of existing theories in educational leadership (How must theory change to include women's experiences?)
6. Transformation of theory so that both women's and men's theory can be understood together (What are theories of human behavior in organizations?)

These six stages provide an excellent historic perspective for examining past and present leadership roles that women assume. Much of the information in this chapter is drawn from studies which focus on Stage 4 – Examination of Women Leaders (e.g. Andrews & Basom, 1990; Helgeson, 1990, 1995; Hill & Ragland, 1995; Shakeshaft, 1987). It is evident from these and other studies that new theories such as transformational leadership, which include as major components vision, communication of vision, empowerment, organizational culture, and trust (Bryman, 1992) strongly embrace values and skills found in women educational leaders (Clark, 1995; Hill & Ragland, 1995; Shakeshaft, 1987). It is also evident that these studies are providing the necessary information to confront the existing theories of educational leadership (Stage 5) and will lead to the transformation of theory so that both women's and men's theory can be understood together (Stage 6).

The leadership theories and practices now accepted not only incorporate but appreciate the skills and characteristics of women's leadership. Collaborative leadership practices are not, of course, the exclusive domain of women. Ample evidence exists that male leaders hired within the last ten years are also more likely to use collaborative and facilitative leadership (Helgeson, 1995; Kanthak, 1991). Perhaps the prediction made by Burns in 1978 is becoming a reality:

As leadership comes more properly to be seen as a process of leaders engaging and mobilizing the human needs and aspirations of followers, women will be more readily recognized as leaders and men will change their own leadership styles.

— p. 50

❏ Profiles of Women in Leadership ❏

A profile of women in middle level and other levels of leadership drawn from the research (Hill & Ragland, 1995; Pavan & D'Angelo, 1990; Valentine et al., 1993) shows that women are older than their male counterparts, they were older when they received their first administrative appointment, they have fewer total years as administrators, and they have spent less time in their current position. Women have more years of teaching experience, more preparation (e.g. graduate degrees), tend to be in larger population areas, and represent greater ethnic diversity.

Women principals indicated they chose to go into the principalship to use their special abilities more effectively, to work with people, to make a positive impact on children and teachers, to make a difference, and to improve instruction (Newman, 1993; Valentine et al., 1993; Woo, 1985). When asked to identify factors that were influential in receiving their first principal appointment, females gave high ratings to "contacts in the profession" and "performance in formal and informal assignments outside the class-room." Female principals in the NASSP study (Valentine et al., 1993) at-tached greater importance to networking, mentoring, and sponsorship, av-enues that traditionally have been less available to them, and to the quality of their performance, than did the male principals. Females also indicated number of years and success as a teacher, number of years as an assistant principal, and successful job interview as being influential.

Both female and male middle level principals questioned in the NASSP study (Valentine et al., 1993) believed an important path to the principalship was experience as assistant principals and in teacher leadership roles. Over one-half of the women and one-third of the men were assistant principals at the middle level prior to being appointed to the principalship. Eleven percent of the males moved directly from a teaching position to a principalship. This option appeared to be unavailable to women as none of the female respondents indicated that career path. Slightly more female principals reported that they had held department chairs (40 percent fe-male; 37 percent male), and more females than males had served as team leaders (27 percent female; 24 percent male).

❑ Women's Leadership Emphasis ❑

In drawing from the research on women in educational leadership, Shakeshaft (1987) identified four areas descriptive of female work behav-ior as an educational leader. Three of these descriptors, (1) the centrality of relationships with others, (2) the major focus of teaching and learning, and (3) the importance of building community, provide the focus for the fol-lowing section of this chapter. The fourth area, the gender issues of mar-ginality, token status, and sexist attitudes toward women, while important, will not be addressed as a separate topic in this chapter.

❑ Relationships and networking

Relations with others are central to women administrators and they "spend more time with people, communicate more, care more about indi-vidual differences, are concerned more with teachers and marginal stu-dents, and motivate more" (Shakeshaft, 1987, p. 8). The importance of relationships may partially explain the leadership roles that women take. Helgeson (1990), for example, in interviewing women business leaders, found that they referred to themselves as being in the middle of things. Not at the top, but in the center; not reaching down, but reaching out. She also described the importance of group affiliation rather than individual achievement as having the highest value for women leaders.

> In the process of devising ways of leading that made sense to them, the women I studied had built profoundly integrated organic organizations, in which the focus was on nurturing good relationships; in which the niceties of hierarchical rank and distinction played little part, and in which lines of communication were multiple, open, and diffuse. — p. 265

Networking is an important component in building relationships. Networking, according to Hill and Ragland (1995), emphasizes connections and legitimizes social interaction with people. Swoboda and Millar (1986) found networking especially beneficial in helping women develop greater self-reliance and less dependency. While essential to passing along collective wisdom, they also found that the foundation developed through networking supports increased confidence in one's leadership (Swoboda & Millar, 1986). The relationships and support developed through networking may, perhaps, offer an explanation as to why in the NASSP study (Valentine et al., 1993) higher percentages of female principals held memberships in every professional association category on the survey. This included memberships in professional teacher associations (e.g., NEA, AFT), administrator associations (e.g., NASSP, NAESP), subject area professional associations (e.g., NCTM, NCTE, NCSS), honorary professional associations (e.g., PDK), and general professional associations for the middle level (e.g., NMSA).

❏ Curriculum and instruction

Women spend more time on the curricular and instructional aspects of the principalship and are more likely to be perceived by their teachers as exemplifying instructional leadership than are men (Andrews & Basom, 1990). Women principals, according to Shakeshaft's (1987) analysis of research, "are more instrumental in instructional learning than are men, and they exhibit greater knowledge of teaching methods and techniques" (p. 8). The data from the NASSP study (Valentine et al., 1993) are consistent with the findings of Andrews and Basom (1990) and of Shakeshaft (1987). Over half of the women middle level principals in the study reported they spent more than 60 hours per week on the job as compared with less than a third of their male counterparts, and more of that time was spent on program development by women principals than by men. This, along with their strong belief system favoring interdisciplinary teaming and advisory programs, may explain why female principals were more likely to have these programs in their schools then were male principals.

The greater support for and implementation of appropriate middle level programs in schools by female principals may be partially explained by a strong commitment to middle level education. It may also be explained by the fact that they have considerably more teaching experience than male principals (McGrath, 1992; Pavan & D'Angelo, 1990; Valentine et al., 1993) and by their strong interest in curriculum and instructional issues (Andrews & Basom, 1990; Shakeshaft, 1987).

❑ Community building and visionary leadership

Shakeshaft (1987) reported that building a community was an essential part of women's leadership style. Women use language that encourages community building, engage in participatory styles that foster inclusiveness, and reach out to the community (Marshall, 1988). The NASSP study (Valentine et al., 1993), for example, found that female middle level principals were more likely than males to seek participation from citizens and parents in advisory activities. Typically these activities include offering advice and suggestions regarding: student activities; school finances and fund raising; program changes; considering new programs; determining objectives and priories of the school. Female principals are also more likely than males to involve parents and citizens in the operations of the school such as sponsors of student activities, as school and classroom resource persons, and as volunteer aides and tutors. This collaborative behavior is strongly supported by Helgeson (1990) who in her study described the leadership style of women leaders in the business sector. She suggested that women typically place themselves in the middle of the organization rather than at the top. The result is what she calls "a web of inclusion," an organization that includes all, even those on the periphery, in sharing the responsibilities and rewards of major undertakings. Obviously, women middle level principals in the NASSP study (Valentine et al., 1993) are using the web of inclusion in their attempts to involve parents and community members in the operation of their schools.

In addition to increasing the "web of inclusion," community building also requires leaders with a vision for their schools. Women principals in Hill and Ragland's (1995) study when asked to give descriptors of their leadership styles used words and phrases such as "problem solvers" and "creators of vision and ideas." They also used other words that describe behavior critical to building community: high expectations for self and others, trustworthiness, fairness, dependability, and honesty in dealing with people.

References to empowering others and team building, two other important factors in community building, are found frequently in the study of women's leadership. Hill and Ragland (1995) found that women are not threatened by empowering others and that they (women) are more adept at empowering and team building than are men. They also suggested that "in enlightened schools, administrators no longer consider how to handle teachers but instead find ways to empower" (Hill & Ragland, 1995, p. 45).

❏ Implications for Practice ❏

As the research indicates, females in leadership roles are making important contributions to the advancement of developmentally responsive schools for young adolescents. The NASSP study (Valentine et al., 1993) and other research (Hill & Ragland, 1995; Shakeshaft, 1987) in the past decade indicate that not only do females bring more instructional experience into the middle level school principalship, they are more highly educated, they are more involved in professional associations, they are more likely to focus their energies on personnel and program issues, they are more likely to have specifically "identified" middle level programs in their schools, and they are more likely to engage parents and community members in school governance and activities.

It also appears that more females are assuming leadership responsibilities in their middle level schools (Valentine et al., 1993). After a decline in numbers in the 1960s, 1970s, and early 1980s (Marshall, 1984), the numbers of women in middle level leadership positions have increased from six percent in 1981 (Valentine, Clark, Nickerson, & Keefe) to 20 percent in 1993 (Valentine et al., 1993). By assuming the positions of assistant principals, department heads, team leaders, and members of school leadership councils (Valentine et al., 1993), female middle level educators are not only employing their expertise and extending their influence at their schools, they are taking important steps on the pathway to the principalship. It is reasonable to assume that if this trend continues, more and more females will be appointed to middle level principalships.

Women educators who are actively preparing themselves for leadership roles are encountering more comfortable graduate school settings (Hill & Ragland, 1995). Comprising more that 60 percent of the students enrolled in educational leadership programs (McCarthy, Kuh, Newell, &

Iacona, 1988), women are now engaged in programs that are more realistically linked with the reality of the workplace, that are increasing the number of women faculty members, and that are initiating reforms in approaches to preparing school leaders. Women are emerging from these reformed preparation programs with insights and essential skills necessary for redesigning school structures (Hill & Ragland, 1995). Women must continue to seek out opportunities to improve their skills and commit themselves to active participation in leadership preparation programs.

Women educators must also be more proactive in seeking out leadership positions in their schools (Hill & Ragland, 1995). Teacher leadership, an area where women appear to be actively involved (Valentine et al., 1993), provides opportunities for women to showcase their leadership skills (Hill & Ragland, 1995). Although it is still ill defined in its application and untested in its contribution to student achievement (Smylie, 1994), teacher leadership offers one of the most promising opportunities for teachers to gain valuable skills, become more visible, and to network with school, district, and community leaders. Seeking out and actively participating in the variety of leadership opportunities in their schools should be a high priority of women desiring administrative positions.

The research is very clear about the contributions of women leaders. With only 20 percent of the nation's middle level schools being led by women principals, it is evident that a rich pool of potential leaders remains largely untapped. It is critical that continued efforts be made to encourage women to consider administrative positions as a career option; to involve them in leadership experiences in the school, district, and community; and to facilitate opportunities for participation in programs that will assist them in acquiring the skills and insights necessary for success. ⓡ

References

Andrews, R., & Basom, M. (1990). Instructional leadership: Are women principals better? *Principal, 70* (2), 38-40.

Bryman, A. (1992). *Charisma and leadership in organizations.* Newbury Park, CA: Sage.

Burns, J. (1978). *Leadership.* New York: Harper & Row.

Clark, S. (1995). Women in middle level school administration: Findings from a national study. *Middle School Journal, 26* (4), 34-38.

Dunlap, D. (1995). Women leading: An agenda for a new century. In D. Dunlap & P. Schmuck (Eds.), *Women leading in education* (pp. 423-435). Albany, NY: State University of New York Press.

Gardenswartz L. & Rowe, A. (1987). Getting to the top: The 5 success secrets of women who have made it, *Executive Female*, X (6), 34-38.

Helgeson, S. (1995). *The web of inclusion*. New York: Doubleday.

Helgeson, S. (1990). *The female advantage: Women's ways of leadership*. New York: Doubleday.

Hill, M. & Ragland, J. (1995). *Women as educational leaders: Opening windows, pushing ceilings*. Thousand Oaks, CA: Corwin Press.

Kanthak, L. (1991). *The effects of gender on work orientation and the impact of principal selection*. Unpublished doctoral dissertation, University of California, Riverside.

Kempner, K. (1991). Getting into the castle of educational administration. *Peabody Journal of Education, 66* (3), 104-123.

Marshall, C. (1988). Analyzing the culture of school leadership. *Education and Urban Society, 20* (3), 262-275.

Marshall, C. (1984). The crisis of excellence and equity. *Educational Horizons, 63* (1), 24-30.

McCarthy, M., Kuh, G., Newell, L., & Iacona C. (1988). *Under scrutiny: The educational administration professorate*. Tempe, AZ: University Council for Educational Administration.

McGrath, S. (1992). Here come the women. *Educational Leadership, 49* (5), 62-65.

Newman, N. (1993, November). *Making it to the top: Results of structured interviews with women in university level administrative positions*. Paper presented at the annual meeting of the Mid-South Educational Research Association, New Orleans, LA.

Noddings, N. (1990). Feminist critiques in the professions. In C. Cazden (Ed.). *Review of Research in Education, 16* (pp. 393-424), Washington, DC: American Educational Research Association.

Pavan, B., & D'Angelo, J. (1990, April). *Gender differences in the career paths of aspiring and incumbent educational administrators*. Paper presented at the annual meeting of the American Educational Research Association, Boston, MA.

Rutherford, W. (1985). School principals as effective leaders. *Phi Delta Kappan, 67* (1), 31-34.

Shakeshaft, C. (1987). Theory in a changing reality. *Journal of Educational Equity and Leadership, 7* (1), 4-20

Smith, W. & Andrews, R. (1989). *Institutional Leadership*. Alexandria, VA: Association for Supervision and Curriculum Development.

Smylie, M., (1994). Redesigning teachers' work: Connections to the classroom. In L. Darling-Hammond (Ed.), *Review of Research in Education, 20* (pp. 129-169), Washington, DC: American Educational Research Association.

Swoboda, M. & Millar, S. (1986). Networking-mentoring: Career strategy of women in academic administration. *Journal of the National Association for Women Deans, Administrators, and Counselors, 50* (1), 8-12.

Valentine, J., Clark, D., Irvin, J., Keefe, J. & Melton, G. (1993). *Leadership in middle level education, Vol. I: A national survey of middle level leaders and schools.* Reston, VA: National Association of Secondary School Principals.

Valentine, J., Clark, D., Nickerson, N., Jr., & Keefe, J. (1981). *The middle level principalship: A survey of middle level principals and programs,* Vol. I., Reston, VA: National Association of Secondary School Principals.

Woo, C. (1985). Women administrators: Profiles of success. *Phi Delta Kappan, 66* (4), 285-287.

Jerry Valentine, Susan Trimble, and Todd Whitaker

The Middle Level Principalship

Middle schools have been involved in the restructuring work of reform for the past two decades, a period of time when the number of middle level schools has steadily increased while the number of junior highs has decreased (*Digest of Education Statistics*, 1995). Less dramatic is the increase in specific middle level practices implemented in schools for young adolescents, a fact which may bear witness to a general resistance to educational change (Wehlage, Smith, & Lipman, 1992), the persistence of standard operational procedures reinforcing old behaviors (Leithwood & Duke, 1993), and a variety of other explanations (Cuban, 1996). In many ways, this transition taking place in schools for young adolescents with its accompanying setbacks, gradual progress, and numerous successes has been the forerunner of the general restructuring movement currently taking place in elementary and secondary schools. At this time, elementary and high schools are adopting practices similar to middle school concepts, such as block scheduling, interdisciplinary faculty teams, and various programs to provide group and individual advisement. Similar to middle level reform, reform efforts in K-12 schools often encounter conflicts and challenges – what Lieberman (1988) termed "turf, tension, and new tasks." At the center of this dynamic change process is the middle school principalship.

Recent studies provide evidence that for reform and restructuring to occur, effective school leadership is essential (Leithwood, Begley, & Cousins, 1990). Principal practices in many cases are associated with changes in the school's culture, student achievement and behavior, attendance, and teachers' willingness to change instructional practices (Leithwood & Duke,

1993). The importance of the principal in the area of restructuring and the change process is therefore central to this review of the research on middle level principals and its meaning for practitioners. We begin this chapter with a description of the roles, characteristics, and knowledge of effective middle level principals. That section is followed by a discussion of research studies specifically addressing behavioral aspects of more effective middle level principals. We conclude with a synthesis of the research on principals and restructuring.

Compared to the many years of study of the K-12 principalship, the systematic study of principals in middle level schools is relatively new. In fact, the term "middle level" first appeared nationally as recently as 1981 in a Dodge Foundation/National Association of Secondary School Principals (NASSP) study report titled *The Middle Level Principalship, Volume I: A Survey of Middle Level Principals and Programs* (Valentine, Clark, Nickerson, & Keefe, 1981). Throughout the eighties "middle level" grew in acceptance as a viable alternative to the terms junior high school and middle school. While the formal initiation of the term can be traced to that study, the popularization of the term was due in large part to the tireless efforts of George Melton, NASSP's Associate Executive Director.

❏ Middle level principal roles, characteristics, and knowledge

In many ways, the middle level principalship has been at the forefront in the reform movement. Middle level principals have helped to establish environments for curricular and instructional change developmentally appropriate for young adolescents. With the drastic evolution of middle level education from the all-too-often less than child-centered programs of the junior high to the more child-centered programs of the middle school, effective principals became leaders of change, establishers of moral and ethical principles, creators of empowering environments, and promoters of collegiality and collaborative decision making in schools for young adolescents.

We see each of these roles enacted in team, school, and district meetings, where decisions are made regarding scheduling, curriculum, intramurals or scholastic sports, and the formation of partnerships with stakeholders. Spindler & George (1984) noted an essential role of middle school principals, "Principals must be a good moderator for open meetings, where divergent thinking must be expressed or recognized while working towards consensus" (p. 294).

Clark and Clark (1989) emphasized that middle level administrators must have a passion for middle level schools. They noted that the passion must be a burning desire to do everything humanly possible to create a developmentally responsive school that meets the unique needs of young adolescents. Other characteristics include a willingness to share decision making and an attitude of support, care, and nurturance for all people in the school. Many of these characteristics are similar to previous findings where the effective middle school principal is (1) perceived by teachers as high in people orientation, (2) perceived by parents as extremely effective in working with parents and the community, and (3) perceived by both parents and teachers as the key to a good school climate (Keefe, Clark, Nickerson, & Valentine, 1983).

The Clarks (1989) provided insight into the unique knowledge bases for principals of middle level schools. They argued that significant knowledge in five areas is essential to make informed decisions: young adolescent characteristics and behavior, successful middle level programs, the school's strengths and weaknesses, parental and community expectations, and the change process.

Other researchers have cited the importance of the knowledge base for principals. George and Grebing (1992) listed the demonstration of "a compassionate understanding of the characteristics and needs of the developing adolescent" (p. 3) as the first of seven essential skills of middle level leadership. Visionary leadership was examined by Stillerman (1992) who found that the visions of principals were shaped by their knowledge of exemplary middle school practices, and as visionary principals, they were successful in implementing their vision. Knowledge of exemplary practice and educational research, such as the impact of staffing in the middle grades on instruction and relations (McPartland, 1990), may also guide principals' decisions related to the hiring and maintaining of quality faculty and staff or influence any of the other numerous daily decisions made by principals.

❑ Effective middle level principals

Several studies are particularly noteworthy for their contributions to the knowledge of effective middle level leadership (Ingersoll, 1994; Johnson, 1992; Keefe et al., 1983; Stillerman, 1992; Whitaker and Valentine, 1993). An NASSP research team (Keefe et al., 1983) identified the following characteristic behaviors of effective middle level principals.

1. Effective principals work significantly longer work days than the average middle level principal.
2. Effective principals view themselves as more democratic and participative than their teachers view them. The teachers do perceive them

as very humane, fair, democratic, and high in people orientation and task accomplishment.

3. Effective principals are rated extremely effective in staff relations and frequently interact with students, and involve a variety of persons and groups in new program development.

4. Effective principals involve faculty in the planning and implementation of staff development activities and value in-service over university training.

Ten years later Whitaker and Valentine (1993) used a pool of 163 middle level schools to identify schools with "more effective" principals and schools with "less effective" principals. They studied eight schools that were one standard deviation above or below the group norm based on (a) teacher responses to the Audit of Principal Effectiveness, a nationally normed assessment of principal skills, and (b) teacher responses to instruments from NASSP's Comprehensive Assessment of School Environments (CASE) instrument set. On-site visits and interviews with teachers and the principals revealed three key differences between the more effective and less effective principals.

1. *Effective principals view themselves as responsible for all aspects of their school.* Though these principals regularly involved staff, parents, and others in decision making, they believed it was their responsibility to do whatever was necessary to make their school be the best it could be. The less effective principals were much more willing to "blame" outside factors for problems in their schools.

2. *In effective schools, teachers and principals share the same perspectives of how much input teachers have in decision making with their schools.* More effective principals and their teachers have the same perspective as to how the teachers are involved in decision making. Less effective principals indicated that they involve their teachers much more than their teachers feel that they do.

3. *Effective principals identify key teachers and informally involve them in decision making.* Regardless of formal decision-making structures in their schools, effective principals went to their informal teacher leaders for input on major decisions or changes affecting the schools.

In a study comparing more effective middle level principals with randomly selected ones, Bauck (1987) reached three conclusions supported by the studies of Keefe and associates (1983) and Keefe, Valentine, Clark, and Irvin (1994). His conclusions addressed the use of time, degree of authority, and perceptions of roadblocks of effective principals:

1. Effective principals spend less time on student behavior and district office responsibilities and more time on professional development and planning.
2. Effective principals had more authority to fill teacher vacancies and to allocate budget funds than non-effective principals.
3. Effective principals perceived roadblocks to accomplishing their objectives as less constraining than did their peers.

Stillerman (1992) looked at the visionary aspects of effective principals at five middle schools to understand how they communicate and implement a vision in their schools.

> *In the current study, visionary leadership is portrayed as an interactive, recursive process in which the principal is continually drawing on his/her own knowledge, values, personal and positional authority, and technical know how, to shape school culture toward a vision of exemplary middle grades schooling. Simultaneously, the influence of district expectation/regulation and the status quo of school culture are shaping the principal's vision in an ongoing manner.* — p. 60

The George and Grebing (1992) list of principal skills needed to create and sustain middle level practices provide a link between research and practice. The applications of the essential skills which follow each listed skill were everyday examples of many researched tenets of successful middle level principal behaviors. These applications include building interdisciplinary teams, establishing a process for continual school improvement, being an instructional leader, and hiring and maintaining quality faculty and staff.

Each of these studies of middle school principals had certain similarities and differences in findings. The Whitaker & Valentine (1993) study revealed the engagement of effective principals with their faculty and key teachers while feeling responsible for their schools. Bauck (1987) on the other hand highlighted the use of time, degree of authority, and perceptions of roadblocks of effective principals, while Stillerman (1992) found an association between shared decision making and building a shared vision. The Keefe studies were very broad in nature and generally supported these conclusions and provided many other pertinent aspects of middle level leadership. Clearly, effective schools have strong principals who promote quality collaboration and shared decision making.

❑ The middle school principal and restructuring

The middle school principal operates within a context of forces that Rowan (1990) labels as two inconsistent reform strategies that form the organizational design of schools. The first strategy is centralized control, with bureaucratic, top-down, hierarchical structures for decision making. This perspective of centralized control focuses on greater accountability and state controls, illustrated by the number of state legislatures and districts this decade that responded to problems by increasing bureaucratic control (Furhman, Clure, & Elmore, 1988; Rowan, Edelstein, & Leal, 1983; Trimble & Herrington, 1997). The other strategy is the professional autonomy of teachers in schools where supportive environments enhance the commitment and expertise of teachers (Darling-Hammond & Wise, 1985; Rosenholtz, 1987). This strategy is exemplified by the recommendations to replace hierarchical structures with networks and collaborative partnerships for decision making (Carnegie Task Force on Teaching as a Profession, 1986).

These two perspectives play out in everyday life at the school level. It is the principal who must have the knowledge, skills, and positive mental frameworks to address and balance the forces representative of these perspectives. We find, therefore, that the concept of "leadership for restructuring" is pervasive throughout contemporary literature of the principalship (Barth, 1990; Boyer, 1995; Goldring & Rallis, 1993; Hopkins, Ainscow, & West, 1994; Lieberman, Ed., 1995; Newmann & Wehlage, 1995; Sergiovanni, 1996). Two books of such magnitude focus specifically on the middle level principalship.

In 1994, Sally and Don Clark's *Restructuring the Middle Level School: Implications for School Leaders* was published. From the first chapter to the last, the Clarks articulately apply the research and literature of change and restructuring within the middle level context. They note that middle level schools are continually "under construction." They described four factors necessary to sustain this process of change, or as they call it, "work in progress." Their message is simple, but it succinctly reflects a major portion of the restructuring literature and thus the research about the contemporary role of the middle level principal.

1. Middle level educators must look to themselves for answers. Within each school community there is considerable expertise to solve problems, implement new programs, improve school climate, and provide professional development. These schools' successes come from a group of people who believe they can make a difference.

2. Middle level educators must reduce the sense of isolation that exists in their schools. They must find ways for teachers, administrators, parents, and community members to collaborate, to share expertise, and to participate in decision making.

3. Middle level educators must recognize that parents are powerful allies in the education of young adolescents. Steps must be taken to establish structures that will involve parents in the everyday life of the school. — p. 296

A discussion of the importance of the role of the principal in restructuring middle level schooling was a part of a comprehensive study of the middle level leadership sponsored by the National Association of Secondary School Principals from 1991-1994. The first book report from that study, entitled *Leadership in Middle Level Education, Volume 1: A National Survey of Middle Level Leaders and Schools* (Valentine, Clark, Irvin, Keefe, & Melton, 1993) described in detail middle level principals, assistant principals, and leadership team members. The second report, *Leadership in Middle Level Education, Volume II: Leadership in Successful Restructuring Middle Level Schools* (Keefe, Valentine, Clark, & Irvin, 1994) provided a rich description of educational programs and practices used in successfully restructuring schools. In that second volume, the authors reported characteristics of middle level principals of successfully restructuring schools. Those principals created environments with high levels of involvement and collaboration in problem solving, governance, staff development, team operations, and decision making. Systemic approaches for restructuring were evident in the successful schools. The concept of "community" was also evident, as were high standards, trust, empowerment, and consensus-based decision making. The restructuring schools had unique cultures that reflected the values, beliefs, and behaviors of the faculty.

Turning Points: Preparing American Youth for the 21st Century (Carnegie Council on Adolescent Development, 1989) may, in time, be recognized as the most influential writing of the contemporary middle level era. While the report was not designed to address leadership per se, it does serve as a means to underscore the key concepts that have emerged from this review on the role of middle level principalship at the school site. Creating a community for learning cannot be accomplished without the skills and competencies associated with restructuring. Empowering teachers and administrators necessitates collaborative decision making and an emotionally safe school climate.

Evident to even the modest observer of the principalship is the drastic change in the role of the principalship over the past two decades, requiring special skills of the principal to unify the school as a whole, involve stake-holders, satisfy the demands of parents and the community, and comply with state mandates. The complexity of the forces acting upon the principalship calls forth a variety of principal styles. Leithwood and Duke (1993) noted, "It seems unlikely that any single existing leadership focus or theory can capture adequately the range of qualities required of future leaders" (p. 329). As a result, the principalship transitioned from a "managerial" focus to an "instructional" focus that includes skills in team building (Trimble & Miller, 1996), in enabling adult growth and involving all stakeholders (Leithwood & Dukes, 1993), and in creating environments for shared participative management (Shedd & Bacharach, 1991). Now the principalship is in the midst of an era described by Sergiovanni (1996) and Clark and Clark (1996) as transformational and pedagogical.

❏ Conclusion

More is known today about the persons called middle level principals than ever before. For example, the percentage of women in the middle level principalship is steadily increasing, moving from 4% in 1966 to 6% in 1981 and 20% in 1992. Thirty-five percent of assistant principals and 66% of leadership team members were female in 1992. Female leaders were very evident in the restructuring schools, with women principals serving as leaders in 32% of the successful restructuring schools studied by Valentine, Keefe, Clark, Irvin and Melton from 1992-94 (Valentine et al, 1993; Keefe et al, 1994). Middle level principals have more formal education than their predecessors, as evidenced by the nearly doubled percentage of principals with doctorates from 1966 (4%) to 1992 (11%). Nine percent of assistants and three percent of leadership team members have a doctorate. Female principals continue to be more formally educated than their male counterparts, with 17% holding a doctorate (Valentine et al, 1993). Higher levels of graduate preparation have been a consistent pattern for all middle level leaders for the past twenty-five years (Keefe et al, 1994).

Such changes in the demographics of principals coincide with the changes in the roles, characteristics, knowledge, and behaviors of effective principals. Numerous pressures place the middle school principalship at the center of an arena where innovative practices are implemented within the framework of educational policy and school/community norms. The next decade will no doubt produce more research on specific elements of leadership that are conducive to bringing about change within the context of political pressures, reform initiatives, and limited resources. Current research points to middle level principals continuing to act not only as instructional/management leaders, but also as "enablers" of the transformation of middle level schools to become more developmentally responsive to the nature and needs of young adolescents. Ⓡ

References

Barth, R. S. (1991). *Improving schools from within: Teachers, parents, and principals can make the difference.* San Francisco: Jossey-Bass Publishers.

Bauck, J. (1987). Characteristics of the effective middle school principal. *NASSP Bulletin, 71* (500), 90-92.

Boyer, E. L. (1995). *The basic school: A community for learning.* Princeton, NJ: The Carnegie Foundation for the Advancement of Teaching.

Carnegie Council on Adolescent Development. (1989). *Turning points: Preparing American youth for the 21st century.* New York: Carnegie Corporation.

Carnegie Task Force on Teaching as a Profession (1986). *A nation prepared: Teachers for the 21st century.* New York: Carnegie Forum on Education and the Economy.

Clark, S., & Clark, D. (1996). The principal's role in interdisciplinary curriculum: Bridging the gap between research and practice. *ERS Spectrum: Journal of School Research and Information, 14* (1), 15-23.

Clark, S. N., & Clark, D. C. (1994). *Restructuring the middle level school: Implications for school leaders.* Albany, NY: State University of New York Press.

Clark, S. N., & Clark, D. C. (1989). School restructuring: A leadership challenge for middle level administrators. *Schools in the Middle.* Reston, VA: National Association of Secondary School Principals.

Cuban, L. (1996). Reforming again, again, and again. *Educational Researcher, 19* (1), 3- 13.

Darling-Hammond. L., & Wise, A. E. (1985). Beyond standardization: State standards and school improvement. *Elementary School Journal, 85*, 315-335.

Digest of Education Statistics. (1995). National center for education Statistics. Washington DC: Department of Education Statistics (1-800-424-1616).

Furhman, S., Clure, W. H., & Elmore, R. F. (1988). Research on Education reform: Lessons on the implementation of policy. *Teachers College Record, 90*, 237-257.

George, P.S., & Grebing, W. (1992). Seven essential skills of middle level leadership. *Schools in the Middle, 1* (4), 3-11.

Goldring, E. B., & Rallis, S. F. (1993). *Principals of dynamic schools: Taking charge of change.* Newbury, CA: Corwin Press, Inc.

Hopkins, D., Ainscow, M., & West, M. (1994). *School improvement in an era of change.* New York: Teachers College Press.

Ingersoll, R. M. (1994). Organizational control in secondary schools. *Harvard Educational Review, 64* (2), 150-172.

Johnson, M. (1992).Principal leadership, shared decision-making, and student achievement. *Research in Middle Level Education, 16* (1), 35-62.

Keefe, J. W., Valentine, J. W., Clark, D. C., & Irvin, J. L. (1994). *Leadership in middle level education, Volume II: Leadership in successfully restructuring middle level schools.* Reston, VA: National Association of Secondary School Principals.

Keefe, J. W., Clark, D. C., Nickerson, N. C., & Valentine, J. W. (1983). *The middle level principalship, Volume 11: The effective middle level principal.* Reston, VA: National Association of Secondary School Principals.

Leithwork, K., Begley, P., & Cousins, B. (1990). The nature, causes and consequences of principals' practices: An agenda for future research. *Journal of Educational Administration, 28* (4), 5-31.

Leithwood, K. A., & Duke, D. L. (1993). Defining effective leadership for Connecticut's future schools. *Journal of Personnel Evaluation in Education, 6,* 301-333.

Lieberman, A. (Ed.). (1995). *The work of restructuring schools: Building from the ground up.* New York: Teachers College Press.

Lieberman, A. (1988). Teachers and Principals: Turf, Tension, and New Tasks. *Phi Delta Kappan, 69* (1), 29-34.

McPartland, J. M. (1990). Staffing decisions in the middle grades: Balancing quality instruction and teacher/student relations. *Phi Delta Kappan, 71* (6), 465-469.

National Governors' Association. (1986). *Time for results.* Washington DC: Author.

Newmann, F. M., & Wehlage, G. G. (1995). *Successful school restructuring.* Madison, WI: Center on Organization and Restructuring of Schools.

Rosenholtz, S. J. (1987). Educational reform strategies: Will they increase teacher commitment? *American Journal of Education, 95,* 534-562.

Rowan, B. (1990). Commitment and control: Alternative strategies for the organizational design of schools. *Review of Research in Education, 16,* 353-389. Washington DC: AERA.

Rowan, B., Edelstein, R., & Leal, A. (1983). *Pathways to excellence: What school districts are doing to improve instruction.* San Francisco: Far West Laboratory for Educational Research and Development.

Sergiovanni, T. J. (1996). *Leadership for the schoolhouse: How is it different? Why is it important?* San Francisco: Jossey-Bass.

Shedd, J., & Bacharach, S. B. (1991). *Tangled hierarchies: Teachers as professionals and the management of schools.* San Francisco, CA: Jossey-Bass.

Spindler, J., & George, P. (1984). Participatory leadership in the middle school. *The Clearing House, 7,* 293-95.

Stillerman, K. P. (1992). Successful North Carolina Middle School Principals' Visions. *Research in Middle Level Education, 16* (1), 62-74

Trimble, S., & Herrington, C. (1997). *Beyond schizophrenia: Sustaining long-term educational reform and maintaining short-term political viability.* Poster session and roundtable at the Annual Meeting of the American Education Research Association. Chicago, IL.

Trimble, S., & Miller, J. W. (1996). Creating, invigorating, and sustaining effective teams. *NASSP Bulletin, 80* (584), 35-40.

Valentine, J. W., Clark, D. C., Irvin, J. L., Keefe, J. W., & Melton, G. (1993). *Leadership in middle level education, Volume I: A national survey of middle level leaders and schools.* Reston, VA: National Association of Secondary School Principals.

Valentine, J. W., Clark, D. C., Nickerson, N.C., Jr., & Keefe, J. W. (1981). *The middle level principalship, Volume I: A survey of middle level principals and programs.* Reston, VA: National Association of Secondary School Principals.

Wehlage, G., Smith, G., & Lipman, P. (1992). Restructuring urban schools: The new futures experience. *American Educational Research Journal, 29* (1), 51-93.

Whitaker, R., & Valentine, J. (1993). How do you rate? *Schools in the Middle, 3* (2), 21- 24.

Issues and
Future Directions

Hough | David Hough
Southwest Missouri
State University
Springfield, Missouri

Irvin | Judith L. Irvin
Florida State University
Tallahassee, Florida

David Hough and Judith Irvin

Setting a Research Agenda

Perhaps for the first time since the onset of the great reorganization effort begun at the turn of the 20th century, middle level education reform initiatives can now be studied empirically. While serving as catalysts for future studies, past research has been neither coordinated nor comprehensive. The last decade of the 20th century and the first decade of the 21st century should provide researchers with a number of bona fide middle schools (encompassing age appropriate programs, policies, and practices for young adolescents) to embark on a new and exciting era of scholarship never before realized on a national scale. At the crux of the entire middle grades reform movement will remain the crucial issue of student achievement relative to middle school programs, policies, and practices.

Contrary to popular belief, middle level education research is actually ahead of its time, not behind. In fact, middle level education research is ahead of almost every other reform initiative – whether it be accelerated schools, essential schools, state standards, assessments, or teacher preparation. In terms of education research as a whole, middle level efforts stand at the forefront. No other field, be it anthropology, medicine, psychology, or chemistry, for example, has advanced as quickly in methodologies and design as middle level education. While these other fields enjoy a long and substantial history (often spanning three hundred years or more), middle level education reform as a field of study did not really begin until after 1900. While some research was performed during the first five decades of the 20th century, most substantive studies began well after the 1960s. Momentum created by the 1960s movement away from junior highs to middle schools "jump-started" research that escalated throughout the 1970s. The national call to alarm in the 1983 report *A Nation At Risk* and subsequent indictments against American public education fostered interest by the Carnegie Corporation to create a Task Force on Education of Young Adolescents. An initial report by this task force, *Turning Points: Preparing American Youth for the 21st Century* (Carnegie Council on Adolescent Development, 1989) created widespread interest and compelled schools throughout the United States to begin implementing bona fide programs, policies, and practices for young adolescent learners.

Now, the crucial question being asked of middle grades education (as well as all education reformers) is: "Does it work?" or "To what extent are the reform efforts leading to improved student performance?" When legitimate questions such as these are broached, researchers tend to turn their attention to designs that will address them. The problem, however, is that researchers may spend an inordinate amount of time simply discovering that the "wrong" questions are being asked, or that the questions are being asked in the "wrong" way. Hence the need for a national middle school research agenda.

To ensure that the "right" questions are being asked the "right" way the National Middle School Association is supporting an effort to establish a national middle grades research agenda. This concluding chapter of *What Current Research Says to the Middle Level Practitioner* takes a look at what has been done, what is being done, and what will be done to guide future efforts.

Student achievement has been and continues to be the "bugaboo" of educational research as well as reform initiatives at every level of schooling. Over the past three decades, a veritable smorgasbord of studies have addressed subtle understandings regarding relationships of a number of different middle level programs, policies, practices to various student and teacher experiences. While some researchers (most often using ethnographic approaches) have sought to understand school cultures and social interactions, only a precious few have tackled student outcomes, most notably academic achievement. Qualitative approaches, of course, cannot be generalized and, in the past, quantitative researchers have shied away from studying student achievement. The so-called "shadow studies" (Lounsbury & Clark, 1990; Lounsbury & Johnston, 1985, 1988; Lounsbury, Marani, & Compton, 1980; Lounsbury & Marani, 1964) provide keen insight into student life in schools as well as schooling in general; but, again, learning outcomes are not addressed.

The culmination in 1996 of a five-year ethnographic study begun in 1991 by a team of UCLA researchers took a thorough look at the impact of *Turning Points* as well as state and local initiatives on middle level school reform (Oakes, Serna, & Guiton, 1996). While school programs, policies, and practices across different middle level grade spans were not specifically identified for study, researchers found significant efforts to make positive changes in the school community and culture to effect school improvement (Gong, 1996; Oakes, Vasudeva, & Jones, 1996; Quartz, 1996; Ryan & Freidlaender, 1996).

Most quantitative studies have used self-report perceptional data that have not controlled for threats to internal or external validity. Merely asking principals, for instance, to what degree they believe specific middle school components impact student achievement (as well as other outcomes such as behavior and attendance) does not provide the empirical data needed to validate student outcomes, especially achievement. Much more sophistication in design is necessary to validate causal variables and examine accurately cause-effect relationships. A significant improvement over past efforts is demonstrated in the latest attempts by researchers to identify causal relationships. Bruce & Singh (1996), for example, used path analysis techniques to examine the effects of a number of different school learning variables on eighth-grade student achievement.

In 1993, a group of researchers in Illinois began collecting and analyzing school-level data including but not limited to achievement for a number of middle level schools. First in Illinois, then in neighboring states, and now throughout the country, researchers are engaged in data collection efforts that should help begin to answer the student achievement question.

Preliminary results from the Illinois or AIMS study show that middle school components seldom have direct, linear relationships to achievement; but that varying combinations of programs, policies, practices at various levels of implementation have significant positive effects on student achievement (Felner, Jackson, Kasak, Mulhall, Brand, & Flowers, 1997). "The central question of these analyses is the extent to which schools that have attained different levels of implementation show concomitant differences in student achievement, behavior, health practices, and socio/emotional adjustment for all students and for targeted subgroups" (Felner et al., 1997, p. 543). The findings of this multi-year study have thus far affirmed that students in schools with high levels of implementation of middle school programs and practices demonstrated higher levels of achievement in mathematics, language, and reading than students in schools with middle or low levels of implementation of middle school practices. Additionally, "reforms

353

implemented independently of one another are likely to produce little or no significant rise in student achievement, especially for disadvantaged youth" (Lipsitz, Jackson, & Austin, 1997, p. 519). That is, when practices such as interdisciplinary team organization and advisory groups are implemented together and in proper sequence, with leadership support and with adequate staff development, gains in student achievement and other outcomes are likely to be positive (Felner et al., 1997). "Our findings to date strongly support the view that high quality schooling, well implemented, can make profound contributions to the achievement, mental health, and socio/behavioral functioning of students who are often left behind and for whom there is often a sense that school cannot make a difference in their lives" (p. 550).

From the AIMS study data and from years of experience with middle level reform efforts, Lipsitz, Mizell, Jackson, & Austin (1997) recommended that the necessary elements of reform included:

- professional development
- technical assistance
- coordination from district and/or state level
- networks between and among schools, universities, and state departments
- data-driven decision making
- leadership from superintendents
- state-level leadership
- improved teacher preparation
- well-informed public constituencies
- comprehensiveness of reform efforts (p. 535-538).

The AIMS study, while ongoing, has assisted middle level educators in answering the question "Does it work?" The preliminary results indicate that implementing only a piece of the *Turning Points* (19890 recommendations does not have the positive impact on student outcomes (achievement, health, behavior) but that implementing a number of recommendations simultaneously, properly sequenced, and properly supported does have a positive impact. While these preliminary discoveries hold promise, various nonlinear hierarchical models will need to be tested and re-tested over time to understand fully both the significance and importance of these relationships.

Recognition of the current state of middle level research along with the need to address achievement issues has led the National Middle School Association to develop a research agenda. A Research Agenda Task Force met in January 1996 to draft both an agenda and an action plan to operationalize the agenda. Using *This We Believe* (1995) to develop research questions, this NMSA action plan could lead to research activities that determine the relationship between various types of middle level programs, practices, and curricula and student outcomes such as achievement.

Coordinated efforts among professional organizations, universities, and middle level schools can eventually add pieces to the research agenda puzzle. The last two decades have provided rich and useful information for school reform in middle level schools. In the past five years, researchers have found ways to answer the big "Does It Work?" question. The next decade holds promise for more definitive answers of "What Works?"and "Under What Conditions?" ℝ

References

Bruce, F.A., Jr., & Singh, K. (1996). Academic achievement: A model of school learning for eighth grade students. *Research in Middle Level Education Quarterly, 19* (3), 95-111.

Carnegie Council on Adolescent Development (1989). *Turning points: Preparing American youth for the twenty-first century.* New York: Carnegie Corporation.

Felner, R. D., Jackson, A. W., Kasak, D., Mulhall, P., Brand, S., & Flowers, N. (1997). The impact of school reform for the middle years: Longitudinal study of a network engaged in *Turning Points-* based comprehensive school transformation. *Phi Delta Kappan, 78* (7), 528-532, 541-550.

Gong, J. (1996). Becoming just: The role of power in ensuring the democratic ends of participatory policymaking processes, *Research in Middle Level Education Quarterly, 20* (1), 69-102.

Lipsitz, J., Jackson, A. W., & Austin, L. M. (1997). What works in middle-grades school reform. *Phi Delta Kappan, 78* (7), 517-519.

Lipsitz, J., Mizell, M. H., Jackson, A. W., Austin , L M. (1997). Speaking with one voice: A manifesto for middle-grades reform. *Phi Delta Kappan, 78* (7), 533-540.

Lounsbury, J. H., & Clark, D. C. (1990). *Inside grade eight: From apathy to excitement.* Reston, VA: National Association of Secondary School Principals.

Lounsbury, J.H., & Johnston, J.H. (1985). *How fares the ninth grade?* Reston, VA: National Association of Secondary School Principals.

Lounsbury, J.H., & Johnston, J.H. (1988). *Life in the three 6th grades.* Reston, VA: National Association of Secondary School Principals.

Lounsbury, J.H., & Marani, J. (1964). *The junior high school we saw: One day in the eighth grade.* Alexandria, VA: Association for Supervision and Curriculum Development.

Lounsbury, J.H., Marani, J., & Compton, M. (1980). *The middle school in profile: A day in the seventh grade.* Columbus, OH: National Middle School Association.

National Commission of Excellence in Education. (1983). *A nation at risk.* Washington, DC: Author.

National Middle School Association. *This we believe: Developmentally responsive middle level schools.* (1995). Columbus, OH: Author.

Oakes, J., Serna, I., & Guiton, G. (1996). Introduction, *Research in Middle Level Education Quarterly, 20* (1), 1-10.

Oakes, J., Vasudeva, A., & Jones, M. (1996). Becoming educative: Reforming curriculum and teaching in middle grades. *Research in Middle Level Education Quarterly, 20* (1), 11-40.

Quartz, K. H. (1996). Becoming better: The struggle to create a new culture of school reform, *Research in Middle Level Education Quarterly, 20* (1), 103-130.

Ryan, S. & Freidlaender, D. (1996). Becoming caring: Strengthening relationships to create caring school communities, *Research in Middle Level Education Quarterly, 20* (1), 41-68.

About the Authors

Lynley Hicks Anderman is Assistant Professor of Educational Psychology at the University of Missouri, Kansas City. A graduate of the University of Auckland, New Zealand (B.A., M.A.), she taught for nine years in elementary and middle schools in New Zealand before earning her Ph.D. at the University of Michigan. Her research interests include young adolescents' motivation and social relationships, and teacher education. She has published in journals such as *Journal of Early Adolescence*, *Middle School Journal*, and *Educational Psychologist*.

Joanne Arhar is Associate Professor of Curriculum and Instruction at Kent State University in Ohio. A graduate of Case Western Reserve University (B.A. and M.A.) and the University of Cincinnati (Ed.D.), she taught high school English and was an administrator at the high school and middle school levels in both Ohio and Colorado. Joanne is currently Chair of the Research Committee of the National Middle School Association. She received the Distinguished Dissertation Award from ASCD and NASSP for her research on interdisciplinary teaming. Her current research focuses on middle school student engagement and belonging and action research for teachers, and she is the author of *Leading Into the 21st Century* (1992).

James A. Beane is Professor in the National College of Education at National-Louis University. He has taught junior high/middle and high school and was a Project Director for New York State Regional Education Planning Centers. He is author of *Curriculum Integration*, *Affect in the Curriculum: Toward Democracy, Dignity and Diversity* (1990) , and *A Middle School Curriculum: From Rhetoric to Reality* (1990; 1993) ; co-author of *Self-Concept, Self-Esteem and the Curriculum* (1986 with Lipka), *Curriculum Planning and Development* (1986 with

Toepfer and Allesi), *The Middle School and Beyond* (1992 with George, Stevenson, and Thomason), and *When the Kids Come First: Enhancing Self-Esteem at the Middle Level* (1987 with Lipka); co-editor of *Democratic Schools* (1995 with Apple); and editor of the 1995 ASCD Yearbook, *Toward a Coherent Curriculum.* In addition he has written forewords and chapters for many books and articles for a variety of professional journals.

Betty J. Bennett is a graduate of Florida State University (Ph. D.) and the University of Central Florida (B. S and M. Ed.). She worked at the junior high, middle, and high school levels for 15 years as a teacher, administrator, and coordinator for at-risk programs. Betty was the 1995 Florida State University Herbert J. Reese Fellowship Award recipient. Her research interests include discipline, middle level education, and leadership, and she has published in *Middle School Journal.* Presently she is a co-author on *The Three Faces of Discipline for Young Adolescents* (In press with Wolfgang and Irvin).

Edward N. Brazee is Associate Professor of Education at the University of Maine in Orono. A graduate of the State University of New York at Oswego (B.A.), Colgate University (M.A.T.), and the University of Northern Colorado (Ed.D.), he taught in middle schools and high schools in New York and Colorado. He has authored many articles for such publications as *Middle School Journal*, *The Journal of Early Adolescence*, and *Journal of Reading*, as well as several chapters in books of readings. Ed writes and edits two newsletters for parents of young adolescents, *The In-Between Years* and *The Family Connection* and is co-author of two books on middle level curriculum, *Dissolving Boundaries: Toward an Integrative Curriculum* (1995 with Capelluti) and *Second Generation Curriculum: What and How We Teach at the Middle Level* (1994 with Capelluti). His middle level interests include curriculum development, parent engagement, and school change.

Judith Allen Brough is Professor and Chair of the Education Department at Gettysburg College in Pennsylvania. She studied education at Shippensburg University of Pennsylvania (B.S. and Ed.M.) and the State University of New York at Buffalo (Ed.D) where she specialized in curriculum planning and middle level education. Her earlier professional experience includes ten years of teaching in grades six through nine. Among her publications and presentations are those which focus on middle level education, reading and the language arts, cognitive implications for learning, home-school partnerships, teaching strategies, and curriculum development and evaluation. Her most recent work includes contributions to the

Scott Foresman's grades 6-9 literature series and the study of schools which have implemented alternative curriculum delivery systems.

Donald C. Clark is Professor and Head of the Educational Administration/ Leadership Program at the University of Arizona, Tucson. He earned degrees from Pasadena College (B. A.), California State University at Los Angeles (M. A.), and the University of Southern California (Ed. D). He has been active in middle level education for more than thirty-five years as a teacher, building level and school district administrator, and university professor. He has served as a member of two national research teams which studied middle level schools and their leaders and he was co-director of the National Study of Eighth Grade reported in *Inside Grade Eight: From Apathy to Excitement* (1990 with Lounsbury). He has also been a member the National Association of Secondary Principals' Council on Middle Level Education, the research Committee of the National Middle School Association, and he currently serves as co-director of research for the Western Regional Middle Level Consortium. He has authored and edited eight books including his most recent books *Restructuring the Middle Level School: Implications for School Leaders* (1994 with Clark) and *The Middle Level Principal's Role in Implementing Interdisciplinary Curriculum* (1995 with Clark), written more than 50 journal articles, and has served as a consultant to numerous school districts and professional organizations.

Sally N. Clark is Senior Lecturer in Secondary and Middle Level Education at the University of Arizona in Tucson. A graduate of California State University at Los Angeles (B. A.), Pasadena College (M. A.), and the University of Arizona (Ed. D.), she teaches undergraduate and graduate classes in middle level and secondary education and has authored more than 45 articles and monographs on middle level education, school leadership, and women in middle level administration. She has also written and co-edited four books, including *Restructuring the Middle Level School: Implications for School Leaders* (1994 with Clark) and *The Middle Level Principal's Role in Implementing Interdisciplinary Curriculum (1995 with Clark)*. She is a reviewer for *Research in Middle Level Education Quarterly* and is on the editorial board of *The Journal of Adolescent Research*. She has served as guest editor for *Schools in the Middle,* coordinated two forums for women in administration sponsored by the University of Arizona and NASSP and was Co-Director for three years of the Greater Tucson School-University Partnership, Middle Level Support Group. Currently she is on the Executive Board of the Western Regional Middle Level Consortium and is Co-Director of its Research Committee.

Thomas S. Dickinson is Associate Professor of Education at Indiana State University in Terre Haute. A graduate of Wake Forest University (B.A.) and the University of Virginia (M.Ed. and Ed. D.), he taught middle and secondary students in his native Virginia for eight years before moving to the college teaching ranks. He has co-authored and edited a number of books including *We Gain More Than We Give: Teaming in Middle Schools* (1997 with Erb), *America's Middle Schools: Practices and Progress—A 25 Year Perspective* (1996 with McEwin and Jenkins), *A Vision of Excellence: Organizing Principles for Middle Grades Teacher Preparation* (1995 with McEwin, Erb, and Scales), *The Professional Preparation of Middle Level Teachers: Profiles of Successful Programs* (1995 with McEwin), *Readings in Middle School Curriculum: A Continuing Conversation* (1993), and *On Site: Preparing Middle School Teachers Through Field Experiences* (1991 with Butler and Davies). His primary interests in middle school education include the professional preparation of middle school teachers and the role of standards in teacher education.

Nancy M. Doda is Professor at National-Louis University at the Washington, D. C. Center where she teaches in the Interdisciplinary Studies Program in the Graduate School of Education. A graduate of Wake Forest University, she taught middle school language arts in a multiage grouped middle school for many years while completing her Master's and Ph. D. at the University of Florida with a specialization in Middle Level Education and Anthropology and Education. Nancy has designed and conducted professional development opportunities for teachers, administrators, and parents in over 48 states, Canada, Europe, and the Far East in an effort to improve middle level schooling and classroom practices. She was the author of the column, "Teacher to Teacher" in *Middle School Journal* for many years and co-authored *Team Organization: Promise-Practices and Possibilities* (1989 with Erb) and has written numerous articles on various aspects of middle school education with particular attention to assisting practitioners struggling to visualize and implement best practices. Her current agenda includes work in urban education, educational equity, and continued work on sustaining and refining comprehensive middle school reform.

Jacquelynne S. Eccles received her Ph.D. in psychology at UCLA in 1974. She did her undergraduate work at University of California at Berkeley and is currently a Professor of Psychology and a Research Scientist at the University of Michigan. She is also the director of the Combined Program in Education and Psychology at the University of Michigan. She was Assistant Vice-President for Research at the University of Michigan from 1987-88 and is a member of the MacArthur Foundation Network on Successful Adolescent Development and is the chair of the new MacArthur Foundation Network on Successful Pathways through Middle Childhood. She is author or co-author of many articles and book chapters on topics ranging from gender-role socialization, teacher expectancies, and classroom influences on student motivation to adolescent development in the family and school context. Her current work focuses on: (1) contextual influences on the development of self and task perceptions and activity preferences, (2) successful development during middle childhood and adolescence, and (3) the transition into early adulthood. She is the Principal Investigator on three longitudinal studies investigating these three sets of issues.

C. Victoria Faircloth, a former elementary and middle level teacher, is Assistant Professor at Western Carolina University in Cullowhee, North Carolina. A graduate of the Toccoa Falls College (B. S.), Georgia State University (M. Ed.), and University of Georgia (Ed. D.), she has served as President of the Special Interest Group in Middle Level Education for the American Educational Research Association. Victoria has co- authored *Beyond Separate Subjects: Integrative Learning at the Middle Level* (1995 with Siu- Runyan), written other chapters and articles on middle level education, and presented at conferences and workshops.

Laurie E. Hart is Associate Professor of Elementary Education at The University of Georgia in Athens. A graduate of Purdue University (B. S.), University of Texas at Austin (M. A.), and University of Wisconsin-Madison (Ph. D.), she has taught at the middle, high school, and university levels. Her research focuses on middle school education, mathematics education, and equity issues in education. Her work has been published in many journals, including *Middle School Journal, Research in Middle Level Education, Journal for Research in Mathematics Education, Elementary School Journal, Teacher Education Quarterly, Action in Teacher Education,* and *Arithmetic Teacher.* For the past five years she has directed a federally-funded initiative in Georgia to improve the mathematics and science components of preparation for middle level teachers.

Rebecca A. Hines is currently an Assistant Professor in the Department of Secondary Education at Southeast Missouri State University, Cape Girardeau. Her dissertation received the 1995 Distinguished Dissertation Award from the National Association of Secondary School Principals' Council on Middle Level Education. She has worked in inclusive settings as a regular educator, a special educator, and as a co-teacher in a fully inclusive middle school. She continues to examine inclusive settings and publishes and presents nationally on this topic.

David Hough, Editor, *Research in Middle Level Education Quarterly,* the National Middle School Association's official publication for the dissemination of research findings, is also Associate Dean, College of Education, Southwest Missouri State University, and Director, Southwest Professional Development Center. David has authored several research reports regarding middle level program components and grade-span configuration. His most recent research published in the *Journal of Research in Rural Education* addresses student achievement. He coauthored a college text, *Middle Level Teaching: Methods and Resources* (1995 with Kellough and Kellough), and drafted the new NMSA document, *A Middle School Research Agenda for the 21st Century* (1997). After earning a Ph.D. in educational policy analysis from the University of California, Riverside, in 1991, David joined the faculty at Southwest Missouri State University, Springfield.

Judith L. Irvin is Program Coordinator for the Department of Educational Leadership at Florida State University in Tallahassee. She served as Editor of *Research in Middle Level Education* for the National Middle School Association (1989-1994) and Chair of the Research Committee (1990-1996). A former social studies teacher, she obtained a Ph. D. in reading/language arts. She authored numerous books including *Reading and the Middle School Student: Strategies to Enhance Literacy* (Second Edition, 1997) and edited *Transforming Middle Level Education: Prospectives and Possibilities* (1992). She also co-authored *Enhancing Social Studies Through Literacy Strategies* (1995 with Lunstrum, Lynch-Brown, and Shepard), *Starting Early with Study Skills: Learning and Remembering in the Elementary Grades* (1995 with Rose), *Leadership in Restructuring Middle Level Schools: Volume II: A National Study of Middle Level Leaders and their Schools* (1994 with Valentine, Clark, and Keefe), and *Leadership in Middle Level Education: Volume I - A National Survey of Middle Level Leaders and Their Schools* (1993 with Valentine, Clark, Keefe, and Melton). She writes the What Research Says to the Middle Level Practitioner Department for *Middle School Journal* and is current Chair of the Task Force on Literacy for Young Adolescents, a collaborative effort between NMSA and International Reading Association.

J. Howard Johnston is Professor of Secondary Education at the University of South Florida. Howard has been a junior high and high school teacher and is now a well-established author, lecturer, and researcher. He has written over 100 works on middle level education, among the most notable is *How Fares the Ninth Grade?* (1985 with Lounsbury) and *Life in the Three Sixth Grades* (1988 with Lounsbury), *The New American Family* (1990), *What Research Says to the Middle Level Practitioner* (1986 with Markle), and *Effective Schooling for Economically Disadvantaged Students: School-Based Strategies for Diverse Student Populations*

(1992). Howard is the recipient of the of the National Middle School Association's Presidential Award, the National Association of Secondary School Principals' Distinguished Service Award, and the New England League of Middle Schools' Distinguished Achievement Award. In recent years, he has been interested in the ability of middle schools to accommodate student diversity and assure success for all youth.

Richard P. Lipka is Professor of Education at Pittsburg State University in Kansas. A graduate of the State University of New York College at Buffalo (B.S., M.S.) and the University of Illinois (Ph.D.), he taught sixth grade as a member of a four person team in Amherst, New York. His research interest is affective development with an emphasis upon self-concept and self-esteem. To that end, he served as co-editor of *Self-Perspective Across the Life-Span* (1992 with Brinthaupt) and co-author on *When the Kids Come First: Enhancing Self-Esteem* (1987 with Beane) and *Self-Concept and Self-Esteem and the Curriculum* (1986 with Beane).

Douglas J. Mac Iver is the Associate Director and a Research Scientist at the Center for Social Organization of Schools, Johns Hopkins University in Baltimore, MD. A graduate of Occidental College (B.A.) and University of Michigan (Ph.D.), he has been engaged in middle level research for 18 years. His research focuses on the impact of middle school reform on students' learning opportunities, motivation, and achievement. He has authored articles for the *Annual Review of Psychology*, *Educational Psychology*, *Child Development*, *Developmental Psychology*, *American Educator*, and many other journals. He has also co-authored *Education in the Middle Grades: National Practices and Trends* (1990 with Epstein).

Janet E. McDaniel is Associate Professor at California State University San Marcos, where she serves as Coordinator of Middle Level Teacher Education. A graduate of Whitman College (B. A.), she taught middle school social studies for twelve years before earning her M.Ed. and Ph. D. at the University of Washington. Her research interests are middle school teaching and teacher education. With her CSUSM colleagues, she has published regularly in journals such as *Middle School Journal*, *Research in Middle Level Education*, and *Teacher Education Quarterly*. Her recent co-authored book is *Working with Middle School Students* (1996 with Stowell, Rios, and Christopher).

C. Kenneth McEwin is Professor of Curriculum and Instruction at Appalachian State University, Boone, North Carolina. A graduate of East Texas State University (B. S. & M. Ed.) and North Texas State University (Ed. D.), he taught sixth grade and was an elementary school principal in Texas. A past-president of the National Middle School Association (1983) and recipient of the Lounsbury Award (1989) from that association, he has co-authored *America's Middle Schools: Programs and Progress - A 25 Year Perspective* (1996 with Dickinson and Jenkins), *A Vision of Excellence: Organizing Principles for Middle Grades Teacher Preparation* (1995 with Dickinson, Erb, and Scales), and *Growing Pains: The Making of America's Middle School Teachers* (1994 with Scales). Ken has been a leader in the development of criteria for assessing middle level teacher preparation programs in conjunction with the National Council for the Accreditation of Teacher Education. He also has a particular interest in interscholastic sports for young adolescents.

H. James McLaughlin is Assistant Professor, Department of Elementary Education (Middle School Program) at The University of Georgia in Athens. He taught school for eight years, primarily on a 7th-grade team in middle school. Jim graduated from the University of Kansas and the University of Wisconsin-Madison before receiving a Ph.D. from the University of North Carolina-Chapel Hill. His recent research interests center on studying multi-year groupings in middle schools and he also writes about teacher reflection, classroom management, and Vygotskian theory. Most of his work is done with teachers and principals in schools, developing action research projects on a team and school level. Jim has published in journals such as *International Journal of Qualitative Studies in Education, Middle School Journal*, and the *Journal of Teacher Education*.

Carol Midgley is an Associate Research Scientist with the Combined Program in Education and Psychology, University of Michigan, Ann Arbor, Michigan. A graduate of the University of Michigan (Ph.D.), her research has focused on the relation between the learning environment and adolescent development. She recently co-authored *Transforming School Cultures* (1996, with Maehr) and has published in journals such as *Middle School Journal, Journal of Early Adolescence, Journal of Educational Psychology and Child Development*. She is on the editorial board of the *American Educational Research Journal* and the *Journal of Early Adolescence*.

Rebecca A. Mills is Associate Professor of Instructional and Curricular Studies at the University of Nevada, Las Vegas. A graduate of the University of Central Arkansas (B.S.E., M.S.E.) and the University of Arkansas (Ed.D.), she taught at the junior high, high school, and university levels. Her research on middle level teaching and interdisciplinary teaming has been published in *Research in Middle Level Quarterly* and *Middle School Journal*. She has written articles for *Schools in the Middle, Action in Teacher Education*, and *Clearinghouse*.

Nancy B. Mizelle has been a member of the faculty of the Department of Elementary Education at the University of Georgia. A graduate of Meredith College (B. A.), Clemson University (M. Ed.), and the University of Georgia (Ed. D.), she taught middle grades in North Carolina and in South Carolina. Her research focuses on young adolescents and middle school education and she is particularly interested in the transition from middle school to high school and in student literacy learning and motivation. She has presented at the annual meetings of the National Middle School Association and the American Educational Research Association; her publications have appeared in *Research in Middle Level Education Quarterly* and the *Middle School Journal* and she recently guest-edited a themed issue of the *Middle School Journal*, Creating Literate Environments (1997, with Irvin and Gay).

Emmett R. Mullins is Technology Coordinator at Harbins Elementary School in Dacula, Georgia. He earned his B.S.Ed. and M.Ed. in Middle Level Education at the University of Georgia and recently completed his doctoral work there, as well. He has been a teacher of young adolescents for thirteen years and his doctoral research examined effects of school transition on this age group. Additionally, he has been author or co-author for numerous social studies curriculum materials for the Georgia Department of Education.

Stephen B. Plank is Associate Research Scientist at the Center for Social Organization of Schools and Adjunct Assistant Professor of Sociology, both at Johns Hopkins University. A graduate of Northwestern University (B.A.) and the University of Chicago (M.A., and Ph.D.), his published research focuses on middle school reform, barriers and access to postsecondary schooling, and peer relations in classrooms. He also has co-authored a book on alternative organizational designs and incentive systems in schools (1997 with Coleman, Schneider, and others).

Elizabeth Platt is Associate Professor of Education, Multilingual/ Multicultural Education, Department of Curriculum and Instruction, Florida State University. She obtained her doctorate in educational psychology from the University of Illinois in 1989 and subsequently was project director of a national study on limited English proficient students in vocational education. Elizabeth's main mission is to improve instruction of children in the public schools. Though grounded in theoretical issues in psycholinguistic aspects of second language acquisition, she has more recently begun participant observation work in classrooms and has become interested in sociocultural approaches to language learning. In recent contributions to the *Modern Language Journal* she has challenged the prevailing model of second language acquisition. She has just completed a publication for the Center for Applied Linguistics entitled *The Vocational Classroom: A Great Place to Learn English.*

Richard R. Powell is Associate Professor of Curriculum and Instruction at Texas Tech University in Lubbock. A graduate of West Texas State University (B. S., M. S.) and Indiana University (Ph. D.), he taught at the middle school, high school, junior college, and university levels. Additionally, he has taught technical laboratory training in the Middle East for two years. He has co-authored several works, including *Field Experience: Strategies for Exploring Diversity in Schools* (1996, with Zehm and Garcia) and *Classrooms Under the Influence: Addicted Families, Addicted Students* (1994, with Zehm and Kottler). He has also co-authored a monograph titled *Classrooms Under the Influence: Helping Early Adolescent Children of Alcoholics.* His research on teacher education has been published widely, including such journals as *Teaching and Teacher Education, Qualitative Studies in Education, Journal of Research in Science Teaching,* and *Curriculum Inquiry.* His primary interest in middle school education is in alternative curriculum contexts and curriculum reform.

Joan Schine, an independent consultant specializing in service learning, early adolescence, and school reform, was the founding director of the National Center for Service Learning in Early Adolescence at the Center for Advanced Study in Education, CUNY Graduate Center. Prior to establishing the Center, she directed the Early Adolescent Helper Program, and has been Senior Program Associate at the National Commission on Resources for Youth. She is editor *of Service Learning,* the 1997 Yearbook of the National Society for Education. She was a middle school visitor for the U.S. Department of Education School Recognition Program. At present, she serves on several advisory committees, among them Chapin Hall's Program on Caring, sponsored by the Lilly Endowment, the advisory board for the University of Pennsylvania's Western Philadelphia Improvement Corps Replication Project, and the Bridgeport, (CT) Child Advocacy Coalition. A former member and chairperson of the Westport, CT Board of Education, Joan has spoken and written extensively on service learning in the middle school and related topics.

Hilda Rosselli is Associate Professor in the Department of Special Education, University of San Francisco, where she coordinates the Graduate Training Program in Gifted Education, directs the College of Education Honors Program, and teaches a variety of undergraduate and graduate level courses. She also established the university's first Professional Development School where she spent five years at a middle school supervising over 100 interns and collaborating with faculty on curriculum and school reform initiatives. Prior to her appointments at the university, she worked as a middle school teacher specialized in gifted education and curriculum development. She has co-edited two texts in special education and authored or co-authored more than a dozen articles or chapters. She has presented at over 100 local, state, national, and international conferences and is a board member of the National Association for Gifted Children. Currently her research focuses on application of multiple intelligence theory, gifted education, and university/school partnerships.

Laura P. Stowell is Associate Professor of Language and Literacy, California State University, San Marcos. She taught middle school language arts and reading for eleven years while also earning her M.A. and Ph. D. at Ohio State University. Her research interests are middle school literacy, literacy and technology, and assessment. With her CSUSM colleagues, she has published regularly in journals such as *Middle School Journal, Research in Middle Level Education,* and *Teacher Education Quarterly.* Her recent co-authored book is *Working with Middle School Students* (1996, with Rios, McDaniel, and Christopher).

John H. Swaim is a Professor at Otterbein College in Westerville, Ohio. Previous to coming to Otterbein he taught 25 years at the University of Northern Colorado where he was awarded emeritus status in 1994. While at UNC he was a middle school teacher and principal of the Laboratory School and later developed and directed the middle school teacher education program. He received his B.S.E. and M.S.E. at Emporia State University and his Ed.D. from the University of Northern Colorado. He is a past president of the National Middle School Association (1980) and a recipient of the John H. Lounsbury Award (1995). He has co-authored *Meeting the Standards: Improving Middle Level Teacher Education* (1996, with Stefanich) and *Middle Level Teachers: Portraits of Excellence* (1995, with Arth, Lounsbury, and McEwin). An additional interest of John's is in the area of young adolescent sports. He has frequently written and presented on this topic on several occasions.

Conrad F. Toepfer, Jr. is Professor of Education, Department of Learning and Instruction, State University of New York at Buffalo where he teaches and advises graduate students in curriculum planning and development. Connie has worked with middle level schools throughout the North America and abroad. A junior high school teacher and administrator before moving to university work in 1965, he is a Past President of the National Middle School Association and chaired the National Association of Secondary School Principals' Middle Level Education Council from 1981 through 1993. Over the past forty-two years, he has contributed to thirty-five books and monographs and authored over one-hundred-fifty articles in general curriculum and middle level educational journals.

Susan B. Trimble is a faculty member in the Department of Middle Grades and Secondary Education at Georgia Southern University in Statesboro. Susan has been involved with middle level education for the past fifteen years as a classroom teacher, researcher, and teacher educator. Her professional work and publications target middle level teacher preparation and development, interdisciplinary teams, and middle level reform, particularly the role of principals. Her doctorate is from Florida State University.

Jerry W. Valentine is Professor of Educational Leadership, University of Missouri at Columbia. A graduate of Louisiana Tech University (B.A.), University of Southwestern Louisiana (M.Ed.) and the University of Nebraska-Lincoln (Ph.D.), he taught at the elementary, middle, and high school levels and has been a principal. During his tenure as a professor he chaired two national studies (1980-83 and 1990-93) of middle level education for the National Association of Secondary School Principals. He has served on numerous national committees for the principalship and middle level education, authored or co-authored five books and several book chapters, published dozens of articles in professional periodicals and is currently working with three co-authors on *The Middle Level Principal: Leadership for a Child-Centered School*. He directs the Missouri Center for School Improvement and is in the process of combining that role with his interest in middle level leadership to establish a National Center for the Study of Middle Level Leadership.

Jill L. VanNess is a doctoral candidate at Florida State University. A graduate of Westmont College (B.A.), she taught middle school English as a second language in Costa Rica for one year and in West Sacramento, California, for four years. She has a California language development specialist credential and a Master's degree in Educational Leadership, from Florida State University. Her research interests include the role of inclusion and facilitation of linguistic minority students in middle level schools.

Gordon F. Vars is Professor Emeritus at Kent State University, Kent, Ohio. A graduate of Antioch College (A. B.), Ohio State University (M. A.) and George Peabody College for Teachers (Ed. D.), he has taught middle level young people almost continuously since 1949. He also has taught both graduate and undergraduate college students at the University of Maryland, Kent State University, and State University of Wisconsin at Platteville. His extensive publications and research deal with middle level curriculum, integrative/interdisciplinary/core programs, and evaluation of student progress. His dedication to the education of young adolescents has been recognized by the Ohio Middle School Association, the National Middle School Association, and the National Association for Core Curriculum. He continues to share his experience with middle level educators through workshops, inservice sessions, and presentations at local, state, and national conferences.

Todd Whitaker is Associate Professor of Educational Leadership, Administration, and Foundations at Indiana State University, Terre Haute. A graduate of the University of Missouri, he was a middle level principal for eight years. In addition, he was middle school coordinator responsible for the development of two new middle schools in Jefferson City, Missouri. His research interests include teacher leadership, the principal, change, and middle level programs and practices. He has presented and published in the areas of motivating reluctant teachers, teacher leadership, effective change, technology in middle schools, and the middle level principalship.

Allan Wigfield is Associate Professor of Human Development at the University of Maryland at College Park. He received his Ph.D. in educational psychology at the University of Illinois. He has done extensive research on how the transition from elementary to middle school influences children's motivation and self-esteem. He has published in journals such as *Developmental Psychology*, *American Psychologist*, and *Elementary School Journal*. He also co-edited (1994 and 1995, with Jacquelynne S. Eccles) two special issues of the *Journal of Early Adolescence* devoted to middle grades schooling and young adolescent development. At the University of Maryland, he teaches a course on adolescent development for students in the secondary education program.

NATIONAL MIDDLE SCHOOL ASSOCIATION

National Middle School Association was established in 1973 to serve as a voice for professionals and others interested in the education of young adolescents. The Association has grown rapidly and now enrolls members in all fifty states, the Canadian provinces, and forty-two other nations. In addition, fifty-six state, regional, and provincial middle school associations are official affiliates of NMSA.

NMSA is the only association dedicated exclusively to the education, development, and growth of young adolescents. Membership is open to all. While middle level teachers and administrators make up the bulk of the membership, central office personnel, college and university faculty, state department officials, other professionals, parents, and lay citizens are members and active in supporting our single mission – improving the educational experiences of 10-15 year olds. This open and diverse membership is a particular strength of NMSA.

The Association provides a variety of services, conferences, and materials in fulfilling its mission. In addition to *Middle School Journal*, the movement's premier professional journal, the Association publishes *Research in Middle Level Education Quarterly*, a wealth of books and monographs, videos, an association newsletter, a magazine, and occasional papers. The Association's highly acclaimed annual conference, which has drawn over 10,000 registrants in recent years, is held in the fall.

For information about NMSA and its many services contact the Headquarters at 2600 Corporate Exchange Drive, Suite 370, Columbus, Ohio 43231, TELEPHONE 800-528-NMSA, FAX 614-895-4750.